Interpreting Archaeology

Interpreting Archaeology

Finding meaning in the past

Ian Hodder, Michael Shanks, Alexandra Alexandri,
Victor Buchli, John Carman, Jonathan Last and
Gavin Lucas

London and New York

First published 1995
by Routledge
11 New Fetter Lane, London EC4P 4EE

Simultaneously published in the USA and Canada
by Routledge
29 West 35th Street, New York, NY 10001

First published in paperback 1997

© 1995 Ian Hodder, Michael Shanks, Alexandra Alexandri,
Victor Buchli, John Carman, Jonathan Last and Gavin Lucas

Typeset in Sabon by
Ponting–Green Publishing Services, Chesham, Bucks
Printed and bound in Great Britain by
T.J. International Ltd, Padstow, Cornwall

British Library Cataloguing in Publication Data
A catalogue record for this book is available from the
British Library

Library of Congress Cataloguing in Publication Data
Interpreting Archaeology / [edited by] Ian Hodder. . .
  [*et al.*].
      p.   cm.
   Includes bibliographical references and index.
   1. Archaeology–Philosophy.
2. Interpretation (Philosophy).
I. Hodder, Ian.
CC72.I57   1995
   930.1'01–dc20 94–8756

ISBN 0–415–07330–8 (hbk)
ISBN 0–415–15744–7 (pbk)

Contents

Tables and figures

Contributors

Alexandra Alexandri, Victor A. Buchli, John Carman, Jonathan Last and *Gavin Lucas*, Department of Archaeology, University of Cambridge.

Maurice Bloch, Department of Anthropology, London School of Economics and Political Science.

Felipe Criado, Facultad Geographia e Historia, Santiago de Compostela, Spain.

Robert A. Foley, Department of Biological Anthropology, University of Cambridge.

Peter J. Fowler, Department of Archaeology, University of Newcastle-upon-Tyne.

Clive Gamble, Department of Archaeology, University of Southampton.

Ernest Gellner, Department of Social Anthropology, University of Cambridge.

Joan Gero, Department of Anthropology, University of South Carolina.

Aron Gurevich, Institute of History, Moscow Academy of Sciences.

Mary Hesse, Department of History and Philosophy of Science, University of Cambridge.

Phyllis C. Lee, Department of Biological Anthropology, University of Cambridge, Cambridge.

Mark Leone, Paul R. Mullins, Marian C. Creveling, Laurence Hurst, Barbara Jackson-Nash, Lynn D. Jones, Hannah Jopling Kaiser, George C. Logan, Mark S. Warner, College Park Department of Anthropology, University of Maryland.

David Lowenthal, Department of Geography, University College London.

Henrietta Moore, London School of Economics and Political Science.

Michael Parker Pearson, Department of Archaeology, University of Sheffield.

Colin Richards, Department of Archaeology, University of Glasgow.

Alain Schnapp, Centre d'Archéologie Classique, Université de Paris 1 (Sorbonne).

James Steele, Department of Archaeology, University of Southampton.

Kevin Walsh, Department of Archaeology, University of Leicester.

Introduction

Archaeology is increasingly important in contemporary society. Some archaeologies provide a narrative of prehistory and a complement to documentary history. But archaeological materials are also being referenced more and more in relation to local and national identities. They are being used by commercial interests in entertainment and leisure industries. The archaeological past is being quoted and interpreted in many diverse cultural fields. Archaeologists are also continuing to ask questions of themselves – the procedures, questions and interests appropriate to a discipline which focuses often on the past but which is concerned with its role in the present. This book is about the state of the discipline in the 1990s. It is a perspective of Anglo-American archaeology, but one which has an eye also on other parts of the world, and one which is prepared to shift with new outlooks and learn new ways of thinking the material past in the present.

ARCHAEOLOGY AND THE INTERPRETATION OF MATERIAL CULTURE: A REPORT ON THE STATE OF THE DISCIPLINE

This book arises from a gathering of 140 archaeologists for three days, late in the summer of 1991 at Peterhouse of the University of Cambridge. The college has long been associated with radical and reflective thought on the nature of the discipline archaeology, and this was the purpose: to explore the latest thinking on the issues associated with interpreting the material remains of the past – and, indeed, understanding material culture generally, past and present. The meeting was not composed of people gathered to hear the opinion of a few designated 'experts', but of professional academic and archaeological fieldworkers, students, amateurs, and those in associated fields, whose experience and opinions were canvassed widely. Most time was given in the conference to short papers to raise issues (rather than to communicate definitive statements) and small-group discussions. An 'agenda' was precirculated to all, proposing some questions and themes which an organising committee of over fifteen members of the Department of Archaeology, Cambridge, considered significant and worthy of debate; comment and suggested amendments were sought and received. The conference attracted people from the United States, many parts of Europe, Africa, India, Japan and Australasia, as well as Britain – an international gathering.

The specialised and narrow atmosphere of many academic meetings was side-stepped both by the exchange of many opinions and also by the emphasis on issues common to most of the human and social sciences – questions of how to explain and understand the material culture dimension of society and its development. These questions run through archaeology, history, anthropology, sociology, ethology and behaviour studies, philosophy and social theory, design studies, archaeological heritage management and interpretation, and museology.

The international and interdisciplinary scope and the multivocal discussions are reported and developed in this book, which can consequently lay claim to representing a cross-section of thinking, a poll of opinion about the present state and future of an archaeology or archaeologies (to retain the pluralism) actively concerned with interpreting and explaining, rather than simply discovering and codifying, the material past for the present.

The main body of this book consists of five sections, each taking a distinct theme and containing editorial statements and short papers. The editorials set the scene, provide a context for the points raised in the short papers and also, importantly, assimilate the conference discussions (based on tapes and notes made by organising committee members and conference participants themselves). The papers vary in their style and format. Some are many-referenced and carefully worded, even guarded, statements. Others are lighter pieces intended to raise issues and provoke thought. To retain a sense of multivocality, editorial control was not exercised heavily in an attempt to achieve uniformity. Informality was encouraged. The book begins with an essay on the character of interpretation and some of the areas of contention (from an Anglo-American perspective) in contemporary archaeology. There follows an outline of some of the questions and issues tackled by the book and which form its intellectual context. This outline is a development of the conference agenda – modified, of necessity, after the event. At the end there is a report of other comment which was less easily assimilated into the main body of the book. A glossary of some key terms provides further orientation.

The opinions and ideas of over fifty people are here reported directly; those of over ninety more lie immediately in the background. This book depends on all of these. Their meeting would not have been possible without the facilities of the Department of Archaeology, Cambridge, the generous assistance of the British Council, the British Academy, the Macdonald Institute of Archaeology, Cambridge, Routledge Publishing, and particularly the Master and Fellows of Peterhouse.

Chapter 1

Processual, postprocessual and interpretive archaeologies

Michael Shanks and Ian Hodder

The theme of this book is the character and scope of archaeologies which may be termed interpretive. However, in spite of the use of the word 'interpretive' in this way as a label, the authors are not proposing and outlining another 'new' archaeology. There have been many such gestures over the last three decades with programmatic statements of panaceas for archaeology's perceived methodological maladies. We do not wish to add to the host of methods and approaches, but present here a general examination of current states of thinking in archaeology via the topic of interpretation. Our interest is interpretation in archaeology.

More particularly, it is proposed that 'interpretation' is a term which helps clarify current debates in Anglo-American archaeology between processual and post-processual approaches (see, for example, Preucel (ed.) 1991, *Norwegian Archaeological Review* 22, 1989, Yoffee and Sherratt (eds) 1993).

Processual archaeology[1] is the orthodoxy which emerged after the reaction, beginning in the 1960s and calling itself 'new archaeology', against traditional culture-historical and descriptive approaches to the material past. Its characteristics are as follows:

- Archaeology conceived as anthropological science rather than allied with history.
- Explanation of the past valued over description.
- Explanation via the incorporation of particular observations of the material past into cross-cultural generalisations pertaining to (natural and social) process (hence the term 'processual').
- Explanation via explicit methodologies modelled on the hard sciences.
- An earlier interest in laws of human behaviour has shifted to an interest in formation processes of the archaeological record – regularities which will allow inferences about processes to be made from material remains.

For many, and although it may not explicitly be described as such, processual archaeology is a good means, if not the best, of acquiring *positive knowledge* of the archaeological past. Positive archaeological knowledge is *of the past*, which means that it aspires to objectivity in the sense of being neutral and, indeed, timeless (the past happened in the way it did; that much at least will not change). Under a programme of positive knowledge, archaeologists aim to *accumulate* more knowledge of the past. The timeless and objective quality of knowledge is important if the aim is to accumulate and build on what is already known; it would be no good building on facts which cannot be relied upon, because they might change. The aspiration to timeless and value-free knowledge also enables high degrees of specialisation, knowledges isolated in their own field and disconnected from the present. The cultural politics of the 1990s does not affect what happened in prehistory, it is held. The archaeologist can live with one while quite separately gaining knowledge of the other.

To secure this timeless objectivity is the task of method(ology), and in processual archaeology this may be described as coming down to reason or rationality working objectively upon data or the facts. Reason is that cognitive processing which is divorced from superstition, ideology, emotion, subjectivity – indeed, anything which compromises the purity or neutrality of logical calculation. To attain objectivity means carefully relying on those faculties which allow access to the past – particularly observation, controlled perception of those empirical traces remaining of what happened. Theory-building may be involved in moving from the static archaeological record of the present to past social dynamics (Binford 1977), but to move beyond controlled observation is to speculate and to invite bias and subjectivity, contamination of the past by the present.

These aspirations to positive scientific knowledge, neutrality, and reliance on controlled observation of facts have led to processual archaeology being described as positivist and empiricist (see, among others, Shanks and Tilley 1987a).

Processual archaeology is anthropological in the sense of being informed by an interest in social reconstruction of the past. The following form the main outlines of processual conceptions of the social as they developed from the late 1960s.

- Society is essentially composed of patterned sets of behaviours.
- Material culture and material residues, the products of processes which form the archaeological record, *reflect* the patterned behaviours which are society, or they are the result of natural processes which can be defined scientifically (the decay of organic materials; the corrosion of metals).
- Society is a mode of human adaptation to the social and natural environment.
- Accordingly, explaining social process means focusing on those features of the society which most relate to adaptation to environments: resources, subsistence and economic strategies, trade and exchange, technology. Attention has, however and more recently, turned to symbolism and ritual.
- The interest in cross-cultural generalisation and patterning is expressed in societal typing (identifying a particular society as band, lineage-based, chiefdom, state, etc.) and schemes of cultural evolution.

Postprocessual archaeology, as the label implies, is something of a reaction and supercession of this processual framework (especially after Hodder, ed., 1982; see also Hodder 1985, 1986). Since the late 1970s issue has been taken with most of these tenets of processual archaeology: the character of science and aims of objective explanation; the character of society; and the place of values in archaeology, the sociopolitics of the discipline, its contemporary location as a mode of cultural production of knowledges.[2]

Doubt, from theoretical and empirical argument, has been thrown on the possibility of an anthropological science, based upon observation of residues of patterned behaviours, detached from the present and aspiring to value-freedom (as positive knowledge). So the processual–postprocessual debate has centred upon the forms of knowledge appropriate to a *social* science, how society may be conceived (reconciling both patterning or structure and individual action, intention and agency), and upon the workings of the discipline of archaeology, its ideologies and cultural politics, its place in the (post)modern present.

The debate has tended towards a polarisation of positions, and it is this which has led to an obscuring of the issues. Postprocessual has come to be seen by some as anti-science, celebrating subjectivity, the historical particular in place of generalisation: the cultural politics of the present displacing positive knowledge of the past. Above all, the authority of a scientific and professional knowledge of the past is posited against particular and subjective constructions, a pluralism of pasts appropriate each to their own contemporary constituency: science is pitted against relativism (Yoffee and Sherratt (eds) 1993, Trigger 1989b, Watson 1990).

We refer to an obscuring of the issues because this polarisation is unnecessary indeed, damaging. We are proposing that a consideration of the character and scope of interpretation may help overcome the polarisations. And, to begin, a renaming may be appropriate. The label 'postprocessual' says nothing about what it stands for, other than a relative position in respect of processual archaeology. If we are to use interpretation as an epithet, *interpretive archaeologies* may be used as a more positive label, perhaps, for many of those approaches which have been called postprocessual. These are archaeologies (the plural is important, as will become clear) which work through interpretation. And we hope it will become clear that a careful consideration of interpretation entails abandoning the caricatures of science versus relativism, generalisation versus the historical particular, and the objective past versus the subjective present.

The main aspects of archaeologies termed interpretive might be summarised as follows.

- Foregrounded is the person and work of the interpreter. Interpretation is practice which requires that the interpreter does not so much hide behind rules and procedures predefined elsewhere, but takes responsibility for their actions, their interpretations.
- Archaeology is hereby conceived as a material practice in the present, making things (knowledges, narratives, books, reports, etc.) from the material traces of the past – constructions which are no less real, truthful or authentic for being constructed.
- Social practices, archaeology included, are to do with meanings, making sense of things. Working, doing, acting, making are interpretive.
- The interpretive practice that is archaeology is an ongoing process: there is no final and definitive account of the past as it was.
- Interpretations of the social are less concerned with causal explanation (accounts such as 'this is the way it was' and 'it happened because of this') than with *understanding* or *making sense* of things which never were certain or sure.
- Interpretation is consequently multivocal: different interpretations of the same field are quite possible.
- We can therefore expect a plurality of archaeological interpretations suited to different purposes, needs, desires.
- Interpretation is thereby a creative but none the less critical attention and response to the interests, needs and desires of different constituencies (those people, groups or communities who have or express such interests in the material past).

TO INTERPRET, THE ACT OF INTERPRETATION: WHAT DO THE WORDS MEAN AND IMPLY?

We particularly stress the active character of interpretation: one is an interpreter by virtue of performing the act or practice of interpreting. An interpreter is a translator, an interlocutor, guide or go-between.[3]

Meaning

To interpret something is to figure out what it means. A translator conveys the sense or meaning of something which is in a different language or medium. In this way interpretation is fundamentally about meaning. Note, however, that translation is not a simple and mechanical act but involves careful judgement as to appropriate shades of meaning, often taking account of context, idiom and gesture which can seriously affect the meaning of words taken on their own.

Dialogue

A translator may be an interlocutor or go-between. Interpretation contains the idea of mediation, of conveying meaning from one party to another. An interpreter aims to provide a reciprocity of understanding, overcoming the lack of understanding or semantic distance between two parties who speak different languages or belong to different cultures. Interpretation is concerned with dialogue, facilitating and making easier.

In a good dialogue or conversation one listens to what the other says and tries to work out what they mean, tries to understand, to make sense. Translation may be essential to this, performed either by a separate interpreter or by the parties of the dialogue themselves. Further questions might be asked and points put forward based on what has already been heard and understood. The idea is that dialogue moves forward to a consensus (of sorts) which is more than the sum of the initial positions. This *fusion of horizons* (a term taken from hermeneutics, the philosophy of interpretation, discussed below) is potentially a learning experience in which one takes account of the other, their objections and views, even if neither is won over.

It is not a good and open dialogue if one party simply imposes its previous ideas, categories and understandings upon the other. Preconceptions are simply confirmed. It is not good if the interpreter does not recognise the independence of the interpreted, their resistance to control and definition. A good conversation is one perhaps which never ends: there is always more to discover.

What might be a dialogue with the past? One where the outcome resides wholly in neither side but is a product of *both* the past and the present. Archaeological interpretation here resides in the gap between past and present. Such a dialogue is also ongoing. We will take up these points again below.

Uncertainty

Interpretation involves a perceived gap between the known and the unknown, desire and a result, which is to be bridged somehow. There is thus uncertainty, both at the outset of interpretation (what does this mean?) and at the end of the act of interpretation. It could always have been construed in a different way, with perhaps a different aspect stressed or disregarded. Although we might be quite convinced by an understanding we have managed to achieve, it is good to accept fallibility and not to become complacent. Is this not indeed the character of reason? Rationality is not an abstract absolute for which we can formulate rules and procedures, but is better conceived as the willingness to recognise our partiality, that our knowledge and reasoning are open to challenge and modification. Final and definitive interpretation is a closure which is to be avoided, suspected at the least.

Exploration and making connections

Interpretation implies an extension or building from what there is here to something beyond. We have already mentioned that interpretation should aspire to being open to change, exploring possibility. Exploration of meanings is often about making different connections.

Here can be mentioned the structuralist argument that meaning, if it is to be found at all, resides in the gaps between things, in their interrelationships. A lone signifier seems empty. But once connected through relations of similarity and difference with other signifiers it makes sense. In deciphering a code different permutations of connections between the particles of the code are explored until meaning is unlocked.

Judgement

A sculptor or woodcarver might examine their chosen material, interpret its form and substance, taking note of grain and knots of wood, flaws and patterning in stone, and then judge and choose how to work with or against the material. An archaeologist may examine a potsherd, pick out certain diagnostic traits and judge that these warrant an identification of the sherd as of a particular type: they choose an identification from various possibilities. Interpretation involves judgement and choice: drawing sense, meaning and possibility from what began as uncertainty.

Performance

In this way interpretation may refer to something like dramatic performance, where a particular interpretation of a dramatic text is offered according to the judgement of performers and director. The text is worked with and upon. Focus is drawn to certain connections within the characters and plot which are judged to be significant. Interpretation is here again reading for significance, where significance is literally making something a sign.[4]

Dramatic interpretation has further dimensions. A text is read for significance and courses of action inferred. A past work (the text of a play) is acted out and in so doing it is given intelligible life. Now, there is no need here to take a literal line and think that archaeological interpretation involves those experimental reconstructions of past ways of life that are familiar from television programmes and heritage parks (though there is here a serious argument for experimental archaeology). We would rather stress that interpretation is in performance an *active apprehension*.[5] Something produced in the past is made a presence to us now. It is worked upon actively. If it were not, it would have no life. An unread and unperformed play is dead and gone. Analogously an archaeological site which is not actively apprehended, worked on, incorporated into archaeological projects, simply lies under the ground and decays. The questions facing the actor-interpreters are: How are the characters to be portrayed? What settings are to be used? What form of stage design? What lighting, sound and ambience? Simply, what is to be made of the play? (Pearson 1994).

Courses of action inferred, projects designed: these are conditions of interpretation.

Critique

Judgement here involves taking a position, choosing how to perform, what to do, which meanings to enact or incorporate. Involved is a commitment to one performance rather than another. Any interpretation is always thus immediately critical of other interpretations. Performance is both analytic commentary on its source, the written play, but also critical in its choice of some meanings and modes and not others.

The ubiquity of interpretation forgotten in black boxes

Interpretation is insidiously ubiquitous. There are always choices and judgements being made even in the most mundane and apparently empirical activities. Describing and measuring an artefact, for example, always involves acts of interpretation and judgement. Which parts of a stone axe-blade are to be measured, for example, and from where to where?

But some interpretation is often overlooked when people accept certain interpretive conventions. So, for example, plants are most often described according to scientific specie lists. But these species lists are not 'natural': they are the result of scientific interpretation concerning the definition and classification of plants and creatures. Such interpretation may have occurred a while ago now, and be more of interest to historians of science, but it should be recognised that the choice or judgement is made to accept that interpretation. Interpretations such as this concerning the classification of plants are often worth following simply because so much work would be required, starting almost from first principles, to redesign natural history. The idea of a species is tied in to so many other things: evolutionary theory and ecology, botany and zoology, etc.

When an interpretation or set of interpretations is accepted, treated as uncontroversial and no longer even seen for what it is, the term *black-boxed* can be used. Interpretation is made, accepted and then put away, out of sight and often out of mind, in a black box. It allows us to live with the world more easily; we would otherwise be as infants, asking whether this thing in front of us really could be interpreted as a table with a box upon it which is most difficult to interpret, a computer.

Indeed, all archaeology is hereby interpretive, concerned intimately with the interpretation of things. However, some archaeologists refuse to accept this, or choose to overlook or black-box acts of interpretation. Excavation, for example, is so thoroughly interpretive. Many students on their first dig find the uncertainty very disturbing. Where does one layer end and another begin? How can you tell? How can it be ascertained that this scatter of traces of holes in the ground was once a wooden house? Yet this pervasive interpretive uncertainty is the construction of 'hard' facts about the past.

Hermeneutics[6]

'The theoretical and philosophical field of interpretation, the clarification of meaning and achievement of sense and understanding, is covered by *hermeneutics*.[7] Hermeneutics addresses the relationship between interpreter and interpreted when that which is to be interpreted is not just raw material to be defined and brought under technical control, but *means* something. The term traditionally applied to the reading of texts and the understanding of historical sources – Is the source authentic? What does it mean? What were the author's intentions? We do not propose a simple import of hermeneutic principles into archaeology, but will be noting their relevance to the topics and issues of this book.

Having unpacked the idea of interpretation, we will now develop some of the observations.

UNCERTAINTY

Interpretation is rooted in a world which cannot be tied down to definitive categories and processes. Consider classification. Articles are grouped or a group divided according to their similarities. Each class or taxon contains those articles judged the same. There are two fields of remaindering or possible foci of uncertainty where judgement is required. First, it may not be absolutely clear where a particular article belongs, particularly if the criteria for inclusion in a class are not specific, if an article is approaching the edges, the margins of a taxon, or if it is somehow incomplete. Second, there is always a remainder after classification. Classification never completely summarises. There are always aspects or attributes of an article which are disregarded and which remain outside taxa, embarrassing classification.

Classification operates under a 'rule of the same'. Taxa are characterised by relative *homogeneity*. This is a legitimate strategy for coping with the immense empirical variety and particularity that archaeologists have to deal with. However, we should be clear that classification does not give the *general* picture; it gives the *average*. It is not a general picture because there is no provision in classification for assessing the norm, the taxa (where do they come from; they are supplemental or external to the classification), nor the variations within a class, nor the variability of variability. Classification is less interested in coping with particularity: Why are the members of a class of pots all in fact slightly different?

Things are equivocal. A pot can be classified according to its shape and decoration as of a particular type. But thin-sectioned under a polarising microscope it explodes into another world of micro-particles and mineral inclusions. The pot is not just one thing which can be captured in a single all-encompassing definition. There is always more that can be said or done with the pot. A single pot is also multiple. It depends on the trials we make of it, what we do with it, how we experience it – whether we attend to surface and shape or slice it and magnify it.

Instead of smoothing over, we can also attend to that which does not fit, to the rough and irregular, to the texture of things. Everyday life is not neat and tidy. History is a mess. We can attend to the equivocal, to the absences in our understanding, focus on the gaps in neat orders of explanation. Conspicuously in archaeology there can be no final account of the past – because it is now an equivocal and ruined mess, but also because even when the past was its present it was to a considerable extent incomprehensible. So much has been lost and forgotten of what never was particularly clear. Social living is immersion in equivocality, everyday uncertainty. What really is happening now? There are no possible final answers.

Uncertainty and equivocality refer to the difference of things: they can be understood according to a rule of the same, but difference escapes this rule, escapes homogeneity. Because an attention to texture which escapes classification is outside of qualities of sameness (the homogeneity of what is contained within the class), the term *heterogeneity* may be used. To attend to difference is to attend to heterogeneity – the way things escape formalisation, always holding something back.

Nietzsche's and Foucault's projects of *genealogy* involves revealing the difference and discontinuity, the heterogeneity in what was taken to be homogeneous and continuous. Nietzsche reveals the 'uncertain' origins of morality (1967). Sexuality is shown to be far from a biological constant by Foucault (1979, 1984a, 1984b).

The social world is thoroughly *polysemous*. This is another concept which can be related to uncertainty. That a social act or product is polysemous means that it can always be interpreted in various ways. Meanings are usually negotiated: that is, related to the interpersonal practices, aspirations, strategies of people. We repeat the classic example of the safety pin, the meaning of which was radically renegotiated by punk subculture in the 1970s (Hebdige 1979).

The forms of social life are constituted as meaningful by the human subjects who live those forms. People try to make sense of their lives. This ranges from interpreting the possible meanings of a politician's speeches and actions to trying to make sense of the fact that you have been made redundant and may never work again even though you are highly skilled.

Giddens (1982, 1984, p. 374) has related this characteristic of the social world (that it is to do with interpretation and meaning) to the hermeneutic task of the sociologist. He describes the difficult *double hermeneutic* of sociology. First, it aims to understand a world of meanings and interpretations (society). Second, sociologists themselves form a social community with its own practices, procedures, assumptions, skills, institutions, all of which in turn need to be understood.

Shanks and Tilley (1987a, ch. 5 especially pp. 107–8) have described a fourfold hermeneutic in archaeology, four levels of interpretation and the need to develop understanding: understanding the relation between past and present; understanding other societies and cultures; understanding contemporary society, the site of archaeological interpretations; and understanding the communities of archaeologists who are performing interpretations. Thus, not only do archaeologists translate between 'their' and 'our' world, but they also have to deal with worlds separated in space and time. But it is difficult to argue that sociologists deal with a double hermeneutic, anthropologists with a threefold hermeneutic and archaeologists with a fourfold. Certainly the societies with which prehistoric archaeologists deal are often remote, and there are many social and cultural layers that have to be bridged. But a palaeolithic archaeologist is not dealing with more hermeneutic layers than a historical archaeologist, and it is inadequate to assume that some cultures in space and time are more 'like us' than others. It is better to assert with Giddens that all the social sciences can be contrasted with the natural sciences in that they face a double rather than a single hermeneutic. Certainly at the methodological level the problem is always one of fusing two horizons, the scientific and the past society. Other information from Western and other ethnographic contexts may be brought into the argument, but always through the scientific community. The archaeologist faces the distant past in the same way that any social scientist faces 'the other', even if the scanty nature of the evidence and the great spans of time involved greatly increase the uncertainty of interpretation.

When the uncertainty of an interpretation declines it is black-boxed and need no longer be subject to suspicion and negotiation. The controversy over an interpretation is settled and closed. What allows one interpretation to prevail over another? Archaeological cultures, for example, are no longer interpreted by many as racial groups; it is not something now usually entertained as a possible interpretation. What allows or brought about the closure? A common answer might be reason and the facts. Close examination of empirical examples shows that ethnicity is not reflected in what archaeologists call cultures. But the history and philosophy of science indicate that such an explanation for the closure of scientific controversy is not enough. The central principle is that of *underdetermination*. This is the Duhem-Quine principle which holds that no single factor is enough to explain the closure of a controversy or the certainty acquired by scientists. It is the philosophical basis of most contemporary history and sociology of science.[8] Theory is never fully determined by the facts or by logic. There is always something which sets off doubts about the certainty, always something missing to close the black box for ever.[9] David Clarke (1968) was very willing to relate material culture patterning to ethnicity after his ethnographic investigations. Cultural and, by extension, racial identity are clearly established with reference to material culture, though perhaps not in the precise terms of the archaeological culture concept (Conkey and Hastorf, eds, 1990).

CREATIVITY AND THE TECHNOLOGY THAT IS ARCHAEOLOGY

The equivocality, heterogeneity or multiplicity of the material world means that choices must be made in perception and to what we attend. The archaeological record is an infinity in terms of the things that may be done with it and in terms of how it may be perceived. Which measurements are to be made? Are some aspects of an artefact to be disregarded in coming to an understanding? How is justice to be done to the empirical richness of the past? How is an archaeological monument such as a castle to be represented? Measured plans may be prepared and descriptions made of masonry and sequence of construction from observations of structural additions and alterations. Here attention is focused upon certain aspects of the architecture deemed worthy by conventional archaeology. But what of other experiences and perceptions of such a monument? This is hardly an exhaustive treatment of architecture. A technical line drawing may direct attention essentially and almost wholly to the edges of masonry – a subjective choice. Turner, in his sequence of picturesque renderings of castles in the early nineteenth century, focuses upon situation in landscape and attempts to convey the passage of light across monumental features. Both approaches are selective; but both also, we suggest, attend accurately to the empirical, albeit in different ways.[10]

Archaeological interpretation requires that some things be connected with others in order to make sense of what remains of the past. Circular features in earth of contrasting colour are associated with removed wooden stakes, and then in turn associated with other post-holes to trace the structural members of a building. To interpret is in this way a creative act. Putting things together and so creating sense, meaning or knowledge.

We are concerned to emphasise that the person of the archaeologist is essential in coming to understand the past. The past is not simply under the ground waiting to be discovered. It will not simply appear, of course, but requires work. Consider discovery. Discovery is invention. The archaeologist uncovers or discovers something, coming upon it. An inventor may be conceived to have come upon a discovery. Discovery and invention are united in their etymology: *invenire* in Latin means to come upon, to find or invent. Invention is both finding and creative power. The logic of invention, poetry and the imaginary is one of conjunction, making connections. It is both/and, between self and other; not either/or. The pot found by the archaeologist is both this and that (surface decoration and mineral inclusions). A castle is both technical drawing and romantic painting. It is there in the landscape and here in a painting. It is both of the past and of the present. Archaeology's poetry is to negotiate these equivocations and make connections. It is the work of imagination.

This is to deny the radical distinction of subjectivity and objectivity in that the subjective is simply the form that the objective takes.

Foregrounding the creativity of the interpreting archaeologist is to hold that archaeology is a mode of production of the past (Shanks and McGuire 1991, Shanks 1992a). This would seem to be recognised by those many archaeologists and textbooks which talk at length of archaeological techniques – archaeology seen as technology. The past has left remains, and they decay in the ground. According to their interest an archaeologist works on the material remains to make something of them. So excavation is invention/discovery or sculpture[11] where archaeologists craft remains of the past into forms which are meaningful. The archaeological 'record' is, concomitantly, not a record at all, not given, 'data', but made. 'The past' is gone and lost, and *a fortiori*, through the equivocality of things and the character of society as constituted through meaning, never existed as a definitive entity 'the present' anyway. An archaeologist has a raw material, the remains of the past, and turns it into something – data, a report, set of drawings, a museum exhibition, an archive, a television programme, evidence in an academic controversy, and perhaps that which is termed 'knowledge of the past'. This is a mode of production.

To hold that archaeology is a mode of production of the past does not mean that anything can be made. A potter cannot make anything out of clay. Clay has properties, weight, plasticity, viscosity, tensile strength after firing, etc., which will not allow certain constructions. The technical skill of the potter involves working with these properties while designing and making. So there is no idealism here which would have archaeologists inventing whatever pasts they might wish.

To realise archaeology as cultural production does introduce a series of important illuminations. Technical interest in the empirical properties of raw material, the viability of a project, is but one aspect of production. Other essential considerations include purpose, interest, expression and taste.

Purpose and interest: products always attend needs and interests, serving purpose. Here is an argument for engaging with and answering a community's interests in the archaeological past, because a discipline which simply responds to its own perceived needs and interests, as in an academic archaeology existing for its own sake ('disinterested knowledge'), can be criticised as a decadent indulgence. Different archaeologies, different interpretations of the material past, can be produced. We suggest that a valuable and edifying archaeology attends to the needs and interests of a community, interpreting these in a way which answers purpose while giving something more, enhancing knowledges and experiences of the past and of the material world. Some issues and questions, a basis perhaps for discussion and establishing such interests, form the substructure to this book and are presented in the next chapter. Reference to publics and communities can be found particularly in Part 3. A strong political argument is that archaeology should attend to the interests of the diversity of communities and groups that it studies, works and lives among, and draws funding from (Potter 1990).

Expression and taste

The expressive, aesthetic and emotive qualities of archaeological projects have been largely down-played or even denigrated over the last three decades as archaeologists have sought an objective scientific practice. In popular imagination the archaeological is far more than a neutral acquisition of knowledge; the material presence of the past is an emotive field of cultural interest and political dispute. The practice of archaeology also is an emotive, aesthetic and expressive experience. This affective component of archaeological labour is social as well as personal, relating to the social experiences of archaeological practice, of belonging to the archaeological community and a discipline or academic discourse. Of course such experiences are immediately political (Shanks 1992a, *Archaeological Review from Cambridge*, 9:2).

The essentially creative character of production is also one of expression: taking purpose, assessing viability, working with material, and expressing interpretation to create the product that retains traces of all these stages. This expressive dimension is also about pleasure (or displeasure) and is certainly not restricted to the intellectual or the cognitive. Pleasure is perhaps not a very common word in academic archaeology, but an interpretive archaeology should recognise the role of pleasure and embody it in the product made. This means addressing seriously and with imagination the questions of how we write the past, our activities as archaeologists and how we communicate with others.

In archaeological interpretation the past is designed, yet is no less real or objective. (We can expect some to dispute the reality of a past produced by such an interpretive archaeology which realises the subjective and creative component of the present: such a product cannot be the 'real' past, it might be said, because it has been tainted by the present and by the person of the archaeologist. This is precisely like disputing the 'reality' of a television set. Here is a technological product which looks like a television set. To ask whether it is real is a silly question. A far better question, and one that applies to the product of archaeological interpretation, is: Does it do what is required of it – does it work?) The question of archaeological design is: What kind of archaeology do we want?

A product of technology is both critique and affirmation; it embodies its creation, speaks of style, gives pleasure (or displeasure) in its use, solves a problem perhaps, performs a function, provides experiences, signifies and resonates. It may also be pretentious, ugly or kitsch, useless, or untrue to its materials and creation. In the same way each archaeology has a style; the set of decisions made in producing an archaeological product involves conformity with some interests, percepts or norms, and not with others. As with an artefact, the judgement of an archaeological style involves multiple considerations, many summarised by the term 'taste'. We need to consider its eloquence: that is, how effective and productive it is. We should also make an ethical appraisal of its aims and purposes and possible functions. Technical matters are implicated, of course, including how true it has been to the material past, the reality and techniques of observation that it uses to construct facts. Judgement refers to all these aspects of archaeological production: purpose, viability and expression.

PROJECTS AND NETWORKS

The 'objective past' will not present itself. The remains of a prehistoric hut circle will not excavate themselves. A pot will not thin-section itself and appear upon a microscope slide beneath the gaze of a cataplectic archaeologist. Work has to be done in the sense that the remains of the past have to be incorporated into *projects*. An archaeological project has a temporality of presencing (Heidegger 1972, p. 14): the past is taken up in the work of the present which is projecting forward into the future, planning investigation, publications, knowledge, whatever. There is here no hard and fast line between the past as it was and the present. This temporality also refers us back to the character of dialogue. On the basis of what one already knows, and on the basis of prejudgement, questions are put, answers received which draw the interpreter into further prejudged questions. This is an ongoing *hermeneutic circle* (see note 6 for references) better termed, perhaps, a spiral as it draws forward the partners in dialogue.

Archaeological projects are about connecting past, present and future, but what empirical or concrete form do they take? An archaeological project involves the mobilisation of many different things or resources. Landowners are approached, funding needs to be found, labour hired, tools and materials convened, skills operated to dig, draw and photograph, computers programmed and fed with data, finds washed and bagged, workforce kept happy, wandering cows chased off site. This is a great and rich assemblage of people, things and energies which achieve what are conventionally termed data. An archaeological project is a *heterogeneous network*.[12] A network because different elements are mobilised and connected, but unlike a bounded system there are no necessary or given limits to the network; it is quite possible to follow chains of connection far beyond what are conceived as the conventional limits of archaeology (in pragmatic terms think of the ramifications of funding; in institutional terms the relations with the education system; in affective terms all the associations of 'working in the field' (Shanks 1992a)). These networks are heterogeneous because connected are entities, actors and resources of different kinds: interests, moneys, academics, career trajectories, volunteers, landowners, wheelbarrows, JCB mechanical diggers, cornfields, decayed subsurface 'features', laboratories. . . .

All these are brought together in an archaeological project which constitutes the reality of the past, makes it what it is. It is within such contingent (there is nothing necessary about them) assemblages that the past comes to be perceived and known. If we were to report objectively the detail of an excavation, all the resonances and associations, all the thoughts, materials and events, the result would be very confusing and of perhaps infinite length. This is again the paradox that specificity of detail brings into doubt the validity of sensory evidence, and points to the necessity of creative choice.[13]

That data are constructed or crafted in (social) practices is the central contention of 'constructivist' philosophy of science (see note 8). Anthropological attention has been focused on communities of scientists and how they work with the physical world. In archaeology Joan Gero has recently considered the role of recording forms (basic now to excavation practice) in constructing archaeological facts.

CONTEXT AND DIALOGUE

A pot without provenance is of limited value to archaeological interpretation. It has long been recognised that placing things in context is fundamental to understanding the past. Much of conventional archaeological technique is about establishing empirically rich contexts of things.

A 'contextual archaeology' makes much of the associations of things from the past (Hodder (ed.) 1987b, Hodder 1986). Meanings of things can only be approached if contexts of use are considered, if similarities and differences between things are taken into account. It is often argued that, since the meanings of things are arbitrary, archaeologists cannot reconstruct past symbolism. There are two ways in which archaeologists avoid this impasse. First, artefacts are not like words in that they have to work in a material way and are subject to universal material processes. Thus, an axe used to cut down a tree must be made of rock of a certain hardness and the cutting action will leave wear-traces. An axe made of soft chalk and without wear-traces can thus be identified, on universal criteria, to be of no use for tree-cutting – an aspect of its meaning has been inferred. Archaeologists routinely think through why prehistoric actors built this wall, dug this trench, using common-sense arguments based on universal criteria. In all such work universal characteristics of materials are linked to specific contexts to see if they are relevant. Interpretation and uncertainty are involved in deciding which aspects of the materials are useful in determining meaning. Hence, and second, the archaeologist turns not to universal characteristics of materials but to internal similarities and differences. Thus, perhaps the chalk axes are found in burials with female skeletons, while the hard stone axes are found in male burials.

Such internal patterning not only supports the idea that stone hardness is relevant to meaning in this case, but it also adds another level of meaning – gender. The task of the archaeologist is to go round and round the data in a hermeneutic spiral, looking for relationships, fitting pieces of the jigsaw together. Does the patterning of faunal remains correlate with the two axe types or with male and female burials? Is there any difference in axe-type deposition in different parts of the settlement system? And so on. The more of the evidence that can be brought together in this way, the more likely is one able to make statements about meaning – for example, that chalk axes were of high value and were associated with women in ritual contexts.

It is important to recognise that a contextual emphasis does not mean that archaeologists can interpret without generalisation. It is impossible to approach the data without prejudice and without some general theory. But the interpretive challenge is to evaluate such generality in relation to the contextual data. So much of what archaeologists assume in a general way is 'black-boxed'. But even terms like 'pit', or 'ditch' or 'wall' or 'post-hole' should be open to scrutiny to see if they are relevant in each specific context. Archaeologists always have to evaluate relevance – are there aspects of this context which make this general theory relevant? However well defined the theory, some contextual judgement has to be made.

The same or similar things have different meanings in different contexts. It is context which allows a sensitivity to diversity and to local challenges to social meanings. But, if context is so important, is not each context, each pit different with different meanings? Certainly, at a precise level this is probably true. But most contexts are grouped together in larger contexts – a group or type of pit, a site, a region and so on. The problem then becomes one of defining the context relevant for each question. Context itself is a matter of interpretation, based on defining similarities and differences. Thus a group of pits might be described as a context because of their spatial clustering, or because they are a distinctive type, or because they have similar contents. By searching for similarities and differences some contextual variation can be identified as more relevant than others, but context and content are always intertwined in a complex hermeneutic spiral. The meaning of an artefact can change the context, but the context can change the meaning.

Thus, archaeologists, working in their own contexts, are likely to pick out certain types of context in the past and look for patterning in relation to them. There can be no context-free definitions of context. A pit, ditch or post-hole is not a 'natural' context. As already stated, archaeologists have to evaluate such general assumptions in relation to specific similarities and differences in the data.

Interpretation, in its concern with context, can also be described as being to do with *relationality* – exploring connections in the way we have been describing.[14] However, an important point to re-emphasise is that context cannot only refer to the things of the past. They are inevitably bound up in archaeological projects. We will clarify with some points from hermeneutics.

Involved here is the context (historical, social, ethical, disciplinary, whatever) of interpretation itself. In coming to understand we always begin with presuppositions. There can be no pure reception of a raw object of interpretation. We begin an interrogation of an historical source with an awareness of its historical context – we view it with hindsight; the flows and commixtures of earths, silts and rubbles in the archaeological site are understood as layers. As interpreters we have to start from somewhere; what we wish to interpret is always already understood *as* something. This is prejudgement or prejudice. And it is essential to understanding. Prejudgement and prejudice are legitimate in that they furnish the conditions for any real understanding.

Another aspect of this is that the acts of looking, sensing and posing questions of things always involve intentional acts of giving meanings. These meanings (rubble as layers, for example) derive from the situation of the interpreter. So the archaeological past is always *for* something. At the least an archaeological site under excavation is part of an archaeological project, and, as we have just argued, *would not exist* for us if it were not. It is understood in terms of its possible applications and relevances in the present. So the 'prejudice' of the interpreting archaeologist's position (ranging from social and cultural location to disciplinary organisation to personal disposition) is not a barrier to understanding, contaminating factors to be screened out; predjudice is the very medium of understanding – indeed, *objective* understanding.

Prejudgement and prejudiced assumptions regarding what it is we seek to understand bring us again to the hermeneutic circle introduced above. Realising that interpretation is about establishing connections and contexts involves realising interpretation as dialogic in character.

This is partly recognised by the idea of *problem orientation*, strongly supported by processual methodology. This maintains that research projects, archaeological observation and study should be designed around meaningful questions to be posed of the past. The correct methodological context is one of question and answer. Questions are considered meaningful if they fit into an acceptable (research) context. So, rather than digging a site simply to find out what was there, archaeological projects should be organised around questions which fit into a disciplinary context of progressive question-and-answer. Theory: complex society can be observed in settlement hierarchy. Hypothesis: region R has a settlement hierarchy at time T. Question: Does site S display features correspondent with a level of the supposed hierarchy? Investigate. Do the data require modification of the hypothesis? This is indeed a dialogue of sorts with the archaeological past: the archaeologist questions the past in relation to their accompanying 'assumptions' of theory and hypothesis; the response of the past may demand the archaeologist thinks and questions again.

But we hope that the notion of interpretation as dialogue suggests a more sensitive treatment and awareness of the relationship between interpreter and interpreted. There is much more to interpretive context. First, the interpreted past is more than something which exists to supply responses to questions deemed meaningful by male and middle-class academics of twentieth-century Western nation states (as most processual archaeologists are). The past has an independence of research design, procedures of question-and-answer (this independence is accommodated in the notion of heterogeneity). It overflows the questions put to it by archaeologists. It may be recognised (Charles Redman, in discussion) that strict problem orientation may miss a great deal, and that simply being open to what may happen to turn up in an excavation is a quite legitimate research strategy. There is nothing wrong with sensitive exploration, being open to finding out.

Second, the past is constituted by meanings. By this is meant that the past is not just a set of data. Some archaeologists have responded to the Native American request for respect for the spiritual meanings of their material pasts with a cry 'They are taking away our database.'[15]

This relates closely to our third and most important point: a dialogue with the material past is situated in far more than *methodological* context. The means of archaeological understanding include everything that the interpreting archaeologist brings to the encounter with the past. The context includes method, yes; but also the interests which brought the archaeologist to the past, the organisation of the discipline, cultural dispositions and meanings which make it reasonable to carry out the investigations, institutional structures and ideologies. We repeat that the archaeological past simply could not exist without all this, the heterogeneous networking of archaeological projects.

MEANING AND MAKING SENSE

Interpretation may suggest meanings for things from the past. A sociological argument is that social practice is to do with interpreting the meanings of things and actions; society is constituted through meanings ascribed and negotiated by social agents (Giddens 1984). So an understanding of the past presupposes that interpretation is given of past meanings of things.

Meaning is a term which requires examination. For example, archaeologists have tried to distinguish functional from symbolic meanings, primary from secondary, denotative from connotative (Shanks and Tilley 1987a, ch. 7, Conkey 1990). In practice, however, it is difficult to separate functional, technological meanings from the symbolic realm, and conversely symbols clearly have pragmatic social functions. In the material world function contributes to abstract symbolic meaning. Much symbolism is entirely ingrained in the practices of daily life, in the rhythms of the body and the seasons, and in the punctuated experience of time. The notion of abstract symbolic code, arbitrarily divorced from practice, has little role to play in current understanding of meaning and its interpretation. There has been a gradual shift in archaeology from a consideration of material culture as language, to a concern with material culture as text and then to an emphasis on practice (see the discussions in Part 5).

It thus often becomes difficult to ask 'What does this pot mean?', since it may not 'mean' in a language-type way (a point well illustrated by Maurice Bloch in this volume). There may be no signifieds tied to the signifier in a code. Rather it may be the case that, even if people cannot answer what the pot means, they can use the pot very effectively in social life. This practical knowledge of 'how to go on' may be entirely ingrained in practices so that the meanings cannot be discussed verbally with any readiness – the meanings are *non-discursive*. This does not, of course, preclude verbal meanings being construed by an outside interpreter. And at other times – for example, in conflicts over uses and meanings – non-discursive meanings may be brought into 'discursive consciousness', although in doing so actors often embellish and transform.

The meanings that archaeologists reconstruct must on the whole be assumed to be general social and public meanings. Archaeologists have sufficient data to identify repeated patterning within large contexts (sites over many decades, regions over centuries or even millennia). The meanings reconstructed must be public and social in nature. Individual variation may be expressed in variability in the archaeological record, but it is rare that the data allow repeated patterning in an individual's action to be identified. Nevertheless it is important at the theoretical level to include the dialectic between individual and social meanings since it is in such terms that the negotiation of change is conducted (Barrett 1988, Johnson 1989).

There is also the question: Whose meanings? We have argued for a fusion of horizons as being characteristic of effective interpretation. A fourfold hermeneutic places great distance and interpretive problems between past and present. There are problems with defining the concept of meaning, and some of these are elaborated in Part 2 which deals with (cultural) meaning in relation to early hominids and primates.

Archaeological interpretation deals with the meanings of the past for the present, so it is perhaps better to think of *making sense*. Emphasis is again placed on the practice of interpretation. As a go-between, guide or interlocutor, the archaeologist makes sense of the past, providing orientations, significances, knowledges and, yes, meanings, relevant to understanding the past. The question of whose meanings is superseded.

PLURALISM AND AUTHORITY

A guide interpreting a map and the land can follow equally feasible paths which may offer different returns or benefits, different vistas. There are different ways of achieving the same ends. Interpretations may vary according to context, purpose, interest or project. Interpretation, we have argued, implies a sensitivity to context. With the equivocality and heterogeneity of things and the underdetermination of interpretation, there are many arguments for pluralism.

But pluralism introduces the problem of authority. On what grounds are different interpretations of the same field to be judged? The problem arises because finality and objectivity (residing in and with the past itself) have been abandoned for an attention to the *practice* of interpretation (making sense of the past as it presents itself to us now). Charges of relativism have been made (Trigger 1980). Relativism is usually held not to be a good thing. If interpretations of the past depend on present interests and not on objectivity, then there is no way of distinguishing a professional archaeological explanation from the crazed views of cranks who may interpret archaeological remains as traces of alien visitors (Renfrew 1989).

The issue of relativism crops up in Part 3. Part 1 deals with this issue of truth, objectivity and knowledge, and argues that the real issue in the debate over pluralism and relativism is that of *absolutes*. Truth and objectivity are not abstract principles inherent in the past, but have to be worked for. That Anglo-Saxon cemetery in the countryside will not excavate itself. It needs the archaeologist's interest, efforts, management skills, excavation teams, finds-laboratories and publisher to be made into what we come to call the objective past.

There are very important issues here to do with the value of interpretation in relation to what science is commonly taken to be. Relativism has not been adequately dealt with, so we present some possible lines which can be taken regarding judgement, authority, objectivity and science.[16]

Objectivity

It is argued that objectivity is not an absolute or abstract quality towards which we strive. Objectivity is constructed. This is not to deny objectivity, but rather, ironically, to make it more concrete. So let it be agreed that an objective statement is one which is, at the least, strong; and that, indeed, we would wish our interpretations to be full of such strong statements. What makes a statement strong? The conventional answers are that strength comes from logical coherence, or because the statement corresponds with something out there, external to the statement, or because of some inherent quality called objectivity. But who decides on how coherent a statement must be? How exact must correspondence be? And in historical and sociological studies of scientific controversies there appear many other sources of strength such as government or religious support, good rhetoric in convincing others, even financial backing.

We have been arguing that the archaeological past will not excavate itself but needs to be worked for. If objectivity is an abstract quality or principle held by reality, how does it argue for itself, how does it display its strength? No, people are needed, their projects. Gravity does not appear to all and everyone on its own. Microbes needed the likes of Pasteur (Latour 1988). So a statement about the archaeological past is not strong because it is true or objective. But because it holds together when interrogated it is described as objective. What, then, does a statement hold on to, whence does it derive strength, if not from objectivity? There is no necessary answer. It can be many things. An objective statement is one that is connected to anything more solid than itself, so that, if it is challenged, all that it is connected to threatens also to fall.

An archaeological report usually aims to present data as objectively as possible – a strong basis for subsequent inference. Its strength comes from all those diagrams and photographs, the many words of detailed description, the references to comparative sites and materials which give further context to the findings. These all attest to the actual happening of the excavation and to the trustworthiness of the excavation team. Where otherwise is the quality of objectivity? Because the report is coherent and reads well (no contradictions betraying lies and artifice), and the photographs witness things actually being found, because its style and rhetoric are found acceptable, because it delivers what is required (from format to types of information), it is described as sound. Objectivity is what is held together. If a report holds together, it is considered objective.

Challenge a fact in the report and you have to argue with all of this, with the happening of the excavation, that great heterogeneous assemblage of people, things and energies. Ultimately the only way to shake its strength is to excavate another similar site, mobilising another army of resources and people. The skill of crafting objectivity is heterogeneous networking – tying as many things together as possible.

Relativism

If the abstract and independent principle of objectivity is denied, relativism is held to result. Here an important distinction is between *epistemic* and *judgemental* relativism (Bhaskar 1979).[17] Epistemic relativism, which we follow, holds that knowledge is rooted in a particular time and culture. Knowledge does not just mimic things. Facts and objectivity are constructed. Judgemental relativism makes the *additional* claim that all forms of knowledge are equally valid. But judgemental relativism does not follow from epistemic relativism. To hold that objectivity is constructed does not entail that all forms of supposed knowledge will be equally successful in solving particular problems. Epistemic relativism simply directs attention to the reasons why a statement is held to be objective or strong; it directs attention to the heterogeneous assemblages of people and things and interests and feelings, etc., mobilised in particular projects. To argue a relativism which maintains objectivity is socially constructed is to argue simply for *relationality*.

But on what grounds is judgement to be made? If objectivity is constructed, are different interpretations of the past to be judged according to their place in the present? Constructed objectivity would seem to imply that there is no real past. Common sense says that it is silly to think that the distance between survey transects is something to do with society or politics (Bintliff 1992). Is an archaeological interpretation to be explained not by the past but by the politics of the Council for British Archaeology or the Smithsonian?

The reality of the past

But what is the *real* past? Reality is what resists, and trials test its resistance. Kick a megalith and it hurts – it is very real. But you cannot conclude that if you used a bulldozer it would have the same result. This is not to deny reality at all, but it has to be specified which trial has been used to define a resistance and hence a *specific* reality. Look at a ceramic thin section down a microscope and there is a reality different from that of its surface decoration. Reality is plural; the artefact is a multiplicity. It depends on what 'work' is done upon and with it.

So what are the conditions of trials of resistance which define reality? Interpretive encounters. They are those heterogeneous networks or projects described above – mobilised mixtures of people and things.

But there is still the problem of the authority of academic science. What is to be done about those cranks who purvey what are clearly mystical untruths about the archaeological past?[18] It has been argued that objectivity is to be sought when the term refers to a strong statement which is held together. Relativism of the sort described here does, indeed, cherish a sense of reality when the real past is conceived as that which resists *specific* trials of resistance.

Introducing an abstract and absolute objectivity into this comparison of academic and fringe archaeology confuses things because thereby trials of resistance are made incommensurable.

Consider the opinion that scientific archaeology is objective and people who believe in ley-lines are cranks. Archaeologists have objectivity on their side; they are clever and professional. What do ley-liners have? Stupidity? Science and pseudo-science are here incommensurable; they cannot be compared. This takes us nowhere and, most important, it makes impossible an understanding of scientific controversy. Does the truth always win? What force does it have? How is it that ideas which are now totally discredited, such as the presence of phlogiston in combustible materials, were once held to be objective truths? Were people stupid then, or at least not as critical as later?

Maintaining an absolute objectivity makes it impossible to understand the reasons for there being different versions of the past. So it seems reasonable to abandon abstract objectivity and make trials of resistance commensurable. This means treating, at the outset, objectivity and 'falsity', science and 'pseudo-science' as equal (many scientific ideas began as cranky ideas). Trials of resistance are perfectly in order. Talk to people, understand them, persuade if necessary; instead of patronising them by playing the expert.[19] Maintain an open and reasoned dialogue. Test what holds the respective objectivities together.[20]

But can fringe archaeologies ever be treated in such a way? Surely there is no controversy? The general point is that it is not possible to argue with the independent reality of the past. It happened. It is not possible to argue with the laws of nature. The environment, for example, sets immovable constraints on what people can do. How can a relativist argue with this?

What were constraints in the past are often not constraints now – nature has a historical relationship with people. Indeed, it is not possible to negotiate with gravity while falling out of a tenth-storey window. But neither is it easy to negotiate with an IRA bomber. These circumstances do not often occur, however. 'Hard' reality does not often suddenly impose itself. It is usually more gradual, during which time 'society' may negotiate and change its practices: consider environmental change. Gravity is not so much a constraint upon an engineer as a resource used, for example, in the building of a bridge. Clay is a very real resource used by potters, but of course many things cannot be made with it. Why be obsessed with the things that cannot be done? Why not try to understand the creativity?

There still remains the issue that the past happened when it did. If it is argued that archaeology is a mode of cultural production of the past, does this mean that things did not exist before they were so constructed? Was the Bronze Age hut circle not there before being excavated? And, conversely, were prehistoric stone tools once thunderbolts?

Here it is important not to confuse existence and essence. Existence is when you specify times and settings; it is local and historical. Essence makes no reference to time and space. If something exists at time 1 (the excavated cemetery), can we conclude that it always existed, even at time 2 (i.e., in essence)? Conversely, can we conclude from the fact that something existed between time 1 and time 2 (a stone thunderbolt) that it never existed (i.e., never had an essential quality)? The same questions can be set with regard to space.

The dualism between existence and essence corresponds with the following:

existence	essence
history	nature
society	objectivity

Why should the object world be credited with essence while people only have subjectivity and historical existence? Deny the dualisms. Society then becomes more than just people, receiving objective materiality, and is no longer opposed to the natural world of objects, and nature becomes truly natural history with things having a history which is often tied to that of people. The specific realities of the past are now historically connected with those of archaeologists in particular projects – heterogeneous and historical mixtures of real people and things. If timeless essences and abstract qualities such as objectivity are put to one side as products of theology, we do not lose the solidity of archaeological facts. They are still real and important; but so, too, are archaeologists, volunteers, publishers, television companies, photographers, feelings, interests, tools, instruments and laboratories which gather and bring to historical reality those facts. There is no necessary monopoly of one particular archaeological mobilisation of people and things which is tied to objectivity. We are hereby more attuned to different archaeological projects. Reburial issues, treasure hunting, landscape art and fringe archaeology become commensurable with professional archaeology: they are but different assemblages of resources (things, practices, people, aspirations, projects, etc.).

It may be objected that this leads to the apparent nonsense that Thomsen 'happened' to stone and metal tools. But this is indeed the case, because the object world is now credited with a history. Grahame Clark did happen to the settlement at Star Carr.

How could Star Carr be defined and pictured before Clark? Perhaps we should apply Clark's excavation retrospectively and suppose that the site was there all along. It is quite legitimate to believe this, but how could it be proved? There is no time machine to take archaeologists back to 1182 or 431 to check that Star Carr was there then, albeit perhaps less decayed.[21] Rather than jumping to conclusions about total existence or non-existence – essences – why not stick with reality defined as that which resists particular trials made of it? The confusion of existence and essence is a damaging one.

A site such as Star Carr does not have an abstract essence or timeless objectivity. We argue that its objective existence has a history. Clark is part of the reality of Star Carr, just as the excavations at Star Carr are part of the biography of Grahame Clark. The reality of Star Carr includes the excavation team, the tools, the whole project.

Are we otherwise to project Clark's and our present back into the past? It is good to remember that Nazi archaeologists find their political realities in the past, projecting back from their present, tinkering with *real* history.

If objectivity is accepted as constructed, a criticism may be voiced that thereby is subjectivity unleashed. This may be countered with the argument that if objectivity is denied as an essence, so, too, must be subjectivity. The opposition between objectivity sticking to the facts and subjectivity giving way to mystical and personal feelings is a false one. Why deny that it is people who do archaeology, and that people are indeed constituted as subjectivities in historical dealings with others and with things? If objectivity is denied as an essence, subjectivity becomes the form that the object world takes – through the looking, digging, thinking, feeling, the projects, those heterogeneous mobilisations of people.

If it is accepted that archaeology is a technology, a mode of cultural construction of the past, reality, objectivity and the past are not lost. Troublesome essences and dichotomies are, however, discarded. The solidity, beauty, originality of archaeological facts are still there and may be described with terms of 'fact', 'reality' and 'objectivity'. But present also are archaeologists, volunteers, publishers, film makers, television companies, photographers, feelings and desires, instruments and laboratories which make these facts live and hold together.

CRITIQUE

Another aspect of judging the relative value and worth of different interpretations of the same field is critique.[22]

Awareness of the dialogues at the heart of interpretation requires self-reflexivity regarding the situated and contextualised interpreters and interpretands. Vital here is the project of ideology critique, now well established in archaeology. Ideology may hinder or make impossible the project of making good sense of the past.

Another dimension of critique is rooted in the heterogeneity, otherness and consequent independence of the material past. The past may become grounds for a critique of the present in that its forms and meanings may defamiliarise and throw into contingency what is taken in the present to be natural or unchanging.

The terms 'equivocality' and 'heterogeneity' were introduced above to describe how something always escapes its classification, there always being more to say and consider. The old pot found by an archaeologist is equivocal also because it belongs both to the past and to the present. This is its history; it has survived. And the equivocality confers upon the pot an autonomy because it is not limited to the moment of its making or use, or to the intentions of the potter. It goes beyond. The archaeologist can look back with hindsight and see the pot in its context, so time reveals meanings which are accessible *without* a knowledge of the time and conditions of its making. The pot transcends. In this it has qualities which may be called timeless.

Here also historicism (understanding in historical context) must be denied, otherwise we would only be able to understand a Greek pot by reliving the reality of the potter, a reality which anyway was indeterminate and equivocal. We would be fooling ourselves in thinking that we were appreciating and understanding the art and works of other cultures.

Pots are often used as a means to an end by archaeologists. They are used for dating a context; they may be conceived as telling of the past in different ways. Historicist interpretation reduces the significance of a cultural work to voluntary or involuntary *expression*: the pot expresses the society, or the potter, or the date. This is quite legitimate. But there is also the pot itself, its equivocal materiality, its mystery and uncertainty, which open it to interpretation.

The pot does indeed preserve aspects of its time and it can be interpreted to reveal things about the past. So the integrity and independence of the pot does not mean that it does not refer outside of itself. It means that no interpretation or explanation of a pot can ever be attached to the pot for ever, claiming to be integral or a necessary condition of experiencing that pot. The autonomy of the pot is the basis of opposition to totalising systematics: systems of explanation or understanding which would claim closure, completeness, a validity for all time. We must always turn back to the pot and its particularity. This autonomy brings a source of authority to interpretation, if it is respected.

The autonomy of the past is also the reason why archaeological method has no monopoly on the creation of knowledges and truths about the material past. Does a painting of a castle by Turner reveal no truths of its object in comparison with archaeological treatment? Were there no truths about the material past before the formalisations of archaeological method from the late nineteenth century onwards?

There is a gap between the autonomy and dependency of the pot. If we were back in the workshop where the pot was made, we might have a good awareness of its meaning. If we were the one who actually made the pot, then it would very much be dependent upon us. But its materiality, equivocality, heterogeneity always withhold a complete understanding: the clay is always other than its maker; the pot is always more than its classification. People may interpret it in all sorts of different ways. The material world provides food for thought, for negotiation of meaning, as we have already indicated.

So the tension within the pot between dependency and autonomy is a tension between its expressive (or significative) character and its materiality. It is a gap between, for example, an image (which has an autonomous existence) and its meanings. Or between the sound of a word and its meaning to which it cannot be reduced. To bridge these gaps requires effort, work, the time of interpretation. This work is one of reconstruction and connection, putting back together the pieces which have been separated.

When a pot becomes part of the ruin of time, when a site decays into ruin, revealed is the essential character of a material artefact – its duality of autonomy and dependency. The ruined fragment invites us to reconstruct, to exercise the work of imagination, making connections within and beyond the remnants. In this way the post-history of a pot is as indispensable as its pre-history. And the task is not to revive the dead (they are rotten and gone) or the original conditions from whose decay the pot remained, but to understand the pot as ruined fragment. This is the fascination of archaeological interpretation.

Commentary and critique

The tension within the (temporality of an) artefact between past and present, between autonomy and dependence upon its conditions of making, corresponds to the complementarity of critique and commentary. Commentary is interpretation which teases out the remnants of the time of the artefact, places it in historical context. Critique is interpretation which works on the autonomy of the artefact, building references that shift far beyond its time of making. It may be compared artistically with artefacts from other times and cultures in critical art history. Critique may consider different understandings of the artefact in our present. Critique may use the integrity of the artefact as a lever against totalising systems, undermining their claims to universality.

Both are necessary. Commentary without critique is empty and trivial information with no necessary relation to the present. Critique without commentary may be a baseless and self-indulgent appreciation of the aesthetic achievements of the past, or a dogmatic ideology, an unedifying emanation of present interests.

Commentary is made on the dependency of things upon their time of making, fleshing out information of times past. But the flesh needs to be brought to life, and this is the task of critique: revealing heterogeneity, yoking incongruity, showing the gaps in the neat orders of explanation, revealing the impossibility of any final account of things. This is a living reality because it is one of process rather than of arrest. It is the ongoing dialogue that is reasoned interpretation.

DESIGNED PASTS: DISCOURSE AND WRITING

The archaeological past is written or told. It is translated into other forms. This is the focus of Part 3, but some general points can be appended here.

Archaeology is a practice in which language plays a dominant part. The archaeologist comes literally to the site with a coding sheet, labelled with words, to be filled in. In addition there is a large implicit 'black-box' coding sheet, never discussed, which defines walls, pits, sections, layers and so on. If the excavation process starts with language, so, too, it finishes with language. The events which take place in practice on an archaeological excavation are contingent and they are experienced differently by different participants. Interpretations are continually changed and contested. But in the end a report has to be written, the diversity and contingency subsumed within an ordered text. A story has to be told which not only describes what happened on the site (usually a minor part of the report) but also describes how the layers built up, when and perhaps why the walls were constructed, and so on. The story has to be coherent, with a beginning, a middle and an end. The site has to be moulded into a narrative using rhetoric which makes the story persuasive. A practice has been translated into words and narrative.

Archaeology, like any other discipline, constructs its object past through the workings of *discourse*.[23] This is a key concept in directing attention not so much to the content, but to the way something is written or told, and the social and historical conditions surrounding writing and telling. Discourse can be treated as heterogeneous networkings, technologies of cultural production (of a particular kind) which enable and are the conditions within which statements may be made, texts constituted, interpretations made, knowledges developed, even people constituted as subjectivities. Discourse may consist of people, buildings, institutions, rules, values, desires, concepts, machines and instruments. These are arranged according to systems and criteria of inclusion and exclusion, whereby some people are admitted, others excluded, some statements qualified as legitimate candidates for assessment, others judged as not worthy of comment. There are patterns of authority (committees and hierarchies, for example) and systems of sanctioning, accreditation and legitimation (degrees, procedures of reference and refereeing, personal experiences, career paths). Discourses include media of dissemination and involve forms of rhetoric. Archives (physical or memory-based) are built up providing reference and precedents. Metanarratives, grand systems of narrative, theory or explanation, often approaching myth, lie in the background and provide general orientation, framework and legitimation.

Discourses may vary and clash in close proximity. In a factory the discourse of the workforce may differ considerably from that of the management. Academic archaeology probably includes several discourses: Near Eastern and classical archaeology being distinct from Anglo-American processual archaeology. The discourse of commercial excavation is different again. Fowler (in this volume) considers aspects of discourses on the countryside, though he focuses as much on the content of the writing. The notion of the English countryside and landscape, its development and relation to national identity could be termed part of a metanarrative. J. Thomas (1991a) has challenged the metanarrative of earlier British prehistory, that it was then just as it always has been – hearty peasants in the English countryside. Other metanarratives include the stories of cultural diffusion from centres of excellence accompanied by conquest and population movement: an explanatory scheme based on nineteenth-century experiences of imperialism. Larsen (1989) has related Near Eastern archaeology to an ideology of orientalism (Said 1978). Evolutionary theories, when treated uncritically, often also form neat formulae for bringing the past to order (Shanks and Tilley 1987b, ch. 6), which is a function of metanarrative.

Archaeological poetics

An awareness of discourse implies an attention to technique, to style, to the way archaeology designs and produces its pasts. This is the project of an *archaeological poetics* (Shanks and Tilley 1989, Shanks 1992a, Tilley 1993) and involves a shift from validation to signification, from anchoring our accounts in the past itself (divorced somehow from our efforts in the present to make sense of it) to the ways we make sense of the past by working through artefacts.

In Part 1, Lucas discusses clarity and density of styles of writing about the archaeological past, arguing not for obscurity, but for contingency: a dependency of writing on its conditions of production. Some other papers in this volume explicitly consider issues of writing the past. Fowler, as already mentioned, discusses writings on the countryside and their styles. Lowenthal introduces the central theme of rhetoric in his discussion of appeals to the past in contemporary self-definition. Shanks considers archaeological historiography and the place of individual agency. Hodder takes a different line and uses rhetorical tropes or features of style to suggest structures in prehistory.

Some concerns of an archaeological poetics include *narrative; rhetoric; rhizomatics; quotation; illustration.*

Narrative, telling stories, is a basic human way of making sense of the world as particular details are given sense by incorporating them into story forms. The following are components of narrative.[24]

- story: a temporal sequence
- plot: the causation and reasoning behind the story
- allegory: metaphor, the story and plot may stand for something else
- arrangement of parts: this need not necessarily be a linear sequence of events (there may be temporal slips and changes of pace, condensation and focus on key points)
- agency: the medium through which the story is told
- point of view: given to the reader

Archaeological narrative is often very predictable. Arrangement is usually linear or analytical, the agency is anonymous or impersonal powers, and the point of view is academic, white, Anglo-American, middle-class (but cf. Leone *et al*. in this volume). Little experiment is encouraged even though it might considerably improve archaeological writing and attend more to the interests of *different* audiences (an essential component of narrative after all).

Archaeology almost of necessity has to quote because so much of the past is destroyed in excavation. *Quotation* here refers to bits of 'reality' brought into the picture in the form of photographs or lists of actual objects lodged in a museum (quotation is thus distinct from referencing or citation of other texts). In archaeology this is usually to witness and legitimate the writing. Quotation is to do with collage and montage – direct quotation, literal repetition of something taken out of its context and placed in another. But there is no archaeological discussion of the theory and poetics of collage that we know of (other than Shanks 1992a, pp. 188–90 and passim). Collage is of essential importance to museum display, and there are many effective exhibitions (on art and anthropology, see Schneider's review 1993). Walsh (in this volume) touches on some issues with reference to the concept of ecomuseum and multimedia display, but again the literature in the archaeological field seems weak. Objects need not only credit a statement with concrete validity, but also be used for their heterogeneity, treated in terms of their autonomy from what is written about them, overflowing the words. This aesthetic principle is familiar from art museums and books but can be greatly extended (see, for example, Greenaway 1991 and 1993).

The field of *rhetoric* is coextensive with all communicative and expressive acts.[25] Classically it comprises the following.

- *Inventio*: the discovery of ideas and arguments. Here are included modes of creative generation covering the history of ideas, historiography, the sociology of knowledge, and also interdisciplinary connections.
- *Dispositio*: the arrangement of ideas into sequences and narratives. Logical and aesthetic links may be considered.
- *Elocutio*: forms of expression and figures of speech, stylistic treatment. This may be divided into *aptum* – appropriateness to subject-matter and context (for example, is a line drawing appropriate?); *puritas* – correctness of expression (according, or not, to rules of discourse and the discipline); *perspicuitas* – the comprehensibility of expression (clarity and density); *ornatus* – the adornment of expression.

   Tropes or figures of speech provide a great insight into varieties of text structure within *elocutio*. Here are included strategies such as antithesis and irony (figures of contrast), metaphor (identity in difference), metonymy. These particularly would seem to be very relevant to archaeology in its translation of material pasts into a different medium, text and image (on metaphor, see Shanks 1992a and Tilley 1990b). Another issue is that of humour (so successfully used by Gamble in his conference presentation); mention has already been made of the importance of pleasure as a constitutive principle in interpretation.
- *Memoria*: the techniques of storage and the retrieval of speech or text.
- *Pronunciatio*: delivery, gestures and setting. Included here are the design and delivery of lectures and television programmes, books and publishing projects, museum displays.

Illustration may be treated simply as a visual appendage to a written text, not intended to add anything to verbal description, for example – simply exemplifying. It may approximate to quotation, a photograph witnessing what is written. But illustration can also perform a summarising function, particularly in the form of diagrams. This, arguably, is one of the great strengths of systems thinking in archaeology: diagrams of neat boxes and arrows brought the complexity of the empirical to order. Renfrew's classic conception of the social system (1972) provided a synoptic structure of chapter topics for over half of his book on the prehistoric

Aegean. Illustration or graphic representation can draw together things, establishing and mobilising connections which are made all the more effective by being visible at a glance in one place. Thought is hereby guided, possibly even conditioned (Lynch and Woolgar, eds, 1990). Latour (1990) has argued that graphic representation can perform a key role in scientific controversy by performing this function.

Illustration involves working with the relation between words and pictures. It refers to multimedia production, a topic which has long been around in the form of the illustrated book or lecture, but which is now receiving attention through the development of computer-based hypermedia (see Miller 1992). Illustration can be related to breaking the linear flow of text, having a disruptive power: 'a picture, labelled or not, is a permanent parabasis, an eternal moment suspending, for the moment at least, any attempt to tell a story through time' (Miller 1992, p. 66). Illustration, grafted upon text, can be an alien addition which produces more than the sum of text and image.

Rhizomatics is a term borrowed from the philosophy of relations of Deleuze and Guattari (1988). A contrasting pair is formed with tree-thinking. Both refer to the way connections can be made, the way things can be thought and interpreted, so the way texts may be construed and constructed. The two are complementary, but rhizomes thinking is often forgotten or overlooked.

Tree-thinking is unified and hierarchical (trunk and dendritic structure), concerned with the place of things, their meanings and identities (by virtue of position). It is conceived that there are roots and bases to what is known. The purpose is to reproduce the object of thought (either by means of an image or in terms of structure).

Rhizomes belong with plants which spread insidiously. Rather than fixed and centred structure, there is shifting, motive connection. Connections spread, shifting through analogies and associations. Rhizomes thinking does not aim to reproduce an object in thought, image or words, but to connect with it, construct with it. Final and definitive identities are denied as the object world is forever reconstructed.

Through our discussion of the general field of interpretation we hope to have shown openings for such relational work.[26] J. Hillis Miller has drawn upon similar distinctions in his essay on cultural studies (1992). He discusses how binary oppositions or dualisms (such as those above) permeate cultural studies (the academic (inter)discipline): high versus popular culture, theory versus practice, hegemonic versus marginal culture, artefact as reflecting culture versus artefact as creating culture, for example. They are difficult to avoid. As a resolution he puts forward Abdul JanMohamed's distinction between binary negation (twinned oppositional pairs subject to hierarchical ordering) and negation by analogue. The latter treats each element of the dualism as part of a *differential series* without hierarchical priority or fixed origin or end. He comments: 'I see this distinction as a crucial theoretical point. It is crucial because cultural studies must hold on to it firmly if they are to resist being recuperated by the thinking of the dominant culture they would contest' (1992, p. 16).[27]

Interpretation, if followed through and as implied by this discussion of archaeological poetics, implies a blurring of the absolute distinction between factual and fictional writing. The archaeological text becomes a literary form. Fact and the fictive form a continuous field. They share the same techniques of production. As Tilley (1993) has pointed out, the real purpose of a radical and absolute distinction would seem to be an interest in the validation of some interpretive practices over others. It should carefully be noted that fictional writing and 'creative imagery' can be a tremendous resource in working with and learning about reality.

Tilley (1993) has remarked upon the paradox that what we now term interpretive archaeology hardly exists, yet all archaeology is interpretive. The number of empirical studies which are self-consciously postprocessual or interpretive (in the senses outlined here) is growing, and the range of issues discussed in this volume attests to the wide applicability of the concept of interpretation, but it is less important that archaeologists adopt the label. We are simply proposing that archaeologists, whatever their claims, always have done and can do no other than interpret the past. This places archaeology in symmetry with those in the past who are studied, and with those who are not archaeologists but who try to make sense of the material past. They, too, interpreted and interpret their world, engaging in cultural production. Foregrounding the interpretive character of archaeology deprives archaeologists of an authority which would lie in their restricted access to scientific method, abstract truth and the objectivity of the past. But they can potentially offer to others their skill in crafting and interpreting material pasts, cherishing their creative responsibilities.

NOTES

1 For definitions and literature, see Trigger 1989a, Willey and Sabloff 1980; a recent textbook expression is Renfrew and Bahn 1991.

2 For general introductions to the issues see Hodder 1984, Gero, Lacy and Blakey (eds) 1983, Gero and Conkey (eds) 1991, Shanks and Tilley 1987a, 1987b, 1989, Miller, Rowlands and Tilley (eds) 1989, Layton (ed.) 1989a and 1989b, Gathercole and Lowenthal (eds) 1989, Leone 1986, Leone, Potter and Shackel 1987, Leone and Preucel 1992, Shanks 1992a.

3 Etymology is of relevance in supporting this choice of epithet for archaeology which stresses an ongoing practice of mediation and translation. 'Interpret' and 'interpretation' are derived from *inter-pres*, Latin. The prefix *inter-* refers, of course, to mediation or reciprocity. *-Pres* is of uncertain root, but perhaps relating to the Greek verbs φράζειν (*phrazein*), to speak, or πραττειν (*prattein*) to act or do; the Sanskrit root may be *prath*, to spread abroad, celebrate, disclose or unfold, reveal or show. And should we speak of 'interpretative' or 'interpretive'? Both have long histories of English usage; 'interpretive' is not a recent and by implication unorthodox elision or American usage. We prefer 'interpretive' because it is an adjective derived not from the noun 'interpretation', but from the *verb* 'interpret' – attention is drawn to the practice.

4 Signification: composed of the Latin *signum facere*, to make a sign.

5 Mike Pearson, director of Brith Gof performance theatre company, Cardiff, has been exploring the connections between performance (theatre without conventional text) and archaeology: see his paper 'Theatre/archaeology' (1993).

6 We draw on Gadamer 1975. See also Warnke 1987 and Bleicher 1980, 1982. Ricoeur has great potential for archaeology: 1981a–d, 1989: see Moore 1990. For archaeology: Shanks and Tilley 1987a, ch. 5, Shanks 1992a, Johnsen and Olsen 1992.

7 Etymology again reveals a rich range of deep and relevant cultural references. The Greek is ἑρμηνεύω (*hermeneuo*) related to the actions of the god Ἑρμῆς, Hermes. Messenger and herald, thief and inventor of the lyre, guide to the souls of the dead; the rhetorician Hermes presided over commerce and exchange, markets and traffic, science and weights and measures. He dealt in stratagems and secret dealings, was a god, like craftsman god Hephaistos, of practical intelligence or knowhow. Termed μῆτις, the field of application of this ingenuity or worldly knowledge is ambiguity and equivocality – finding a way out of sticky situations (Detienne and Vernant 1978, especially pp. 122–3, 281–3, 301–3). Hermes takes us from the philosophical circuit of hermeneutics into a semantic and interdisciplinary field of translation, communication, movement and equivocality, messages and interference, transference and exchange, connections, hermeticism and mystery. The five-volume interdisciplinary epic of Michel Serres on such themes in language, literature, philosophy and science takes the name of *Hermès* (1968–80; selected translations 1982).

8 The collections Knorr-Cetina and Mulkay (eds) 1983 and Pickering (ed.) 1992

provide introductions and bibliographies to the work of people such as Latour, Knorr-Cetina, Woolgar, Collins and many others.

9 Gavin Lucas has pointed out (in discussion) that not only is theory underdetermined, but it is also *overdetermined* by the facts – there is always a surplus or excess of data which any theory cannot cover. This also contributes to uncertainty.

10 Shanks 1992a and 1993; more generally on phenomenologies of landscape see J. Thomas 1993a and 1993b, Tilley forthcoming. For a background in humanistic geography, see Seamon and Mugerauer (eds) 1989 and Seamon (ed.) 1993.

11 The analogy is owed to David Austin, Lampeter.

12 For this important concept in the sociology of production and technology, see Law 1987, Law and Callon 1992, Callon 1986 and 1991.

13 On the idea of ethnographies of archaeological excavation and project see Shanks 1992a, pp. 192–3.

14 For philosophies of relationality, see Ollman 1971, Sayer 1987, Deleuze and Guattari 1988; in archaeology: Shanks and Tilley 1987a, Shanks 1992a, McGuire 1992.

15 This was repeated, in various ways, at a conference held at Hunter College, Manhattan, April 1990; cf. Leone and Preucel 1992.

16 The following arguments can all be found thoroughly rehearsed in much recent history, sociology and philosophy of science, particularly that which is sometimes called 'constructivism': above, note 8.

17 The terms are unfortunately ambiguous. Judgemental relativism maintains that judgement cannot be made of different interpretations which arise authentically from their social context, though interpretations are judged to be equal. Epistemic relativism allows judgement of different interpretations. We have used the terms because Bhaskar is well cited and himself continues their use.

18 A question posed forcibly by Renfrew in his critique of postprocessualism (1989) and by Renfrew and Bahn (1991, p. 430).

19 An important point is, however, that professional archaeologists deal with the material past on a day-to-day basis, amateurs when and if they can. Archaeologists *should* have achieved an authority through developing the skills involved in interpreting material remains of the past; though, of course, they may not have. This is based on the premiss that archaeology is a mode of cultural production of the past – skills which involve practical reasoning as well as propositional knowledge (Shanks and McGuire 1991). A key set of issues, and relevant to epistemology, here concerns the regulation of the profession and monitoring of the acquisition of interpretive skills.

20 This is a possible answer to the dilemma posed by Rhys Jones and reported in Part 1 concerning possible conflicts between accounts of human origins presented by academic scientists and Australian Aborigines. Reference may also be made to the issue of professionalism raised in note 19. The skill of interpreting the material remains of the past should, if characterised as in the present paper, carry with it a persuasive authority.

21 But, it may be argued, scientific observation shows that materiality has duration. Excavate Star Carr and its materiality (and any C-14 dates) signifies its duration. This is precisely the point. A house does not stop being real when it is abandoned and collapses, when it ceases to be tied to the history of the people who once lived in it. That house has *its own* history.

22 See Connerton (ed.) 1976, Held 1980, Kellner 1989; for archaeology, Leone, Potter and Shackel 1987, Olsen 1986, Shanks and Tilley 1987a and 1987b.

23 See Foucault 1972 and 1981, together with secondary literatures, for example Macdonell 1986. Tilley has presented a programme for what he calls a discourse analysis of archaeology: 1989b, 1990a and 1990b, 1993.

24 See Cohan and Shires 1988, Ricoeur 1989, Rimmon-Kenan 1983, H. White 1973 and 1987.

25 On archaeology and rhetoric, see Shanks 1994.

26 Further examples can be found in Shanks 1992a, 1992b and 1992c, and Tilley (ed. 1993). *A Thousand Plateaus* by Deleuze and Guattari (1988) is full of historical references.

27 This point cannot be overstressed. Consider the distinction within representation between repetition as *copy* and repetition as *simulacrum* (Derrida 1972, Foucault 1973, Deleuze 1969). Bruno Latour (1987 and elsewhere) adopts a similar relational strategy in dealing with the connections between science, technology and society. It should, however, be pointed out that relational thinking encompasses that described as tree thinking. A radical dichotomy which simply denies the validity of one pole of the opposition is to be avoided. In describing features of rhizomatics the intention is to open space for experiment rather than to deny the usefulness, in specific circumstances, of dendritic organisation.

Chapter 2

Interpretive archaeologies

Some themes, and questions

Michael Shanks and Ian Hodder

Some may see the 'big issues' of archaeology to be concerned with substantive questions of, for example, the origins of agriculture, or the emergence of civilisation. As has been explained, this volume takes another perspective on the discipline. To provide further orientation, here is presented a series of questions and issues which seem to be at the heart of discussion about the character of the discipline archaeology, and which we expect will be the foci for future developments.

1 SOME GENERAL, PHILOSOPHICAL AND POLITICAL QUESTIONS OF HOW TO GO ABOUT ARCHAEOLOGY

The long-standing debate about the fundamental character of archaeological method, whether it should be more or less modelled on the natural sciences, has deepened and widened with awareness of the subtlety of the social practices that are commonly termed *science*. Philosophical alternatives and complements to positivism and objectivist analysis of the past have been proposed for archaeology. These include traditional hermeneutics and modern revisions (particularly those of Ricoeur and Gadamer), critical and dialectical approaches to cultural interpretation and criticism (through Western Marxists to Habermas and beyond), and poststructuralist positions (derived especially from Derrida and Foucault's archaeology and genealogy). The following questions seem now pertinent for philosophies of archaeological interpretation.

- On what grounds are different approaches to the archaeological past to be judged – epistemological? ethical? political?
- Can scientific archaeologies which aim at objectivist explanation of the past accommodate the criticisms made of them from hermeneutic and critical standpoints – particularly that they ignore that archaeology is of necessity acts of contemporary cultural production?
- Are there different forms of science, some of which are more or less appropriate as models for archaeology?
- Is the notion of (hermeneutic) dialogue (between archaeological finds and researcher, past and present, subject and object of knowledge) appropriate or workable in archaeology?
- What is the politics of hermeneutic and poststructuralist interpretation in archaeology?
- Is it necessary or possible to get to the original meaning of the past?
- If it is not, and there is or was no original comprehensible meaning, does the past have an indeterminate and shifting meaning, subject perhaps to the desires and interests of the present?

- What authorities may be invoked to distinguish good from bad archaeological explanation or interpretation?
- If empirical 'fact' and the objective are not the only sources of authority for different archaeological explanations and interpretations of the past, what others are there?

Further discussion of these and other relevant issues can be found in the following books and papers: Tilley (ed.) 1990, Shanks 1992a, Shanks and Tilley 1987a, Warnke 1987, Eagleton 1983, Renfrew 1989, Hollis and Lukes (eds) 1982, Lawson and Appignanesi (eds) 1989.

2 ANIMALS AND HUMAN MEANING; EVOLUTION AND THE EMERGENCE OF THE HUMAN 'MIND'

Interpretive approaches, as outlined particularly by Shanks and Hodder in this volume, may be concerned with understanding the *meaning* of things and practices. To the extent that such frames of meaning may be cultural, rooted in self-reflection and complex modes of communication, questions are raised about the human species as an animal species and its evolutionary development.

- To what extent were humans more 'animal' in the remote past?
- To what extent are contemporary studies of non-human animals relevant the further back in time one inquires?
- Are there radical differences between the conceptual abilities of humans and animals?
- What is the nature of these differences?
- To what extent are interpretation, understanding and intentionality present in animal behaviour?
- If they are, what are the implications for early hominid development, the development of language, tool-use and symbolic behaviour (for example, style and mortuary practices)?
- What generally is the evolutionary significance of the development of symbolising abilities and linguistic communication?
- Is the interpretation of the earliest phases of prehistory going to be different from that of later phases?
- If so, how?

Cheney and Seyfarth 1990, Parker and Gibson (eds) 1990, Haraway 1989, Hinde 1987, Wynn 1989, Mellars and Stringer (eds) 1989, Midgley 1979, Foley (ed.) 1990, Lutz 1990.

3 INTERPRETING, WRITING AND PRESENTING THE PAST: INTERFACES BETWEEN PAST AND PRESENT

Archaeologists work on the past to produce specialist papers, excavation reports, works of synthesis, popular books, museum displays, television programmes and other 'texts'. Different rhetorical strategies are employed which have implications regarding power, authority and relationships with audiences. Audiences, for example, may be conceived as subjects or objects of marketing, education, administration, or as partners in a constructive dialogue. There have been recent exhortations to shift from the singular voice of the expert to multivocal and participatory dialogues. This has been related to the contemporary cultural (and postmodern) scene with its tension between a comercialised and fragmented past of 'heritage' and desires for meaning and 'genuine' (historical) points of cultural reference. Here are issues of the cultural value of the past. In the terms of archaeology there is a potential tension between the archaeological find treated as an object of analytical treatment or as a subject of affective responses.

- What is the place of archaeological work in (post)modern society?
- What is the place of something such as 'English heritage' in a multicultural society?
- What are the boundaries of the discipline of archaeology, particularly in relation to popular writing, novels, art, travel-writing, etc.?
- How should archaeologists create and attend to audiences?
- Are there distinct 'genres' within archaeology?
- Is there a place for experimental writing in archaeology?
- What can archaeologists learn from the experiences of 'interpretive anthropology' and the attempts there to revaluate the anthropological encounter in terms of writing?
- How should museums present the past?
- Are they the best medium and forum?

The literature on these matters falls into three distinct groups: that concerned with museums and museology; works on and about writing the material past; and those concerned with cultural values and the past. On museums and presentation, some critical perspectives include Hudson 1987, Hooper-Greenhill 1992, Vergo (ed.) 1990, Lumley (ed.) 1988, Pearce (ed.) 1989, Pearce 1992, Walsh 1992. Writing the material past: Bapty and Yates (eds) 1990, Barrett *et al.* 1991, Hodder 1990, Shanks 1992a, Tilley 1991, Spector 1991. Values and the past: Chippindale *et al.* 1990, Hewison 1987, Lowenthal 1985, Lowenthal and Binney (eds) 1981.

4 THE NATURE OF HISTORY AND ITS RELATIONS WITH ARCHAEOLOGY

There have been moves in both anthropology and archaeology to encompass aspects of the discipline history. Some anthropologists are coming to recognise the importance of historical studies. Archaeologists have been reflecting on the relations between the disciplines particularly through encounter with the *Annales* school. An issue is that of timescale and forms of appropriate interpretation. Social and cultural structures and other forces (such as environmental) may affect scales of historical change in different ways. Contingency and unintended consequences of action may play different roles. Intentionality and agency in social practice are crucial points of debate here – can they ever be ignored? Further relevant notions include the totality of history, periodisation, and the character of historical and archaeological narratives.

- Do different timescales require different kinds of history?
- Is archaeology only suited to long-term historical perspectives, and, if so, what form of interpretation is implied?
- Can history be without periods?
- Do historical periods reflect or affect change?
- Could history have been otherwise?
- Are general structures always reinterpreted locally?
- Are the large-scale trends sometimes identified by archaeologists the product of small-scale and varied practices?

- What holds 'history' together?
- What is the relation of narrative to history and scale?
- Are there inappropriate archaeological timescales and narratives?

Sahlins 1985, Hodder (ed.) 1987a, H. White 1973, Bintliff (ed.) 1991, Knapp (ed.) 1992, Veyne 1971, Deleuze and Guattari 1988, Duby 1980, Ricoeur 1989.

5 THE INTERPRETATION OF MATERIAL CULTURE

The category of material culture unites all the different interests and concerns of archaeology addressed in the other sections. Issues concern the relation of material artefacts and material dimensions of practice to social structures and to social change. Architecture and environmental space or place form one theme. There is the matter of the design and use of things, their relationships to propositional and practical knowledges. Some archaeologists – after a (post)structuralist model – have come to see material culture as a text; the emphasis in its interpretation is upon reading, meaning and context. Others, particularly drawing upon a French tradition, are developing sophisticated accounts of the organisation of practical knowledges or skills. A challenge to be considered is the relationship between these two views: the relationship between or independence of language and 'higher' symbolic functions and practical skills or knowhow.

- What are these 'things' that archaeologists talk about?
- What are the main dimensions of the design and making of things?
- How is practical knowledge organised?
- Are practices always socially and symbolically mediated?
- Is meaning always socially and symbolically practised?
- What is the distinction between meaning and being?
- What are the dimensions of the experience of materiality?
- How can information from psychology and ethology contribute to understanding material practices?
- How does the organisation of space engender particular social understanding and practices?

Bourdieu 1977, Tilley (ed.) 1990, Hodder (ed.) 1989, Miller 1987, Patrik 1985, *Archaeological Review from Cambridge*, 9:1, Tilley (ed.) 1993.

Part 1

Philosophical issues of interpretation

Chapter 3

Interpretation in contemporary archaeology
Some philosophical issues

Gavin Lucas

INTRODUCTION

A tale of two narratives

Apparently, before the 1960s we were all sleeping virgins. Somewhere in those heady days, we lost our innocence, and awoke to a new state of consciousness (D. Clark 1973, Renfrew 1982). This Romantic narrative of the experience of archaeology in Britain at this time was matched by a rather more religious experience in the United States. Binford describes it in his own words: 'I had a message, and I wanted them to hear it. . . . The first that I knew there was applause, and people began rising to their feet clapping their hands. It continued until I was back in my seat. I was choked up and wondered if Huxley had ever cried' (Binford 1972, pp.12–13).

Apart from differences in rhetoric, English and American archaeology share a similar Origin myth for contemporary philosophical and theoretical debate. A kind of enlightenment, as the story goes, occurred in which archaeology became for the first time truly self-conscious, and began to look back, both on its own past and its present presuppositions. It was a New Archaeology. And the characteristic feature of the New Archaeology was its explicitly scientific foundation. Papers were (and many still are) packed with formulae, mathematical or quasi-mathematical symbols, phrases which evoked the classical language of science, such as Schiffer's C and N transforms (Schiffer 1976), though surely the most audacious has to be the pre-revolutionary Leslie White's (White 1943) equation for Culture as $C = E \times T$ (where C = cultural development, E = energy, and T = technology). But behind all this rhetoric of science (for I do not think that archaeologists – at least, in Britain – thought any less that they were doing science in the earlier part of this century) lay one dominant urge – to extend the limits of what you could say about the past. They wanted to scale the heights of Hawkes's famous ladder (Hawkes 1954). And invoking a scientific foundation for archaeology provided a means of legitimating extended inferences, but more than that, of legitimating the claim for extended inferences. The popularity of science reached a peak in the 1960s, with the 'wonders' of technology and the ostensible rise in the standard of living which accompanied the new technology, and this played a large part in legitimating the New Archaeology (Patterson 1986, Redman 1991).

Those who still live this narrative today, including the original authors of it, have not by any means remained loyal to all their proclamations – or, indeed, agree between themselves on all issues. Most particularly, many have now rejected, if they ever accepted, the ideal of producing firm laws of human behaviour; and second, they have continually expanded, in accordance with their original programme, the limits of inference, most clearly in the extension of a social to a cognitive archaeology (Watson, LeBlanc and Redman 1984, Renfrew 1983). The new strands of various social theories, such as Structuralism and Marxism, were cautiously accepted as adding to the base on which to expand our understanding of the past (Renfrew 1982); and so today processual archaeology is still moving, and opening horizons. It is a narrative of continued but measured progress and optimism.

Yet there is another story which has been growing in Anglo-American archaeology since the early 1980s, of an archaeology which needs to break itself away from the Origin myth, away from the scientific foundation which controls and constricts it. This other, 'Oedipal' archaeology defies the authoritarian structure of processualism, yet is still tied to it like son to father; the term *postprocessualism* encapsulates this ambiguity. Renfrew's indignation at the arrogance of the 'post' in postprocessualism (Renfrew 1989) is not surprising when the developments in the 1980s are considered in terms of the narrative described above; the continuity with the original pro-gramme is what he no doubt sees. But this 'post' is far less arrogant than the 'New' in New Archaeology.

As processual archaeology has invested its authority in the Scientific Method, the processual–postprocessual debate is inevitably focused on this issue. For the processualists, the matter is simple: you attack the Scientific Method and you therefore threaten the possibility of any authority in archaeology; without a scientific basis of empirical and objective means of evaluating views of the past, you renounce any possibility of such an evaluation. Intellectual castration. Authority is absolute or it is nothing. In general discussion, this manifests itself as charging their opponents with relativism, while with reference to particular studies, it is a familiar cry of overextended inference. Postprocessualists either step too close or overstep the razor's edge of acceptable interpretation (Watson 1990). And this threat of relativism, of emasculation, is exactly what ties postprocessualism to its father. Processualism, in fact the processual–postprocessual debate, is patriarchal, both authoritarian and masculine. Only through the dissolution of the relativist issue, and more generally of the question of Method, can postprocessual archaeology develop a viable philosophy, and even perhaps drop its patronymic.

Archaeological neuroses

A strong theme of contemporary thought is the breaking down of disciplinary boundaries; as philosophy and social theory merge, the significance of philosophical issues in archaeology is perhaps more acute now than ever before. Yet ironically the chasm between theoretical and practical archaeologists widens, though this is by no means translatable into armchair and field archaeologists. Nor is it synonymous with critical and uncritical thinking. Such stereotypes are untrue and harmful. The key difference lies in those archaeologists who generally think archaeology is a self-contained discipline with fixed boundaries and those who do not. This is why, for the latter, philosophical issues take on increasing importance, often to the bewilder-ment of the former.

Furthermore, within the theoretical debate in Britain, there is still a gap between processualists and postprocessualists, albeit rather subdued. Although it has been shown how perhaps the divide is exaggerated – for example, through a common acceptance of the theory–data interdependency and pluralistic perspectives (Wylie, conference paper) – a fundamental philosophical difference still resides in the opposing positions. Again, the positions can be stereotyped, but the crux lies in a notion of the purity of Method. Processualists maintain that any work can be evaluated by a fixed and absolute standard, the basis of which is empirical, while postprocessualists have no such faith. While the question of Method remains central to processualists, postprocessualists tend to be more concerned with the situated nature of interpretation, and how that feeds back into the kinds of questions they ask of their data. So there are still quite basic differences, and one has to be careful about exaggerating lines of convergence, and thereby pointing to a consensus which is in fact spurious (see commentary below).

Finally, these internal tensions within Anglo-American archaeology are crossed by a wider tension within archaeology as an international discipline. This is particularly apparent between the Anglo-American tradition and others, where the theoretical debate in Britain and the United States often assumes a universal importance by virtue of their political hegemony. It is, as Olsen points out, scientific colonialism (Olsen 1991). Archaeological discourse, whether internally in Britain or globally, is always channelled through political structures which suppress or sustain vocality. Yet each country has its own rich tradition of archaeology, a genealogy of problems which are particular to itself (e.g., see the papers in Hodder, ed., 1992), and often not at all on the same course as the Anglo-American concerns.

At whatever level you look at our discipline, it appears to be fragmenting; internal divisions are more fundamental than ever before. It is not a question of disagreements of interpretation as it might have been fifty years ago – it is a disagreement over the very nature of archaeology. How coherent is it today, and, more significantly, how coherent should it be? And if there are different ways of doing archaeology, can we still sustain some dialogue between them? These questions apply at all levels of our fragmenting discipline, and have never seriously been addressed. Perhaps because it was assumed that, whatever internal debates arise, archaeology is archaeology is archaeology.

COMMENTARY

Spurious consensus

All the papers in this section express a somewhat similar perspective, in that a major theoretical divide is not what fuels their arguments. Hesse embraces some of the postpositivist critiques in her conception of science, while both Gellner and Moore warn of the dangers of excess in postpositivist positions. Yet this apparent concordance is misleading, especially in the case of Gellner and Moore who approach the issue from quite different viewpoints. Although pluralism and diversity of opinion appear to be widely approved, as in all so-called democracies, there are limits to how far people are willing to accept such diversity, particularly when pluralism looks like it is going to accelerate into relativism.

Thus, consider the following hypothetical dilemma (Rhys Jones, conference comment):

> Say, for example, you are trying to construct different sorts of histories in a museum, and the museum is there for the people, for the public. Consider the question (and I am taking an Australian example) where there is a positivist archaeological statement that human beings have been on that continent for, say, 40,000 years, and that they arrived across water barriers from Asia at about the time of the global spread of modern settlement. Say you put forward that view. And somebody comes to you as curator, with a lot of political pressure and says, 'Aborigines right across the continent firmly assert they have always been on that continent. That they are autochthonous, they came from the land, they have

always been there.' Now, do you place that view side-by-side with the positivist, scientific view, and say here is one view, here is another, as equal forms of truth; or, do you say, in the second one, Aborigines believe that this is the case, and respect their view as a religious statement – but it is false, because human beings are placental mammals, they are primates, they evolved in Africa, they did not evolve on a continent of marsupials. Now, that is a dilemma.

Crisis of confidence

Jones's dilemma, of course, raises the threat of relativism. One way of answering him might be that the way you tell it depends very much on who you are telling it to. But what this means is not altogether clear. Do you change conviction according to who you address, like some kind of intellectual chameleon? In which case, you lose all credibility. Or is it merely the manner of expression which changes, the style of rhetoric used? If so, a basic distinction between truth and style is maintained, and Jones's dilemma has still to be answered.

Criticisms of the positivist position are not lacking in the archaeological literature, particularly from Shanks and Tilley (1987a); however, the issue is really how to answer the main charge of the positivists, as presented in Jones's dilemma. Why do archaeologists not feel confident to tackle this dilemma directly? There does appear to be a lack of confidence in postpositivist positions (John Barrett, conference comment), and more generally a lack of conviction when presenting our work to the public, who expect us to know it all (Peter Fowler, conference comment). Is archaeology facing a crisis of confidence? Is there a feasible philosophical alternative if we reject positivism?

Philosophising with a hammer

I do not deny that there is an uneasiness when faced with Jones's dilemma; but, as in all dilemmas, their rhetorical force comes precisely because they draw the attention to sharp and contradictory consequences, and away from the blurred premises from which the dilemma is generated. Nietzsche's attitude (1968) to his contemporaries was to philosophise with a hammer; that is sometimes the only way to break through the consequences to undermine the premises. It is impossible to defend relativism, because it is based on the same premises as positivism: the primacy of epistemology. If all philosophy begins with the question of knowledge and truth, then relativism spells the end of philosophy; but, as Nietzsche says, why do we want the truth at all?

The basis of the dilemma is that truth and knowledge are objective – that is, independent of what we believe. Immediately you accept this, the dilemma is painful and violent, because it means beliefs can be true or false, and two contradictory beliefs cannot both be true. The value of my conviction therefore depends on its truth, and there is no way I can hold the Aboriginal view as equal to my own with any credibility. But – and this has never been satisfactorily answered by any positivist – how can you distinguish between belief and truth? On what grounds? The expected answer is, of course, Method. It is only through (the scientific) Method that we can hope to attain any kind of confidence of the independent validity of our knowledge. But the Method is impure – any method is impure, contaminated by our beliefs, and if so it cannot serve the function positivists want it to. Yet no matter how hard critics deconstruct the Method, believers will always attempt to save a fragment which is pure, and which guarantees the probity of the whole.

This clinging to the purity of Method is ultimately based on an alienated view of humans and the world; the familiar subject–object split. It starts from the premiss that we are separated from the world, and try to understand it yet avoiding simply projecting ourselves on to it. Hence the desire for an uncontaminated Method and the primacy of epistemology. But there are alternative starting-points, not the least that we are *always already in the world*. This is the radical thrust of Heidegger's ontology (Heidegger 1962), and why he describes Humans not as subjects or consciousnesses but as Being-there (*Dasein*). This radical hermeneutic tradition, which began with Heidegger, is extended by others such as Gadamer and Ricoeur, who especially articulate it in the spheres of interpretation. Method is no longer a problem, nor is relativism. The chasm between our understanding and the world which existed in positivist philosophy, and which gave rise to all their problems, is no longer of any relevance. Because we are always already in the world, situated, the problems are not how to decide the truth or falseness of different views – as in Jones's dilemma – but how to decide our reaction to different views. This means that I can say I believe the archaeological version rather than the Aboriginal one, but not that it is true in any independent way from my belief. Our problem is whether their view is represented, since we hold the power of vocality.

Interpretive archaeology

Jones's dilemma presented a rather extreme case of different cultures – and this, of course, is intentional, because it sharpens the dilemma; but it is really a political rather than an interpretive issue. However, as archaeologists facing each other with our interpretations, the dilemma becomes more blurred – we share more assumptions in common, and the question of evaluation on academic or intellectual grounds is far more pressing. How do we assess our colleagues' work? 'How do you get a story which has authority?' (Ian Hodder, conference comment).

Before going into a postpositivist arena for raising some answers to the question of the 'authority' of interpretations, and means of assessment, it is worth anticipating some of the more common positivist critiques of the postpositivist claims.

Positivist prejudices

1 *Science*. In itself, post-positivist philosophy is not so much anti-science as against 'The Scientific Method'; it is not a call for archaeologists to stop doing scientific work in the analysis of their data, or to stop using scientific equipment or techniques. (e.g., see Thomas 1991b).

2 *Data*. Nor is it an abandonment of the role of data. 'Data' (Latin: 'given') – that which is given; in positivist language, what is presented to our senses as empirical, independent and objective. But, if twentieth-century philosophy teaches us anything, it is that nothing is given, in the sense of primordially, i.e., antecedent to anything else. It is not that data do not exist so much as that data are not primordial. This does not mean they are not relevant in considering a particular interpretation, and evaluating it, however; and, although data are not independent of our interpretation, one can still talk of a certain degree of distanciation between the object and the interpreter (Ricoeur 1981c). Yet what is interesting here is the treatment of data in practice; essentially, someone's presentation of their data is taken on trust. Rarely do we question its integrity – data are hardly ever really the issue in evaluation. Of course we can insist on larger samples to strengthen a claim, or consider other

dimensions of variability; but a sceptical attitude is often a cheap attitude to adopt, especially when what is really irritable is not the lack of data but the nature of the interpretation.

3 *Meaning.* A point raised by Colin Renfrew (conference contribution) concerned the current and misguided trend, as he saw it, to get at meaning in the past: 'If meaning is what you believe and what I believe but not in any real sense what we believe, because there is no such thing as a collective meaning or a longer-term meaning, then it is a very slippery concept indeed and it may be that the current panacea, the current grail, the holy grail that we are after – "meaning" – is indeed a misleading one.' And he also makes a distinction between meaning and the mind, such that his cognitive archaeology would address operations of the mind as evidenced in the material record, e.g., the Indus Valley weights, but could in no way hope to recover the meaning of those weights (also see Renfrew 1983).

What Renfrew seems to be saying is that mental phenomena have an objective and a subjective element; by deciding that these stone cubes comprise a system of weights, a string of inferences follow which say something about the way the users of those weights thought – the weights are an objective representation of those thoughts. The thoughts themselves, however, are purely subjective and inaccessible. We can never know what those weights meant to the Indus Valley people, but we can know in a general way the mental operations they imply. This same reasoning leads him to make a distinction between written texts and material culture – with texts, we can actually gain access to meaning because the thoughts are actually down there in black and white or wedge on clay: 'the experience of "aha! I see it now", I know what she meant or what he meant . . . that experience may well be a possible one when you read the text . . . but it is a rare experience . . . and one that does not particularly come from archaeological data' (Renfrew, conference contribution).

From all this, it appears that Renfrew's understanding of meaning is that it is co-extensive with an individual's experience, and therefore with an individual's existence; meaning does not exist outside the mind of individuals. I can no more know with certainty what you mean when you say something than I can know how you feel when you experience something. Second, he does seem to associate meaning with language, and although he recognises that art can be meaningful, too, there is clearly a certain priority between meaning and words. It seems to me that these two misconceptions of meaning are responsible for the greater part of the positivist misunderstanding of postprocessual approaches.

The trouble, first, with the subjective conception of meaning is that, by insisting on the subjective/objective split, the nature of sociality or intersubjectivity becomes inherently insoluble. It is impossible to explain how communication is possible at all, not merely any certainty of understanding in communication, since meanings are locked within each individual; but, and implied in that, meaning itself becomes incomprehensible without that social base. Contrary to what Renfrew states, meaning is not what you or I believe, but is exactly what we believe (although 'believe' is not perhaps the right word here). Meaning is first and foremost social, not individual. When Renfrew expresses agreement with the ambiguity of meaning, again he seems to see it in terms of subjectivity; but the ambiguity does not come from the subjectivity but from the signifiers (e.g., words) – my own thoughts are no less ambiguous to myself, *because* they are mine, than someone else's.

The link between meaning and language is also a very restricted conception of meaning; actions are meaningful, a gesture such as a wink can mean all kinds of things – and this is not simply a conflation of two different senses of the word 'meaning'; there is a real continuity between a gesture and an exclamation. Yet there is a deep prejudice in Western intellectual traditions which privileges language, and the quality which language is supposed to possess, namely its ability to refer, and therefore to transcend itself, its context. Indeed, this may be an ineluctable prejudice because of the very nature of philosophy as referential discourse, and it is no wonder that Derrida causes such consternation when he looks at philosophy as language stripped of its ability to refer, language in its context, philosophy as simply writing.

If, following Derrida, we release the repressed side of language, as situated (whether speech or text), the continuity between the exclamation and gesture is much clearer. It is in phenomenology that many of the directly non-linguistic but meaningful aspects of human life are investigated – from Husserl's pioneering work to Heidegger (1962), Schutz (1967), Sartre (1956) and Merleau-Ponty (1962). From the exclamation and meaningful gesture, which both use the body in a temporarily transformative manner, we can equally look at the hairstyle and tattoo as meaningful transformations of the body in a semi- or fully permanent manner. Moving from the body to other objects as means of expression is no different in kind; to stress a boundary between the body and the world is to repeat the error of a subjectivistic notion of meaning, i.e., that it emanates from a human subject. The boundaries between language, gestures and material culture are not fixed but fluid, not discrete but continuous. The boundaries are simply one way of carving up the phenomenon of the world, and it is phenomenology which discloses such perspectives. When Renfrew says we can only have the 'aha!' experience with a text, I believe he is wrong. There is no anamnesis involved in understanding material culture, any more than there is in understanding a text. Just a complex and sometimes very difficult labour, involving a dialectic between the part and the whole, the general and the particular.

4 *Politics*. Gellner's phrase 'Descartes, therefore Kipling' is a way of trying to demonstrate the absurdity of deriving oppression from a philosophy of clarity, of trying to imbue science with politics. What possible reasoning could link Descartes and the Enlightenment, the quest for clarity, with Kipling and colonialism, the oppression of other communities? How does clarity entail colonialism?

Again there is this sense of the Absolute here – clarity, something which is clear, the truth revealed finally. It is not so much clarity itself which is the problem, but absolute clarity as a guiding standard or ideal (even if unattainable). No one is arguing for deliberate obscurity, rather the recognition of the contingent and relative nature of clarity. It is the old ideal of Philosophy as the Mirror of Nature (Rorty 1980), to be able to grasp Reality as it is by some kind of reflection. Metaphors of the Mirror abound, especially through the associated notions of *reflection* and *clarity*. However, there is a sinister side to these metaphors. The idea of reflection is ultimately alienating, violent in wrenching us away from the world, separating Mind from Nature, Subject from Object. Similarly, clarity sets up an Absolute, a view of the Object, the World, Nature as ultimately Perfect, complete, and the degree to which we attain a grasp of this Reality is measured by this standard.

These sinister aspects to Enlightenment rationalism are precisely what makes it political; by presuming alienation, Reason then offers itself as the means of bridging the gap between subject and object, and by presuming the absolute nature of the object it restricts the nature of the object to what Reason defines. This notion of Rationalism is in fact totally tautologous, and indeed tyrannical. Violence is engendered, and pain and suffering follow. Clarity does entail oppression. Science is political.

Postpositivist projects

Beyond scientific techniques and data, there are other factors which we employ in evaluating work; for example, those discussed by Hesse (this volume), though her approach seems to imply a kind of grading of such factors with the data being primary. Hodder, in taking up this issue (Hodder 1991a and 1991b), invokes a more hermeneutic approach by suggesting factors such as the historical tradition of the discipline, rhetoric and the status of the author. But what is clear is that more attention needs to be paid to the contexts within which research and interpretation take place – a sociology of archaeological practice. The structure of archaeological education in terms of student–teacher relations, peer rivalry, groups (such as the processualists and postprocessualists), and intradisciplinary special-isations. All these are examples of the social relations within which archaeological discourse operates, and one cannot be blind to the political aspects than run through them, and therefore of the effect they have on evaluation. The idea that we are all neutral scientists and our work is judged purely on its own merit cannot be maintained. The power of the work is intimately tied up with the networks of 'academic capital', which surely operate within a wider sphere of cultural capital (e.g., see Bourdieu 1988).

What we could produce, then, is an archaeology conscious of the dialectical tension between that which is 'distanced', the data, and that to which we 'belong', the discipline. This is what prevents the hermeneutic circle from being vicious – the dialectic between tradition and texts. But what mediates this new consciousness? This brings us to a central debate between Critical Theory and Hermeneutics (e.g., see Ricoeur 1981b), where Gadamer would simply place this consciousness within a wider hermeneutic circle (Gadamer 1977), whereas Habermas, with more than a tinge of positivism, would prefer to see the possibility of an 'ideal speech situation', in which discourse can be carried out impartially (Habermas 1980). Between the ontology of Gadamer and the epistemology of Habermas, the debate seems to fluctuate unendingly. If we do not wish to wallow in an exercise of deconstruction, yet still feel we can move beyond this debate, a postpositivist philosophy needs some new ideas. In this respect, one might turn to Adorno and his critique of the new ontology and the old Marxism alike (Adorno 1973).

In practice, perhaps all that really matters is that debate is sustained, and debate which seeks dissension rather than unanimity. One can go no further perhaps at this point than to reaffirm the objectives which Shanks and Tilley put forward in the their programme for an archaeology of the 1990s (Shanks and Tilley 1989).

ACKNOWLEDGEMENTS

I must thank everyone who read and commented upon the drafts of this paper, some of whose comments caused me substantially to rewrite it: Alexandra Alexandri, Victor Buchli, John Carman, Ian Hodder, Jonathan Last, Janet Miller and Michael Shanks.

Chapter 4

Past realities

Mary Hesse

Archaeologists speak of 'reading the past', and this is usually taken to be a non-realist view about the past – we can only read the world as constructed through our languages. But the metaphor of the world as text is not original to the decon-structions of the twentieth century. Ironically it was the metaphor that underpinned an ideological defence of realism about natural science in the seventeenth century. Galileo said that God wrote the book of nature in the language of mathematics; and Francis Bacon spoke of the 'alphabet of nature', by which he meant that the ultimate atoms were letters combining into words combining into well-formed sentences, all of which constituted the 'grammar' of the laws of nature. This metaphor, however, did not imply a two-way dialogue between symmetric participants in language, as do our differing interpretations of the world, but a one-way communication of truth from God to humankind. Spiritual truth is written for us in the Scriptures; secular truth is written in the world, but obscurely, so that it has to be decoded from immediately sensed phenomena. The method of recovery was the new experimental philosophy, according to which all subjectivity and prejudice must be stripped from our eyes and we must 'put nature to the question' to elicit her hidden secrets by experiment, often aided by instruments of observation: telescopes, microscopes, pendulums, alchemical reactions, lodestones, etc. Bacon claimed that his inductive logic gave the recipe for doing this.

The 'new science' was objective and capable of reaching truth. Thus its theories, if produced correctly by the method, were literal descriptions of hidden realities – of atoms, of forces, of the very small and the very large, of what has happened in the past, and what will happen in the future. The eighteenth century extrapolated from the natural world to the human world, in the claim that the method would ultimately reveal all truth about minds, societies and history.

This intellectual dream had clear ideological roots. Particularly after the English civil war, when the Royal Society was founded, it was necessary to believe that somewhere there was an attainable objective truth transcending ideological disputes: 'nullius in verba' – truth is not found in disputatious words, but in experimental action. The 'meaning' of nature is God's meaning, an arbitrary will to be accepted with piety. In another sense, however, its meaning is that there is no meaning: nothing of human interest should be read into nature; she must be approached with an entirely open mind transcending subjective hopes and fears.

Two main snags about this dream have been amply documented in all the sciences. First, data are not open to the unprejudiced eye like the letters of a familiar alphabet; data are constituted by background theories or expectations – they are theory-laden. Second, in any case there is no unique way to arrive at true theories by Bacon's method – they are always underdetermined by data, and the history of the sciences is a history of conflicting theoretical models, giving no final answers to the metaphysical questions What is there? How does it work? These two logical snags were primarily responsible for the postpositivist revolution in philosophy of science familiarised by Kuhn, Feyerabend and their successors.

On the other hand, something does remain of the seventeenth-century aspiration towards objectivity. The experimental method depends crucially on testing theories, often in artificially contrived situations, and, more important, on checking the success of predictions derived from the theories. Where this works, it spawns not only better theories, but also the means of control of the natural world, and eventually the artificial environment of technology. The realism of natural science survives in a modified form, not because it attains an ultimate alphabet or grammar of nature, but because in comparatively limited space–time regions it comes up with locally valid regularities and successful predictions based on these (to call these laws of nature would be too strong). That we depend on these regularities at every turn, and can artificially control as much as we can control of the natural world, demonstrates that we have partial but genuine and realistic, though localised, knowledge.

In my view this residual instrumental realism, depending on successful control, still constitutes a criterion of demarcation for natural science. Popper's original demarcation criterion failed because it was a criterion of testability, not of successful prediction. Popper's emphasis was still on the attainment of true theories (or at least the detection and rejection of false theories), not on instrumental outcomes, which he dismissed as mere technology. But testability alone is put in question by the theory-ladenness of the test data to a degree which successful prediction is not. If we want to know what constitutes 'success' here, look around. Amidst a multitude of failed attempts to predict and manipulate the environment, which are obvious and undeniable, the successes must not be overlooked. No academic élitism about pure knowledge and truth should be allowed to obscure the fact that it is essentially Bacon's method that has produced the technology by which the modern world lives.

So far all this refers to the natural sciences, where the empirical control criterion has successes and failures – the successes more obvious the nearer we are to physics and the farther from complex open systems such as brains, evolution, ecology. We do, however, have well-established regularities from physics and chemistry which can be infiltrated into the problematic domains of complex systems. Since we are concerned here principally with theories about the past, note that locally successful physics and chemistry have given us some testably successful knowledge about the past of nature: the origins of life and species, of geological formations, even of cosmic galaxies. But of course such extrapolations in time, even in natural science, are hit by theoretical underdetermination. Where successful prediction and control is ruled out as a direct criterion, as in theories about the past, theories are also chosen for the way they organise conceptual schemes and integrate them with other cultural interests. Such extra-empirical criteria may be entirely pragmatic, such as ease of manipulation, or they may be sociopolitical constraints, or aesthetic, metaphysical or theological ideologies.

This is how intersubjectivity and meaning enter natural science, and of course such criteria and constraints are even more evident in the human sciences where the test-and-control criterion is generally inapplicable both for logical and moral reasons. First, the systems involved are too complex to be wholly predictable; and, second, even where they are predictable it is generally undesirable in a free society to manipulate them as we manipulate nature. An additional characteristic of the human sciences is what Giddens calls the 'double hermeneutic': all theories interpret the world in accordance with various kinds of human interest, but theories about humans also have to interpret what those humans' own interpretations are – for a start, their languages have to be learned and then the meanings and interests they themselves project on to the world.

It is not surprising that this whole concept of science begins to look like a vicious circle of relativistic interpretation and counter-interpretation, where, for example, the past is at best a present construction. What has become of objectivity? This is where I think a demarcation criterion between natural and human science still has to be used. We have to maintain the objectivity of the test-and-successful-prediction model and use it where it can be used: that is, where natural science methods can be made to infiltrate human subject-matter. This will at least provide constraints on interpretation: constraints with respect to such things as dates, reconstructions of skeletons, crop and food remains. Archaeology is almost unique among the human sciences in being more open to these constraints because more concerned with material objects which can be investigated by physical methods.

Sometimes these sorts of constraints will not carry us very far. Are there other sources of objectivity? In the original Baconian sense, which has informed all subsequent empiricist philosophy, I think not. But there are other sources of constraint. I conclude by suggesting three, in decreasing order of Baconian acceptability:

1 Use of uniformitarian principles of analogy, similar to those used in natural-science extrapolations to the past. For example, human beings with demonstrably similar anatomies and metabolisms are likely to have had similar basic physical needs, and faced with similar practical problems they may have solved them in similar ways, or at least in ways we can understand and appreciate if they are reconstructed.

2 Use of hermeneutic principles extrapolated from the way we have learned to do more recent history, and more contemporary sociology and anthropology. We do not, for example, have to go to Neolithic burials to find alien cases of symbolic use of materials – these are already evident in the history of science as recently as alchemy or field theory. By normal processes of historical interpretation we have learned to construct intelligible theories about such symbolisms. These 'meanings' do not always have to be elicited by subjective empathy: they can sometimes themselves be studied 'objectively'. From this point of view they are just the human cognitive ability to classify and reconstruct the environment, both practically and conceptually, by shifting about both things and ideas, and the ability of social groups to share such systems through symbolism and language.

3 More fundamental sources of theorising are those ideological principles and constraints derived (whether intentionally or unintentionally) from contemporary interests and power structures. In a culture dominated by the Baconian model of objectivity such principles generally remain implicit, but they are always operative below the surface – as, indeed, the Baconian ideology of 'objective science' itself has been for so long. More insidious, now, than overt ideologies is a kind of professional inertia which takes over when the historical relativity of theories comes to be recognised. Scientists, both natural and human, become wedded to certain assumptions and ways of doing things that are elevated to unquestionable principles of 'entrenchment', 'fruitfulness', 'aesthetics', or just 'fun', and then claimed as 'objective' by the consensus of the professionals. In my own field certain habits of mathematical physicists would be examples. With respect to all such ideological principles, the moral is surely to make them as far as possible explicit, so that they can criticise and debate with each other.

Chapter 5

Interpretive anthropology

Ernest Gellner

If one were to ask what has been the major, or, at any rate, the most conspicuous and visible theoretical development in social anthropology in recent years, the most plausible answer would be: the emergence of so-called interpretive anthropology, the hermeneutic twist, the switch from social structure to meaning as the principal focus of interest. The justification or validation of this shift of vision would run something as follows: earlier anthropological styles had forgotten, or neglected, the fact that the accounts of alien cultures were offered, not by some culturally disembodied spirit endowed with a divine objectivity and transcendence of all cultural assumptions, but, in reality, by a culturally embodied observer, whose vision is as suffused by his own culture as the vision he is claiming to fix in the ethnographic record. A sound anthropology is one which is as acutely sensitive to the cultural idiosyncrasy of the anthropological object. To single out the former for special treatment, to give him or her licence and exemption from critical scrutiny is, all at once, a disastrous methodological error and a mark of moral and political fall from grace.

At this point our protagonist of the interpretive turn goes over to the counter-attack. Consider, for instance, what might be called the Malinowskian-functionalist or British-imperial school of anthropology, the first generation of a fully institutionalised anthropological profession in what may be called the intellectual sterling zone (which survived the dismantling of the British Empire). This school was forged in Malinowski's seminar in London during the interwar period, dominated the discipline during the postwar period, and it could be claimed that the general profile of the subject still remains in the mould which it received then. Unquestionably, the fieldwork practised by the members of this school benefited from the Pax Britannica; more questionably, it can be claimed (and has been claimed from the left) that it in turn served the Empire, either by helping train its colonial administrators, or by providing it with a rationale, or both. Functionalism, on this view, was a kind of ideological fig leaf for indirect rule. It is not entirely clear why the imperialists had to turn to Bronislaw Malinowski for ideas they could just as well find in Edmund Burke, but let that pass. But the important thing is that the members of this school strove to write clearly and well, and that they succeeded in this aspiration. Their ideal of good prose was that of a style characterised by great lucidity and personal unobtrusiveness: there was a kind of Savile Row unostentatious elegance about their prose. Their artfulness attained a degree of simplicity which, to the simple-minded, would give the impression that no art was being deployed, that the author was simply not present in his work. He simply told it like it was, without interfering with his material.

Practitioners of a limpid but self-effacing style, beneficiaries of imperial power and privilege, and pillars of it: that, roughly speaking, is the picture. The hermeneutic movement presents itself, amongst other things, as the reaction, the corrective, of the cunning delusions fostered by the colonialist practitioners of good prose, or the practitioners of lucid style in the service of imperialism. It presents itself as both a methodological and a moral revolution. The discovery of the anthropological self, of the culture of the observer, is at the same time also a recovery of equality, or moral symmetry, of the restoration of dignity to the investigated object, of the (strangely belated) repudiation of colonialism and superiority, of an expiation and atonement for it. The movement is linked to the repudiation of all kinds of moral asymmetry, including that between the sexes or genders, so that the enemy is not only the imperialist, but also the patriarch, or presumably the patriarchal imperialist or imperial patriarch.

The overall alignment is now becoming clear. We know our friends; we can identify our enemies. In the enemy lines, there is clarity of style and thought, and pretence of objectivity, an absence of any recognition of subjective interference. So, in our hermeneutic or interpretive camp, there is an anguished recognition of subjectivity, a proudly recognised inner turbulence reflected in a correspondingly murky style of expression. The oppressed and exploited ones of the world, who of course have not yet fully emerged from their weakness and poverty, may now at least and at last find some consolation in the knowledge that their erstwhile oppressors and exploiters no longer add insult to injury by writing about them with an implicitly condescending lucidity, but that, on the contrary, their accounts are now impenetrably tortuous, and are more concerned with the moral and epistemic anguish of the objects of the inquiry. This, presumably, is meant to bring them a measure of solace.

So the interpretive position presents itself as the accompaniment of global decolonisation, of an intercultural egalitarianism, of the restoration of human dignity to those who had been deprived of it by, amongst other things, the stylistic fastidiousness of a school of anthropology. Let me say first of all that this assiduously propagated self-image ought not to be accepted without some scepticism. Is it really the case that clarity is on the side of oppression, and obscurity the ally of liberation? Is it really the case that Descartes entails Kipling, and that the repudiation of Kipling (who incidentally can hardly be accused of lacking a sense of the diversity of cultures, and was acclaimed for this quality, quite some time ago, by Noel Annan) requires us to repudiate the values of Descartes and the Enlightenment? I find it hard to accept any of this.

The hermeneutic turn, which reached anthropology mainly through literary studies, has a number of historic roots, including Marxism, phenomenology and Wittgenstein. The Marxist origins are paradoxical, in as far as the central intuition of Marxism is that of a stress on the objective determination of society and culture. But for a long time, as the actual course of history was becoming less and less favourable to the claims of Marxism, Marxist intellectuals came to concentrate more and more on the false consciousness of their opponents than on the consciousness they credited to themselves (and whose actual content inspired an ever-diminishing account of confidence). They became great experts in false consciousness and its crucial role in maintaining social order, particularly (this was a great speciality of the so-called Frankfurt School, which provided many of the ideas or slogans of the dissent of the sixties). Here is one of the ancestors of interpretivism.

Phenomenology, once again, is a paradoxical ancestor: it originally consisted of the aspiration to carry out a really scientific study of subjectivity, rather than of a subjectivistic replacement of scientism. All the same, it did prepare the ground by encouraging a curiosity about the subjective. Wittgenstein, by insisting on a shift of philosophic focus from the referential use of language to its social use, encouraged the idea of the centrality of meaning, and of the social-specific, culturally rooted nature of meaning. Having initially tried to anthropologise philosophy, in a subsequent generation he could also be used to make anthropology more philosophical. The Malinowskians already had shifted from material culture to social practice, and the move could be continued, from practice to meaning.

So much for (some of) the roots of the movement. What is wrong with it? At least three things: its subjectivism, its exaggerated sense of cultural symmetry, and its style.

Human societies are perpetuated by various mechanisms, which include the systems of meanings employed by the members of the said societies, but are not exhausted by them. Social order is also maintained by economic and physical coercion. Semantic coercion is perhaps indispensable, but probably not sufficient. In any case, the precise proportion or relative role of different forms of coercion is something to be investigated, and it may well not be the same in all societies. It is not something which can be prejudged by the very method employed. Hermeneuticists do not say, in so many words, that non-semantic constraints are irrelevant or absent: but they tend to acknowledge their presence only in the small print. Their very method tends to make it hard to look at them, because to do so would be acknowledgement of preoccupation with objective fact.

The stress on the equality of all cultures sounds generous and humane. In fact it is patronising and disingenuous. The central fact about the current transformation of the world is that one particular cognitive style engenders a technology which, economically and militarily, easily dominates all others. This does not, of course, mean that any particular segment of mankind can claim superiority over others. On the contrary: it looks as if the culture within which this cognitive style originated is not necessarily the one best adapted to its further exploitation, and that the originators are being left behind in the economic and technological race. The circumstances favourable to the birth of the new science are not necessarily favourable to its subsequent development. There is a further asymmetry: the new wisdom works in some fields, but not so much, or not at all, in others. The new technology has led to a completely new ecological predicament: certain past problems have disappeared, and grave new ones have emerged. All this needs to be explored: a vision which begins with a denial of the asymmetrical nature of our condition, of the basic premises required for the handling of our predicament, cannot be much use.

Ironically, the hermeneutic twist makes little contribution to the advancement of our understanding of meaning. In fact, the idea of meaning is, in its practice, less a tool of analysis than a means of self-titivation. The awesome difficulty of gaining access to the meanings of others, or even one's own, the chasms of communication, the contemplation of the precipices which separate us – all this is used more to soften us up than to illuminate us.

We have always known that the world is mediated by meanings. The world is, if you like, the totality of meanings rather than of things. But things do have their reality and exercise constraints over us, and some ways of knowing them are more effective than others. An exaggerated meaning-centredness, which obscures all this, cannot be salutary.

Chapter 6

The problems of origins

Poststructuralism and beyond

Henrietta Moore

Can we know the past or know anything about it? In recent years the status of the question itself has moved anachronistically from the ridiculous to the sublime. Where once we thought knowledge of the past to be a matter of discovery and technique, we now perceive the impossible and deceitful nature of the enterprise. Are we enlightened or self-deluding in our convictions?

Archaeology as a discipline is more concerned with origins, as in the origins of the state, the origins of language and the origins of agriculture. The whole notion of origins and of the originary has been subjected, of course, to dismissive critique by a number of theorists whom we shall conveniently designate postmodernist. A saner version of this enterprise has been conducted by professional archaeologists whose purpose has been to unsettle a variety of well-known, long-playing narrative accounts of the origin of various human institutions, activities and capabilities whose domination of the professional imagination is rivalled only by their popular appeal. The link between the professional and the popular, and its constituted nature in terms of fields of power and fantasy, is too obvious to need explanation here. The problem of origins is twofold. On the one hand, we look to the past for the origins of specific things, such as the state or sociality, language or gender, the family or sexual division of labour. On the other, we use the notion of origins to make a number of originary moves in our thinking and writing. These originary moves are designed to authorise certain accounts, to establish them as authoritative. These two aspects of the functioning of origins in the interpretation of the past work so as to produce continuous narratives.

Narrative may or may not be essential for an understanding of ourselves as human, and it might or might not be a prerequisite for the human comprehension of time. However, what does seem clear is that narratives in archaeology and anthropology often mislead and they mislead because they present themselves as concerned with beginnings, with the moment when something began, was invented and so on. The preferred professional term here is 'emerged', which gives people more room for manoeuvre and carries a sense of the appropriate mix of cataclysm and process which is now so essential to disciplinary rhetoric. However, narratives are in fact, as so many have discussed, determined not by their beginnings but by their endings. Our stories of the past must end with the present.

This determination of origins by ends necessarily means that the past is constructed or reconstructed in terms of the present. Our creative representations of the past are shaped not by what we know to be true of the past, but by what we believe to be true of the present. This simple proposition has been presented by many as a problem of back projection. Archaeologists have discussed this problem a good deal and did so at greater length in the days when they aspired to be positivists than in the period since a few of them have been self-designated poststructuralists or versions thereof. Such discussions were evident, for example, in the treatment of analogy and in much famous talk about smudge-pits and frying-pans. This having been said, it seems that archaeological talk of analogy perhaps missed the crucial point about the role of analogy in the reconstruction of the past. Paul Ricoeur, who might be termed poststructuralist, but whose commitment to moral value debars him for ever from the label 'postmodernist', has considered the question of whether historical narrative refers to a real past: that is, to events which really happened in the past. His contention is that historical knowledge represents, in the sense of 'stands for', the past. This analogical relation is paradoxical because to stand for something is both to be it and not to be it. The very fact of standing for is premissed on both identity and difference. The relationship of historical narrative to the past is not therefore one of replication or equivalence, but one of metaphor (Ricoeur 1989).

Postmodernism plays on this metaphorical relation to the past. The simultaneous assertion of identity and difference unsettles and disrupts any narrative search for closure. The irony, of course, is that we did not need to go to postmodernism for this revelation; a point made by many a literary critic and social theorist when discussing the unstable boundary between high modernism and postmodernism. This is not, of course, to assert that there are no differences between modernism and postmodernism in their developed forms – the crucial difference being one of political motivation and purpose. Modernism wanted to inaugurate a new era through the destabilisation of the old; postmodernism seems happy to content itself with a constant process of disruption which promises nothing for the future. In some very profound sense, postmodernism does not seek to change the world at all. The charge against postmodernism of designer radicalism is a familiar one, and it would not bear repeating if it were not for the fact that disciplines like archaeology cannot afford to embrace a politics of style which is devoid of any notion of improvement or aspiration or value. One story about the past is not as good as another, and, if it were, there would be no purpose in the practice of archaeology. What is strange about postmodernism's designer radicalism is that it is often not particularly self-reflexive in spite of protestations to the contrary. There is a curious irony in the fact that a methodological and theoretical commitment to disruption, fragmentation and critique in the context of a chronic instability of meaning ultimately makes self-reflection futile, drains it of its critical purchase and of its potential for motivated change. The temporary and shifting nature of value to which postmodernism is committed undermines any purpose it might have in the world. This may be one reason why postmodernism, while able to deconstruct the old certainties of archaeological thinking, is powerless when it tries to apply the same critical tools to itself.

When applied to archaeological knowledge, postmodernist critiques of totalising narratives, the subject–object distinction and the nature of representation have much to offer. Archaeology's constant quest for origins and for missing links – gaps that do not exist, but must be created in order to make the story coherent and complete – should be evidence enough. The back-projection of concepts, categories and values on to the past is standard procedure, as many feminist archaeologists have demonstrated. It is for these reasons that facile and dismissive critiques of post-modernism in archaeology should not be countenanced, but it is equally important to point out that postmodernism does not provide archaeology with a ready-made solution to evident problems. The inappropriateness of postmodernism as a panacea has to do with issues of value, time and agency.

The postmodern critique in the humanities and social sciences, as many have remarked, is a manifestation of the workings of high capitalism. Postmodernism's commitment to anti-empiricism constructs a strange kind of market-place where everything has equal value and everything is equally valueless. In the context of meaning endlessly deferred, a market of interpretation takes over, and such values as there are are merely the commoditised products of a series of exchanges. Since one story is as good as another, everything is up for sale, and proffers itself for consumption. Explanation and interpretation are reduced to description in the process because no mechanisms can be adduced or permitted for choosing between alternatives. Description is thus left to speak for itself. There are no values other than the facts of description. Such descriptions are a form of brute empiricism, for there is nothing behind them, they have no depth, there is no further meaning to be plumbed. Since nothing is permitted to be authentic, superficiality reigns. The world just is. It exists, 'replete in its own brute positivity' (Eagleton 1986, p. 132).

The valueless world of postmodernism thus threatens to return archaeology to a strange unmediated empiricism, and it is the self-evidential nature of the world as implied in this move which raises the question of time. In terms of the postmodern critique, the present becomes co-extensive with the past and with the future. There is therefore no past but simply a present past, a present future, and a present present. The affects of time are abolished. This does not matter greatly if all we are saying is that what is important about the past is that we recognise that it is constructed as an object of knowledge in the present, with all that implies. However, an overweening presentism seems an impoverished way of dealing with the past. As Ricoeur implies, what is important about the metaphorical representation of historical knowledge to the past is that it is a relation premissed both on identity and on difference. Archaeologists have as part of their political purpose in the world to recognise that the past is the present, but that it is also not the present. The collapsing of time implied in an overwhelming presentism threatens to erase important differences, and this in turn raises the question of agency. A past which is simply co-extensive with our present, as well as constructed in our own image, is a passive past. Whatever the motivations and actions of individuals and groups in the past, they merely come to serve our present needs, and are not treated as if they had any independent existence. There may be no way of knowing anything about their existence except through the prism of our own, but it seems unduly cavalier simply to erase all differences between the present and the past. Archaeologists are charged, of course, with the task of paying close attention to such differences, and in the postmodern world we all now inhabit they have the unenviable job of maintaining that the past did once exist independently of our understandings of it. Paradoxically, it is the archaeologists rather than the postmodernists to whom we look to sustain our awareness of the plurality of social times.

Part 2

The origins of meaning

Chapter 7

The origins of meaning

Alexandra Alexandri

'There is a particular pleasure to see things in their origin and by what degrees and successive changes they rise into that order and state we see them afterwards, when completed.'

Thomas Burnet, *Telluris Theoria Sacra*, 1689

The title of this section is rather deceptive. I will not attempt to define 'meaning', nor will I suggest where its 'origins' might lie. Instead I will use the title as a springboard for the discussion of some of the issues and problems that arise from attempting to understand and construct meaning. The contributions included in this section cover a variety of areas ranging from primatology and hominid evolution to Palaeolithic archaeology. The papers contain excellent discussions on the recent developments and problems in their respective fields, so here I will take the opportunity to point out the areas that usually create tension in inter- and intradisciplinary dialogue and to highlight some of the insights that could be of benefit to archaeology in general. I hope that this discussion will entice archaeologists to reconsider the potential merits of a dialogue, both within their own discipline and with other disciplines which deal with the problem of meaning from different perspectives.

Looking for the origins of meaning is essentially another way of attempting to define the moment and the process through which we became human. In this sense it is one of the most enduring and fascinating subjects, capturing the imagination of both scholars and the public.[1] This, however, is neither a recent development nor a new question, despite the fact that we have phrased it in terms that are now 'meaningful' for us. In fact, although we now conceptualise the problem along different lines, we are still concerned with the same questions that have been answered in various ways from the Bible to the Theogony and centuries before that. Today, the persistent popularity of questions concerning the emergence of modern humans, and consequently of meaning the way *we* construct and understand it, is the subject of psychological, existential, social, or political explanations and critiques. We now go so far as to question our motives for wanting to define the boundaries between humans and animals; but, regardless of how critical we try to be, we always seem to return to questions of origins one way or another.

Why, then, would we want to phrase our quest for meaning as a question of origins? The underlying idea is, of course, that if we know how something came to be we will understand it better. And 'meaning' requires explanation, since it is one of those vague, broad terms that we all somehow know but would be hard-pressed to define. Obviously, the concept of evolution (as we have come to understand it) may play a crucial role in creating a link between 'cause' and 'explanation'. However, knowledge of the theory of evolution is not essential to the perception of 'Origin' as the ultimate explanation as the colloquial use of the term attests. Indeed, only a small part of research on origins makes use of modern evolutionary theory.

Meaning is perhaps ambiguous and purposefully vague so that we can use it as a measure of value, a way of defining ourselves in a variety of circumstances. Yet in our work we tend to require a more precise definition of meaning, and here the difficulties start. The term is understood differently not only across disciplines but also within disciplines themselves. This, of course, is not a unique terminological problem, as different disciplines or in fact theoretical traditions use common terms in disparate ways (e.g., see Parker and Baars 1990). However, in the case of 'meaning' we run into further problems because it is usually broken down into component parts (cognition, consciousness, language, intelligence, etc.) which are themselves problematic, both in terms of their definition and in their perceived relationship to meaning. Each discipline, and in turn each theoretical position within that discipline, tends to privilege its own perspective as far as the construction of meaning is concerned. Thus, if you want to talk about meaning, you ought to talk about the brain. Or you can only talk about meaning in terms of language and text.

Obviously we can agree to disagree. Then, again, we can accept the challenge: we can ask a deliberately complex and 'loaded' question like the 'origins of meaning' and discuss it within an interdisciplinary framework. We can use it to critique the concepts we employ to talk about meaning, to discuss the implicit and explicit assumptions we make about meaning, to question our motivations, or even to challenge the notion of a universality of meaning. We can also be constructive and try to define new ways of approaching meaning by combining different perspectives and breaking down many of our 'either/or' prejudices.

ASPECTS OF MEANING

A question of origins

Henrietta Moore (in this volume) suggests that the search for 'Origins' characterises much of the discipline of archaeology. Drawing from the work of Paul Ricoeur (1989), she describes origins research as a twofold process in which we search in the past for the beginning of specific things and at the same time make a number of *originary moves* which are designed to authorise particular accounts. This twofold process produces a continuous narrative, where gaps are constantly created and filled. She further points out that such narratives are essentially misleading because, although they appear to be concerned with beginnings, they are actually defined by their endings.

As Meg Conkey observes, we don't need to invoke recent trends in post-structuralism to 'realize that origins research derives from and constitutes a methodology of narration' (Conkey with Williams 1991, p. 104). The aim is to produce logical, coherent stories using the concepts, terms or 'institutions' that we are familiar with. These accounts, because they are rooted in the present, tend to naturalise and present as inevitable the phenomena they study. They also function as a means of providing the researcher with intellectual control over the point of origin and therefore over all subsequent stages or areas of research (figure 1).

Of course, all this may not seem to be saying much, since obviously we search for the beginning of something that we 'know' or 'think' exists/existed and we cannot search for the beginning of something we have no conception of. Furthermore, we usually study the things that we feel affect us or grab our interest, not things that we perceive as totally irrelevant to us. We somehow tend to forget these 'simple truths', however, and these critiques are insightful by virtue of reminding us of how influenced we are by our experiences and of the difficulties involved in entertaining

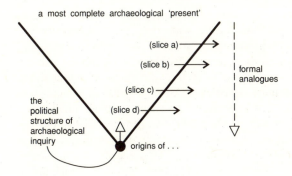

a most complete archaeological 'present'

(slice a)

(slice b)

formal
analogues

(slice c)

the
political
structure of
archaeological
inquiry

(slice d)

origins of . . .

Figure 1 The 'research cone' (from Conkey with Williams 1991, after Wobst and Keene, 1983).

alternative explanations. But the critiques are not themselves without problems. First of all, there is the question of what actually qualifies for the term 'origins research'. The confusion centres on whether the critique of 'origins research' refers to the enterprise itself of wanting to define the beginning of familiar concepts, to a particular *type* of inquiry about beginnings, or to the usual subject-matter of these inquiries. Conkey, for example, seems to oscillate between identifying origins research from its ideological content on the one hand and on the other criticising the choice of the objects of such inquiry. She claims that origins research is essentialist since it promotes the definition of phenomena in terms of their essential features, as opposed to focusing or concentrating on the variability of the cultural construction of these phenomena. She also considers the origins of agriculture, or the state, or gendered behaviour as paradigmatic 'originary narratives'. This seems to imply that we are not dealing with material things but rather with concepts or phenomena that have a broad applicability, some kind of 'universals'. In this light the search for 'the origins of meaning' is archetypal originary research, in that it is the ultimate point of authoritative control over all other research and can easily result in essentialism – after all, the ultimate meaning of a thing is its essence.

Obviously the ideological content, the mode, and the subject-matter of any inquiry are connected, but the specific pattern or relationships we observe are not inevitable or predetermined. In other words, the questions we ask do not predetermine the answers we choose to give. For example, we can see the search for the beginning of a particular house-type or pot-decoration of a specific culture as a kind of origins research. Moore suggests that an important aspect of originary narratives is to draw a link between then and now. In this light, even humble research into the beginnings of a pot-type is eventually presented as relevant to us, as part of the broader picture of who we are and used to be. It can be used as part of a story that explains, naturalises, and renders inevitable the ideas or conditions we live in. It can become an 'archetypal' pot against which all other pots are measured. And it can serve the production of authority, by obliging everybody to 'get to know' these pots with such accusations as 'you do not know your data' (see Part 4). On the other hand, the same research can be used to challenge the inevitability of our institutions or even serve simply to establish a chronological sequence without necessarily being imbued with any further 'cultural meaning'.

Here I have shifted away from the question of 'meaning' in an attempt to blur the distinction between research on grand unifying scales and more mundane projects, since we sometimes fall prey to the use of easy criticisms – a kind of 'one size fits all' enterprise. Conkey and Moore presumably object, not to the idea *per se* of looking for the beginning of something – after all, a widespread and popular human enterprise – but rather to what can result from particular agendas: essentialism, reductionist interpretations and the authorisation of currently dominant institutions. A solution to this problem could be to avoid asking 'origin' questions altogether, focusing instead on the particularities of specific cultures. Suggesting, however, that a contextual approach is by definition antithetical to the production of undesirable ideas makes it easier to become less reflective of what we do, both in dismissing *a priori* all so-called 'non-contextualised' research and in assuming that by dint of concentrating on variability we are avoiding previous pitfalls. Similarly, and more to the point, a total rejection of a question like that of the 'origins of meaning' loses sight of the durability and general public appeal of this question and its role in shaping our identity as humans; in so doing, we may distance ourselves from an important ongoing discourse.

Stories about origins are inevitably linked to the production and consolidation of identity, whether individual or collective. In this respect they enjoy the continued interest and attention of both academics and our public, perhaps more so than other areas of archaeological investigation. 'Origin' stories are the creation myths of our time.[2] They play an important part in explaining the world and our place in it. The narrative structure of 'origin stories' discussed above is to some extent necessitated by their function as myth. The connection between the search for origins and the making of myths is not necessarily a comment on the objectivity or reality of such stories. In turning 'myths' into an anthropological study far removed from us, belonging to the domain of 'other' cultures (whether we consider them primitive or important in their own right), we tend to forget that myths and especially creation myths *are* reality. Their 'objectivity' is questioned only by outsiders and by the same token our creation myths will stand unchallenged until they are supplanted by another reality, be it the product of scientific discovery or of the advent of a new religion.

Given that we don't operate removed from the desires and needs of the rest of the human population, it is noteworthy that we actually believe that we are the ones who ultimately decide which origin stories are going to be told, in terms of both the subject-matter and of the designation of the 'point of origin'. Yet our choices are not simply the outcome of internal disciplinary decisions but also a product of our social realities. We can gain much from a better understanding of the 'practical' aspects of our discipline in terms of how it is organised, what experiences shape our methodological and theoretical choices, and how external influences (funding, publishing possibilities, etc.) affect us (e.g., see studies by Latour and Woolgar 1979, M. Lynch 1982, Heritage 1984, Livingston 1987).

At the end of the day any archaeological research can be 'origins' research, in that it produces accounts with beginnings and endings, and these accounts both influence and are influenced by the present. In order to make sense to more than just its author, any account, however contextual, will ultimately be placed within specific spatial and temporal boundaries, and will be understood in terms of difference from and similarity to us. If it does not authorise current beliefs, it will eventually authorise others. What we really need is not a vague notion of 'contextual research' defined in negative terms (i.e., what it should *not* be), but a better understanding of how we use concepts like 'meaning', 'context' and 'variability'. Contexts, after all, can be as broad or as restricted as we like, they can be spatial and temporal, and variability ultimately depends on a sense of norms.

Universals and contexts

The tension between notions of variability and notions of 'universals' and their intrinsic relationship to 'meaning' is a central problem in archaeology. As Steele suggests in his paper, there is currently a revival of the study of 'human universals'. This renewed interest in universals is partly generated by research questioning the definitions of unique human traits, and invites a more integrated and comparative approach between various disciplines (e.g., ecology, sociology, etc.). Indeed, most recent research would suggest that traits previously considered 'uniquely human' are often shared with other animals. It all becomes to some extent a question of degree, and the shift in terminology suggested by Foley (1990a and in this volume) reflects these observations. Hinde (1987, 1992), for example, draws a clear distinction between hard-wired universal characteristics and basic propensities. The template exists, but the manner in which and the extent to which this will be realised are highly variable, depending upon context and environment. He further rejects the notion of innate versus learned behaviour (nature versus culture), and favours the continuing interplay of an organism and its environment.

The study of 'human universals' is usually perceived to be at odds with post-processual archaeology. However, the current emphasis on the dialectic relationship between a biological template and context or environment would suggest otherwise. The problem seems to centre on a confusion regarding what each type of study or area of interest involves. Postprocessual archaeology is often conflated with post-structuralism, while the prominence of contextual analysis gives rise to heated and often misleading debates on the notion of relativity. Placing an emphasis on context and variability, however, is not the same as saying that everything is relative. Indeed, nobody suggests that universal characteristics do not form the basis of any contextual analysis. Most of the terms and concepts regularly employed in post-processual archaeology are taken to be universal. Postprocessual archaeology rejects, not all notion of universals, but rather those paradigms that leave little scope for understanding and explaining the particularities of and differences among cultures. There is a further problem in that once a 'universal' becomes entrenched in our thinking it is very difficult to dislodge it. The contention is that doing 'epic' archaeology, in which everything becomes assimilated into a homogeneous entity, makes it easier to establish gross generalisations and to draw rigid and uncontested boundaries between cultures or people. In contrast, the emphasis is now increasingly placed on why people in a specific time and a specific place produce a particular culture. Nevertheless, we still need and in fact would gain much from a constructive discussion on what we could claim as universal, and here concepts developed in other disciplines, such as the notion of basic propensities, might be helpful.

Robert Hinde (conference contribution) proposed some ways in which archaeology could benefit from research in the behavioural sciences. His basic contention was that the term 'culturally constructed' provides only a partial view of culture and cultural artefacts. He suggested that in order to understand culture and cultural artefacts we should think in terms of the dialectic between human basic propensities and what he identified as successive levels of social complexity (Hinde 1992, fig. 2). The concept of basic universal propensities is crucial and, as Hinde warns, should not be confused with a notion of rigid, hard-wired, universal characteristics. It should rather be understood as behavioural or psychological predispositions (e.g., aspects of perception, motor patterns, motivation, etc.) that can be realised to variable extents in different contexts and environments. Furthermore, the aim is not to attempt a distinction between human 'nature' and 'culture', but rather to suggest a basis for understanding both cultural similarities and diversities.

We *should* be cautioned against forgetting that humans are grounded in biology –
even though it may no longer be viewed as destiny – and that our distinction between
biology and culture is as arbitrary as any other human construct. Steele (in this
volume), for example, attempts to bridge this perceived gap by defining distinct *types*
of behaviour and examining their relationship to human conversational talk. On the
other hand, Hinde's contention that 'culturally constructed' is a misleading term
because it provides only a partial view loses sight of the variety of questions we
might be interested in examining. We can approach a question in many ways,
different emphases requiring different levels of abstraction or detail, and it would
be wrong to suggest that these are necessarily mutually exclusive. Similarly, any
research on human basic propensities is bound to be constrained by a number of
factors. To begin with, the choice itself of the potential propensities will be heavily
influenced by contemporary evaluations (e.g., gender differences in the propensity
to be promiscuous). Also, claims for the 'testability' and hence potential proof of
these propensities will not always be easy to make. To take some of the examples
that Hinde (1992) uses, you can probably test the notion of a basic propensity to
fear snakes more easily than you can the notion of gender differences in the
propensity to be promiscuous. The problem arises because we have (at least now,
in Western cultures) more at stake in gender differences or similarities than we have
in fearing snakes. In addition, the social implications of these propensities are
radically different. Archaeology can enter the propensities debate constructively by
trying to provide a view of what could have happened in the past, rather than
unquestioningly accepting the proposed propensities.

All this is not to deny that there is a tension between 'universal' paradigms and
postprocessual archaeology. Part of the problem lies in claims of authority:
biological characteristics, whether they be 'universals' or propensities, are seen as
more basic and fundamental than social or cultural attributes, and consequently
research in these fields is considered of greater importance than other types of
research. The tension is partly caused by the preference of our society for 'science'
and 'unifying' theories. Disciplinary authority expands in ever-increasing circles. In
addition, the social consequences and accountability of scientific research have
emerged only fairly recently as valid areas of discussion. Still, the notion of a
dialectic between biology and society, no matter how arbitrary or culturally specific
this distinction may be, should imply a balanced evaluation of the components
involved. Similarly, if we are going to engage in interdisciplinary dialogue we need
an equal footing, as well as a 'common' language.

Here, we return once more to the problem of the science/humanities divide,
especially the terminology and by extension language-barrier. Comments about
'humanities babble' are to some extent valid, but ignore the manner in which even
scientific language can affect our construction of knowledge and may actually hide
contemporary evaluations under the guise of objectivity. This does not necessarily
mean that authors always intend to produce this effect, but scientific prose
and scientific terminology can be conducive to using words, and by extension
concepts, unthinkingly (see, for example, studies like Bazerman 1981, Yearley
1981, Law & Williams 1982). Calling for a clarification of the various assumptions
implicit in any theory, and criticising our use of language (from terminology to
metaphors) in propounding and supporting scientific discourse, whether it be in
archaeology or in other disciplines, does not constitute 'babble'. And, to return
to the relationship of language and meaning, perhaps we should be cautious,
since many learned articles contain passages which suggest that language can be
quite 'meaningless'.

Language (use and abuse) and interdisciplinary communication

The difficulties we encounter in agreeing on and defining the constituent parts of any problem highlight our great dependence on language. Language is considered cardinal in understanding how we construct culture and meaning, and the evolution of the capacity for language in humans has been a consistently central issue in searching for the origins of meaning. Language development and acquisition is a domain in which a number of different disciplines have traditionally met. Perhaps this is not surprising given our privileging of the capacity for language. Language is probably the only remaining bastion of human difference from non-human primates, which have recently claimed most of the other characteristics previously thought to be unique. Hinde (conference comment), for example, suggested that humans have a propensity to learn language, a fact that differentiates them from other animals and ultimately enables culture and cultural differentiation. The case for uniqueness, however, is now being questioned by a number of studies on non-human primate vocalisations, as well as symbol manipulation and the use of sign language by chimpanzees and gorillas in captivity (e.g., Savage-Rumbaugh 1986; articles in Byrne and Whiten, eds, 1988, and in Parker and Gibson, eds, 1990).

Most theoretical debates on the evolution of the capacity for language and language acquisition have tended to concentrate on and produce stage-based interpretations. These debates have been influenced to a great extent by studies of intellectual and linguistic development in children, and consequently the notion of progression from simplicity to complexity is inherent in many of the proposed models. For example, the Piaget–Chomsky debate (a good if rather daunting presentation in Piattelli-Palmarini, ed., 1980) has been central to discussions of language acquisition. Chomsky supports a species-specific innate structure which is expressible through formal language universals. This accounts for the spontaneous, uniform and complex character of rules of sentence production or comprehension, and explains why children are capable of learning (any) language without in-struction, thus suggesting that language is preprogrammed in us. Piaget, on the other hand, rejects the notion of an innate structure of language and believes that general intellectual development is a necessary precursor to the acquisition of language. Intelligence, for Piaget, is an organisational ability and has a number of innate functions which through interaction with the world (through senses and motor activity) construct a series of cognitive structures. It is worth noting that both Piaget and Chomsky agree that there must be a cognitive organisation of some kind present from the start, and that the individual must interact with his or her environment. In contrast to Chomsky, Piaget has proposed a stages theory that distinguishes levels and rates of development across domains. Perhaps for this reason, this theory has been widely favoured in studies of non-human primates as well as in Palaeolithic studies (e.g., Wynn 1990).

Theoretical debates are also founded on studies focusing on the physiological development of the brain, neurological connections and vocal cords (for example, Eccles 1989). Recent studies of the brain and attempts to discern its relationship to 'mind' have increasingly revealed the manner in which neural structures serve for storing concepts or representing internally the outside world.[3] The existence of fossils would seem to facilitate an analysis of at least some of these physiological developments of the brain, but see Foley (in this volume) for a few of the problems. Furthermore, as Steele (in this volume) notes, the notion of discontinuity in the neural circuits involved in producing human language and non-human primate vocalisations is now being questioned. Moreover, non-human primate vocalisations appear to be much more complex and nuanced than was previously thought.

The effort to understand the nature and function of non-human vocalisations and their relationship to human language has also been characterised to some extent by the use of concepts based on notions of progression and stratification. For example, a number of researchers have used the concept of intentionality in an attempt to classify the mental states and intentions of non-human primates (see Dennett 1987, 1988; also summary in Cheney and Seyfarth 1990, pp.141–4). The aim is to distinguish between different levels of intentionality by determining the mental state and intentions of an individual (i.e., the signaller) during particular acts (in this case vocalisations). It is interesting to note that one has to presuppose that the individual is rational. In first-order intentionality, the signaller has beliefs and desires, and acts on them in order to modify the behaviour of others, without, however, having beliefs about beliefs and desires – that is, without attributing a mental state to others. In second-order intentionality, the signaller attributes mental states to others and communicates in order to modify their behaviour and mental states. Higher-order intentionality includes all subsequent levels, which are elaborations of second-order intentionality and require that the individual must recognise that both s/he and others have knowledge, and that others' knowledge may not correspond to his or her own. For effective linguistic communication higher-order intentionality is required (see Premack 1988 for difference of belief from desire).

Whether or not non-human primates have higher-order intentionality is currently one of the most hotly debated issues. As Lee (in this volume) puts it: 'Monkeys and apes do not think the way we think, but they do think.' Her statement should alert us to the possibility that their lack of 'language' as we understand it may not imply a lack of meaning. We should also consider the possibility that our reliance on hierarchical stage-based interpretations of language development may potentially steer us towards unreliable connections between different domains and contexts and actually diminish the role of the surrounding environment. For example, comparisons between children and primates or early hominids are frequent, and they are inevitably accompanied by implicit assumptions about 'child-like' nature and behaviour.

In a different vein, Foley's contention (in this volume) that language is externalised thought suggests that our current understanding and privileging of human language may require some revaluation. Similarly, Steele (in this volume) attempts to situate the development of language within both a biological and a social context and to highlight the *continuities* between human talk and behavioural traits shared with other species. Furthermore, recent advances in the study of the brain should not be dismissed so lightly. Most of these studies arise from observing the changes that occur in perception, language-use, or even personality when a small section of the brain is damaged or altered. If a small knock on the head can, for example, alter radically our perception of space or shapes, or our comprehension of language, how can we easily divorce 'meaning' from the function of the brain? And, if we don't understand properly the ways in which meaning is produced, how can we even attempt to 'reconstruct' it in archaeological contexts? Certainly we would not be off the mark in suggesting that our understanding of culture cannot always be reduced to a linguistic analysis. Consequently, textual analogies in archaeology should be reconsidered in the light of the emerging realisation that 'meaning' can be attained in various ways.

The wide range of approaches to the development of language and its relationship to meaning suggested very briefly above are admittedly daunting. Obviously, no one can be expected to gain an in-depth understanding of all the relevant issues. After all, these studies are not all of equal importance to archaeology nor are they always applicable. On the other hand, it is necessary to be at least aware of both the negative and the positive implications of such studies before choosing to reject or to accept their relevance for archaeology. Lack of specialist knowledge should encourage caution but need not always act as a deterrent to the critical evaluation of the implicit and explicit assumptions in various theories.

DIFFERENT MEANINGS

Given the apparent consensus on the *contextuality* of 'meaning' that emerges from the issues discussed above, as well as from the contributors' papers, it might be worthwhile to ask how we can get at different meanings. This is not really an evasion of the original question of how to determine the beginnings of meaning but, rather, a realisation that we need a better understanding of the concepts we are dealing with.

In this light, the study of cognition in animals, especially non-human primates, is important, but perhaps not in terms of identifying a traditional linear evolutionary path leading from non-human primates (somehow seen as closer to our ancestors) to us. Rather, such studies should be seen as an attempt to examine alternative ways of viewing and comprehending the world, and thus to understand 'meaning' through its variability. To some extent this enterprise may involve the much criticised anthropomorphising of animals. This may be inevitable, since at present we don't really have any other channels for the mediation of the perceived differences between ourselves and animals. Furthermore, such studies are primarily understood in terms of the production and consolidation of our identity, and as such involve emotional responses to our object of study (Haraway 1989). To a certain degree, anthropo-morphising has been used as an effective strategy to sensitise us to the similarities between ourselves and animals, and has perhaps even invited us to accept differences in a non-derogatory manner. In short, attempts to discern certain universal features that are related to cognition should not be abandoned since our understanding of the issues involved is at present far from comprehensive. However, one major idea has to be abandoned if we are to avoid the pitfalls of essentialism and functionalism. The notion of difference must be divorced from a framework that devalues it.

Obviously, to accept and even to value difference is not to uphold absolute relativism – value judgements will always occur, and are actually necessary if we are to make any choices in life and work. However, the problem of negotiation of difference is central to all the studies we conduct. We look for how similar or different we are from our objects of study, and frame our research according to this constantly shifting boundary between 'us' and 'them' – be 'they' non-human primates, Neanderthals, or medieval monks. An important factor which influences research but is hardly ever discussed is the extent to which we like or dislike our objects of study. Discussion of this issue is avoided because emotional responses are believed to hinder objectivity, yet emotionality is constantly present in all theoretical discussions, as many conference debates can attest. Furthermore, emotionality has been traditionally linked (in philosophy and science) with gender differences: men are rational, women are emotional (Lloyd 1984). Perhaps discussion of the role of human reactions and emotions during research can be one of the arenas within which we not only re-examine a number of the concepts we uncritically employ, but also identify and try to rectify our prejudices – for instance about gender.

In view of the fact that difference itself has to be mediated through channels that we are familiar with, a strategy that would allow us to get at different meanings is not easy to develop. Although talk about the necessity of alternative approaches abounds, it very rarely leaves the confines of generality by providing viable examples (but see Gamble's suggestions in this volume). Conkey (conference contribution), for example, has cautioned us extensively regarding the uncritical acceptance of the terms and concepts we employ in order to 'recover' meaning. However, she did not follow through her discussion in order to illustrate how our concepts could be replaced for the better, other than by suggesting the creation of new social realities – in many cases a desirable goal, but hardly readily and easily attainable. Similarly, as Gamble observes in his paper, the use of anthropological examples, instead of inspiring us, usually frustrates us by pointing to the (irrecoverable from our perspective) innumerable levels of variability existing around us.

Yet the enterprise should not be abandoned. Looking for the origins of meaning, set as a broad agenda, may not be helpful except in highlighting our need to revaluate our concepts. However, we can try to understand what constitutes meaning, and here a strategy of breaking it down to its 'potential' constituent parts, as suggested by Foley, may be the best way forward. In this light, looking (for example) for the emergence of language as we understand it becomes an enterprise far removed from the initial 'origins' question, since it forms part of the picture rather than its explanation. Similarly, as was mentioned above, primate studies or early hominid studies will help us to understand the various forms which meaning can take and possibly the underlying template of cognition. However, classic evolutionary interpretations cannot provide the definitive explanation of meaning, since much of what we look at in archaeology belongs, as Gamble aptly puts it, to the domain of exaptation (Gould and Vrba 1982). This, of course, does not mean that there is no need for a strong evolutionary basis in archaeology. Rather, the call is for a revaluation of our current understanding of the developments in an active theoretical tradition in other fields.

Breaking down interdisciplinary and intradisciplinary barriers is necessary. Creating and strengthening communication channels across the so-called sciences/humanities divide does not negate the tension that exists nor does it imply that biology will be privileged over 'culture'. By assuming that this divide is a 'philosophical' given, by not problematising it, and by constantly using it as an excuse for the 'unbridgeable' competing ways of defining and using various concepts, we support and (to use the ever-popular term) authorise a particular *modus operandi*, without taking into account the changing nature of our experiences and needs. To some extent our present attitudes are the result of an interdisciplinary communication problem, where only a particular set of notions is popularised and 'exported' from one side of the divide (e.g., sciences) to the other (e.g., humanities). The actual development of internal criticism and competing ideas stays within the discipline (Sperling 1991). Although we recognise the problem, we don't often try to find effective solutions; the matter is left to the initiative of a handful of authors.

Of course, all this sounds like an oversimplification of a deep-rooted problem. However, different generations of archaeologists have varying experiences of nature, technology, or the production of knowledge itself. This has resulted in a renewed questioning of the necessity to maintain a rigid conceptual and practical division between disciplines, without necessarily having returned to biological determinism and a linear functionalist agenda. In fact, a renegotiation of the boundaries between 'nature' and 'culture' is evident in society in general.[4] Again, the point is neither that we should accept any 'new' type of research uncritically nor that we should abandon contextual analysis in favour of grand 'universal' originary narratives. In short, if anything is 'culturally constructed', it is the boundaries and evaluations we set upon various disciplines. We should not aim towards an archaeology of exclusion. This is not simply a matter of allowing 'politically correct' alternative archaeologies to exist in the margins of an agenda-setting, ultimately patronising postprocessual core. It requires engaging in a dialogue with other archaeological traditions and other disciplines.

It can be argued that there have been numerous attempts to bridge the sciences/humanities divide, and that many archaeologists regularly collaborate with other scientists. It seems, however, that there are some 'acceptable' areas of co-operation (e.g., the Palaeolithic, or the analysis of bones and soil), while the greater part of archaeology remains impervious to 'outsiders'. Furthermore, collaborations are usually represented as one-sided, whether it is anthropology or biology we are talking about. Archaeology is seen to benefit directly from such collaborations, but the way in which other disciplines benefit from archaeology remains nebulous, perhaps with the exception of the well-rehearsed contribution of the long term to anthropology.

Borrowing a concept or methodology developed in another field and applying it to archaeological material is a phenomenon frequently encountered in archaeology, and although such enterprises have produced intriguing results, archaeology is still seen as an area of application rather than a potentially important generative and testing ground. The concept of basic propensities is a good example, in that it is 'developed' and 'tested' in the present and offered to archaeology as a readily usable export; the idea that archaeology could be an area for testing the proposed propensities never arises, or, if it does, is not stated as such. The underlying claim is, of course, one of unchanging biology, but seeing that our understanding of various processes like evolution or the transmission of genetic information through genes is constantly challenged and modified, diminishing archaeology's potential contribution to the debate is perhaps not wise. Similarly the importance placed on the interaction of an individual with his/her environment would highlight the significance of archaeology in examining different types of environment and relationship, rather than merely reproducing the familiar. After all, as Phyllis Lee observed (conference comment), the question of meaning is very culturally specific and, in both human societies and non-human primates, 'meaning' means something different in every context.

NOTES

1 For a historical overview of the search for the origins of humans, see Lewin 1989; and, for some current discussions on this and related questions, see the articles in Mellars and Stringer (eds) 1989, Foley (ed.) 1990b, Mellars (ed.) 1991. The most recent example of the intense and general appeal of scientific debates on human origins is the public controversy surrounding the African Eve theory.

2 See also Gould 1987 for a further (accessible) discussion on the study of Origins.

3 For a collection of articles dealing with subjects ranging from language to consciousness, see the 'Mind and Brain' issue of *Scientific American*, September 1992.

4 These changes can be seen in the rise of an 'ecological' consciousness manifested in movements to protect the environment or endangered species, as well as in consumerist trends towards the advertisement of products as 'recycled' or 'not tested on animals'.

Chapter 8

Cognitive and behavioural complexity in non-human primates

Phyllis C. Lee

In this paper, I will attempt to provide a few insights, albeit very briefly, into the ways primatologists think that monkeys and apes think. I hope to establish and define what we humans, who watch these animals, perceive of as cognition in the non-human primates.

Initially, we are looking at the ways in which the animals perceive the world, how they classify, if they do, others and objects, and the use of signals to simplify responses to the environment and to other animals. Most primatologists are somewhat more sophisticated than simply to equate behaviour and its outcomes with cognition (see Candland and Kyes 1986, Griffin 1984). Rather, they try to relate knowledge to behavioural variation; in other words, to assessments of possible outcomes and to how individuals manipulate outcomes of behaviour in dynamic contexts. This variation between individuals or on the part of the same individual under different contexts is often termed *alternative tactics for behaviour* and discussed as part of the cognitive and behavioural complexity of the non-human primates (see Dunbar 1988).

PRIMATE MODES OF COGNITION

Many forms of cognition in the non-human primates relate to food processing and food extraction, its spatial and temporal location, and to memory of where food is and how it varies through time in abundance and quality. While these sound very simple in terms of task performance, if you are a chimpanzee confronted with a termite mound how do you know that there are termites inside? How do you know that if you stick a little twig down that hole you will be able to get the termites to bite it, so that then you can pull the stick out and eat them? Embedded resources, exemplified by termites, are typical of many foods eaten by non-human primates (Gibson 1986, Parker and Gibson 1990). Such resources are hidden from the animal within a defended coating, or inside another kind of object (a tree trunk, or the ground), and they require quite complex skills for perception of the edible within the inedible, memory of previous encounters, some degree of planning in relation to outcomes, and manual skills for processing or extracting the resource. Can these be considered forms of cognition? In attempting to address this question, workers have experimentally manipulated the environmental contexts for food acquisition. Some species, notably capuchin monkeys (Visalberghi 1987, 1988) and chimpanzees (Menzel 1971, Boesch 1991), respond to novel problems in food procurement with novel solutions, learning through interest, observation and exploration. The acquisition of food does seem to provide opportunities for the demonstration of some complex cognitive skills among many primate species (Milton 1988).

Another area of interest is that of social knowledge (Cheney *et al.* 1986, Byrne and Whiten, eds, 1988). This knowledge relates to self and attributes of self (such as age, sex, power), to other individuals and their attributes, and to knowledge about relationships – the self in the context of others both in terms of interactions and the patterning of interactions over time, as Robert Hinde (1976) defines relationships. In examining social knowledge, we are attempting to assess whether or not there is intentionality (cf. Dennett 1987, Cheney and Seyfarth 1990), in that the actions or communications of one individual are given with intent to provoke a specific desired response. Further interest centres on whether or not primates have hypotheses about mental states. Do they have some way of representing the world? Do they have simple representation, abstract representation and cognitive representation? If there is intentionality, do the other individuals recognise this intention? In other words, is there second-order intentionality or high-order intentionality?

These global aims in the exploration of primate cognition are, in principle as well as in practice, difficult to attain and face major methodological problems. Informants, in the classical context of social anthropology, are unavailable and, as stated earlier, the simplistic leap between behaviour and cognition cannot be made. Furthermore we must work within the constraints of a visual, vocal, olfactory and locomotor world that is really quite different from our own. We can only answer these questions by observing behaviour, examining outcomes and their variation, by understanding primate learning, and by attempting to resolve questions of decision-making.

A vast area of exploration has been that of learning – how do primates learn about their physical and social environment? The emphasis on learning is both developmental, with respect to the long period of infant dependence, and in relation to the capacity for adults to acquire new behaviour and solve novel problems. Many workers have focused on the question of whether or not animals have expectancies (see Rumbaugh 1986). Do they expect certain outcomes to follow as a result of behaviour A? Will consequence B inevitably be the outcome? Do they form models of the relations between A and B on the basis of what they have experienced in the past? At a further cognitive level, do they form mental models, hypotheses about the expectations themselves? And what is the role of experience in creating these expectancies – how do they develop and change? Expectancies link into the capacity for both memory and learning, but memory alone is also of significance in understanding non-human primate cognition (see Menzel 1973). Memory is of critical importance in food location, in ranging patterns and in territoriality. With memory comes a cognitive concept of goals. Can these animals perceive a relationship between what they know and what they desire? Do they actually set out to achieve something?

There is good evidence that non-human primates have an excellent memory for relative number and position (Sands and Wright 1980, Rumbaugh 1986). This need not imply that they are counting, although some chimpanzees can indeed count (Matsuzawa 1985), but rather that they are forming mental maps of important elements within their environment. For example, among hamadryas baboons, mental maps appear to set out the position of water-holes in relation to safe sleeping sources, and the routes between foods of different types relative to water-holes and the need to return to safe sleeping sources. All of these elements (foods of specific quality, water, distances between sites) vary over time, in any season, or on any day depending on the presence of, for example, a predator or another group. Baboons may need very complex mental maps of relative number and positions of objects in their environment (Sigg and Stolba 1981, Sigg 1986).

Finally, the social traits are of marked interest, since they specifically require (at least) two cognitive abilities. The first is that of some degree of self-knowledge and the second is that of iterated interactions between recognised individuals. A final element of social transactions is that they require a degree of information-transfer (King 1991). The existence of self-knowledge need not imply a concept of self in the sense of 'self-awareness' or mirror self-recognition (Anderson 1984), but rather some degree of self-knowledge about state and status. These are attributes of individuals expressed in terms of physiological requirements and general categories (old, young; pregnant, lactating, cycling; male, female; high or low ranking), which none the less are specific to the single individual. Since much of the variation we observe in primate behaviour is explained by individual attributes such as these, it would be expected that individuals react as a function of some self-knowledge of these attributes.

The second characteristic, that of iterated interaction, requires further a recognition of other as an individual, also with specific attributes and furthermore with a specific history to the past transactions. That monkeys and apes can distinguish between other individuals as a function of attributes and relationships is well established (see below). Indeed, macaques can recognise and classify others and the relationship between others on the basis of photographs (Dasser 1988a, b).

Information transfer on the part of primates can suggest the ability to use a vocal means of communication, which further implies that some level of symbolic communication is in effect (Cheney and Seyfarth 1990, King 1991). Alternative modes of information-transfer (visual signalling: Snowdon 1990, Bard 1990; grooming: Dunbar 1991) may still carry symbolic intent.

A variety of social transactions has been examined in relation to primate cognition. Those recently at the centre of such studies are interactions described as deception and manipulation (see Byrne and Whiten, eds, 1988). These elements of conflict between individuals, and what recently has been termed conflict resolution (de Waal 1989, Harcourt and de Waal, eds, 1992) are of primary interest in understanding primate cognitive skills. How do animals set about resolving the tensions created by conflicts of interest in their social contexts? The alternative approach is to focus on co-operation as a form of interaction requiring meshing in expectations, actions and outcomes between two or more individuals engaged in a co-operative relationship (Harcourt and de Waal, eds, 1992). Some workers term these forms of social exchange in the context of relationships 'political traits' (Mason 1986, de Waal 1982), with the implication that goals and conscious tactics are pursued. The evidence for complex political traits among primates is growing, but still controversial.

COGNITION, KINSHIP AND CO-OPERATION

As a detailed example of the kinds of social thinking exhibited by the non-human primates, patterns of assistance during aggressive interactions have been examined in great detail. The aid given and received by individuals during an attack is part of the alliance structure of the social group. Many species of cercopithecine primates live in stable social units where the females habitually reside with their genetic relatives over their lifespan. Daughters grow up in their mother's group and remain there to breed while the sons emigrate. A structure with genetic relatedness through the maternal line thus develops. Is this relatedness perceived, and how does it translate into behaviour for the non-human primates? In these 'female kin-bonded' species, intervention in other individuals' aggression is relatively frequent. In a variety of studies of pig-tailed macaques, rhesus macaques, Japanese macaques and vervet monkeys, small-to-medium-sized cercopithecine monkeys that live in these female bonded groups, a clear pattern of preference for providing assistance to relatives can be shown (Fig. 2). Assistance given during aggression is not given at random; it is preferentially directed to individuals that are both familiar and likely to reciprocate. In such societies, familiar individuals are most often members of the same female lineage. Such monkeys do, indeed, seem to behave towards their kin in a way that is different from the way in which they behave towards non-kin. There is an effect of the degree of relatedness on the relative frequency with which more closely related, rather than distantly related, individuals are aided. Despite this marked kin-preference, individuals also help totally unrelated individuals who can be categorised as 'friends'. Friends are other animals who habitually and consistently interact in a helpful, relaxed and supportive fashion. In cognitive terms, neither the discrimination on the part of close kin nor that of friends requires a great degree of

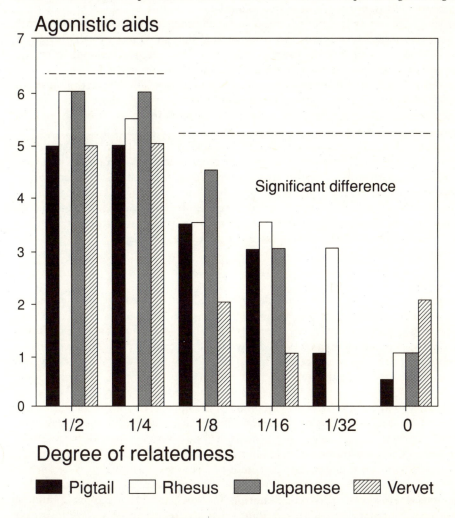

Figure 2 Alliance structure and kinship in primates. Aid given to participants during aggressive encounters as a function of the degree of relatedness between the aider and the recipient. Data from four different species are presented to emphasise the similarity of the patterns across the female, kin-bonded cercopithecine primates.

Sources: Massey (1977), Kaplan (1978), Kurland (1977), Lee (1981).

genetic or mathematical sophistication to effect. It does require knowledge of the social conditions and assessments of individuals; those receiving and providing help alter their behaviour depending on who is nearby, who is involved in the fight, who needs help to change the course of the fight, who is vulnerable, and whether or not there is a reliable partner.

Cheney and Seyfarth (1986) have taken this question a step further and experimentally examined whether or not these kinds of alliance translate into actions outside the context of an immediate threat to the other individual. They were able to determine that simple vulnerability, where, if an individual screams, another will come to its aid, did not explain the pattern of alliances. They assessed the frequency of one vervet monkey threatening another when that other individual had been involved in a fight with the first individual's kin at some time within the previous two hours. They found that if animal A had been fighting with animal B's kin, animal B was much more likely to approach, threaten and attack A than if it had not been fighting with B's kin. This observation suggested a surprising capacity for perception of threat to others over time and space. It further suggested that subsequent retaliation for a threat was likely, even though direct personal involvement was lacking, when the threat was to others between whom some special relationship existed.

The result could have been explained in terms of a fight simply creating arousal, and delayed and redirected aggression due to tension. However, there is no effect if the two individuals fighting previously were related to B. If your sisters are squabbling over in the corner, two hours later you do not go over and threaten one of your sisters, nor do you randomly threaten any other individuals after a fight between your siblings. These results suggest discrimination between individuals who have different relationships and the capacity for assessment of threat to others within the context of that relationship. The monkeys indeed appeared to recognise the relationships between others, both relative to themselves and outside the context of their own relationships. It also suggests at least some level of intentionality in their ability to discriminate in the consequences of their interactions.

CHIMPANZEE 'TECHNOLOGY'

If we turn from the social to the manual, further evidence of cognitive abilities among the non-human primates can be found in their tool-use (see Essock-Vitale and Seyfarth 1987, McGrew 1989, McGrew 1991). While some monkeys will use tools occasionally, it is the chimpanzees in the wild and in captivity and orang-utans in captivity that are the most skilled and varied tool-users. Chimpanzees, as all archaeologists are no doubt aware, make rudimentary tools which involve some considerable skill. They use these tools for a variety of different actions, and the same substrate to a number of tools can be modified to be appropriate for the specific action to be attained (see Table 1). Many observations of tool-use among chimpanzees come from their natural habitat. In captivity, the list extends enormously with the addition of human-induced substrates which chimps can and will take advantage of. If being tool-users and -makers under natural conditions equates with any form of intelligence, or cognitive skill, then we should focus on their capacity expressed in that environment. However, it is worth noting that, when challenged by a human environment, chimpanzees and orang-utans show far greater variety in the form and function of their technology. The basic question is which context allows us to assess their cognitive skills most effectively. The flexibility shown in responding to the novel conditions created by captivity suggests that we are nowhere near understanding the full range of technological or cognitive potential.

Table 1 Examples of the types of actions and substrates used in ape tool technology. W = observed in the wild; C = observed in captivity.

Action	Object	Chimpanzee	Gorilla	Orang-utan
Defence	Stone	W	W	
	Branch	W	W	
	Leaf		W	
Crack	Stone	W		
	Branch	W		
Probe	Stem	W		C
	Twig	W		C
	Branch	W		C
Prod	Twig	W		C
	Branch	W		C
Cut	Stone	C		C
Dig	Twig	W		
	Branch	W		
Lever	Branch	W	C	
Sponge	Leaf	W	C	
Wipe	Leaf	W		
Rake	Twig	W		C
	Branch	W	C	C
Ladder	Branch	C		
Nest	Leaf/twig	W	W	
Symbols	Sign language	C	C	
	Computers	C		

Source: Essock-Vitale and Seyfarth 1987, McGrew 1989, McGrew 1991.

What, then, are the hallmarks of ape tool-use in the wild or in captivity? The first is that manipulation of objects can be placed into a symbolic context. Chimpanzees can manipulate symbols such as lexigrams quite effectively in captivity (Greenfield and Savage-Rumbaugh 1991). Whether this truly reflects a capacity for 'semantic language' is debated (Terrace 1984), but further links between communication skills and tool-use are continually suggested by experimental work and observations (Savage-Rumbaugh et al. 1978, Tomasello 1990). Chimpanzees can alternate between tools, each with a specific design for a specific function. They can use the same 'tool' for a number of different actions, such that the simple relations of stone-equals-hammer do not hold. Stone may equal hammer in one context when there is a nut to be opened, but stone equals weapon to throw at a predator when there happens to be a leopard near by. Chimpanzees thus are quite capable of manipulating their technology and, indeed, the use of different technologies to suit the appropriate context (Boesch and Boesch 1983, 1990).

Chimpanzee tool-use, then, has several physical and cognitive prerequisites. The first of these is the existence of a considerable degree of manual dexterity, opposability of thumbs, and physical strength to carry out repeated and powerful actions. They also have the neural integration to co-ordinate complex and sequential fine-scale motor actions. Tool-use also requires some experience – very few chimps use or make tools de novo without any previous exposure to either humans or other chimps making tools (Goodall 1970, Hannah and McGrew 1987, Boesch 1991). Tool use is apparently not something that is instinctively programmed; it requires learning and teaching in the wild or in captivity. It also requires, at least potentially, the ability for the animal cognitively to make, or to construct, a mental relationship between the object used as a tool and the goal to be attained, as in being able to crack open a nut using a stone tool. Understanding of the consequences of the motor actions and the relations between two objects, stone hammer and nut, are necessary.

Furthermore, it may possibly lead to the construction of relationships between relationships, in that certain tools have to be used in sequence to attain the end or desired goal. There do indeed appear to be goals to the actions of the chimpanzees, in that the outcome is predetermined. In other words, they want to get those termites out of that termite nest; they want to open the nut. They may want to escape from their pen and therefore want to make that ladder. A goal is both implicit and explicit in their actions, and we can measure these goals and the level of motivation required for attaining these goals. There are rewards for success; you get the food, you get out of the pen, while there are time and energy costs for failure. Technology carries risks in that when it goes wrong it is a waste of time and energy, with major implications for energy and nutritional balances.

Tools thus reflect a specific environmental context, in that there are energetic reasons for attempting to use those tools. There are also some interesting sex differences in that females tend to use and make tools somewhat more frequently than do males, and the foods that are obtained are usually high energy high protein foods which are particularly important to lactating or pregnant females (McGrew 1979, Boesch and Boesch 1984, McGrew 1991). There is also a social context, in a sense that there is transmission of information from mother to offspring and possibly across several generations within this familial context. And there is also an opportunity for individual experimentation and consistency with this transmission across generations – what Nishida (1987) and McGrew and Tutin (1978) termed a tradition for tool-use in different areas. Finally, patterns of tool-use relate to novelty and innovation, to the recombination of motor acts, and to alteration of the tool substrates for different outcomes. Innovation allows chimpanzees to challenge their environment through their technology.

SUMMARY

The non-human primates demonstrate a variety of cognitive capabilities. Behaviourally, they are capable of flexible responses to physical and social contexts, which have only briefly been mentioned above. They have the capacity for memory of the physical environment, of some aspects of self, of other individuals, and of relationships. Furthermore, they are capable of assessment of changes in the conditions of both the physical and social environment, and are able to make strategic adjustments to their own behaviour as a result of these assessments. Learning thus plays a critical role throughout the lifespan. Visual, vocal and physical perception is combined with generalisation across contexts, and leads to abstractions. Some components of their behaviour might be classed as potentially cultural in that there is transmission across generations, social roles are evident, particularly from studies of kinship and conflict resolution, and there is the ability to comprehend and use some kinds of signal or symbolic representation, to act on information and to exchange information.

Monkeys and apes do not think the way we think, but they do think. It would be surprising if they did not, for human cognitive capacities, whether technological, linguistic or representational, arose from the primate brains carried by their ancestors. The issue of continuities in form and function have been emphasised here, at the expense of the obvious discontinuities between human and primate, in order to establish that primate template for thinking in an evolutionary context (see also Lee 1991). Furthermore, I hope to have provided some idea of the ways in which primatologists attempt to understand how primates think, and the context for thinking. In this way we may achieve some insight into the diversity of what cognition means, rather than confining ourselves to our own concepts of meaning.

ACKNOWLEDGEMENTS

Some of ideas presented here developed from early introductions to monkey communication by Robert Seyfarth and Dorothy Cheney. I thank them, and Marc Hauser, for making vervet monkeys theoretically interesting in the field. I also thank Professor Robert Hinde for his inspiration with respect to relationships, and Bill McGrew for generating interest in chimpanzee tools.

Chapter 9

Language and thought in evolutionary perspective

Robert A. Foley

THE ORIGINS OF CULTURE REVISITED

I may be wrong but I suspect that the 'origins of meaning' is the new way of talking about the origins of culture, and so, broadly speaking, I have taken that as my brief. It is of course an interesting shift in terminology. On one hand it reflects the change in what the term *culture* means in anthropology. Earlier formulations saw it primarily as a bundle of characteristics that were uniquely human – technology, language, tradition, symbolic systems, etc. – but it is now viewed as the mental template that enables these other traits to occur and to vary. In a sense we are following so-called cultural behaviour up to its source in the mind or ultimately the brain. I take *meaning* to be the ability of the brain to be self-reflective about behaviours and to propagate actions on the basis of those reflections. The other aspects of culture are therefore epiphenomenal to the mental activities. In terms of the problem of seeking the origins of this capacity this at least makes the question more specific. While how exactly meaning might be empirically observable remains rather obscure, we at least have more focus than looking for culture. Indeed, I argued elsewhere (Foley 1990a) that the culture concept, on account of its compound character, is not an appropriate concept in evolutionary studies, and that instead we should focus on its constituent components independently. There are two reasons for this: one is that it is the individual components that we might be able to observe in the past, whereas we can never see culture; the other is that there is no reason why past hominids should have put the bundle together in the same way as modern humans. Characteristics of so-called cultural behaviour may appear and exist independently. Meaning, therefore, I take to be one of the constituents which we might try to track in evolutionary terms. The problem is how to do this.

There are obviously a number of simple questions that we can ask from an evolutionary point of view. When did 'meaning' appear? Why did it evolve (i.e., what was the selective advantage)? What form did it take? In the space available to me I shall simply address the first of these and in doing so tangentially touch on some other aspects. I shall also take a fairly basic empirical approach.

BRAIN SIZE

How can we get at the evidence for the origins of meaning? One possible approach is to say that it is a question of having sufficient information processing power to allow the mind to develop, and therefore we should look to the evolution of the brain for the evidence we need. Here at least we have fossil evidence. Brain size shows a general increase through time during the course of human evolution (Stringer 1984). However, we have learned that absolute brain size is a misleading measure and therefore need instead to look at relative brain size or brain size once body size has been taken into account (Jerison 1973, Martin 1983). The term used here is encephalization quotient, or EQ: the size of the brain relative to the expected size for a given body size. A plot of hominid EQs against time shows an interesting pattern (Fig. 3). The earliest hominids – the australopithecines, living from over 3 million to about 1 million years ago – have EQs that are not significantly larger than extant apes. Enlargement of the brain is not a general hominid characteristic, but it is specific to the genus *Homo* and, indeed, occurs most rapidly in the later parts of hominid evolution.

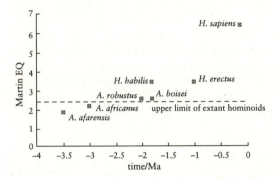

Figure 3 Encephalisation quotients (EQ) of fossil hominid taxa through time. EQs show the relative size of the brain once allometric body size relationships have been taken into account. These data show that encephalisation occurs late in hominid evolution and that the earliest australopithecines display no significant increase in brain size.
Source: Aiello and Dean (1990)

The inference we may perhaps draw is that if we accept that chimpanzees and gorillas do not have 'meaning', then neither did the australopithecines; nor, in all probability, did early members of the genus *Homo*. At the most extreme we might argue that it is only with the origins of *Homo sapiens* (*sensu stricto*) that the event in which we are interested occurs. In other words, by this line of reasoning, the origins of meaning are late.

The caveat here, of course, is whether the other apes have minds. If they do, then the argument collapses, or is at least reduced to saying that early hominids probably had minds like African apes. Certainly the ethological evidence that has been presented in recent years concerning the cognitive capacities of the chimpanzee in particular (Savage-Rumbaugh 1986) should act as a warning against saying that non-human primates do not have significant capacity for complex thought (see Lee in this volume).

TECHNOLOGY

It might be argued that brain size is a poor indicator of mind and meaning. What other evidence might be adduced? One possibility is to say that the evidence for imposed meanings can be found in the detachment of behavioural patterns from genetic and other formal evolutionary ones. This might mean that if we take the archaeological record we should look for discrepancies between that and the hominid fossil record – the same species making different tools, different species making the same tools, etc. This is not easy, and made less easy again by the observations of McGrew (1989) that tool-use in chimpanzees is population-specific and the pattern of tool-use among hominids is not susceptible to simple phylogenetic interpretation.

The relationship between hominid taxa and archaeological assemblages is highly disputed (Foley 1987b, G.A. Clark 1988). Broadly speaking, there is no doubt there is some matching – the Oldowan appears with *Homo*; the development of bifaces is subsequent to the appearance of *Homo erectus*; the East Asian Middle Pleistocene hominids have both a distinctive and simple technology and, according to some authors, a distinctive evolutionary trajectory. African and European late Middle Pleistocene hominids are united by the use of prepared core techniques, although there are also distinct regional characteristics. The dispersal of modern humans is also characterised by a new pattern of technology, associated especially with blades. There are, however, anomalies; the timing of the appearance of new technologies and the appearance of new taxa is not entirely coincident (for example, *Homo erectus* precedes the appearance of bifaces, while anatomically modern *Homo sapiens* precedes the appearance of blade technology and is by no means always associated with it). Furthermore, the complex overlapping of hominid distributions in Western Asia and North Africa is not matched by a similar pattern of artefact assemblages. None the less, at a broad level, it is clear that the pattern of technological change is not entirely independent of changes in hominid morphology. Technology, looked at in this very gross way, seems to be behaving much like any other trait used for phylogenetic analysis.

More important perhaps, the rate of change is very slow. The industries of the Lower Palaeolithic have a duration at a scale of 10^6 years; those of the Middle Palaeolithic of between 10^5 and 10^4 years. It is only in the Upper Palaeolithic, or after the appearance of anatomically modern humans, that we begin to get variation on a scale of only 10^3 or less, and regional variation at scales of less than a continent or subcontinent. It may be argued from this that, whatever else the hominids are doing with their technology, they are not doing much in the way of the imposition of meaning. Or, if they are, they have fairly limited imagination. Once again there appears to be a discrepancy between ancient and modern hominids, and the focus of interest must lie with the origins of anatomically modern humans.

LANGUAGE

Technology, though, may be more to do with ecological determinants than with the mind, or be constrained by motor control rather than by conceptual ability. Perhaps we should try to get closer to the heart of the problem and address what must surely be a reflection of meanings: language. Language is explicitly concerned with meaning, and so if we can find evidence for language, then we might argue that meaning is there.

The origins of language is a well-worn path and, like all well-worn paths, full of potholes for the unwary to fall into. Anatomically it has been argued that Broca's area has been found on australopithecine and early *Homo* endocasts, but this has been disputed – as, indeed, has the notion of Broca's area at all. It has also been argued that the lack of basi-cranial flexion in Neanderthals as well as in other hominids is evidence of non-linguistic species. This has also been disputed, and furthermore a Neanderthal hyoid bone found in Israel a few years ago is morphologically identical to that of modern humans. The fossils do not seem to have any clear indications of the origins of language (see Lieberman 1991 and Noble and Davidson 1991 for recent reviews).

Surprisingly it is the field of genetics that has posed some interesting new insights. Cavalli-Sforza *et al.* (1988) showed recently that there is an interesting overlap between linguistic and genetic evolutionary trees. It seems that the major human

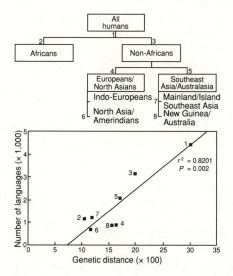

Figure 4 Relationship between the level of genetic diversity and the number of languages spoken for living human populations. The genetic diversity found in each of the major geographical groupings of living populations (top) is plotted against the number of languages spoken by these groups (bottom). The numbers refer to the nodes of genetic relationships. The relationship breaks down at lower levels owing a number of historical and geographical factors.

Source: Foley (1990a)

genetic groups have diverged in conjunction with the major linguistic families. Estimating the rate of linguistic change is fraught with difficulties, but using various assumptions of genetic change Cavalli-Sforza *et al.* (1988) have estimated that the stem human clade lies between 10,000 and 60,000 years. Given the co-variation with the languages it may be claimed that modern languages also had a single stem origin at about this time. This can to some extent be shown by simply plotting genetic diversity against linguistic diversity (Fig. 4). There is a strong correlation between the two, suggesting both a recent common origin and a relatively constant rate of diversification. Again we might look to the origin of modern humans for the origins of what we think of as language, and hence of meaning.

CONCLUSIONS

The implication of these considerations is that the origin of anatomically modern humans at around 100,000 years seems to be a significant evolutionary event, and that a case can be made that major changes towards a modern cognition occur primarily at this stage rather than earlier during the course of hominid evolution.

Palaeontologically and archaeologically we have been downgrading the cognitive and behavioural capacities of the early hominids. To put it crudely, today's *Homo erectus* is a lot dumber that Glynn Isaac's *Homo habilis* of a few years ago. Reading some of the recent interpretations we would seem to have archaic hominids, including Neanderthals, as lumbering, randomly wandering, mindless zombies stalking the earth in utter silence. There is nothing inherently wrong with this newfound modesty of our ancestors, but there is a major anomaly. At the same time the hominids have been sliding down the cognitive scale, the apes and monkeys have been climbing up. Tool-making, language, politics, kinship, hunting and all sorts of flexible sophisticated behaviours have been documented for the non-human primates. They have acquired culture while the non-modern hominids have lost theirs. This change of perspective has occurred in the context of greatly improved comparative analyses of primate and fossil hominid evolutionary biology, and the massive expansion of primary fieldwork with living non-human primates.

The problem that arises is that according to some lines of evidence and interpretations we now have early hominids with larger brains and more complex technology than living apes being viewed as less flexible than chimpanzees. At the same time, one cannot help being struck by the apparent gap between the archaic hominids and the modern ones. How can we resolve this anomaly? My own solution would be a reductionist one. We have come some way in singling out meaning from the generality of culture and focusing on that as the critical variable. I believe we can go further. By and large, what we are seeking and finding in the archaeological record is the external consequences of symbolic or linguistic activities. That, though, is exactly what they are, external manifestations, and we are inferring internal mental states from them on a one-to-one basis.

However, the most exciting work in animal behaviour and cognition, such as that by Cheney and Seyfarth (1990) and de Waal (1982), is significant in that it implies that what is going on inside an animal's head is a lot more complex than what it is communicating externally. Chimpanzees may not be speaking a great deal, but they are thinking a lot. In other words, the external manifestations of non-human primate cognition are far less developed than their internal information-processing capacities. External manifestations seem to under-represent the levels of thought involved. What this implies to me is a reverse of the traditional dogma that thought is internalised language. Instead, I suspect, thought is the primary focus for selection of intelligence, and is largely internal. Selection for communication, which has an entirely different function, is a separate issue. Language, I think, is externalised thought, and built upon thought as an internal information-processing system. This in part explains why chimpanzees and other primates have what is known as unrevealed capacities – the ability to do in captivity (i.e., under social pressure) more than they show in the wild.

When we look at human evolution, therefore, and are struck by the absence of modern forms of symbolic behaviour, I think we should be wary. Our ancestors may have been silent, but they were not necessarily unintelligent. Brains are very expensive metabolic items, and they were not there for nothing. The real key question in the origins of meaning is to detach the reasons why we have developed the ability to think from the reasons why we should communicate those thoughts. These are, I suspect, two different evolutionary events. Selection for intelligence and selection for the ability or need to communicate the products of that intelligence may have been functionally and chronologically detached in hominid evolution, and the trend towards placing considerable emphasis on language as a signifier of other capacities may have been misplaced and misleading.

Chapter 10

Talking to each other

Why hominids bothered

James Steele

INTRODUCTION

As Alexandri notes in her section introduction (above), the relationship between archaeology and evolutionary biology is problematic. On the one hand, evolutionary approaches are concerned with the biological history of those propensities which underlie any situated human actions (including those that archaeologists reconstruct from their fieldwork). This relationship might be graphed hierarchically (Fig. 5).

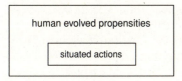

Figure 5 The relationship between archaeology and evolutionary biology

However, many archaeologists take the basic propensities for granted, to the extent that the understanding of variation in human behaviour across contexts becomes the principal or the only goal of their endeavours. Where does that leave the Palaeolithic archaeologist? As a student of the evolution of the human basic behavioural repertoire, or as a student of cultural variation in a data-poor branch of cultural studies?

Jonathan Turner has recently suggested (rather confrontationally) that 'the social sciences, particularly sociology and anthropology, have lost their early vision. They seem afraid to assert that there are universal and generic patterns of human behaviour and organization that can be described and understood with concepts, models and propositions. . . . In all of this new "discourse" – to use a favourite word of humanities-babblers – relativism reigns supreme. *Realism*, *positivism*, and *naturalism* are dirty words, because everything is relative, and, as a result, the only real things are text and talk' (1992, p. 126). In fact, thanks to Turner and others, the study of 'human universals' is currently undergoing a renaissance (e.g., Brown 1991, Fiske 1992), and as Alexandri notes (above) this is producing fertile ground for a hybrid research programme involving the social scientists active in this area in a dialogue with Palaeolithic archaeologists.

The pungency of Turner's critique obscures one vital universal which is the joint concern of humanities 'types' and of students of human universals (sometimes called 'evolutionary psychologists'). That is, of course, talk and the behaviour of talking. In this paper, I shall ask what can be gained by treating talk as an evolved universal – specifically, the kinds of talk which are the focus of Turner's humanities-babblers, as used in status- and identity-negotiation, alliance-building, confirmation of solidaristic intentions, and social manipulation. My perspective will be that of a Palaeolithic archaeologist wanting to understand *why* this behavioural universal evolved.

LANGUAGE CAPACITY AND THE EVOLUTIONARY TREE

Is the study of how talk evolved as a basic propensity a search for origins? Are human cognitive and behavioural abilities qualitatively distinct from those of other species? Do we need a special language and set of analytical tools to explore human capacities? It seems to me that the future of this debate revolves around the scope of comparative and evolutionary analyses to account for language and for rule-governed social behaviour in the human case. Foley, in his book *Another Unique Species* (1987a) and elsewhere, has demonstrated how much can be gained by taking a comparative zoological and ecological perspective on human evolutionary anatomy and behaviour, while Cartmill (1990), in a paper on 'Human uniqueness and theoretical content in palaeoanthropology', has argued that palaeoanthropology should attempt to reduce and if possible eliminate the list of qualitatively unique human traits, since qualitatively unique phenomena cannot be explained by reference to any more general overarching laws or regularities. From the other side of the divide, Wolfe (1990, p. 618) notes that 'Any statement about human uniqueness, for sociologists an introduction to their science, constitutes for many students of animal behaviour a challenge to be met', and asserts the qualitative uniqueness of the human abilities to regulate behaviour (as 'interpreting selves') by reference to rules which are negotiated as social practices, and which are consequently subject to reorganisation from one generation to the next. Philip Lieberman, in his recent book *Uniquely Human: The Evolution of Speech, Thought, and Selfless Behaviour* (1991), argues that humans are distinguished by their possession of a higher moral sense (cognitive altruism), which is mediated by language and related cognitive abilities to extend the concept of 'relatedness' and to regulate conduct by concepts which are only explicable using language. The study of how talk evolved is therefore focal to this clash of paradigms: if talking underwrites the generativity of human culture as a set of contextually bound practices governed by linguistically encoded rules, then the major conceptual headache for Palaeolithic archaeologists is that of trying to understand the evolution of talk in terms of overarching laws and cross-species regularities.

For this purpose, let us define three ways of talking about a behavioural trait or propensity in any given species. *Type '1'* behaviours are those which are shared with other species as a result of a common descent-line – they are 'conserved' traits deriving from a common ancestor. For instance, many ethologists see a continuity between the basic human emotions (and their facial expressions) and the basic facial expressions of other monkeys and apes, with their associated action patterns. This continuity is, then, a conserved human trait – a Type '1' behaviour.

Type '2' behaviours are those which are shared with other species in different descent lines as a result of ecological convergence. Analogous challenges in the environment of adaptation have led to the evolution of functionally analogous traits. For instance, birdsong and mammalian vocalizations may serve overlapping functions – such as territorial spacing – but have evolved independently in separate descent lines.

Type '3' behaviours are unique evolutionary novelties which have evolved in a single descent line and are characteristic of a single species. Most social scientists would class human language as a Type '3' behaviour. This, then, makes the task of Palaeolithic archaeology that of 'origins' storytellers with respect to Type '3' human behaviours. It also makes the analytical task of Palaeolithic archaeology virtually impossible. If unique Type '3' behaviours need to be analysed using a special-purpose terminology, then there can be no overarching generalisations covering both the Type '3' behaviour and other behaviours of other species, and thus no account of the behaviour's evolution as a product of law-like regularities. When animal behaviour students try to account for human language abilities in comparative terms, they are not engaging in disciplinary 'imperialism'. They are simply trying to maintain the overall coherence of the prevalent scientific world-view.

In the next section, I want to itemise some aspects of human talk which come into the categories either of Type '1' or of Type '2' behaviours – respectively, traits which are conserved and those which are the product of ecological convergence. I shall argue that this enables us to make sense of the evolution of any Type '3' aspects of human language propensities as the product of general, law-like regularities in the evolutionary process.

CONSERVED AND CONVERGENT ASPECTS OF HUMAN LANGUAGE PROPENSITIES

A number of components of human language abilities are evidently conserved features shared with other living primates owing to our common ancestry. At the level of the anatomical apparatus which enables speech articulation and comprehension, it appears that the basic neural circuitry linking Broca's and Wernicke's areas in the neocortex, and their connections to the orofacial and laryngeal (Broca's) and to the ear (Wernicke's) muscles are shared with monkeys (Deacon 1988, Heffner and Heffner 1989). The same is true for laterality in vocalisation circuitry. There is some indication that the human brain organization is consistent with primate trends (a 'scaled-up version'): great apes, with brain structures most similar to our own, can also be trained to develop syntactic and semantic abilities paralleling those of young human children (cf. Passingham 1982, Savage-Rumbaugh *et al.* 1993). Monkey vocal gestures involve manipulation of the tongue and lips paralleling human speech articulation (Brown and Hauser 1990); phonological evidence shows that monkeys use acoustic patterns in vocal communication which are common to human language phonology (frequency modulation, changes in power spectrum, amplitude modulation and call duration) (Maurus *et al.* 1988). Emotional messages are conveyed in human talk using simple features of the sound spectrum which do not require linguistic pattern-recognition techniques: many of these features are shared with monkeys, and in one recent study it was found that naïve human subjects had a high probability of recognizing the emotional significance of basic elements of the vocal repertoire of macaque monkeys (*M. arctoides*), suggesting an underlying Type '1' conservatism for this aspect of talk – its ability to convey information about the speaker's emotional and motivational state (Leinonen *et al.* 1991).

In addition to these continuities in the hardware, there are apparent continuities in everyday patterns of use of human language compared with other primate vocalisations and with other aspects of primate social behaviour. Although the generativity and semantic richness is missing, other primates show patterns of vocal behaviour which have some of the elements of human discourse: for instance, squirrel monkey 'chuck' calls (their most commonly heard close-range affiliative vocalisation) are structured by 'conversational' turn-taking and by simple syntactic rules, and occur within established groups principally during quiet, relaxed and unthreatened periods (Biben and Symmes 1991). Gelada baboons use rhythm and melody to introduce a sequential order into their vocal gestures, and to delimit the boundaries of a communicative event: in the long term, the social function of such vocalisations is to form bonds between individuals – for example, through developing patterns of dyadic vocal exchanges (Richman 1987). Dunbar (1988, p. 250) suggests that these data justify the suggestion that 'contact calling (and similar vocalizations) may be used as a form of vocal grooming in the maintenance and servicing of relationships'.

Human conversational talk – the most common, prototypical instance of natural language-use – also serves such functions, negotiating the satisfaction of socially motivated needs (cf. J. H. Turner 1987). A number of studies suggest that the development of physiological self-regulation in humans involves entrainment to repetitive patterns in social interactions, with specific systems regulated by hidden rhythms in specific aspects of interactions and relationships (Hofer 1984). Conversational talk, with its turn-taking and its repetitive, collaboratively scripted and reproduced routines, serves as precisely such a medium of 'mutual adaptation': in conversational speech, partners adapt elements of their conversation to one another, including basic 'paralinguistic' elements of the acoustic speech signal itself (fundamental frequency of phonation) (S. W. Gregory 1986). Gregory et al. (1993, p. 211) have identified this process of mutual adaptation as a means of providing social cohesion at the dyadic level, and suggest that this process 'may indicate [that] a primal form of hominid sociability is still very much with us and sets the scene, acoustically as well as interactively, for the verbal utterances and complex social relations that follow'. Indeed, it has been found that cyclicity increases in the course of a conversational interaction, and can be taken as an index of the success of the interaction in servicing the relationship among participants (R. M. Warner 1992): this has parallels with Deborah Tannen's (1987) analysis of the role of repetition and other non-novel elements in conversations, as consolidating discursive coherence and a sense of participation, in what she calls the 'poetics of talk'.

Although this comparison suggests that the underlying continuity between primate contact calls and human language relates to the affiliative motivations, there are clearly competitive and dominance-seeking aspects of both repertoires, most clearly articulated in models of human talk by Mazur (1985, Mazur and Cataldo 1989) and Burling (1986). Just as some of the most cognitively demanding aspects of primate social behaviour are those involved in deception, and concealment of intention, so in human talk we see repeatedly and across cultures a metalinguistic lexicon of terms devoted to commenting on language use and to analysing conversational intentions and assessing truthfulness in a speaker's utterances (e.g., Stross 1974, V. Turner 1980). These are certainly not restricted to literate cultures, and remind us of the extent to which humans can monitor intentionality in themselves and others outside the linguistic channel – for example, by visual monitoring. Nevertheless, the most immediate parallels between human talk and primate vocal behaviour appear to relate to reassurance gestures and affiliative bonding, and it is my suggestion that the anatomical and behavioural continuities mark out these aspects of human talk as conserved, Type '1' behaviour patterns shared with other living primates.

DERIVED ASPECTS OF HUMAN LANGUAGE ABILITIES

What, then, are the Type '3' (derived, novel) aspects of human language abilities? Clearly these include at least the following: brain expansion and associated expanded working and long-term associative memory capacity; vocal tract re-modelling to permit greater high-frequency acoustic modulation of the speech signal; increased voluntary control of vocalisation circuitry; increased role for linguistically encoded representations in organising memory processes and in regulating behaviour. These are the traits which are the most usual focus of palaeoanthropological reconstruction in 'language origins' research. However, by focusing exclusively on them we risk losing sight of the continuities which I have just discussed, and which may shed light on the evolution of the Type '3' components of human talk as adaptive traits.

As I have suggested, the default social science model starts with these 'novel' components, and therefore treats human language processes in their entirety as effectively novel, Type '3' behaviour. This model has also been associated with what Andresen (1992) calls the 'FAX' model of human linguistic communication: the conventional conduit model of language as transmission of information between two speakers who share a common grammar, lexicon, and set of mental representations.

Dawkins and Krebs (1978) depicted the traditional ethological view of animal signalling in similar terms, as a vehicle of interindividual co-operation, in which signals carry information which is beneficial to the recipient. They argued (from game theory) for a contrasting view of animal signals as a means whereby actors manipulate 'at a distance' the behaviour of reactors. A lot of recent work in primate studies has focused on primate 'mind-reading' abilities as the correlate of such deceptive intentions in signallers (e.g., Byrne and Whiten 1992). However, in a subsequent paper Krebs and Dawkins (1984) argued that, whereas exploitative signalling which had evolved as a means of coercive social manipulation would tend towards repetition, ritualization and conspicuousness, *co-operative* signalling for common interest should lead to 'conspiratorial whispering', minimising the costs (predation risk, energy and time costs) and muting the display: 'if the reactor *benefits* from receiving the signal and responding in accord with the actor's interests, instead of heightened sales-resistance leading to exaggeration of the signal during evolution we would expect to see heightened sensitivity to the signal leading to a *reduction* in the amplitude and conspicuousness of the signal' (1984, p. 391). They cite close-range calls in monkey troops as an example of this kind of 'conspiratorial whispering'.

One of the reasons why the FAX model of human talk has been so successful is, I suggest, simply that in humans the 'conspiratorial whisper' function of vocal behaviour has evolved to such a degree that the elements of the FAX model – shared grammar, lexicon, set of mental representations – are close approximations to the actual substrate of a conversational exchange. However, it is only by excavating the Type '1' components of human talking that we can understand the preconditions of its subsequent evolution into a Type '3' universal. Without the conserved basis in affiliative adaptation, conversational talk could not have evolved to its present rapid rates of information transfer.

CONCLUSION

The approach taken in this short paper has been that of a new kind of 'archaeology' devoted not to the stratified artefactual record, but to the embedded sets of features which make up a biological individual as a member of a species. I have distinguished between conserved and derived traits, and argued that the conserved components of human language ability point to an origin for talk in primate close calls as a form of affiliative 'vocal grooming'. I have then suggested that this provided the basis for the adaptive evolution of the high rates of information transfer characteristic of human talking.

Although the analogy with archaeology (as it is conventionally understood) should not be pressed too far, this kind of approach to human universals and behavioural predispositions is gaining favour in the social sciences, and conventional archaeology needs to find a way of integrating the study of the artefactual record with this kind of behavioural reconstruction based on comparing living species. There are issues in interdisciplinarity here which deserve our thought. They concern both the difficulty of working across disciplinary boundaries, and the potential intellectual rewards (for instance, I would suggest that the Type '1' components of human talk are central to the process which interpretive sociologists deal with in terms of 'permanent communication' – sometimes seen as a non-rational facet of human behaviour). Furthermore, for a hybrid field to evolve in which conventional (primarily Palaeolithic) archaeology is integrated with the new evolutionary psychology, it will be necessary for some researchers to make such hybridization their primary research focus. This process has often paid dividends in the past (cf. Dogan and Pahre 1990).

ACKNOWLEDGEMENTS

Thanks to Alexandra Alexandri for constructive feedback on earlier drafts.

Chapter 11

Interpretation in the Palaeolithic

Clive Gamble

The founding fathers of archaeology had the habit of producing incompatible interpretive offspring. The best-known example is Stukeley, who gave us field archaeology and the Druids – the unhappy twins of ourselves *and* the lunatic fringe. Boucher de Perthes in the first half of the last century is another. In 1847 he demonstrated the great antiquity of chipped stone implements, and hence humans, in the gravels of the Somme. Having established, but not named, the substance of the Palaeolithic, he then went on to classify many other natural stones as flint sculptures. There are, of course, many who think he got it right. At least one amateur collector this century thought he was a flint, possibly a strangled blade, and starved himself to death. Many others, like the Revd Frederick Smith (1926) who scoured the Cambridgeshire gravels for 'sculptures' of Gibraltar monkeys, have garages full of 'hag goddesses' and other dubious objects.[1]

Boucher de Perthes was highlighting what he thought motivated Palaeolithic peoples. In that sense he attempted to understand interpretation *in* rather than *of* the Palaeolithic. Of course he may well have been right. Pebbles could have been selected because they looked like a Gibraltar monkey. Like Columbus, also in uncharted waters, Boucher de Perthes may have been better as a reader of signs, a compiler of significant markers, than at providing accurate observations for those who followed (Greenblatt 1991, p. 86). His pedigree in the history and development of the Palaeolithic as a historical science provides us, like the case of Stukeley before him, with an interpretive challenge.

The reason that most of us continue to think he was wrongheaded stems from our conviction that, even if the world works like that, we would be hard-pressed with Palaeolithic data to prove it. Like Stukeley, Boucher de Perthes relies on little more than assertion. The past is what he said it was. The question of meaning is ignored. As a result he falls easy prey to the materialist camp many of whom are reluctant even to admit that prior to cave art humans had that top rung in Christopher Hawkes's famous ladder.

Consequently there is an obvious unease with alternative interpretations among Palaeolithic archaeologists (e.g., Bettinger 1991, p. 147; Bender and Morris 1991, p. 9). One reason perhaps why the Palaeolithic is regarded as different, somehow apart from the rest of archaeology. Ever since Lubbock named the period in 1865 we have interpreted its data as human by supplying an ethnographic face (Murray 1987), but rarely a text. We prefer instead interpretive arguments validated by a temporal metaphor of controlled attrition to reveal the process of the past, whether that entails dismembering a caribou or reducing flint from nodule to tool. In the Palaeolithic actions always speak louder than words.

But these interpretive arguments are unlikely to crack the problem of the origin of meaning – if meaning can, indeed, be said to have an origin in the same way as agriculture, urbanism or even modern humans. In these traditional archaeological terms I do not think it can; but I find the question intriguing, like asking why Boucher de Perthes was wrong about his sculptures. By asking it we are forced to examine our frames of reference.

MESSAGES AND CONTEXTS

I understand *meaning* as message + context. An interpretive archaeology needs to examine both parts of the equation. The messages are the basis for the interpretation of the past, although they remain obscure to us because they are specific to the past. Moreover, the form and content of the messages are more likely to be exaptively than adaptively derived; the product of selection by reason of their form rather than fit by the selective design of history. As Gould and Vrba (1982, p. 13) comment, 'most of what the brain now does to enhance our survival lies in the domain of exaptation – and does not allow us to make hypotheses about the selective paths of human history'.

It is this crucial distinction between exaptation and adaptation which makes the task of prediction concerning the choice of message (their form and content) so difficult, except in general terms. Cultural choices that involve how pots, flints, textiles, houses, boats, headgear, paintings – whatever – will be elaborated remain almost infinite. The messages may be comparable, but the means to express them can be so widely divergent because they are co-opted from existing forms rather than adaptively constrained. Hence historical circumstance is important in understanding the form of the message and documenting how these change along cultural trajectories. But this is hardly a route to explanation and interpretation. So we need to appreciate that, although the forms messages can take are almost infinite, the information systems of material culture are under selection. Variability within cultural systems has to be understood in that light (Wobst 1977). Any attempt to examine the origin of meaning therefore addresses a question in evolutionary time. The interpretation of meaning is best-regarded as a problem on an ecological timescale (Gamble 1991a).

By comparison, contexts can at least be generalised since the institutions which define them are recurrent as is the power upon which they are reproduced. The resources for this power involve interaction between people and their surroundings. Such forces of interaction are never purely social or environmental but dynamic and interactive (Hinde 1987, p. 27).

The second part of the equation, context, needs closer definition. It refers to lifespace where meaning is both restored and recouped through actions by individuals, groups and institutions. The messages conveyed through routines include technological procedures, while ritual and performance constitute meaning as defined above. Sacred and secular, the interest lies in the regional organisation of power.

At this spatial scale we must expect that meaning will vary enormously within a thousand years let alone 10,000 or even 100,000. For many years it has been commonplace to talk of the monotony of the Palaeolithic (the million years of boredom) with its unvaried material culture and colourless stone tools. It is now increasingly common to discuss the diversity within the uniformity (S. L. Kuhn 1991, Cundy 1991). We need to become interpreters of signs as well as observers of data, appreciative of inner and outer meanings. To do this requires recognising other properties in Palaeolithic artefacts.

LONG-TERM AESTHETICS

The possibilities of alternative interpretation in the Palaeolithic can be illustrated within the wider discourse on aesthetics. Grahame Clark provides a characteristically elegant starting-point in his book *Symbols of Excellence* (1986) that examines the cross-cultural recurrence of similar precious materials as expressions of status. His question why this should be is a good one. He begins by listing the physical attributes: 'Ivory attracts by reason of its smoothness and creamy colour, jade by its translucence, hues and touch, gold by its untarnishable gleam, pearls by their orient and the most precious stones by their fire' (1986, p. 6). These are qualities of excellence according to Clark (ibid., p. 12) where, 'Regardless of social circumstances a concern for excellence and a desire to recognize it through symbols embodying precious substances, is widespread among our species' (ibid., p. 106).

While disagreeing with his explanation, I am struck by the pan-cultural sweep of his vision and the interpretive insights it might offer, if harnessed differently, to an assessment of meaning in the past. Clark remains wedded to his own culture from which he ponders the artistic marvels encompassed in its empire. The alternative pursued by Morphy (1989) in his discussion of aesthetics is to look at the concept from the periphery rather than the centre of such political relationships. He defines aesthetics as how something appeals to the senses (ibid., p. 21). Using the art of the Yolngu of Eastern Arnhem Land as an example, he shows how spiritual power is expressed in their art through the quality of *bir'yun*, or brilliance. This is caught in the shimmering quality of the art as well as being present in natural objects such as ochre and stones. Blood forms a similar important source of spiritual power (ibid., Knight 1983, 1991). People can be made to shine, *wangaar*, by rubbing them with fat, ochre and blood. Bark paintings shimmer like a Bridget Riley with their fine hatched lines and basic colours. *Bir'yun* produces effects that humans find stimulating and appealing. Brilliance, Morphy believes, is an effect that operates cross-culturally (1989, p. 36). Good taste has nothing to do with it, as Gary Glitter and the Crown Jewels both testify.

What catches the eye is aesthetic. If it expresses spiritual power, such meaning will be context-based, the brilliant messages related to it. A T-shirt with Australian aboriginal designs reflects brilliance, is definitely aesthetic but is not necessarily a source of spiritual power. The power of ritual, as Morphy points out, is not an aesthetic effect (ibid., p. 38). That possibility depends upon a belief in Ancestral beings. Although, to be successful as theatre or performance, ritual requires the enhancement of aesthetic qualities of natural and artifical objects brimming with brilliance.

Now down a rung on the ladder of inquiry to the technological procedure of making a spear-point. Jones and White (1988) were privileged to observe this at a sacred Yolngu quarry. These sparkling quartzite spear points are described by the word *djukurr*, which has an outside and an inside meaning. On the outside it refers to a particularly important source of brilliance, animal fat, especially the shining fat around the kidneys. The inside meaning of the word refers to power both ritual and actual (ibid., p. 61). The power of these killing-points is spoken of as *djukurr mirri* (having fat).

Many might dismiss this argument as just so many pretty pebbles on the beach, a magpie model of aesthetics and power. Now, if this were a multimedia text, you could click the movie button on your screen, activate a window to another context, and let the Yolngu do the talking as they do in a Kim Mckenzie film, *The Spear in the Stone* (1983, counter 5.12 to 6.52). The passage I would select to illustrate my argument from this short film highlights both message (spear-points: brilliance:

danger) and context (quarry: regional power: death) that together provide me with an interpretation of meaning in ecological time. The fact that this episode is 'frozen' on tape and can be replayed, recycled, recut, reinterpreted emphasises the shape of meaning (B. Molyneaux, pers. comm.).

The clip follows two traditional owners as they 'rediscover' their sacred quarry. Such an exercise in memory deals with the reproductive power of stone and the power of blood, and ends on a lighter note with one of the principals cutting himself while knapping flint and joking to camera about his companions leaving a wounded man.

THE ARCHAEOLOGICAL CHALLENGE

While such films may be an enriching experience, supplying the missing text to Lubbock's ethnographic faces, they usually frustrate archaeologists rather than inform them. Jones and White (1988, p. 85) talk of the 'impoverished history' that would be available to any archaeological excavator of the quarry who lacked the insights of the traditional owners. They mention (ibid.) extra hypotheses which could be tested with the archaeology, but tantalisingly do not tell us what these might be.

The alternative, as Taçon (1991, Gamble 1991b) has shown for the stone tools of Kakadu in Arnhem Land, is to stress different properties. Rather than measure the points as Jones did as a good and honest observer, read the signs and see how they glitter. Taçon proposes that changes in raw material were constrained not just by provisioning and availability but by their variable brilliant properties that symbolise alteration in regional power relations.

And why not? I would be one of the first to admit to the sterility of many typological schemes for stone tools based on shape and edge. Brilliance can be measured and changes in patterns of regional mobility or transfer documented through sourcing raw materials. Variation in the local and global connotations of brilliance can be compared. Their aesthetic appeal and its relation to sources of power underpins the argument. If required, this appeal could no doubt be pinned down to cognitive and psychological causes. The just-so stories of those like Bender (1985) who descry the functional-technological school (Bender and Morris 1991, Mazel 1989) would now have something other than subjectivity to elaborate their histories of hunters and gatherers.

The key point is to locate the problem of meaning in regional terms. The glitter factor by itself is probably a red herring, rather like the entoptic theory (Lewis-Williams 1991) for all cave art that originally came from the written ethnography of the !San. Such simple universals explaining complex cultural phenomena usually enjoy a brief following. No doubt the brilliance will also soon fade.

Its lasting interpretive value for archaeology would be to link the tools with other aspects of the cultural landscape. The tools become the basis for recognising contexts. As messages in the meaning equation they remain obscure and unpredictable. Instead they signpost contexts where power was reproduced, their variable properties the basis for future interpretation of the symbolic worlds of prehistoric peoples.

CONCLUSIONS, WILD AND DANGEROUS

The origins of meaning will never be a research question like the origin of modern humans. It provides instead a focus for reviewing our interpretive arguments. I have no wish to set up a chase for the earliest shining stones such as the rock crystal tools from Mousterian levels at Les Merveilles (McCurdy 1931) or the swirling multi-coloured jasper hand-axes from Fontmaure-en-Vellèches (Gruet 1976, p. 1092). Local examples of Mousterian brilliance do not necessarily reflect Neanderthal meaning. That requires an altogether wider study. The origin of meaning, if it exists, is an exaptive process, one of those evolutionary 'opportunities' on a par with the meteoric demise of the dinosaurs. Stone tools, as *The Spear in the Stone* shows, continue to do what they have always done since first used some 2.5 million years ago – assist hominids to survive and at some point to interpret existence. In ecological time that must be about 900 million days of selection at an ecological, immediate, timescale. During all that time the routines of existence were repeated as we repeat them today. The stone tools assisted and were available for co-option as elements to change the shape of meaning. They were a resource for exaptation and hence the elaboration of cultural and social life. But there was no requirement that they should be so co-opted, just as there is no requirement or necessity that the stones which forest chimps use to crack open nuts will be exapted to interpret existence and so provide more than just assistance.

Such a conclusion is at variance with Hodder's recent suggestion (1990, p. 283) that at the beginning of the European Palaeolithic there is a contradiction 'between the ordered world of social representation and the physical violent world of the non-social'. Following such initial conditions all that happens during the European Palaeolithic is an extension of a single idea, 'The prestige of the cultural, its value, depends on the presence of an opposite – the danger of the wild. Thus at the centre of the cultural is an absence. The handaxe both celebrates and excludes the wild' (ibid., p. 284). Know the noble savage by his footprints in the forests of time, seems to be the conclusion. The long-term extension of an idea, subject to a form of multiplier effect, leaves me wondering what remains to be explained in the long corridors of the Palaeolithic. Is 'enough time' sufficient explanation for the idea to grow to full expression? If it is, then the origin of meaning in Hodder's sketch can be found in the words of the song 'You're everywhere and nowhere, baby, that's where you're at'. The problem will remain unresolvable because the questions of evolutionary time have been elided with the experience of ecological existence. History has been abandoned in preference to assertion. The spectre of Boucher de Perthes returns to haunt us by casting doubts on what we think we know and how we know it. While it is good to have interpretations challenged, it is unhelpful if the alternative concludes there is essentially nothing to explain in a historical discipline because no changes occurred. The examination of the origin of meaning requires more than hindsight and assertion. Once there is meaning, who, indeed, would abandon a wounded man?

ACKNOWLEDGEMENTS

Financial assistance towards the preparation and research for this paper was generously provided by the Sir Robert Menzies Centre for Australian Studies and the British Academy. I would like to thank Alexandra Alexandri for editorial encouragement.

NOTE

1 For a discussion of the theoretical power of images in the visual language of archaeology, see Gamble 1992.

Part 3

Interpretation, writing and presenting the past

Chapter 12

Interpretation, writing and presenting the past

John Carman

This subject-matter is one on which most participants at most conferences (rightly or wrongly) feel qualified to comment. Whereas in a discussion of 'Origins' participants may feel alienated by the intrusion of non-archaeological specialisms (primatology, cognitive development), here they encounter an aspect of contemporary modern culture – the social context in which we all work and live day-by-day – that of 'the heritage'.

This 'heritage' word is a dangerous one: it is one of those that most people think they understand, but rarely take the trouble to define. Accordingly, some of us are fighting the battle to ban the 'H-word' from use. The 'H-word' should be banned because the field of 'heritage' is strange and wide. At one level, the central issue is that of the *values* to be placed on archaeological material. Key questions concern the rather ambiguous nature of ancient material existing as objects in the *contemporary* world, raising issues concerning the nature of (post)modernity, why the past is considered important, and how specifically *archaeological* material can be distinguished (if it can) from other phenomena – art, antiques, the everyday. This extends into the area of the presentation of the past by way of the processes by which the *thing* is transformed into *language*, the medium of communication – and how this affects the object itself and the audience to which the words are addressed. Connected to this is a close concern with the immediacy of the object – its capacity to engender an emotional response in the viewer, the physicality of the object, the *art* in *art*efact. At the same time, there is the problem of the otherness of the past and its objects (Lowenthal 1985) – as well as its simple difference from modern objects, and all the issues surrounding commodification (Appadurai, ed., 1986) and alienation (Stewart 1984). The problem with this level is that – while very interesting – it inevitably leads away from an attempt to consider the audience for archaeology (our 'public', our 'clients', our readers) and into territory better-served under other rubrics – philosophy, the nature of history, the interpretation of material culture itself.

At another level, 'heritage' encompasses a concern with the production and consumption of archaeological knowledge – a direct concern with our *audience*. Since archaeological knowledge is contained in works that are written, then 'writing' is a convenient and apt metaphor for all kinds of dissemination: books, journals, conference papers, museum displays, television and radio programmes, guided tours. All of these are forms of 'writing' which need to be 'read' by an audience. Reflecting, as it does, the concerns of so-called 'interpretive anthropology', this approach opens up many avenues to thought.

A key text – and one that conveniently raises all the relevant issues – is James Clifford's introduction to *Writing Culture* (Clifford 1986). Clifford's argument starts with the recognition that the act of *writing* is central to ethnography as a discipline, itself a historically constituted framework for organising knowledge in the modern world. If we are now entering a postmodern world, in which the institutions of modernity (those that have dominated since the later nineteenth century) are unravelling – as some have argued (and Kevin Walsh agrees: see below and Walsh 1992) – then the concept of 'Man' as a focus for study is also unravelling (Clifford 1986, p. 4; cf. Foucault 1970), which raises the question of the nature of any academic discipline which studies human society. If, as Clifford goes on to argue, ethnographic writing is determined by its context, by established forms of rhetoric, by its institutional framework, by relations of power, and by historical contingency (Clifford 1986, p. 6), then the same must be true of other disciplines, including archaeology. The consequence is that ethnographic truths – and archaeological ones – are 'inherently partial – committed and incomplete' (ibid., p. 7). In other words, 'power and history work through [texts] in ways their authors cannot fully control' (ibid., p. 7). If 'the writing and reading of ethnography [and archaeology] are overdetermined by forces ultimately beyond the control of either an author or an interpretive community [the readers, then] [t]hese contingencies – of language, of rhetoric, of power, and history – must now be openly confronted' (ibid., p. 25). However, 'an interest in the discursive aspects of cultural representation draws attention not to the interpretation of cultural "texts" but to their relations of production'. This raises questions pertinent to all forms of the production of knowledge: 'who speaks? who writes? when and where? with or to whom? under what institutional and historical constraints?' (ibid., p. 13). It also opens the way to new forms of writing, as is happening in ethnography and in archaeology.

This necessary focus on producers *versus* consumers opens up the question of other kinds of dispute. Who does, after all, *own* the past? Indeed, is there *a* (single) past, or are we faced with multiple pasts that vie for attention from different communities? If this is the case, then how do we cope with competing claims concerning objects and sites of archaeological concern, claims that deny the validity of an archaeological approach? If the archaeologist is only one voice among many, then can any preferential position be claimed? Ultimately, the issue is one of the place of archaeology, and the archaeologist, in society. It is one of the purpose and value of the past and its study – not *a priori* but deriving from a consideration of archaeological practice.

Of course, all practice is historically situated and it is in part a concern for the historical trajectory of a discipline that gives rise to the possibility of new modes of practice. This concern with a historical understanding of our own practices is reflected in much recent literature. It is fairly obvious in the case of Hudson (1987) (a history of museums which have influenced museum design, now nicely complemented by Eilean Hooper-Greenhill's (1992) study of museum history from a Foucauldian perspective and in the historically orientated contributions in Pearce (ed., 1989). Specifically as it affects archaeology, the historical perspective particularly informs Barrett *et al.* (1991) since part of this project was based on efforts to reinterpret Pitt-Rivers's nineteenth-century work in Cranborne Chase in building a new approach to the study of British prehistory.

This interest in how we reached our present situation (soon to be the subject of an encyclopaedia no less: Murray, forthcoming) is combined with a particular concern for audiences, especially in museum studies (Lumley, ed., 1988, Pearce, ed., 1989, Vergo 1990). Out of this combination is derived an imperative to be explicit about one's own approach to archaeology, particularly clearly displayed by Hodder (1990), Shanks (1992a) and Tilley (1991), and in attempts to express the meanings things have for communities other than white, male middle-class professional archaeologists (Spector 1991).

AUDIENCES AND COMMUNITIES

The issue of audiences is reflected in all the papers presented in this section. Fowler exposes the failure of the archaeological community to contribute to an understanding of the phenomenon of the countryside – a point emphasised from a different angle by Greeves (1989). Leone *et al.* and Walsh each display a keen concern for the impact of their work on those to whom it is shown and a willingness to interact with their audience. Leone *et al.*'s use of oral history as a way of making contact between communities and archaeologists is instructive, reflected elsewhere by Mbunwe-Samba's (1989) identification of its value in an African context and McDonald *et al.*'s (1991) combination of oral tradition and archaeology as a 'tool of resistance' against military myth-making in North America. Against this, however, can be offset Walsh's perhaps too sanguine acceptance of the value of the interactive video: in particular, its encouragement of passivity in the viewer (surely one of the faults of postmodern 'heritage'?), and the recognition that, however carefully created, all paths through the system are ultimately dictated by its structure; no system can be created that allows completely random and user-controlled access to its contents. Lowenthal's focus on the use of rhetoric in disputes of ownership perhaps gives the lie to the suggestion that archaeologists do not listen to others: in some respects, at least, they may listen too much to their own (and others') propaganda!

A direct concern with audiences opens up the wider issue of the place of the student of culture in society. Chippindale (as communicated in the Peterhouse conference) argues for the supremacy of the archaeological approach to studies of Stonehenge – thus freeing the archaeologist from outside entanglements. By contrast, Fowler, Leone *et al.* and Walsh advocate a direct involvement of the archaeologist with other communities. Fowler urges us to contribute to a particular literary genre. Walsh, more committed, argues for the creation of particular kinds of community through the use of the museum display and challenges those who dispute its legitimacy. His is a direct political concern which denies archaeology any pretence to neutrality. Similarly, Byrne (1991) recognises that the apparent aims of the field of 'archaeological heritage management' to *serve* the world community mask the imposition on that community of narrowly Western concepts and values.

The suggestion that practitioners of archaeology have ever been politically neutral in their work is undermined by a review of the history of the discipline. As Bradley (1983) has pointed out, a main aim of Pitt-Rivers's work was to teach the unnaturalness of revolution. Similarly, in the final chapter of *Prehistoric Times*, John Lubbock (1900 [1865]) preached a clear political message. At the same time, he, Pitt Rivers and others were conducting fierce political campaigns within a number of learned societies (Chapman 1989, Stocking 1987). Thus, for Walsh to call for the creation of a specific kind of community in line with a particular political agenda is not new for archaeology. Nor should we find Leone *et al.*'s recognition that 'presentations of history are politically powerful' strange or dangerous.

There is, of course, the distinction to be made between (real) *history* and (false) *heritage*. Walsh argues against the 'denial of historical process in heritage', and Lowenthal exposes the close relationship between the use of powerful but deceiving rhetoric in 'heritage disputes'. Hewison (1987) equates 'heritage' with a nostalgic wish for a past-that-never-was in a period of economic and political decline, and Wright (1985) with Thatcherism. We are now forced to recognise that the bulk of 'ancient' European traditions date from no earlier than about 1870 (Cannadine 1983, Hobsbawm and Ranger, eds, 1983, Colls and Dodd, eds, 1986), raising doubts about the 'authenticity' of much we hold dear; nevertheless, we must recognise the problematic nature of 'authenticity' itself (Stewart 1984, Clifford 1988, p. 224; Shanks 1992a, pt 3, *passim*). For Ashworth and Tunbridge (1990, p. 25), 'heritage' is the word that links 'preservation of the past for its intrinsic value and as a resource for a modern community or commercial activity'. Accordingly, the field of archaeological heritage *management* concerns all things from the past and their role in the present (Lipe 1984, Cleere 1989, Carman 1991).

The idea of *community*, in one form or another, is present in all the papers. This provides a link with the context in which they were presented, since any conference is really about social cohesion – building and consolidating a community. Academics are a notoriously individualistic crowd, not least because once formal academic training has been completed (all the theses written and submitted, all the requisite degrees collected) one is on one's own to create new research projects. This makes community-building quite difficult, and we all have to work very hard at doing it. This is where conferences come in. At the conference, we seek out those who are like-minded and seek to avoid those who are not. In so doing, we need tools to help us, and these can conveniently be found in disciplinary shorthand – 'weasel expressions' disguising themselves often as Keywords. A Keyword is a crucial one in understanding a text, written or spoken. A 'weasel expression' is usually also a keyword – used not to clarify but as a well-worn cliché no one bothers to examine any more, a form of in-group cipher, the purpose of which is to bind the group more closely while excluding non-members; the trick is to find a term that no outsider dares admit they do not understand clearly.

It is here, in the discourse of weasel expressions, that many of the issues of this section of the book combine – inclusion and exclusion, authority, the personal anecdote masquerading as general principle, the nature of the 'discipline', the politics of discourse. And the chief principle of community-building (a point that Kevin Walsh seems to forget in his concern for their creation) is always that, while some people are chosen to be included, others have to be excluded. Community-manufacture involves three simultaneous processes on the part of those involved: the construction of networks of contacts in which one strives to be placed at or near the centre; the construction of intergroup boundaries, so placed as to ensure one's inclusion at the expense of the exclusion of others; and the manipulation of resources to ensure non-exclusion from the network and the appropriate positioning of boundaries (M. Thompson 1982, pp. 38–41).

Divisions are manifest throughout this section. On the one hand, archaeologists – experts in the past – are to be distinguished from others who are relegated to the status of 'the public'. On the other hand, Peter Fowler pointed out (in conference discussion) that 'the Public' does not exist – instead there are many 'publics'. Archaeologists from outside the English-speaking world legitimately criticised (in conference discussion) the exclusive concentration on the condition of Anglo-American archaeology, which raises questions of national styles of archaeology, nationalist archaeology, and cultural imperialism. As David Lowenthal put it, answering the suggestion that in re-creating the past we merely think ourselves into it, 'isn't the crucial point that we lie back and think *of England*'?

Another criticism may be raised that this section and others in this book do not explicitly consider 'the social' as a category of archaeological reconstructions of the past: discussion about the character of social practice or behaviour and its relations with material culture is not as prominent in this book as it has been in many other volumes concerned with the character of archaeology. But this charge is misplaced: instead of being ignored, the social was being acted out. Those British prehistorians who, with others, may voice such a criticism (personal communication) are perhaps seeking to distance themselves from both processualist approaches and the creation of a perceived unitary interpretive archaeology which focuses less, in their eyes, upon issues of social practice and agency in the past. Differences are thus established within the discipline and community of archaeologists. Overarching these differences within and between archaeologists and others were divisions between 'heritage' and 'real' history, to which only professionals hold the key; and between the past and the present.

The relationships between these phenomena are relations of power. As M. Thompson (1982, p. 41) comments, 'manipulation is power made manifest' – something akin to Foucault's notion of power as something that permeates all through society and creates possibilities as well as acting as a coercive force (Foucault 1977). Archaeologists control their writings and thus the flow of archaeological information and knowledge to others. Archaeologists, however, work in the present. Thus both – archaeologists and the nature of the present – overwhelm the past with their concerns. The question of the past's resistance to this overpowering is one which can be found discussed elsewhere in this volume.

The concerns of this section resolve themselves into three, roughly corresponding to Thompson's community-building processes (M. Thompson 1982). In the realms of discourse, language and writing are communicated and created networks of contacts. In setting up divisions (between archaeologists and public, the past and the present, 'heritage' and 'real' history, the West and the Rest) are built and strengthened the boundaries that exclude and render silent. In the claims of authority and knowledge, in the exercise of power, are positioned agents or actors in the community of archaeologists.

Chapter 13

Writing on the countryside

Peter J. Fowler

Even the titular phrase involves a positivist concept: 'the' countryside? Who says that such exists?

Even more to the point is the commonplace that everybody perceives something different when they raise their eyes unto the hills or just look out of a train window at the passing scene. The word 'countryside', partly as a consequence but not necessarily so, is also ambiguous, meaning for some merely the boring bits between railway stations, for others the habitat of wildlife, for others a place of aesthetic satisfaction, even stimulation, and for yet others, who have not been blessed or hamstrung by the concept of countryside, nothing. This chapter can mean little to an Eskimo; yet the essential prosaicness of its approach would suggest to a Tibetan monk or Australian Aboriginal that this writer, writing on his countryside, has rather missed the point.

The paradox, however, is that, in the Western world especially, 'Interpretation' of the countryside is not only all around us but is also practised daily by a growing band of professionals paid to be countryside interpreters. This they do by writing on it, in several ways (Lunn 1988, Uzzell 1989). Archaeologists do it, too, walking across it, surveying it, flying over it, digging into it, and then writing on it in the sense of writing about it (Renfrew and Bahn 1991). Meanwhile, the long tradition of rural prose writers continues, and poets and composers, painters and, now, landscape artists and photographers, are as avid as ever for their countryside inspiration, each one seeking his or her singular interpretation (e.g, Blythe 1972, D. Thompson, ed., 1980, Arlott 1988, for writers and poets; for an inspirational archaeological perspective of landscape, see Hawkes 1978, of landscape artists Richard Long and Andy Goldsworthy, see Fowler 1992, pp. 69–70; and for photographers see Godwin 1990 and Fowler and Sharp 1990). While they do so, a Landsat camera zooms invisibly overhead, providing a totally different view interpreted by scientists seeking rather different sorts of meaning.

Despite my diluting positivism with the truism of relativism, an identifiable topic nevertheless exists out there, even if only in the sense that people have written on it, literally as well as in literature. Perhaps that points the way towards a definition of 'countryside': not as something that may or may not physically exist but as a perception that is always interpreted differentially, both visually and also in terms of the 'values' it carries or represents (Jellicoe 1975, Appleton 1986). The 'meaning' of countryside is therefore relative, the conceptions of it expressed by the products of art and science and the preconceptions people bring to it as a result. Farmers' and foresters' views would not fit in with that and they are various, too, but archaeological interpretations would, for they are very much the products of art, science and preconceptions. 'Preconceptions', perhaps, above all, for in essence there has been but one conceptual advance, and that only partial, in archaeological interpretation of the countryside since Camden, Aubrey and Stukeley took to the field 300–400 years ago (Ashbee 1972).

These three sought sites but were well aware of the possibility of spatial, temporal and cultural relationships between them; Stukeley, indeed, specifically sought them out in a very modern way even if his interpretive archaeology, his model, has not subsequently been substantiated (Ucko *et al.* 1991). The advance on Stukeley, reflected methodologically by such as air photography and systematic field-walking, has led via O. G. S. Crawford (1953) and 'field archaeology' and W. G. Hoskins (1955) and his 'man-made landscape' to the like of 'landscape archaeology', the 'historic landscape', 'total archaeology' and 'cultural landscapes' (e.g., Fowler, ed., 1972, Aston and Rowley 1974, Baker 1983, Aston 1985, Birks *et al.*, eds, 1988). All such jargon phrases express the concept that cultural relationship through time and in space is now overt in the seeking, rather than merely a rather surprising result sometimes. Sites in the countryside, in other words, have been contextualised; or, conversely, the countryside is conceptualised as being a whole, not merely containing a lot of potentially related sites but as the matrix within which past life has been enacted and the consequential residues now exist.

This holistic approach to the concept of an entity contrasts nicely with the deconstruction in our own time, respectively physically and intellectually, of so much of both the fabric of the countryside as it is and of the artistic output inspired by it, including, presumably, writing about it as perceived. Yet it was barely twenty years ago that one of the few serious book-length studies of the subject – that is, the writing, not the countryside – began with the statement 'Rural writing is a curiously neglected topic' (Keith 1974, p. ix).

Keith continued: '. . . no scholarly attempt has been made to consider the literature of the countryside as a definable and legitimate field of study' though, as he acknowledged (p. x), Williams (1973) was about to do so, and his own self-imposed limitation to non-fiction reduced the validity of his consideration of a possible 'rural tradition'. Presumably most archaeological writing would nevertheless fall within his scope, at least in intent, though the nearest he came to an archaeologically aware writer was H. J. Massingham (of, inter alia, *Downland Man*, 1926, *The Heritage of Man*, 1927, and a regional study, *The Southern Marches*, 1952). Massingham, of course, did not, and still does not, command any academic reputation, perhaps because in no sense was he an original scholar, perhaps because in his early years he attached himself to the Eliot Smith school of 'diffusionist' cultural anthropology. Nevertheless, it is worth remarking on three aspects of his voluminous writing on the countryside because they are central to present archaeological concerns.

First, in Keith's words (p. 236), 'In travelling widely over southern . . . England to visit prehistoric barrows and encampments . . . [he] came to appreciate the historical complexity of the local regions . . . the continuity of local culture and tradition, the fidelity of the ancient builders to the aesthetic features of the regions in which they settled, all these things gradually coalesced into a discernible pattern . . .'.

Second, an early prophet of modern urban disillusionment and what we would now call 'green thinking', Massingham himself wrote: '. . . I do not really care for landscape which is without sign of any co-operation between Nature and Man' (in *Shepherd's Country*, 1938, quoted by Keith 1974, p. 238). He was, as Keith commented on the same page, 'well aware of the extent to which an apparently "natural" landscape is in fact man-made' – this a world war and half a generation before Hoskins. It is a lesson which, a full generation and more post-Hoskins, is still being learned, as the recent conversion of the Countryside Commission well illustrates (see further discussion below).

Third, in his book called simply *Country* (1934, quoted by Keith 1974, p. 240), Massingham deplored 'a purely ornamental past which has ceased to be in living contact with the present' – a sentiment echoed in many a criticism of the 1980s 'heritage industry' (Wright 1985, Hewison 1987). Writing of the restoration of Tretower Manor in *The Southern Marches* (1952, pp. 96–7), for example, Massingham remarked that what he 'should like to see is the ancient manor restored not only to the appearance of its old self but to the reality of usage by relating it once more to the agricultural life of this fertile region' (quoted by Keith 1974, p. 240). The detail, of course, relates to an issue basic to the preservation movement or, as archaeologists grandly call it, cultural resource management, and, beyond that, to numerous soft-centred activities within the contemporary heritage field such as the travesty of countryside interpretation that blooms in the guise of so much so-called 'living history'.

In the Massingham *œuvre*, therefore, the writing on the countryside of a popular mid-twentieth-century author echoes the values of his early-nineteenth-century predecessor William Cobbett (1967, Sambrook 1973). Both were radical and deeply conservative. We nevertheless find in Massingham three of the main precepts of contemporary archaeological academic thinking about the countryside: cultural relationships expressed spatially; the anthropogenic nature of much landscape; and concern about the very nature of conservation. Yet do Massingham, Cobbett or the other non-fiction countryside writers discussed by Keith anywhere appear on an archaeological reading-list? Given the inevitable answer, one can but remark that more's the pity.

The reason for saying so, anticipation of contemporary concerns apart, is that the countryside is quite unavoidably the subject of the bulk of premodern archaeology; and more wisdom about and understanding of it resides in the writings of Gilbert White (1977), Sturt (1922) and, more recently, George Ewart Evans (1969, for example) than in many an academic report about rural archaeological sites. The two genres are, however, complementary, for archaeology can, of course, decipher much of which even the non-fiction prose-writing country-dweller was unaware; but, while these two sorts of writing on the countryside are not mutually exclusive in principle, they are in practice, if archaeological thinking, however intellectually sharp and informed by high-tech in trying to understand the countryside, looks only at material culture and palaeo-environment without absorbing the readily available firsthand evidence of what it was actually like to live in preindustrial rural communities. Cottagers, for example, were not quite so preoccupied with the rim-forms of their pots as archaeologists; and, while the latter through such studies can reveal several facets of the rural life of the time unknown to those who lived it, to leave it at that without considering, for example, the number of pigs a cottager kept in the back-garden (reflecting Flora Thompson 1973) or, say, what his contribution was to the communal plough-team, is to produce a somewhat idiosyncratic, almost wilfully perverse, sort of writing about the countryside. This is not an argument for bucolic nostalgia or rustic wistfulness, just for a more rounded written 'historic reality' – that is, interpretation.

It is the latter, not the former, sort of writing which characterises the work of Estyn Evans (1973, for example), Fenton (1985, for example) and Jenkins (1976). They listened as well as observed, respectively in Ireland, Scotland and Wales. Ewart Evans (1965, for example) is their nearest contemporary equivalent in England; he was just able to touch the oral tradition extant at the end of the horse-dominated country life of East Anglia before 1914. The obvious archaeological objections can be made that his record is both localised, and therefore suspect as a basis for generalisation, and of such recent times that its validity for the medieval period never mind prehistory is highly questionable.

At least two other major objections can be made to the general line of argument above. The archaeologist is a specialist, runs one of them, an original researcher, moreover, producing primary evidence. His or her role is to make a contribution, small perhaps but hopefully significant, to a team effort from which the data, the 'results', emerge. Somebody writes a conclusion; possibly somebody else then uses the conclusions in a synthesis; at which point an aspect of the original work becomes generally accessible and potentially, particularly if a popular writer like Massingham launders it, part of general knowledge. If such is the process, then the role of the archaeologist is very minor; and it is not one that this author accepts, either personally or for his subject and profession. Yet where are the significant writings on the countryside by archaeologists? And by 'significant' here I have to mean not just academically original, or merely well informed, but also works whose message has been assimilated by a wider, non-archaeological audience to the extent of affecting individuals' perceptions. In my experience, much of it spent on countryside affairs outside archaeological circles, no books about the countryside by archaeologists fall into that category.

My evidence is only anecdotal and personal but, as I work with a fairly wide range of land-based professionals such as estate managers, land agents, foresters, farmers, and various experts concerned with Town and Country Planning, road design and conservation and heritage matters, the work of one man, Dr Oliver Rackham, constantly crops up. He has certainly succeeded in putting his message across; his research, teaching and writing about trees and woodland, including, interestingly, the potential historicity of both (1986, 1990), are now axiomatic in countryside affairs. There is no archaeological equivalent. If any one person is mentioned, it is Hoskins, and irritatingly Hoskins 1955, not Taylor's 1988 modernisation of it. In the case of both Rackham and Hoskins, my impression is that their television programmes have been significant in a general sense in conveying their message, though, at least for the professionals, the existence of their books and papers as back-up to the images is crucial.

(While on the subject of television, since I have probably been involved in as many programmes about the English countryside as any archaeologist, I should perhaps say that my impression is that, educationally, their impact has been minimal but that, perhaps significantly, the ones that 'got through' were the general interest series 'In Deepest Britain', where I was one of a group walking through and talking about particular landscapes from several points of view, and various programmes on a range of topics in regional series produced from Bristol and subsequently repeated nationally. Avoid didacticism and, engaging interest with the local, move from the particular to the general, seem to be the lessons. Looking at the writings of Gilbert White and Ewart Evans, one can but reflect that, in using the late twentieth century's moving-image equivalent of traditional writing on the countryside, *plus ça change*.)

In the contemporary professional milieu referred to above, however, the archaeological message about the countryside has now been taken. By that I mean not just the fact that archaeological sites are extremely numerous and are likely to occur in any given tract of landscape but the proposition that much of the landscape is in fact man-made or at least man-influenced. This proposition, unlike the Rackham perception of woodland (1990), may not be associated with any one archaeologist's name, though in a list dominated by non-archaeologists, Taylor (1988), Taylor and

Muir (1983), Muir (e.g. 1985, 1989a, 1989b), Darvill (1987a) and Jones (1986) have doubtless all contributed through their synthetic, at least semi-popular writing, to a communal effort which has brought about a paradigmatic shift in at least professional perceptions of the countryside. Darvill 1987b helped crystallise these perceptions.

That shift has recently been expressed, for example, by such countryside-managing but non-archaeological bodies as the Forestry Commission (Yarnell 1992), the National Trust (1992) and the Countryside Commission. It was the Director of the last, no less, who wrote: 'we are increasingly involved in protecting and interpreting the historic elements in the landscape of this long-settled country. From drystone walls to camping barns, from hillforts to inland waterways, our programmes have enabled many historic features to be protected and to find new life . . . we can now put money into agreements with farmers to protect and restore historic landscapes, meadows and old pastures and orchards. These achievements . . . reflect the intimate link between different elements in the landscape . . .' (Dower 1992). Shades of Massingham fifty years later but none the less welcome and clearly indicating that now, more often than not in places where it matters, there exists at least some grasp of a holistic concept of rural landscape including the time/cultural dimension.

I certainly find that, at the practical level, it is now usually accepted as one of the 'givens' in landscape considerations, along with other well-established factors like floral interest, rights of way and rental values. The questions tend to be not whether archaeology exists or matters but rather what we do about it: e.g., change the estate management policy, reshape the proposed tree-planting, or adjust the road alignment (Fowler 1992, chs 7 and 8). Not every battle has been won, as is sadly illustrated, for example, by a recent and otherwise excellent report on countryside conservation in Northern Ireland (Milton 1990, who writes of a countryside which apparently has no historic dimension – oh! Estyn Evans and Dudley Waterman long ago); but that a sea-change has occurred compared to the indifference and antagonism of just twenty years ago is clearly evidenced. Curious writings on the countryside like the relevant parts of County Council Structure Plans and the Department of the Environment's Policy Planning Guidelines no. 16 (November 1990) exemplify that. Perhaps all our own writings on the countryside have not, after all, been in vain; though it was a journalist (or headline-writer?) who used what is surely the best phrase for, not the writing but the countryside itself: 'our oldest asset' (Halsall 1992).

The absorption of this archaeological dimension, the rural historic environment, into landscape concerns has led to the development of a new type of writing about the countryside, a type familiar to those involved with Planning Authorities in particular but currently reaching its apogee, not necessarily to the adornment of English literature, in Environmental Statements and Environmental Impact Assessments. By their very nature, references are difficult to give since, in the first instance anyway, such are prepared privately for the would-be developer and technically only become available to others at some later stage in the planning process such as a Public Inquiry. While some may concentrate on the archaeology for practical reasons, others ignore it; while, in between, the historic dimension of the rural area in question is likely to be described, assessed for significance, and made the subject of proposed mitigation including enhancement (for example) included in some form of public amenity such as a country trail subsequent to the development (Ralston and Thomas forthcoming). Whatever the requirement, the point here is not only that a considerable amount of archaeological work in the countryside is, quite suddenly, being funded for such purposes but that its written product is having to be cast in a format and expressed in a prose which owe everything to bureaucratic processes rather than to the work of, say, Ronald Blythe (1982, for example) as a contemporary exponent of the literary tradition of writing about the countryside.

Clearly different sorts of 'countryside' are perceived to exist (Coones 1985, Cosgrove and Daniels, eds, 1988); it is equally clear that several different sorts of 'writing' about them exist, too. Archaeological writing about archaeological countryside is only a small part of a complex, and is by no means central to it. A morphology of writing on the countryside – and, like Keith (1974), we must confine ourselves to non-fiction – can identify at least nine types:

1 The good, well-informed 'countryman' writing in book form, exemplified by Collis (1975), Geoffrey Grigson (1984, for example), Paul Jennings (1968, for example) and Henry Tegner (1970, for example) until recently, and by A. G. Street (1932, for example) a generation or two ago. Blythe (1982, for example) continues that tradition, as do two modern classics, both dealing with fundamental change in the countryside on the boundary between first-class local history and traditional country writing (Reeves 1980, Tindall 1980). Some of the articles carried in 'quality' periodical journalism such as *Country Life*, *The Countryman* and the *Weekend Telegraph* continue this peculiarly English tradition of high-class writing on the countryside. Contemporary individuals working in this genre would include Clive Aslett and R. W. F. Poole who, whatever their viewpoints, do at least know what they are writing about; and, collectively, the writers of the *Guardian*'s Country Diary (though whether any could sustain a book-length treatment in like vein is uncertain). In truth, however, it is difficult to discern the contemporary White or Cobbett; and their function, serious description of what is happening in the countryside during their lifetime, may well now have passed to popularising academics in category 3 (below).

2 Really a subclass of 1 and often attempting to look like the real thing, is a large quantity of an inferior sort of writing, characteristically journalism, in numerous country-type magazines at national, county and local level. Unoriginal, cliché-ridden and often dangerously sentimental, such need not detain us, though its existence is significant in considering, if not the writing about, then perceptions of the countryside. The sentimental nostalgic strain in such writing carries over into avowedly literary and quite sincere writing of the sort, often all soft-focus photographs and expressions of personal 'meanings', characteristic not only of many commercial books about the countryside but also of some serious publications, for example CPRE 1987. Their good intentions and objectives nothwithstanding, such seemingly perpetuate a rose-tinted view which is out of step not just with rural reality but also with informed concern about it; so they fall here with such magazines as *Country Living*, *Country Homes* and *Interiors and Heritage* (see Hewison 1987, pp. 77–9; a classic of this subclass, 'A gentle tale of village folk', occupied the front page of the *Weekend Times*, 29 August 1992).

3 Scientific, academic writing about the countryside is now a large category embracing journal papers, conference proceedings, symposia, books and edited collections ranging in topic from ard to zymosis. Archaeology, but a small part of a voluminous literature, fits in here together with all the other '-ologies' such as geology, geomorphology and zoology, and 'non-ologies' like history, botany and geography. The crucial qualities of this class of writing include being backed or even prompted by original research and being authored by scientists/academics. Thus, Mingay (ed., 1981), about the countryside in one period, and Costen (1992), as a modern local history using a lot of archaeology and a landscape approach to a particular countryside, are good examples; while, for the archaeological component

of this class, the Coleses' (1986) *Sweet Track* and C. Thomas's (1985) *Drowned Landscape*, for example, would be included as works of synthesis arising from detailed scientific investigation, despite their overt (and successfully achieved) aim of *haute* popularisation. Similarly, two other outstanding archaeologists' books, Morris (1989) and Hodges (1991), and Newby's several rural sociological books (e.g., 1988, for example) would come in here. On the other hand, for example, Clive Ponting's (1991) well-written and interesting but unoriginal study is excluded (not least because it very much echoes Haines 1973 and, on the global scale, Seymour and Girardet 1988).

4 The overtly educational writings follow: not necessarily written by the academics whose work is used, the material being recast specifically for educational purposes as textbooks on a subject or course-books for a particular syllabus. Jones (1986) exemplifies the former, though, since he synthesises a great deal of work including his own original research, another textbook written by non-academics can also be quoted (Lane 1992); the Countryside Commission books to go with an Open University course on 'The Changing Countryside' provide an obvious example of a course-book (Blunden and Curry, eds, 1985; Blunden and Turner 1985; Rogers *et al.* 1985).

5 Professional interpretive writing on the countryside must now justify a category of its own, its media ranging from the conventional booklet and pamphlet through interpretation panels on-site and along the trail to brief written instructions and explanations, literally, on the countryside. It is the motivation rather than the media, however, which characterises the output: by definition it is well intentioned, altruistic, informative and seemingly interpretively neutral, though in practice it has to be selective and therefore cannot convey other than chosen messages.

6 Tourist literature of the sort put out by Tourist Boards and Local Authorities (see Fowler 1992, ch. 10).

7 The next category, more overtly propagandist writing to argue a cause about the countryside rather than the (supposed) merits of a particular part of it, might be thought to be a recent phenomenon, but in fact its origins lie in the early stages of the rural literary tradition. Aubrey (Fowler, ed., 1972, p. 96; Hunter 1975, p. 166) and Cobbett (1967, Sambrook 1973) were both protesters about the changes they saw happening to their countrysides; contemporary writers like Christian (1977) and Shoard (1980, 1987) are themselves within a tradition. Archaeology has played a role in it, too, perhaps one of its more significant contributions to writing on the countryside. Lubbock (for example, in the preface to Kains-Jackson 1880), among others, encapsulated a considerable amount of liberal concern about a component of the countryside which, after years of failure, finally brought about the first Ancient Monuments Act in 1882, the first English legislation directly affecting landowners' property rights in the cause of what we would now call conservation; and Crawford frequently protested about what was happening to archaeology in the countryside in his *Antiquity* editorials throughout the thirties, forties and fifties (a tradition continued up to the present in different voices).

It was very much rural destruction (mirrored in Fowler, ed., 1972) which led to a unified archaeological protest, formalised in the creation of Rescue, the Trust for British Archaeology in 1971 (Rahtz, ed., 1974). Propagandist writing, in the sense of seeking to publicise archaeology as a rural issue and persuade people of the extent and significance of damage and destruction, has continued over the last two decades, in parallel with a deliberate highlighting by others of other countryside changes such as hedgerow removal, species deterioration and access restrictions. While many archaeologists feel that their specialist interest fits in well with such issues as part of a greater, and increasingly 'green', whole (for example, Greeves 1989, Macinnes and Wickham-Jones 1992), neither archaeology nor the historicity of either landscape or country life-ways are often mentioned by others, let alone expressed in terms consonant with modern scientific knowledge (Pryor 1990; Fowler 1992, pp. 156–9).

8 The eighth, and newest, type, increasingly including an archaeological element, is that meeting bureaucratic need, what we might call 'professional' writing on the countryside (as discussed above). The volumes of assessment accompanying the English Heritage/National Trust outline planning application for development of new visitor facilities at Stonehenge are so far probably the most ambitious writing of this type publicly available (Debenham, Tewson and Chinnocks 1991).

9 A final type can be identified as 'alternative' writing on the countryside; some archaeologists used to call it 'lunatic fringe' writing but that is to misunderstand and antagonise quite unnecessarily. Scientifically, of course, archaeologists and others not only have a right but a duty to characterise that which they can demonstrate to be spurious; but, nevertheless, many people happily believe in a whole range of irrational rusticana (Bord 1978, for example), as the burgeoning shelves of 'New Age' writings illustrate, and choose to pursue will-o'-the-wisps like ley-lines and mysterious phenomena (some of which, unlike ley-lines, actually 'exist', see Cavendish, ed., 1989). Crop-circles are a case in point.

They certainly exist as physical phenomena and, indeed, could well be construed as 'writing on the countryside' in a literal sense, whether they be created by little green men or jocular *Homo sapiens* (for these, and other attempted explanations, see *The Cerealogist* 1990–2, and the considerable literature on the subject advertised therein). '[C]rop circles . . . could be viewed as a vital clue to a cosmic crossword. The clues are a developing language, on whose meaning we can only speculate . . . . They are not signs giving directional information, but symbols of meaning . . .' (Davis, ed., 1992, p. 6).

Among all the pseudo-science, bogus claptrap and emotional outpourings, the scientist should nevertheless note a continuum in the interest in the rural para-normal, notably in relation to 'Antiquities' (Michell 1982), a residue of the unexplained by rational or 'alternative' theory, and an earnest desire on the part of some working in this fringe area to test their hypotheses by recognisably scientific methods (Devereux 1991, 1992). It is also interesting to note how mainstream archaeological data (e.g., Fleming 1988, for example) can be converted to alternative uses, not as von Daniken *et al.* did by cheating, but in serious (if misconceived, in this writer's view) attempts to construct a different sort of countryside in prehistory.

Which brings us to the nub of the matter. Having indicated the range of perceptions about the countryside and outlined a rough classification of writing stemming from them, it is clear that our topic is not about writing at all: it is about editing – editing in as well as editing out. And that point introduces the thought about audience. Who is all this writing for? Some of it may well be primarily for the writer, the motivation and justification being primarily in performance itself, the act of writing; but most of it was written with an audience in mind, and hence the editing, tailoring the text to suit the intended readers. *Country Living* knows what its intended audience is, so an unreal, almost surreal image of countryside is created and purveyed; similarly, a totally different audience conditions the nature of the 'professional' writing about the countryside in category 8 above.

The great bulk of writing about the countryside by archaeologists has been intended only for archaeologists, and some of it only for some archaeologists. No archaeologist, as far as I am aware, has deliberately set out to write a popular book about the countryside *per se* as seen from an archaeological point of view; and maybe that point of view is too narrow anyway. Hence, at best, the inclusion of archaeological perspectives in countryside books by others, notably numerous books by Richard Muir, an academic geographer who turned to writing full-time, sometimes with his wife (1989a). But otherwise 'interpretive archaeologies' of the countryside as perceived by most people simply do not exist from the pens of archaeologists, so the failure of archaeology to impinge on those perceptions other than as a specialist topic of little general relevance and a particular set of rather arcane activities can be laid squarely at archaeologists' feet. We write well for ourselves, and sometimes for other specialists and professionals, but we edit out the other 99.99 per cent of humanity.

The past and present of writing on the countryside, with some omens for the future perhaps, can be summed up from an archaeological perspective in a number of propositions:

1 That, for some, the validity of writing on the countryside lies in the act of verbal creation as performance, not in its product.
2 That wide communication with others is seldom the primary purpose of writing about the countryside, especially in writing about rural pastness.
3 That the word 'countryside' is itself so value-loaded that it is at one and the same time both meaningless and a powerful epistemological trigger to aspiration, expectation and, usually, disappointment: for example, 'I want a day out in the countryside'; 'We shall enjoy a day out in the countryside'; 'Gawd! Those midges, those smells, and that crowd at the Interpretation Centre – it will be a long time before we go out into the countryside again.'
4 That to discuss writing on the countryside actually involves a consideration of two other activities: editing by the writer, another or others; defining function – for example, what, if any, is the intended message and/or audience?
5 That archaeology plays a small and often non-existent role in writing about the countryside.
6 That archaeology is far too narrow a concept by which to interpret, or just write about, the countryside, yet it can provide dimensions of time-depth and development, understanding and interest, potentially significant for public interest and recreation and crucial for land management.
7 That most archaeological writing on the countryside is one, some, or all, of the following: badly written, introspective, tendentious, tedious, unilluminating, and irrelevant to most people's perceptions.
8 That, to correct this, archaeological understanding of the countryside must, for popular consumption, be repackaged in its written form into other people's language and forms of expression (as can be done relatively easily using the spoken word with any group of people standing on a hilltop and prepared to look and listen).
9 Among dozens of interpretive models for the countryside, the old one of Professor Appleton (1986) that much in the landscape can be considered as either prospect or refuge is very helpful in illuminating not just rural mechanisms but also rustic psychology.
10 That most people in the world live in the countryside and aspire to live in towns; while, in the Western world, most people live in towns and many dream of living in the countryside. The former do not write about the countryside, while the latter do.

The more you think about it, the more it appears extraordinary that so land-based a subject as archaeology, devoting so much of its time and effort to rural landscapes and the peoples who lived in them through all the millennia of human history, has not developed, outside professional and academic circles, a distinctive voice in writing about the countryside. The outstanding challenge for future interpretive archaeologies is to develop that voice.

Chapter 14

Can an African-American historical archaeology be an alternative voice?

Mark P. Leone, Paul R. Mullins, Marian C. Creveling, Laurence Hurst, Barbara Jackson-Nash, Lynn D. Jones, Hannah Jopling Kaiser, George C. Logan, Mark S. Warner

INTRODUCTION

We consider ourselves to be part of a debate within historical archaeology about its role within the United States. On one side, the debate features a conventional role for archaeology as a way of discovering the pasts of those normally ignored or thought to be anonymous. On the other side is our position, which sees historical archaeology as capable of providing a critique of our own society by using its history. We will describe this debate in order to situate an African-American historical archaeology within it.

Historical archaeology is considered an exploration of European expansion and settlement through material remains. It can be thought of as an exploration of the spread of Europeans around the world, primarily through the process of establishing colonies. Thus, historical archaeology can trace the remains of forts, ports, factories, cities, suburbs, mines, plantations and farms, among other institutions. Archaeology is associated with these institutions as they facilitated European expansion since the fifteenth century.

The expansion of Europe was led, if one reads the documents and looks at the pictures, by white men of status and stature. But, since we all know that many people were involved in and were absorbed by this process, how are we to know the past from their perspective? Their perspective is of value either because it offers unvoiced comments which could be useful to us today, or because in a democracy all voices deserve a hearing, regardless of their content. And, additionally, it has been argued that those alive now count on an appropriately presented past in order to safeguard a reasonable future.

Historical archaeology has access to the material remains and thus, people reason, the daily lives in the past of women, children, foot soldiers and sailors, slaves, freed slaves, Native Americans from the moment of contact, the insane, the gaoled, as well as anybody else who has ever used a dish, chamberpot, room, privy, or medicine-bottle. While many, many such people have gone unrecorded historically, such people did often live in and were spatially segregated in countless ways. Consequently, there is a distinctive archaeological record for them. And studying it is worthwhile.

It is worthwhile because if people alive now have unrecognised and undiscussed histories, then we are all poorer because only one view – or very few views – is not enough to understand history.

This argument acknowledges that presentations of history are politically powerful. Power is involved because it is derived from the production of the histories themselves or their ability to produce behaviours that can be influenced successfully by picturing models of noble natures, patriotism, actions, achievements, probity, or a thousand other culturally desirable traits. Consequently, historical archaeology can be a vehicle to give voices to the silenced, power to the disfranchised, recognition to the ignored, and a historical signature to the anonymous. And thus it can help do the same to any interested descendants. We will therefore have a more plural and democratic society if we do historical archaeology.

Since the creation of Archaeology in Annapolis in 1981, we have attempted to explore the multiplicity of voices in the archaeological record of Annapolis. During that time we have been fairly successful in exploring histories of the white residents of Annapolis. However, we also realised that we were overlooking a large portion of the city by not explicitly addressing the historic experiences of African Americans in our work. To address this problem we began an initiative in 1988 to explore the histories of African Americans. Based on our experiences of the past five years we believe that an African-American historical archaeology is an illustration of the contemporary relevance of historical archaeology. There is a distinct African-American voice; it can be heard; and it may or may not be critical.

Hodder (1986), Beaudry (1990), Beaudry *et al.* (1991), M. Brown (1992), and Yentsch (1991), among others, claimed that our use of Althusser (1971) meant that only the ideology created by dominant groups was available through our work in Annapolis. Neither Althusser nor, by extension, we, had considered whether any of the subordinated groups had been convinced or infected by a dominating ideology. They claimed that the historical archaeologists' achievement was to recapture alternative and muted voices. Consequently, historical archaeology had little or no need of the dominant ideology thesis since it had the ability to present voices and resistance – voices which had the capacity to determine the actual efficacy of any dominating ideology.

Byron Rushing has said that African Americans want to know how and why they are here now – they want to know why there is no change for them now. White people typically don't want to know these things. They choose to remain blind (no date, personal communication). Within this paraphrase of Rushing's quote, we argue, may lie the solution to the critique of the dominant ideology thesis and of how to realise historical archaeology's role of exemplifying anonymous histories. If an African-American voice, or a woman's voice, or anyone else's can protest current circumstances and unify class membership sufficiently by showing common roots, the goals of both ways of doing historical archaeology might be achieved, we will argue in the essay.

The nine of us, as authors, conceived of a project that involved discussions about the questions to be asked by archaeologists, places to excavate, members of the black community to be interviewed about their history, exhibiting all the results in local public museums, and visitor evaluations of the results. None of us was involved in every phase of this joint work, but the resultant whole would not have been the same without each part and person, as well as the co-operation that produced the whole. We have found it easier to refer to ourselves as 'we' in this essay, rather than using specific names all the time when specific parts of the project are described.

In order to explore the possibility of African-American historical archaeology as an alternative voice, we were guided by Shanks and Tilley's (1987a) fourfold hermeneutic and Habermas's (1976, 1984, 1989) theory of communicative action. The hermeneutic suggests that there are many contexts to be understood and attended to in conceptualising archaeology. One part of the hermeneutic is that of living within contemporary society as an active participant. More broadly, it entails gaining knowledge of that which is to be human, in order to interact and participate with others and to be involved in struggles about beliefs and social and political values (Shanks and Tilley 1987a, p. 108).

Habermas (1976, 1984, 1989) uses language to enhance life in a democratic society in a way which enables participation within a living community that cared about archaeology. He outlines various speech acts or situations needed to have discussions, or a dialogue, about decisions affecting all parties. These acts include establishing comprehension, the ability and capacity to establish beliefs and intentions, equal participation, and access to alternative interpretations. This ideal speech situation should enable the colonised to speak to the coloniser, the subordinate to the dominant, the muted to the vocal, and the enfranchised to the disfranchised, if there is a desire to do so. Habermas's ideas could make 'the hermeneutic of living within contemporary society as an active participant' work.

One of the first actions of an African-American historical archaeology in Annapolis involved discussion with the two leaders of the Banneker-Douglass Museum, the home of the State of Maryland's Commission on Afro-American History and Culture. Steven Newsome and Barbara Jackson-Nash asked of Mark Leone and Mark Warner three questions which have guided Archaeology in Annapolis since 1988: 'Do African Americans have archaeology?', 'We're tired of hearing about slavery; tell us about freedom!', and 'Is there anything left from Africa?'. These questions have such great value because they are at once political and historical. They speak for a community that sees unbroken continuity and considers history as political action. These were and remain archaeological questions, anthropological questions, political questions, and questions which invited being 'involved in struggles about beliefs and social and political values' (Shanks and Tilley 1987a, p. 108).

The archaeological answers to these questions are still tentative from the point of view of standard archaeological scholarship. There are intact sites all over Annapolis from the nineteenth century to today that are African American. Several have not been excavated by our project and, since they are locales where free people lived, they not only answer the first question, but they also deal with daily life in conditions of freedom. The archaeology of sites where free people lived produces three kinds of information. Analysis of the artefacts from excavations shows both how similar the artefacts are to sites occupied by contemporary whites and also shows some evidence of economic and even ethnic differences. And, when combined with oral history, it provides a partial look into local American racism from within. There is thus in our joint work beginning to be knowledge useful to blacks, knowledge about how they are the same as whites, knowledge about differences with whites, and some knowledge of what creates the deeper differences within American society.

ARTEFACTS

Since 1988, Archaeology in Annapolis has excavated three sites occupied by free African Americans and one occupied by both enslaved African Americans and their white masters. Each of those excavations recovered a significant volume of material culture including ceramics, bottle glass, food remains, and other household refuse which was acquired, used and discarded by African Americans.

These excavations have established that there is indeed a rich archaeological record of the African-American experience in Annapolis, particularly of the free black community, and some excavated objects have documented the persistence of cultural practices with links to African cultures. In response to scholarly criticisms of our use of ideology, we have begun to use these artefacts to interpret how African

Americans simultaneously have been absorbed by dominant ideologies while resisting certain elements of those very ideologies. These fundamental dimensions of the African-American archaeological project are intended both to serve the social interests of local black constituents and to demonstrate to the academic community the social and intellectual viability of our perspective.

Our first excavation of a site exclusively occupied by African Americans was at Gott's Court. Gott's Court was a series of twenty-five connected, two-storey wooden houses built about 1906 and occupied exclusively by African-American renters into the early 1950s. Gott's Court's tenants were primarily employed in service positions in Annapolis, such as day labourers, laundresses and cooks. The Court was located on the interior of a city block within sight of the State House dome two blocks away; yet, like other contemporaneous 'alley' communities in Annapolis and other American cities, the Court was invisible from the surrounding streets (Warner 1992b).

Although the excavations at Gott's Court were limited, the artefact assemblages suggested several points for investigation on subsequent African-American sites. The first insight was that excavated artefacts could indeed be very effective in stimulating dialogue about how to interpret the histories of peripheralised people. We confronted this after excavating a steel comb (Fig. 6). After the archaeologists fruitlessly tried to determine the object's function, an African-American woman explained that

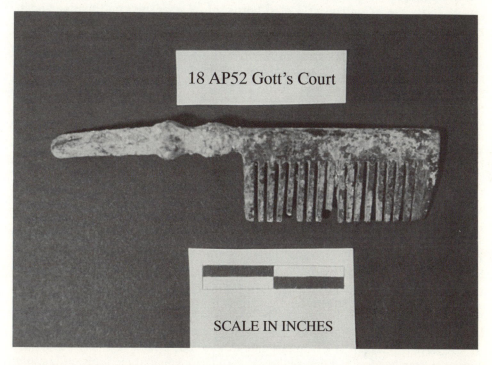

18 AP52 Gott's Court

SCALE IN INCHES

Figure 6 A point of archaeological dialogue: this steel comb was excavated by Archaeology in Annapolis in 1989 at Gott's Court. Known as hot combs or straightening combs, such combs were used by African Americans to style and straighten hair. As a group of white archaeologists, we initially saw this as an object which reflected the functional act of straightening hair, an indication of some integration into dominant society. However, our African-American constituents see the meaning of hair-straightening as prudent social negotiation. They consider the hot comb as an object which African Americans used to *appear* assimilated so that they could ensure their cultural survival. They see the hot comb as such effective resistance that its meaning is still being misinterpreted by the white community.

the object was a 'hot' or 'straightening' comb, a steel comb which was heated to straighten hair. The archaeologists initially surmised that straightening hair was an effort to assimilate, but this notion was quickly rejected by African Americans. They instead saw the comb as an artefact which was used merely to give the appearance of assimilation. Indeed, some African Americans saw racism in the archaeologists' initial inability to recognise hair-straightening as a conscious social strategy. The archaeologists were forced to acknowledge that this single object and all its associated cultural connotations could have quite different meanings between different contemporary and historical communities. In that sense, the comb was able to foster dialogue between contemporary African Americans and at least one group of white archaeologists.

The Gott's Court assemblage also stressed that African-American consumption strategies sometimes are quite subtle in their differences from dominant strategies. We were not surprised to recover a large collection of bottle glass from our excavation, since post-1900 bottle-production technologies were sufficiently special-ised to manufacture large quantities of inexpensive bottled goods. The goods contained in these vessels can be identified by embossed designs and bottle forms, so they provide reliable information on the types of bottled goods being consumed: for example, pharmaceutical, soda, wine, liquor, etc. Bottles also tend to enter the archaeological record rapidly, because they are bought for their contents rather than for the bottle itself. Consequently, glass bottles provide sensitive information about the type and time of consumption.

When we compared the types of bottle glass goods to those from a con-temporaneous white-occupied site in Annapolis called Main Street (Shackel 1986), there were no significant differences which seemed 'African American'. Pharma-ceutical, that is, patent medicines, were the most common type of early twentieth-century bottled product at Gott's Court; 38% of the total assemblage, and 45% at Main Street, a few blocks away (Warner 1991, p. 9). The percentages of all alcoholic goods, which includes pharmaceutical as well as liquors and wine, was also quite similar, comprising 69% of the Gott's Court assemblage and 58% of that on Main Street. Consumption of bottled goods appears to be similar between these two assemblages.

The appearance of partial economic assimilation is being more thoroughly analysed at an African-American residence on nearby Duke of Gloucester Street, occupied circa 1847–1980. The Maynard-Burgess house was built about 1847 by John and Maris Maynard, free blacks, and was subsequently occupied by the Burgess family from 1915 until the 1980s, who were also African Americans (McWilliams 1991). After two years of excavations, the Maynard-Burgess assemblage has provided a larger and more diverse collection of objects to investigate African-American consumption strategies, particularly through the analysis of bottles and food remains.

In 1991, a cellar containing 85 bottles with a mean date of 1881 was excavated at the Maynard-Burgess site (Mullins and Warner n.d.). Of those vessels, 25% (21 bottles) were classified as liquor/whiskey, the most common type in the cellar, and 19% (16 vessels) were pharmaceutical. Yet, of those 21 bottles classified as liquor, six were Udolpho Wolfe's Schiedam Aromatic Schnapps, a highly alcoholic, very popular 'medicinal gin' advertised to have multi-purpose therapeutic effects (Schulz *et al.* 1980, pp. 37–8). These may well have been consciously consumed as 'medicines', regardless of their alcoholic content. Six mineral water bottles were also included in the cellar assemblage, and this bottled water from natural springs was typically consumed for its medicinal effects as well (ibid., p. 111). If just the Wolfe vessels and the mineral water bottles were reclassified as pharmaceutical, then pharmaceutical would comprise 33% of the assemblage (28 vessels). That percentage is slightly lower, yet still comparable to the percentage of medicines recovered from Gott's Court (38%) and Main Street (45%).

What this similarity in bottled-good consumption suggests is that this one form of material consumption was indeed quite effectively homogenising different social groups. A high percentage of bottled foods (16%, 14 vessels) might at first glance seem to suggest further assimilation of the Maynards into the market in the late nineteenth century. Yet in examining the very diverse and well-preserved food remains from the site we saw a very wide range of acquisition strategies. This diversity indicates that these African-American households resisted the trend to acquire food through the market.

Food remains – animal bones, shells, fish scales, etc. – were recovered in large quantities at the Maynard-Burgess site. An addition built on to the rear of the house in about 1875 preserved dense deposits of yard refuse and construction debris dating to the period 1847–75, and upper layers included deposits of quite recent food remains which had been taken under the house by small animals and rodents. Although these deposits have not been fully analysed yet, we can offer some initial analyses and insights which suggest both ethnically distinctive and class-specific food-consumption strategies.

Turtles as a source of food were not unique to African Americans. Turtle remains have been consistently recovered in small amounts from many sites in Annapolis (Lev-Tov 1987, Reitz 1987). On the Maynard-Burgess property turtle remains were slightly more prevalent than what was recovered from the Main Street site (Mullins and Warner n.d.). However, the quantitative similarities between the two sites do not address potential differences in the social significance of turtles as a food source. Oral history accounts recall that turtles were caught as part of individual fishing excursions and not purchased at the market – a point which suggests that African Americans avoided and consequently resisted the market through the private acquisition of foods. Additionally, the turtle shells were decorated by children and used as doorstops in the house (Kaiser n.d.).

A more explicit example of the significance of foodways is the recovery of a large number of pig mandibles and feet from the Maynard-Burgess property. Oral accounts have frequently mentioned the importance of hog's head and black-eyed peas for holidays such as New Year's Eve (Kaiser n.d.). The combination of archaeological and oral history data suggests that household consumption patterns were not exclusively based on the market economy but were at least partially related to ethnic food preferences.

Analysis of one deposit from the Maynard-Burgess house indicates both similarities and quite clear differences from the faunal assemblage recovered from Main Street. At both sites, the percentage of fowl was quite similar (30% at Maynard-Burgess and 39% at Main Street), suggesting that birds were a relatively basic part of most Annapolitan diets, although their preparation and mealtime presentation may well have differed between groups. Mammals accounted for 43% of the bones recovered from the Maynard-Burgess deposit, yet they comprised only 20% of the Main Street assemblage. Fish accounted for 24% of the Maynard assemblage, but only 7% of the Main Street faunal assemblage was fish (M. Warner 1992a).

The differences in the percentage of mammals consumed probably reflects both ethnicity and class. The Maynards were by no means impoverished, so any reference to economics accounts only partially for the differences. They may have had restricted access to the market – that is, they probably could not shop with some of

Annapolis's butchers – but that influence reflects racist ideology more than it indicates an inability to afford certain cuts of meat.

The presence of fish and turtle remains suggests more reliance on foods which could be obtained readily from the Chesapeake Bay, which is just two blocks from both the Maynard-Burgess and Main Street sites. Such reliance, though, may have been experienced by African Americans as a way of gaining some economic independence from the market.

In analysing these artefacts, which are individually no different from those on any other site in Annapolis, it became clear that we needed a persuasive way to contextualise African-American consumption. We felt confident that the context in which these objects were acquired, consumed and discarded was quite distinctive in the African-American community, yet documents provided only suggestive information about the cultural context. To interpret the everyday African-American world and its relationship to material culture, we incorporated interviews with African Americans which discussed how excavated objects were part of African-American society.

ORAL HISTORIES

Members of the project posed general questions to elicit stories about artefacts, and in some cases asked specific queries, such as questions about children's games and china. In turn we heard rich accounts about playing marbles, eating large Sunday breakfasts with the family, going to church, paying fifty cents a week for fine china bought on the instalment plan, three generations of women doing the laundry on wash days, and fishing expeditions.

Some of the stories provided an African-American context to the artefacts. The former Franklin Street residents described how extended families acquired and made clothing for children; what it was like as children not to attend the same school as their white playmates; the experience of being allowed to buy food to carry out, but of being prohibited from eating food at the counter of the Little Tavern Restaurant; and the experience of listening to your grandmother read to your illiterate grandfather the *Saturday Evening Post* in the evening by the light of a kerosene lamp.

We understood from the beginning that we were not collecting oral history in order to do better archaeology. The request to listen to the recollections of residents of the former houses being excavated was initiated by a member of the African-American community, Barbara Jackson-Nash, and we understood that the stories were not only valued in and of themselves but that they had a special status for the community, rather like that of written records for the white community. We understood, too, that this enterprise could offer us the opportunity to see the other side of life in Annapolis, including economics and racism, and, through archaeology, the history of both, which might extend beyond memory. Thus oral history might provide access to a critical commentary of contemporary and past society in Annapolis.

The oral history entailed, as Hodder (1991b, p. 15) has described interpretation, 'listening, understanding and accommodation among different voices rather than [being] solely the application of universal instruments of measurement'. Based on conversation with Banneker-Douglass staff, an outline of general questions was prepared for interviews with five former residents of Franklin Street. These people, identified by Jackson-Nash, were interviewed in the summer of 1991 by several archaeologists about the layout of their houses and backyards. When Kaiser, who did most of the key oral history, met with them in the spring of 1992, they were already familiar with the project and interested in helping the archaeologists interpret the artefacts.

The former residents of Franklin Street were first asked broad open-ended questions about the neighbourhood, what it looked like, where the children played, what the adults did, and generally what went on outside. They were then asked about the interiors of the houses, the preparation of food, and family life, since archaeologists wanted to learn how the artefacts were used and what they meant to African Americans. Respondents in general were not guided or influenced, so that they were given the opportunity to describe their world as they remembered it. This showed that, as Margaret Purser (1992, p. 28) has described it, 'oral history is an inherently collaborative process, between interviewer and interviewee, between story teller and audience'.

EXHIBIT

Two factors led all these authors to participate in an exhibit that contained both the archaeological material and the oral history. The Banneker-Douglass staff felt that the African-American community would be interested in the archaeology since it was virtually unique in everyone's experience; and the archaeologists, long involved in public explanation of archaeological method, wanted to continue to try to reach black and white audiences with views of Annapolitan society from an alternative and, they hoped, a critical perspective, one that developed consciousness of society as it was and is.

Once the interviews had been transcribed, Archaeology in Annapolis and the Banneker-Douglass Museum staffs met to decide what texts would be selected for the exhibit. This was a dialogue about the past, one 'enabled by an assumption of momentary political equality, one which recognizes competing interests in the past and suggests negotiating these interests' (Leone and Potter 1992, p. 140). One result of the dialogue was a general agreement about which texts should be included, with one exception. Stories about taking food from the Naval Academy as a way of getting food during the Depression were not included. The Banneker-Douglass staff thought they were too negative. The archaeologists did not think the stories reflected negatively on African Americans but, rather, revealed the consequences of racism and limited economic opportunity – circumstances the archaeologists thought were important to include.

The exhibit was planned and mounted three times, twice in Annapolis and once in southern Maryland. Laurence Hurst, designer for the Banneker-Douglass Museum, created the floor plans, case arrangement, and integration of the exhibit for its two installations in Annapolis (Figs 7–10). The exhibit design was straightforward, and was done with a $1,200 mini-grant from the Maryland Humanities Council and many hours of volunteer labour.

The exhibit separated the archaeological sites shown – Franklin Street, Gott's Court, and Benjamin Banneker homesite – and then divided cases into kitchen artefacts, architectural artefacts, and toys. The artefacts in the exhibit included bits of ceramic, bottle glass, buttons and parts of porcelain dolls. To the museum staff, and to the archaeologists, most of the artefacts could have belonged to anybody. Only one artefact was identifiably 'African American', and that was the metal straightening-comb.

The novelty of the exhibit came from its very existence – no such exhibit had ever been mounted before in Annapolis and probably in Maryland. And, second, in its use of oral histories as the main texts, we tried something unusual in blending

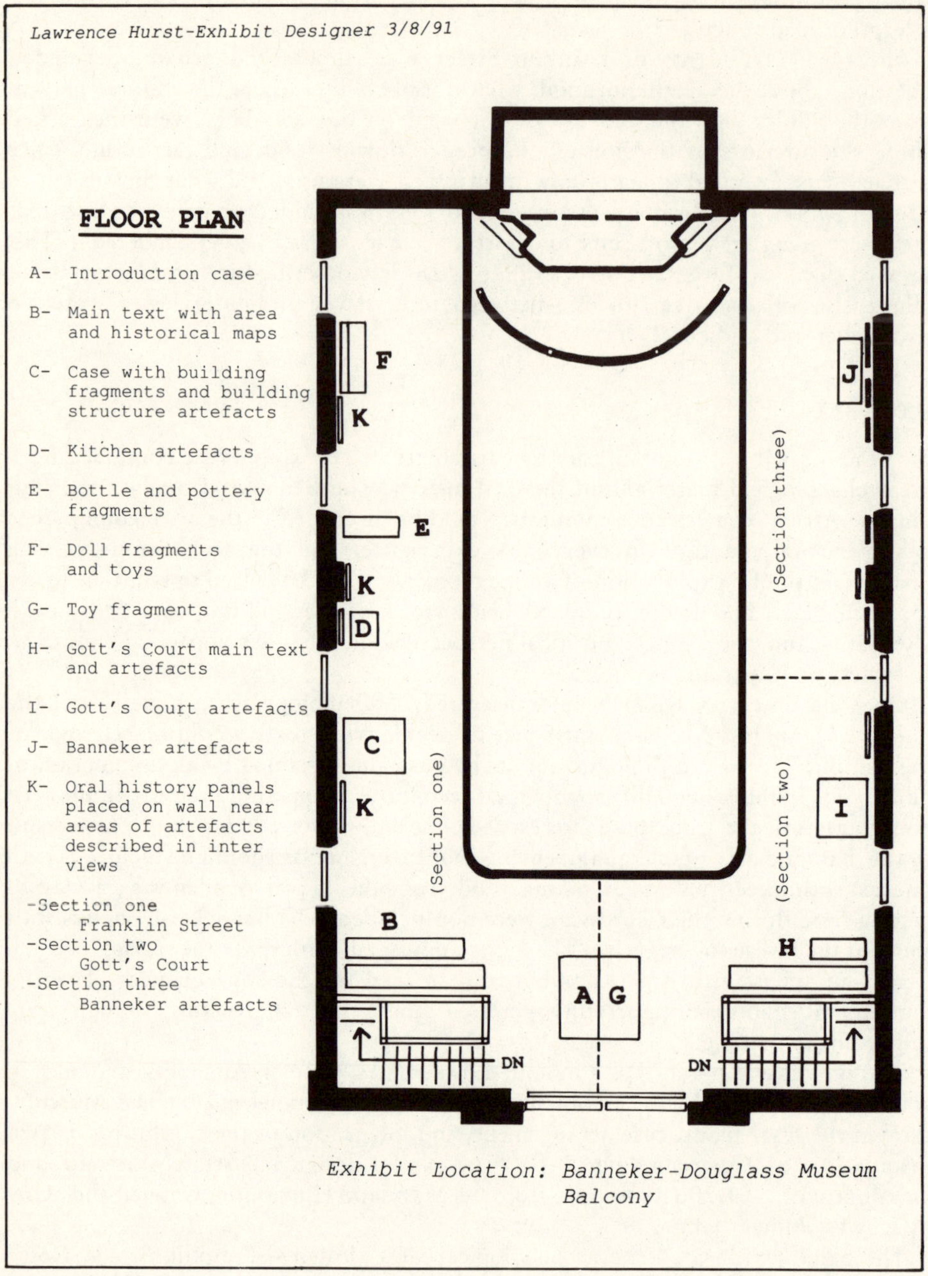
Lawrence Hurst-Exhibit Designer 3/8/91
FLOOR PLAN
A- Introduction case
B- Main text with area and historical maps
C- Case with building fragments and building structure artefacts
D- Kitchen artefacts
E- Bottle and pottery fragments
F- Doll fragments and toys
G- Toy fragments
H- Gott's Court main text and artefacts
I- Gott's Court artefacts
J- Banneker artefacts
K- Oral history panels placed on wall near areas of artefacts described in inter views
-Section one Franklin Street
-Section two Gott's Court
-Section three Banneker artefacts
F
K
E
K
D
C
K
B
A
G
H
I
J
DN
DN
(Section one)
(Section two)
(Section three)
Exhibit Location: Banneker-Douglass Museum Balcony

Figure 7 The Banneker-Douglass Museum is a former African Methodist Episcopal Church. The exhibit was mounted in the balcony in cases A–J. The balcony forms a U overlooking the main floor.

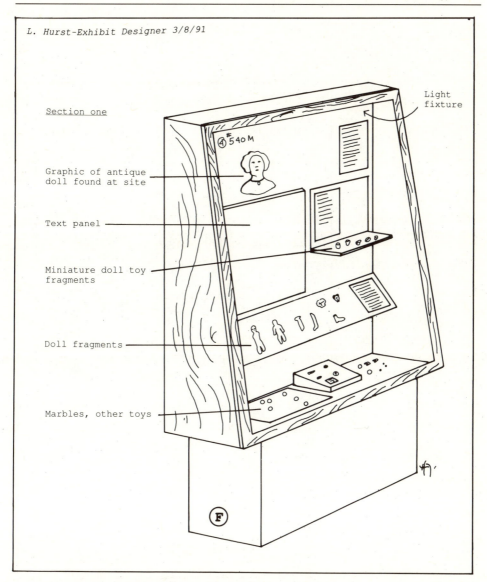

Figure 8 Case F contained doll fragments and toys with accompanying texts.

artefacts and community identification. In this sense, the people who lived in the neighbourhoods and who knew the excavated and exhibited materials made the commentary.

Three of Laurence Hurst's drawings for the exhibit show how a blueprint for an exhibit was essential to integrating exhibit areas, print and artefacts, labels and larger placards, colour, classes of things, numbers and sizes of artefacts. The archaeologists had no idea at first about what to choose, how to display or identify the artefacts. Working in an African-American space with an exhibit designer who knew its special needs and offerings made the exhibition work through the careful selection of material for all these criteria.

We all discovered that the exhibit could be self-sustaining and self-correcting.

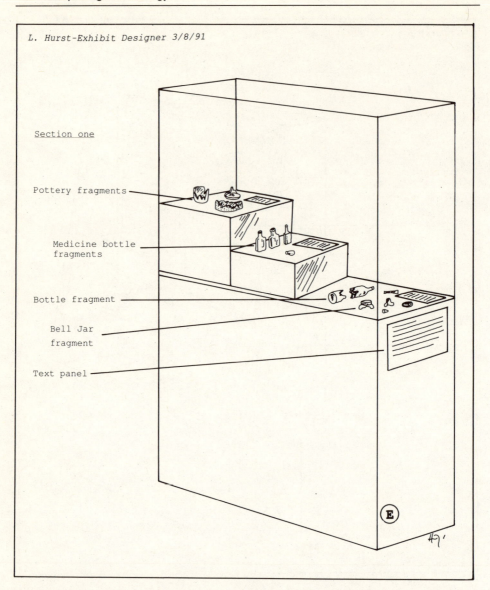

L. Hurst-Exhibit Designer 3/8/91

Section one

Pottery fragments

Medicine bottle
fragments

Bottle fragment

Bell Jar
fragment

Text panel

E

Figure 9 Case E contained bottles, bottle fragments and pottery fragments, with text.

Wherever it was moved, a new community's needs presented new material for display; wherever it was received by new parts of the African-American community, new data, new ideas, opinions and facts became available for inclusion. When the exhibit was moved to the Shiplap Museum, a building owned by the Historic Annapolis Foundation, the archaeologists curated this exhibit. Because of time constraints, the Banneker-Douglass staff and the archaeologists did not meet to decide what texts would be put on the wall, so that there was no dialogue between the two staffs prior to this exhibit's opening. The archaeologists decided to use the quote about taking food from the Naval Academy, but they included additional text that described what it was like to be poor during the Depression in order to give taking food a context. The Banneker-Douglass Museum staff did not object when they read it on the wall.

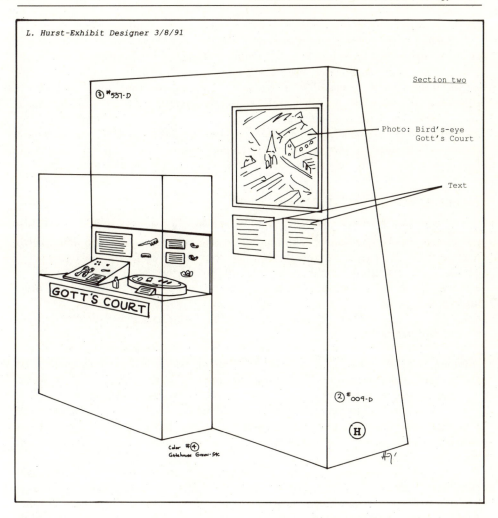

Figure 10 Case H contains the hot comb and other archaeological materials, a photo of Gott's Court and texts.
Editor Figures 8–10 were created originally by Lawrence Hurst and redrawn by Amy Grey with his approval.

The most compelling illustration of the self-correcting aspect of the exhibit process we jointly defined involves the former residents of Gott's Court who were displeased with the newspaper article which resulted from a major excavation on their former homes. The excavation and article were not part of Archaeology in Annapolis. One former resident had contacted Jackson-Nash because of an article in the *Arundel Sun*, a local newspaper, which described the houses in Gott's Court as 'ramshackle'. The residents from Gott's Court considered the article demeaning, believed that it portrayed their neighbourhood as dirty, and they wanted to respond to it. Jackson-Nash suggested that they meet with the Archaeology in Annapolis staff who would interview them about their past and help them develop a response to the newspaper article.

The Gott's Court residents met with project staff, learned about the oral history project and visited the exhibit at Shiplap Museum. They laughed at the quotes about chicken feet soup and strongly disagreed with the stories about taking food from the Naval Academy, claiming that people in Gott's Court did not do that. It was explained that the texts represented other versions of the past. Their memories of Gott's Court, which were just as valid, could be added to the exhibit.

The oral history interviews with Gott's Court residents have followed the same outline used with the Franklin Street residents. Additionally, there have been several group interviews. A preliminary selection of texts related to the artefacts was made and presented to them for their approval. Their stories portray them as a clean close-knit group of people who helped each other. These quotes were added to the exhibit at its third location, the Jefferson-Patterson Museum in Southern Maryland. Discussions about how to respond to the newspaper article are also continuing.

EVALUATION OF THE EXHIBIT

Voluntary, spontaneous visitor participation has always been an important component of Archaeology in Annapolis on-site educational programmes. Such participation has usually taken two forms: tour discussions and written visitor evaluations. Discussions held at the end of every tour have given visitors the opportunity to ask questions, challenge archaeologists' interpretations, and offer interpretations of their own. One-page visitor evaluation forms have asked for demographic information and analysis of programme content and effectiveness (Potter and Leone 1987).

As part of a central commitment to make the African-American initiative a community-based project, archaeologists and museum professionals have used visitors' responses as an important source of information to gather reactions, to see whether messages were acceptable, got across, provoked dialogue, strong dis-agreement, as well as to plan subsequent public programmes. Did a dialogue occur? Was there any hint that alternative voices produced consciousness of conditions within our own society? These are different questions, and this section summarises visitor responses.

More than 300 written evaluations have been collected at the African-American exhibits (Logan 1991). Through the questionnaires, visitors indirectly became decision-makers in developing educational programmes, illustrating the first result.

In September 1990, during Annapolis's annual Kunta Kinte Commemoration and High Heritage Festival, over 350 people visited excavations on the Franklin Street site, adjacent to the Banneker-Douglass Museum. Approximately half of the site visitors that day were African Americans, and 25% of the total number of visitors filled out questionnaires – an unusually high rate of response (Logan 1990).

Many enthusiastically positive responses were passed along to the project members through these evaluations, indicating that programmes in African-American history were long overdue. Furthermore, most respondents indicated that they did not want to see this initiative begin and end with archaeological excavations. For example, when asked, 'What would you like to see in future tours?', most responded that they would like to see examples of the many archaeological finds put on display (Logan 1991, pp. 12–13).

In an effort to satisfy this request and to continue working with the local African-American community in exploring its past, archaeologists and museum professionals created the exhibit entitled 'The Maryland Black Experience as Understood through Archaeology'. The total number of visitors to the exhibit at Banneker-Douglass Museum was 842, and 149 questionnaires were completed – a return rate of 18%; 10,789 visitors viewed the Shiplap House exhibit, yet only 106 questionnaires were completed – a return rate of less than 1%. Although no specific numbers on ethnicity were recorded, a high percentage of Banneker-Douglass visitors were African Americans, whereas most visitors to the Shiplap House were whites.

The general purpose of the evaluations was to help the exhibit's creators answer their own question: Did the exhibit work? Project members developed three questionnaires during the exhibit, but since all were very similar no attempt has been made to analyse each questionnaire-type separately. However, one general observation about the different forms is worth mentioning before discussing individual responses. The forms available to visitors at the Banneker-Douglass Museum consisted of questions that required checks to indicate answers or preferences for future work: that is, they included no spaces for text responses. There were no questions requiring written answers, and nowhere on the form were visitors explicitly encouraged to write down additional thoughts.

Nevertheless, some visitors included very powerful responses on these surveys.

It explains what history books don't about African-Americans.

So few blacks realize through their constant struggle they have a rich background that needs to be remembered and kept in mind.

I felt the oral and archaeological perspectives complemented each other really well, like a call and response from church. I thought that this was a wonderful exhibition and it just pointed out how much more we need to learn and for so many reasons. . . . All in all, this history seems so important (for many reasons!) because so much of the history of this area is one colonial (white) history. . . . How about something from another perspective! Thank goodness for the Banneker-Douglass Museum.

(Logan 1991, p. 14)

Visitors to the Shiplap House exhibit often commented on how similar daily life was for the people depicted in the exhibit as compared to their own daily lives today. When asked, 'What did you learn about the history of African Americans in Annapolis?' many respondents repeated (more or less accurately) basic points from the exhibit texts:

About 1/3 of free people in Annapolis in the 19th century were black.

The most important fact was that there were free black families in the 1800s.

Free blacks comprised a large portion of the population of Annapolis and not all were poor.

They lived more like civilized humans with more rights, freedoms, and privileges than the African Americans about whom I've heard.

I had not known that 1/3 of the population of Annapolis has consistently been African Americans and they they had contributed as much as they did to this community.

I've never been to a free African-American home as an historic site that wasn't famous or a slave. Very interesting to see and about time.

(Logan 1991, pp. 10–11)

One realisation that came as a result of reading these questionnaires is how knowledge of the African-American past is absent from most people's understanding of history. These responses suggest that visitors incorporated at least some of the exhibit's empirical information on African-American history.

Answers to the question 'What would you like to see in future exhibits?' led to a diverse range of recommendations. This is not surprising, given Americans' generally low level of knowledge of the African-American past. Suggestions to the question included:

More artifacts from residences . . . records of work life.

Show successes of blacks from 1700–1900.

Early black literature and other cultural finds.

Types of clothing, currency, pictorials of a typical family.

Things they did for entertainment. More info about African-American life.
(Logan 1991, pp. 12–13)

These responses make it clear that people realise how little they know about the African-American past and that they will take advantage of opportunities to learn more. Evaluations of this exhibit argue that it was a success in promoting some consciousness of African-American heritage. They also point out that there has been a long-standing demand for more information about African-American history (and minority groups in general) that has not been satisfied.

CONCLUSION

We achieved some goals and not others. The archaeologists certainly have learned how to be archaeologists within a living community's needs. There are some new archaeological questions and answers, and we are serving archaeological needs and community concerns in new ways. White archaeologists have felt useful, innovative, and participatory about the focus of their work. African Americans have felt better-served but also felt the need for more exhibits, colloquia, workshops and contacts of all kinds. The demand to know about and contribute more information on black heritage was substantial.

Was consciousness changed? Yes, at some level for most who participated. If the evaluations tell a truth, then certainly awareness of a new source of African-American heritage occurred. Among archaeologists there is a sense of greater understanding of African-American culture, but little truer understanding of what it is like to be black, or how difficult it was or is. But there is the beginning of an understanding of what American culture does to black people and that many black people do see American society with very different, sharper, and both angrier and more tolerant eyes. So, some white eyes are more open. And some black eyes have a better understanding of 'why they are here now'.

ACKNOWLEDGEMENTS

The authors would like to thank the Maryland Historical Trust and the Maryland Humanities Council for their continuing support of the Archaeology in Annapolis project. Additionally, we are grateful to Karen Davis of Jefferson-Patterson Park for the opportunity to present the exhibit on African-American archaeology at their facility. Finally we would like to thank the many former residents of Gott's Court and the Franklin Street neighbourhoods for their willingness to participate in the oral history component of our project.

Chapter 15

'Trojan forebears', 'peerless relics'
The rhetoric of heritage claims

David Lowenthal

Those who treasure memories and artefacts of the past, whatever their motives, characteristically assert impassioned claims. Archaeologists, archivists, genealogists, conservators, patriots of all kinds champion the viewpoints and husband the relics of the epochs they explore. This essay documents the role of rhetorical hyperbole in delineating the past and in staking claims to its heritage.

Rhetoric today is often decried as empty bombast. But in classical and medieval times rhetoric pervaded and enriched learning. The truth or falsehood of an argument mattered less than the eloquence and elegance with which it was presented; the art of persuasion took precedence over pedantic concern with accuracy.

In writings about the past, the topic deemed most worth attention, rhetoric was emphasised to the detriment of other scholarship (Levine 1987, pp. 102, 135–6). History, in Cicero's classic expression (*De oratore* 1979, 2.9.36), was 'the witness to the passing of the ages, the light of truth, the life of memory, the mistress of life, and the ambassador of the past'. History and biography delineated particular events and lives chiefly to exemplify moral principles and eternal verities, in order to promote public virtue. Chroniclers' functions were panegyric and hortatory, not critical. Anecdotes and speeches, conversations and contexts were concocted to heighten interest and to stress the virtues or vices of past notables, themselves often anachronistically displaced or purely mythical. Death-bed scenes (men of fame seem never to have died in their sleep or in a coma) were choice occasions for rhetorical prophecies.

In describing themselves as disinterested purveyors of unvarnished truth, chroniclers were being doubly rhetorical; they knew they were expected to exaggerate and invent. After dismissing precedessors' fictional additions, historians then took them over and went on to devise their own. The distant past was rhetorically more manageable than that within living memory, when the historian's embroidery might be challenged by eyewitness memory (Morse 1991, pp. 16, 87–94).

The law courts were rhetoric's prime locale; here advocates deployed their skills on causes remote from their own interests. It was rhetorically persuasive to start with a *chria*, a gloss on some well-known wise saying; assenting to this memory inclined auditors to agree with the argument that followed (ibid., pp. 53–65). More honour attached to pleading a brilliant losing case than to winning it, though clients may have felt otherwise.

Rhetoric infused famous quarrels over the relative worth of ancient and modern achievements. Humanists often took stances in order to flaunt their virtuosity in the face of common faith, defending moderns not to undermine ancient authority but to parade unusual rhetorical skills. The fifteenth-century Florentine chancellor Accolti thus upheld pro-modern positions seen as notoriously absurd. He contended ancient rhetoric had been made obsolete by the decline of Roman oratory; praised the mercenary system and arts of trickery and deceit as military innovations; defended the luxury of the modern Church and its paucity of martyrs on the ground that 'if there were more martyrs in antiquity, that was because there was more persecution' (Black 1982, pp. 17–19, 25; 1985, pp. 192–208).

Noble families had long advanced themselves by means of historical rhetoric. In late-medieval Europe an ancient lineage became a bona fides of rights to titles and landed estates. 'Written above all to exalt a line and legitimize its power, a medieval genealogy displays the noble family's intention to affirm and extend its place' (Spiegel 1990, p. 79).

Rising English and French aristocrats bolstered the antiquity of their lineages by contriving fabulous pedigrees. Fake modern versions of Homeric epics, the pseudo-Turpin chronicles of Charlemagne, the fantastic history of Geoffrey of Monmouth made available heroic Trojan and mythic ancestors. Working Hercules (not to mention Gideon) into the Duke of Burgundy's family tree enabled him to 'restore' his dukedom to the status of a principality (Morse 1991, p. 107).

Several rhetorical modes added weight to these family tales. Their vernacular style appropriated the authenticating authority of Latin texts. Prose (rather than verse) was used for *gravitas* and to heighten the appearance of truth. Conflating *vita* and chronology upgraded hereditary succession into historical narrative, stressing pro-creation and filiation as metaphors for historical continuity and change. Individual lives were celebrated in rhetorical tropes that affirmed the collective identity of the whole lineage, from mythical forebears to Merovingian monarchs. Tracing ances-tries back to Troy not only earned feudal nobles awesome pedigrees, it at length glorified nascent national identity (Citron 1991, p. 149; McKendrick 1992; Spiegel 1983, 1986, 1990).

Rhetorical histories flourished well into the last century. In praising Boswell's biography of Johnson as a monument more lasting than any material remains, Carlyle (1832, p. 227) both salutes and exemplifies the power of rhetoric:

> Rough Samuel and sleek wheedling James were, and are not. Their Life and whole personal Environment has melted into air. The Mitre Tavern still stands in Fleet Street: but where now is its scot-and-lot paying, beef-and-ale loving, cock-hatted, pot-bellied Landlord; its rose-faced assiduous Landlady, with all her shining brass-pans, waxed tables, well-filled larder-shelves; her cooks, and boot-jacks, and errand-boys, and watery-mouthed hangers-on? Gone! Gone! . . . The Bottles they drank out of are all broken, the Chairs they sat on all rotted and burnt; the very Knives and Forks they ate with have rusted to the heart, and become brown oxide of iron, and mingled with the indiscriminate clay. All, all has vanished. . . . Of the Mitre Tavern nothing but the bare walls remain there: of London, of England, of the World, nothing but the bare walls remain; and these also decaying (were they of adamant), only slower.

Chroniclers today profess to be as soberly unbiased as possible. But the most objective and dispassionate histories need eloquence to be readable. 'Rhetoric is ordinarily deemed icing on the cake of history', but in fact 'it is mixed right into the batter'. Historical knowledge depends on emotive language; if the historian fails to communicate what he believes, it never becomes publicly available. Hexter (1968, pp. 378–91) shows how quotations function as rhetoric. Confronted with a veritable slice of the past, we respond not simply, 'Yes,' but exclaim, 'Yes, indeed!' Historians constantly have to gauge when to be allusive rather than precise, when to sacrifice fact for evocative force. Rhetoric gives us not Frye's (1983, p. 227) 'familiar remembered things, but the glittering intensity of the summoned-up hallucination'.

Unlike earlier times, however, historians' rhetoric is now constrained by narrowly prescriptive and prospective standards of truth. Not so the rhetoric of heritage, which uses history to persuade, to kindle patriotism, to enlist chauvinist passion. Heritage concern normally reflects personal or national self-interest. Things are valued as my heritage or our heritage; rival claimants dispute peerless and indivisible relics. We may be modest about what we are, but not about what we were. Even a shameful past is lauded in unabashed self-admiration. In celebrating the symbols of their identities societies actually worship themselves (Durkheim 1915, pp. 206–14, 230–2).

Social self-admiration has sources in private ancestral pride. Every person's 'past life . . . presents itself through the beautifying glass of fancy', noted a pioneer Nordic scholar (Thorpe 1851, Vol. 1, p. 1–2):

> Among nations the same feeling prevails; they also draw a picture of their infancy in glittering colours. The vain-glory of the people will continue to cherish, to ennoble and diffuse their traditions from generation to generation. Nations proclaim the peerless nature of their own past residues, historical memories along with material monuments. Antiquity and continuity, redemptive hardship and triumphal success are common leitmotifs of such claims.

National anthems graphically confirm the durability of militant rhetoric. The 'Marseillaise' urges French patriots to 'drench our fields with [Prussians'] tainted blood'. 'God Save the Queen' begs Him to 'Scatter her enemies and make them fall'. Danes extol King Christian 'hammering . . . through Gothic helm and brain'. Mozambicans foretell 'the tomb of capitalism and exploitation'. Gaddafi's Libyans repulse the enemy 'with truth and with my gun'. Even citizens of tiny Monaco vow to 'die in defence' of their Prince (Cathcart 1992).

A few British rhetorical flourishes typify the flavour: Mandell Creighton (1898, pp. 14–15, 18), historian and Bishop of London:

> The most important point about English history is that the English were the first people who formed for themselves a national character at all. No nation has carried its whole past so completely into its present. Our long period of steady success [spares us] the centuries of oppression from barbarian conquerers, of long struggles to realize national unity [that make others] fantastic, unreasonable, fanatical.

C. H. K. Marten (1905, in Samuel 1989, Vol. 1, p. 12), Eton provost and Queen Elizabeth's tutor:

> Our history has a continuity [lacking in] many other countries. We have preserved our national character throughout the ages. The medieval, the Elizabethan, and the modern Englishman all show the same individuality, the same initiative, the same independence, the same practical sagacity.

Bernard Levin (1989), contemporary columnist:

> The most noticeable thing about our history is that we have more of it than any other country. Of course, Rome is older, but Italy is a 19th century upstart. The length of time, the depth and richness of our island story, gives us a claim to pre-eminence.

But the British have no monopoly on chauvinist rhetoric. This is a prefatory exhortation from a French school-history text (Chiappe 1989, p. 8):

> Whether you are noble or bourgeois, of worker or peasant origin, you participate in the unrivalled glory of a monument of wisdom and grandeur: the French

monarchy. Thanks to her, you are what you are: superior in knowledge and imagination to all other men.

The seldom-read but oft-cited sacred Finnish epic, the *Kalevala*, is exalted by a historian as Scandinavia's 'richest, most genuine, and most independent [folk creation], a singing testimony of our people's immemorial heroic age and of that toughness and will to survive by which our nation and our culture have grown . . .' (Jalmari Jaakkola 1935 in Wilson 1975, p. 107).

> The *Kalevala* is not only the unquenchable wellspring from which our writers, our artists, and our composers have drawn . . . inspiration; it is also the sounding board which has given power and strength to . . . political awakening [enabling] a nation whose heroes once freed the sun from the mountains . . . to cast off the bonds of slavery, to walk free and independent.
>
> (Niilo Karki 1924, in Wilson 1975 p. 121)

And from an Andalucian spokesman (in Enzensberger 1990, p. 225):

> Our culture survives by allowing itself to be over-whelmed. This strategy has defeated every conqueror: the Phoenicians and the Romans, the Vandals and the Visigoths, the Arabs and the kings of Castile. We corrupted the Napoleonic invaders, and we'll deal with tourism as well. Adaptation is our strongest weapon – it makes us unconquerable.

Along with boasts of superiority and uniqueness, rhetoric is crucial in conflicts over heritage that now suffuse politics and public consciousness. Such disputes are of two principal kinds: contested assertions of prior occupance and creation, or of a privileged divine covenant; and contested demands for relics and icons of identity.

Different heritage realms generate different conflicts. Endemic to archaeology are disputes over national or ethnic primacy, the validity of famed remains, preferred prehistoric and historic epochs, the repatriation of autochthonous skeletal remains, the primacy of scholarly versus sacred values of relics. Those who would restrict excavation rights to nationals are at loggerheads with international scholars. The allocation of finds among national, regional, local and *in situ* display sites is bitterly contested. Impassioned disputes attest the close linkage of heritage and habitat, the felt fusion of identity with locale.

National heritage crusades are couched in highly righteous polemic. To seize or demand land or resources is internationally reprehended; to seize or demand adjuncts of heritage may be condoned as essential to integrity, even if it infringes the integrity of others. A Mexican scholar's theft of an Aztec codex from France's Bibliothèque Nationale was acclaimed as an act of patriotic heroism because his purpose was repatriation (Stetie 1982, pp. 55–6).

The rhetoric of restitution is expressly anti-colonial. Newly independent nations dwell at length on imperial iniquities that deprive them of material relics and icons of identity. For tangible validations of ancestral antecedents, former colonies have to grub for their roots among relics held in Western collections. They term it imperative that 'the former mother country restores to the new State not only its sovereignty but also its heritage', as an Algerian (Tayeb 1979) expressed it. The chairman of the UNESCO committee charged with this issue saw 'the restitution and return of cultural property', embracing architectural structures along with other antiquities, works of art and archives, as 'one of the key problems of the Third World' (Stetie 1981).

UNESCO's then chief was no less dramatic. 'The vicissitudes of history have . . . robbed many peoples of a priceless portion of [their] inheritance in which their enduring identity finds its embodiment. [To] enable a people to recover part of its memory and identity', other lands should relinquish these irreplaceable cultural treasures 'to the countries where they were created' (M'Bow 1979).

Though heritage claims ring with rhetorical bravado, their vehement assertion does not necessarily mean the claimant especially wants what is at issue – at least, not yet. In many disputes honour is satisfied, communal identity secured, simply by fervent reiteration of a heritage claim. It may better serve Greek pride to go on demanding the return of the Elgin Marbles than actually to get them back.

Nothing rouses popular feeling more than a grievance unrectified. To gain Quebecois sovereignty or Scottish home rule would at a stroke deprive separatists of their prime weapon. Identity is more zealously created and husbanded by the quest for a lost heritage than by its nurture when regained. Basque extremism dwindled to querulous impotence once Basques gained substantial autonomy. 'Before, we had answers to our problems,' says a Basque spokesman (in Heiberg 1989, p. 230). 'They were self-government, *conciertos economicos*, the restoration of our Basque culture. All that has been achieved. . . . Now our problems seem to have no answers at all and what we have achieved doesn't seem that important.'

Many conflicts fester unresolved because bereaved claimants are poor and powerless. It is no accident that ex-colonial Asian and African nations spearhead UNESCO's heritage restitution drive. Though now sovereign, these states often seek in vain to regain icons of their identity from European collections. Lacking armed clout, their heritage crusades are limited to moral exhortation, with predictably few victories.

Autochthonous and other beleaguered minorities often assert claims that are blatantly extreme. They do not expect them to be conceded; instead they aim to maintain a high profile, reminding the majority of past iniquities for which guilt can be turned to account. Passamaquoddy Indians in Maine challenged the validity of old treaties that ceded fully half the state; so huge a claim would never succeed, but while legal proceedings went on no land could be transferred; the resulting log-jam of property transactions ensured a substantial out-of-court award to the Indians (Brodeur 1985, pp. 69–141). The Woggle, an invisible Aboriginal spirit, can be found to have inhabited – and hence now inhibits – any locale facing a critical decision affecting conservation or development.

British amenity groups frankly admit they assail agricultural greed to generate public interest in open-space causes. Asked why his countryside pressure group adopted such an aggressive stance towards farmers and landowners, its secretary replied: 'Because it gets us publicity in the media, and that is how we attract new members' (in 'Access' 1991). Populist rhetoric pits heritage amateurs against professionals who invoke the claims of science to protect some legacy from the philistine public. Complaints by geologists about fossil-hunting despoliation along the Dorset coast are countered by accusations that this academic élite exaggerates the risks to palaeontology in order to deprive the public of time-honoured heritage participation (Lowenthal 1985, p. 44; Nicholson-Lord 1991). Accusations that the Council for British Archaeology is a hotbed of Marxist authoritarianism may strike archaeologists as absurd, but metal-detector cowboys get a lot of mileage out of portraying themselves as folk patriots against a haughty and (shades of Anthony Blunt) subversive scientific Establishment (Wright 1991, pp. 39–51).

The gulf between rhetoric and results is symptomatic of heritage issues generally. It is not only the poor and the weak whose aims exceed their grasp. British laments over the drain of national treasures overseas are a case in point. Current export restrictions were, to be sure, tailored to a more prosperous Britain and a stronger pound. But National Heritage Memorial Fund and national museum resources fall woefully short of safety-net needs highlighted by SAVE Britain's Heritage.

The size of this gulf is less startling than the shortsightedness of despondent heritage guardians. Time and again Britain's museums have turned down some proffered private relic as too costly, retrospectively to regret a bargain missed – and sometimes later buying it at twice or more the initial price. To publicize potential loss with alarmist rhetoric – 'comparable to the damage that Cromwell and his Roundheads caused when they executed Charles I and dispersed the greatest private collection the world has ever known' (Leggatt 1978) – makes such heritage at once indispensable and ruinously expensive.

In short, competition encumbers heritage with a sad irony: when we realise we cannot do without some legacy, we find we can often no longer afford to keep or acquire it. Where access rights embroil rival claimants, as at Stonehenge, media reports of hippie intransigence, Druid determination, and custodial fears of criminal damage led to draconian protective measures that have negated most heritage functions for a decade.

I have shown that rhetoric suffuses public debate on heritage matters. Let me conclude by suggesting why this is so. One reason is given above: heritage is seen as intensely personal to individuals and to communities; its ownership and control arouse possessive anxieties. But the very uniqueness of heritage to each claimant means we cannot persuade others to adopt our perspective. Failing rational reasoning, we fall back on rhetorical hyperbole. Finally, rhetoric reinforces our own sense of attachment, shoring up our conviction that we care about heritage as much as we claim to, and reassuring our fellows that we are at one on vital matters of identity.

Chapter 16

A sense of place

A role for cognitive mapping in the 'postmodern' world?

Kevin Walsh

INTRODUCTION

Although there are many characteristics of the so-called postmodern condition, it is my belief that the most important is that of a feeling of placelessness. This placelessness undeniably has its roots in the process of modernisation witnessed during the eighteenth and nineteenth centuries.

In this paper I will consider one possible strategy for coping with this sense of placelessness. It involves the development of an idea mooted originally by Kevin Lynch (1960) and then Fredric Jameson (1988a) – the idea of cognitive mapping.

Essential for an appreciation of how feelings of placelessness have emerged is a consideration, albeit a brief one, of how economic systems have affected people's lives.

Each stage of capital has brought with it a new experience of space. With each 'advancement' of capital there has been a kind of distancing of the social: people have become removed from the economic system of production which they serve. In the early stages of economic development people were closer to the actual market systems within which they operated. During the Industrial Revolution the great migrations to urban centres removed people from the markets in which they worked. For the majority, life was dominated by the locality: personal interactions, economic production and exchange largely occurred within a set of relatively small spatial contexts.

The development of imperial networks heralded the beginnings of a truly global economy; markets which working people in London, Manchester and Liverpool could never really hope to understand or participate in with any power.

If placing oneself in time and space, and therefore gaining a sense of place, was difficult during the nineteenth century at the time of imperial capital, then today, under the regime of multinational capital, it must be well-nigh impossible. Even the nation-state has a limited existence in the truly global economy. It is the multinationals such as Ford and Unilever that call the shots in the postmodern world. Production processes and market networks are so disparate today that people and places are subjected to influences on a global scale. Our consumption and cultural experiences are the result of many varied influences which seem to know no temporal or spatial limits. Few in the Western world would raise an eyebrow at the thought of consuming Taiwanese cooking in a refurbished nineteenth-century dock situated between a French-style street-café and a boutique selling clothes from South America.

Also, the media which have contributed to the ability of capital to transcend time–space boundaries and exacerbate the processes of alienation have at the same time perpetuated an experience of time–space compression – what might be described as a shrinking of the world (Harvey 1989, chs 15–16). Media of mass communication permit both instantaneous transactions of ethereal capital and also communication between people or groups of people. Despite the fact that it is now possible to be aware of events that are taking place all over the world, the media of mass communications serve to deny our understanding of these processes which affect our lives, through the incessant reporting of events both important and specious. This irruption of media imagineering (sic) serves to promote an amnesia which denies the possibility of ever coming to terms with these events.

Since the nineteenth century particularly, people have witnessed ever-accelerating changes, especially within cities. Both architectural styles and consumer goods have been developed with such speed that it seems almost impossible to stop for breath, stand back, and come to terms with the machinations of the (post)modern world. Such perpetual change has brought us to the point where there would seem to be an exhaustion of style; all we can achieve today is the mixing and remixing of styles aggregated from any time and any space. The past is now a pool of timeless images which feed a seemingly ever-growing desire for the retro.

As Jameson considers, late capitalism might be thought of as a set of processes which have increasingly collapsed the differences between the cultural and the economic (Jameson 1991, p. xxi). This has resulted in a lack of distinction between the base and the superstructure (the economic and the cultural): a mythological book, such as J. R. Hartley's *Fly Fishing*, the creation of a television advertisement for Yellow Pages, is eventually published as demand for this non-existent commodity reaches a level where it becomes profitable actually to produce it.

> Aesthetic production today has become integrated into commodity production generally: the frantic economic urgency of producing fresh waves of ever more novel-seeming goods (from clothing to airplanes), at ever greater rates of turnover, now assigns an increasingly essential structural function and position to aesthetic innovation and experimentation.
>
> (Jameson 1991, pp. 4–5)

Postmodern heritage is typical of such a system of production. With its unnerving ability to deny historical process, or diachrony, heritage successfully mediates all our pasts as ephemeral snapshots exploited in the present to maintain an artificial sense of organic unity within the nation, to embellish decaying cityscapes, and to guarantee the success of capital in its attempts to develop new superfluous markets.

The postmodern place is one constituted through an unrestrained plagiarism: the unreferenced quotation, or even misquotation, of styles, images, histories and legends from any time and any space. Such contrived places range from the redeveloped city-centre, with its postmodern architecture and heritage centres (see Walsh 1992, chs 4 and 5) to the hyperreality (Eco 1987) of EuroDisney where the 'most popular rides like Star Tours, Captain EO and Pirates of the Caribbean will be combined with brand new experiences drawn from the rich heritage of European culture, fairytale and legend' (Cresta 1992, p. 2). The wealth of brochures appearing in 1992, enticing those who can afford the more exclusive 'short break', are a bricolage of images of Paris and EuroDisney. Pictures of the Eiffel Tower, Montmartre, St-Germain and the Left Bank are juxtaposed with those of the Sleeping Beauty Chateau, Fantasyland and Big Thunder Mountain.

It would be wrong to claim that the consuming public do not differentiate between the 'reality' that is Paris and the myth or fantasy that is Disney. But it might be prudent to consider whether the strategy of packaging what should be two very different experiences so closely might eventually lead to a blurring of the differences between real and imagined places. Because, despite my contention elsewhere (Walsh 1992, ch. 6) that places constituted by postmodern architecture and heritagised space might not be considered as 'real' places, there is a danger that as experiences such as EuroDisney become established in our mental maps they may take on a reality which erodes the distinctiveness of real places.

It is this blurring of difference and erosion of distinctiveness which as much as anything else contributes to a loss of a sense of place as we approach the end of the century.

MAKING CONNECTIONS

This loss of a sense of place, a product of those experiences outlined above, may be avoided through an attempt at a totalising of 'mapping', based on a strategy of understanding the links that exist between people and places across both space and time. It should also be considered that such processes continue right up to the present, as throughout the (post)modern period the past has emerged as something which is no longer contingent upon our daily lives. The idea that history is over, and that all we should do now is exploit the styles and images of the past, was symbolised by Kenneth Clarke's declaration, in a circular to teachers in January 1991, that these teachers should not cover the Gulf War in their classes, as history has nothing to do with current events. The cut-off date for the study of the Middle East in British schools is about 1967 – a generation ago.

The links which we might wish to articulate are partly related to understanding the nature of markets and, more recently, the movements of capital, as it has been and is these which determine to an extent economic, social and cultural configurations. None of us is removed from these networks, and it must therefore be one aim of museums to help people come to terms with the ways in which these networks affect them.

An appreciation of how these processes affect us is best approached from the locality, defined as 'the space within which the larger part of most citizens' daily and consuming lives is lived' (Cooke 1989, p. 12).

Two geographers, Gould and White, attempted to ascertain how people perceived their own localities; the 'mental maps' that people possessed. They considered the degree of 'emotional involvement' that people had within an area. Unsurprisingly the research revealed that emotional involvement fell off very steeply with distance, and then levelled out after this (Gould and White 1974, p. 42). Therefore, the starting point for any cognitive mapping project must be this kind of locality.

A sense of place is partly constituted through the subjective recognition of 'time marks': elements in the environment, both humanly and naturally constructed. Such marks, in a way, make time 'visible'. To put it another way, one's sense of the past or sense of history is partly developed through an appreciation of age, that is, how old a building, a person or even a mountain is. More specifically, a history is developed through locating these phenomena in some kind of temporal order, and also within spatial contexts relating to this order. A key element in any strategy of cognitive mapping must be the discovery and articulation of the links which have existed, and still do exist, between these phenomena.

Also, we should be concerned to develop strategies which allow people to develop their own mental maps of places rather than impose institutionalised readings of places, as is often the case with orthodox museum and heritage presentations.

A ROLE FOR MUSEUMS

Museums as facilitators should first and foremost be concerned with promoting the skills which might enable people to read their own place, as well as other places which they may visit. One example of such skills would be the ability to date vernacular buildings and to understand how and why they were built. The need to understand this element of the historical environment is all the more important in the light of the impact of postmodern architecture. The unreferenced quotation of historic styles within built environments which consist of 'real' historic buildings and those produced by plagiarising architects can only serve to inhibit a sense of place.

An understanding of place might well be enhanced through a consideration of the 'four-dimensional web'. This requires us to consider localities as nodes developing through time and space, which possess almost any number of links with other nodes, or localities, within a web or network. As far as this discussion goes, the first three dimensions are those of the physical world as perceived at any one moment in time, while the fourth dimension is time. The fourth dimension does not have to be founded on the orthodox framework of the past as linear progression through Western historical dates; but rather as a dimension or, more specifically, a characteristic of a place, or object, which implies process, change and depth.

An emphasis should be put on how places are nodal points in networks of production, how places are physically constructed through the exploitation of material resources, from water, clay and stone, to the manipulation of chemicals and their transformation into commodities, from bricks to nuclear power.

Archaeologists have long been concerned with illustrating trading networks based on the provenance of material; such 'maps' can be developed to show how we have exploited different resources over time and space. The trend towards the distancing of the production of commodities away from the direct daily experiences of those who consume them is an obvious theme. We might consider how early farmers would have produced much of their requirements within the locality, while today commodities manufactured on the multinational scale are consumed. We should consider highlighting the processes which have remodelled peoples' places and have perhaps influenced their perceptions of place. Crucial to peoples' perceptions of place might be the definition of boundaries through time – from the parish, and named areas within towns and cities, through to the nation, and supra-national organisations such as the EEC.

We should be clear that places are continually changing, and our perceived present is always a form of pastness. It is this crucial contingency of the past on our daily experiences which can be articulated through the museum, more specifically the ecomuseum as originally conceived in France by Georges Henri Rivière.

The key to success of the ecomuseum is the fact that it operates as part of the community, within the locality. The ecomuseum is concerned to integrate all of the disciplines which are normally involved in museology, including archaeology, social history, natural history and geology, in fact any discipline which contributes to the understanding of people and places.

> The ecomuseum is an instrument conceived, fashioned and operated jointly by a public authority and a local population. The public authority's involvement is through the experts, facilities and resources it provides; the local population's involvement depends on its aspirations, knowledge and individual approach.
>
> (Rivière 1985, p. 182)

Rivière considered that such a museum should be a mirror, which a local community could hold up to its visitors so that the visitor may develop a respect for that locality as it is constituted by its people and their interaction with their environment through time and space.

Ideally, ecomuseums should be concerned with considering the development of places through time, or at least develop a sequence of temporary projects which deal with this. A theme for consideration might be that of how and why humans have progressively manipulated and, in one sense, simplified ecosystems through an unquestioning belief in the verity of technical rationalisation. Why has the history of the first world especially been one of increasingly labour-intensive modes of production, which have pushed the ecosystem to its limits whilst reducing the amount of free time available to most people?

The ecomuseum is, then, one way in which projects of cognitive mapping may develop. Other ways might include the production of 'maps of feeling' as promoted by the Common Ground organisation. Such maps allow people to represent their place as they see it (see Greeves 1987a, 1987b).

Integrated with this sort of mapping project should be a consideration of people's relationships with objects. Areas for consideration might include the following: people's relationships with everyday objects, including consumables and durables, and objects of 'special' meaning, from heirlooms to souvenirs. How do people 'feel' about these various objects? Are they aware of the object's history? Where, when and by whom was it manufactured?

There might be scope for discourses on the differences between gifts and commodities (Appadurai, ed., 1986, pp. 11–12). Appadurai argues that we should be attempting to consider commodities in the different situations within which they might exist during their 'social lives'. This demands a break 'with the production dominated Marxian view of the commodity and focussing on its total trajectory from production, through exchange/distribution, to consumption' (Appadurai, ed., 1986, p. 13). We should go on to consider the different contexts of consumption and perceptions held by people over a commodity's lifespan: for example, the transformation of everyday objects, such as a cutlery set, into the more psychologically 'valuable' family heirloom. Another – and perhaps a more archaeologically pertinent – example would be that of ceramic assemblages, and their trajectory from the everyday commodities of past societies to the auratic objects of the modern museum display.

We should also consider the ways in which commodities contribute to the construction of relationships between people. The study of the life paths of objects undeniably enhances any study of the human condition. Commodities are 'a universal cultural phenomenon. Their existence is a concomitant of the existence of transactions that involve the exchange of things (objects and services), exchange being a universal feature of human social life' (Kopytoff 1986, p. 68).

Using such information, it would be again possible to 'map' people's relationships, exploitation of, and attitudes towards material culture. Again, such strategies must emphasise the temporal aspects of such relationships.

INTERACTIVE VIDEO

One set of tools that could easily enhance the development of the mapping projects outlined above is Interactive Video and other media environments. The Interactive Video Disc (IVD) is based on an archive of images which can be still or moving. The disc is essentially a larger version of a Compact Disc (CD), and has a capacity of 4 gigabytes which allows 26 minutes of moving images or 55,000 still frames. The image archive can be accessed randomly, which is probably the system's most important characteristic. There is also the facility for two parallel soundtracks, and computer-generated graphics can be superimposed over an image.

At the physical level, the IVD is an indexed collection of images. At a separate logical level, the image archive is controlled by software on a Personal Computer (PC), and it is the software which to a certain extent controls the ways in which the image archive can be accessed and manipulated (Martlew 1988, 1990).

From the museum's point of view the introduction of IVD permits visitors to access not just images of material on display in the museum, but also images of archived material and images of the places where the material was found, including maps. A catalogue approach to the image-archive offers the potential for users to access structured sequences of images and other data in a relatively idiosyncratic manner. The user, through the PC, could structure his own sequences of images and interrogate the archive to his own particular ends. However, it should be made clear that structuring a set of images does require a lot of thought, and is not something that could be achieved by a visitor during a casual visit to a museum.

Interactive Video will allow a user to integrate different types of information, including information on objects, their provenance, date, and so on. It will also permit the user to search for information about the site where it was found, and show maps of similar sites and objects. The information stored and subsequently retrieved can concentrate on any temporal or spatial context. Such video discs could quite easily facilitate the mapping of links between people and places within a county or, perhaps more important for those interested in the (post)modern experience, across the world.

In the context of the community, or ecomuseum, Interactive Video allows individuals, or groups of people, to develop their own presentations on topics of their own choice, or to develop cognitive links between visual and other forms of data (Ruggles, personal communication). The IVD system easily permits the development of linked sequences of images, both still and moving, along with superimposed textual information. It is possible to set up a number of different 'routes' through the presentation. A general topic might start with considering a certain period of a place's history. Routes from a general introduction might go in a number of different directions: economy, religion, leisure, conflict, and many others. Within those subtopics, a number of alternative explanations could be offered. Essentially, Interactive Video offers the potential for a greater democracy in access to information about the past and can allow people to develop their own cognitive maps and, thus, a sense of place.

Eventually such media could be greatly enhanced through their combination with Geographical Information Systems (GIS) which contain data relating to production and consumption patterns, for example. However, some geographers' inclination towards the synchronic spatialisation of data would have to be avoided, and databases concerned with temporal patterns would need to be developed. If GIS were developed as historical tools, the combined strength of the two systems would allow the development of quite complex mapping projects which could employ demographic, environmental, consumption and production data.

The basis for such systems has already in part been developed by the Midland Regional Research Laboratory at the University of Leicester. The development of the Meta-Information Retrieval and Access System (MIRAS) allows users to access and integrate multiple datasets. Such datasets might be constituted by textual, visual and aural information. Therefore the datasets would contain maps, image-archives of buildings, objects, and so on, and structured datasets, which might include 'tape-slide' presentations on various topics (Ruggles and Newman 1991, pp. 189–90).

The system allows people to set up spatial and temporal constraints. For example, a user may be interested in a specific 10-square-kilometre block during the last 500 years, or a 300-hundred-square-kilometre block during the previous five years. The MIRAS system employs spatial and temporal 'tiles'. These are the user-defined temporal and spatial parameters, as mentioned above. Defining spatial tiles is relatively straightforward, while the definition of temporal tiles is more complicated. As Ruggles and Newman observe: 'there is the tricky problem of the wide granularity of time. A dataset of archaeological or geological information could span many thousands or even millions of years, with imprecise starting and finishing dates, while a dataset of traffic flows on a section of motorway may only span a few hours' (Ruggles and Newman 1991, p. 201). Therefore the MIRAS system approaches this problem by offering time-tiles of different sizes: the smallest are those closest to the present, and the largest those most distant in time.

This definition of time-tiles may serve to remove the contingency of historical processes from the present, through the promotion of predefined temporal parameters which do not include the present. It cannot be overemphasised that cognitive mapping must be concerned with helping people to locate themselves in the present through an appreciation of historical processes which potentially have no spatial or temporal limits.

PLACES AND COMMUNITIES

The aim of cognitive mapping and developing a sense of place should be to allow people to develop their own sense of place. This is not an argument for an unfettered radical individualism but, rather, an argument for the promotion of communication between people that allows the development of communities of discourse: 'common meanings are the basis of community' (Taylor 1985, p. 39). People should be encouraged to take 'positions' *vis-à-vis* the past. This engagement with the construction of places demands that people be allowed to assess what they consider to be 'right' or 'wrong' about the processes which have affected their place. As people make value judgements about contemporary issues in society, they should be encouraged to take positions regarding the past, as it is processes through time which have contributed to the construction of societies. Some relativists might argue that such intersubjective communities are objectionable on the grounds that they stifle individuality. For example, one writer has asserted that

> Not only does this ideal of shared subjectivity express an impossibility, but it has undesirable political implications. Political theorists and activists should distrust this desire for reciprocal recognition and identification with others, I suggest, because it denies difference in the concrete sense of making it difficult for people to respect those with whom they do not identify. I suggest that the desire for mutual understanding and reciprocity underlying the ideal of community is similar to the desire for identification that underlies racial and ethnic chauvinism.
>
> (Young 1990, p. 311)

Such a simplistic decrial of the idea of community is flawed on a number of levels. First of all, the promotion of the radical individual, supposedly freed from the constraints of society, is, as I have detailed elsewhere, an uncritical acceptance of Neo-Conservative ideology. More important, it denies the understanding that for an individual to exist with rights there must be a concurring society to confer those rights: 'since the free individual can only maintain his [sic] identity within a culture/society of a certain kind, he has to be concerned about the shape of this society/culture as a whole' (Taylor 1985, p. 207). The individual cannot exist as an isolated entity removed from surrounding societal processes. Second, Young would seem to be assuming that communities are necessarily constituted by people from the same ethnic group, the same sex or even the same class. Young is possibly guilty of assuming that communities are constructed along the lines of simple binary oppositions, black/white, male/female, or working class/landed class. So-called 'postmaterial political communities' transgress the traditional well-defined boundaries in the form of single issue groups.

There is no reason why communities with positions *vis-à-vis* their place should not also flourish. Such communities are of course not restricted to understanding their place purely in terms of the development of the material environment. Although it is a cliché, people do make places, and an understanding of how people affect places is crucial. Projects which aim to develop an understanding of localities should ensure that those people who have recently moved into a place are not disfranchised. The history of many places is one constituted by processes of both emigration and immigration. An overemphasis on material culture, and associated trading networks, should be avoided, whilst emphasis should be placed on the influences of groups of people on places. The myth of the 'traditional' indigenous society should be exposed, while the problems that are associated with immigration should be highlighted and discussed. As Merriman has argued in his discussion of a display on 'the peopling of London', if we look back far enough in time we are all immigrants of some sort, as initially all hominids originated from out of Africa.

It should be emphasised that communities of intersubjective understanding need not be constructed along orthodox class or ethnic lines. '*Ethnic* interests also intersect with class, gender and other dimensions in the community, the workplace, the local and national state, and – sometimes – the household' (Bagguley *et al.* 1990, p. 140). It should be clear that an understanding of place is developed through a commonality which is constructed on the basis of a shared intersubjectivity, not bound by gender, race or class (although positions regarding the past will be necessarily influenced by such factors), but one developed through a common position regarding the processes which affect places. Such communities are not place-specific but are developed along the lines of intra- and inter-place commonality. Since the emergence of multinational capital such communities are potentially global, as many places are subjected to similar processes over time and space. The bottom line in the postmodern world must be *making connections*.

Whatever method is employed, cognitive mapping must be about developing an understanding of those forces which influence places. We have only to look at the success, even if limited, of campaigns against multinationals such as Barclays Bank, or the strategies of Greenpeace, where local organisation has proved crucial for dealing with a problem which is undeniably global. Such strategies are successful because of the realisation that *making connections* across both time and space is the key to an effective politics.

Part 4

Archaeology and history

Chapter 17

The nature of history

Jonathan Last

ANNALES HISTORY AND ITS RELATION TO ARCHAEOLOGY

In recent decades, archaeologists have rarely shown more than passing interest in history and the theoretical issues of historical interpretation. This is somewhat odd given the 'historical' (in the sense of temporally concerned) nature of our discipline. Instead, archaeology's principal influences have come from anthropology and from the sciences: particularly evolutionary biology, which sees change as an externally driven, adaptive process rather than one of historical contingency; and philosophy of science, especially the Hempelian logico-positivism underlying the New Archaeology. Postprocessual archaeology has recently rediscovered the social sciences, and the anti-histories of Claude Lévi-Strauss, whose reified mental structures allow no room for historical change, and Michel Foucault, whose 'history' has been extensively criticised on empirical grounds (Vilar 1985) – although this does not invalidate his theoretical project. For their part, historians have generally been concerned more with methodology and the problems of interpreting texts than with the wider issues of understanding the past. Hence the archaeology of historic periods has had little theoretical input from documentary history and is frequently characterised as an atheoretical 'handmaid of history' (at least in Britain; for America, by way of contrast, see the historically situated structuralism of Glassie 1975, Deetz 1977). Historians have generally distrusted grand theorists – who now reads Toynbee? – and Foucault has contrasted the Hegelian view of history common among philosophers with the real-life practices of the historian (Chartier 1988).

Against this particularist trend in history has been the Annales school in France, named from the journal *Annales d'histoire économique et sociale* (renamed *Annales: économies, sociétés, civilisations* in 1946) founded by Marc Bloch and Lucien Febvre in 1929 (for more detailed discussion, see Stoianovich 1976, Burke 1990). The main aims of Bloch and Febvre were to initiate a multi-disciplinary approach (in the early days the interest was in psychology, sociology and economics) and to overcome the prevailing emphasis on political history and 'great men' by considering economic and social factors. This led to some radical changes in the methodology and theory of history, as Aron Gurevich describes, particularly the rejection of notions of objectivity typified by Ranke's stated wish to write history 'as it really was' (*wie es eigentlich gewesen*), and an interest in *mentalités* – not the history of ideas, which is an élitist, 'great man' concept, but the history of ideologies, worldviews and mental structures, in other words the historical context. In this respect, Febvre was interested in historical psychology, Bloch in the Durkheimian notion of collective representations.

The second Annales generation of the 1950s and 1960s was dominated by the figure of Fernand Braudel. His seminal *La Méditerranée et le monde méditerranéan à l'époque de Philippe II* was published in 1946, although not translated into English until 1972 (translation of the second (heavily revised) French edition). Braudel's history was revolutionary in its approach to time and space. He studied the history of a region in terms of its human geography and topography. Ultimately historical events were constrained or even determined by these geographical structures: Mediterranean life has 'clay foundations' (Braudel 1972, p. 352). For example, the mountainous areas of the Mediterranean basin can be characterised as lawless and places of refuge throughout history because of their topography: 'for the mountains are a refuge from soldiers and pirates, as all the documents bear witness, as far back as the Bible' (ibid., p. 31). 'Their history is to have none, to remain almost always on the fringe of the great waves of civilisation, even the longest and most persistent, which may spread over great distances in the horizontal plane but are powerless to move vertically when faced with an obstacle of a few hundred metres' (ibid., p. 34).

Braudel discerned temporal structures of historical change at three levels: the *histoire éventuellement* of events and individuals, the stuff of traditional history; the *moyenne durée* of economic, social and political structures, 'the history of groups, collective destinies and general trends' (ibid., p. 353), governed particularly by the rhythms of wages and prices; and the *longue durée*, the nearly timeless geohistory of the relationship between humans and their environment. In fact Braudel saw these as abstractions from an infinite number of *durées* or temporal levels, but it is clear from the structure of the work that Braudel privileges the *longue durée*: events are seen as mere foam, exciting but epiphenomenal, on the surface of a sea below which the deep currents of history run undisturbed: 'events are the ephemera of history; they pass across its stage like fireflies, hardly glimpsed before they settle back into darkness, as often as not into oblivia . . . every historical landscape . . . is illumined by the intermittent flame of the event' (ibid., p. 901). Even Philip himself is not a 'free agent', but the prisoner of this historical cage. Musing on the events of 1571, the year of Lepanto, Braudel (ibid., p. 1243) asks: 'What degree of freedom was possessed by Philip II, or by Don John of Austria as he rode at anchor among his ships, allies and troops? Each of these so-called freedoms seems to me to resemble a tiny island, almost a prison.'

This type of history, brilliantly continued in the three volumes of *Civilisation and Capitalism*, and finally in *The Identity of France*, has been greatly influential but has also attracted a number of serious criticisms. These relate to three main areas:

1 The lack of a consideration of *mentalités*. Braudel was less interested in these than was Febvre whose death prevented him writing the planned companion volume to *Civilisation and Capitalism* on thought and belief, but the division of the work in this way was symptomatic of Braudel's belief that the true historical context lay at the much deeper structural level.

2 This naturally led to charges of determinism. It has been suggested more than once that the powerlessness of the individual in the face of long-term structures mirrors Braudel's personal experience of the prison camp in which he first wrote *La Méditerranée*. In any case, the deficient concept of agency is a problem, as with the theories of Althusser and Lévi-Strauss.

3 Moreover, the geographical framework is portrayed as static and not susceptible to human intervention when in fact human practices were significantly altering the environment – through deforestation, for instance – even within the period covered by *La Méditerranée*.

These criticisms of Braudel are crucial as they exemplify the main concerns of attempts to reconcile subjectivist and objectivist approaches seen in other social sciences and discussed further below. The third Annales generation attempted to overcome these shortcomings of Braudel's work, although objectivist strategies also continued. Braudel had, for instance, used statistics in a decorative fashion, but among other historians a serious interest in quantitative methods led to the development of serial history, and the notions of *structure* and *conjoncture* to describe levels of economic temporality were coined by Pierre Chaunu. This may be seen as part of an attempt to make history a science, deriving more from Braudel than from Bloch or Febvre who were more interested in the rather unscientific concept of *mentalités*. Serial history tended to substitute the 'objectivity' of statistics for the narrative structures of traditional history, which were perceived to be too close to the style of literary discourse to be scientific. The natural sciences had long since expunged the narrative mode from their own discourse. But Hayden White (1987, chs 1, 2) has argued that a narrative does not have to suffer from the dramatisation and humanism which were the main Annales criticisms of traditional history. Indeed, philosophers of history like White and Paul Ricoeur have argued that narrative is an integral part of historical discourse, even such as Braudel's (see below).

On the other hand, an interest in *mentalités*, particularly in the work of the medievalists Jacques Le Goff and Georges Duby, was paralleled by a rediscovery of cultural anthropology, seen in works like Emmanuel Le Roy Ladurie's *Montaillou* (1975). Despite doubts about the accuracy of the statements of the 'informants' (which were collected under the duress of the Inquisition) this book about a late-medieval Cathar village is the best-known example of this strain of 'historical anthropology', and shows the regional and microhistorical approaches characteristic of the third Annales generation. But more recently there has been a return, albeit more self-conscious and theoretically informed, to narrative and political history, particularly biography. Paul Veyne typifies the hostility to the old buzzwords of *histoire globale*, *la longue durée* and *mentalités collectives*. The rediscovery of agency can be seen as a reaction against Braudel's objectivist type of history, but perhaps the structural baby has been thrown out with the determinist bathwater.

This discussion of the Annales school is important for a number of reasons. It shows that 'Annales' must not be reduced to Braudel, nor even seen as representing a unified approach (*pace* Bintliff 1991). It needs to be considered in the generational terms outlined here, as part of an ongoing debate concerning the theoretical status of important concepts like structure and *mentalité*. The vigour of the debate is related to the quality of the work produced over the years and begs the question of the lack of archaeological concern with or input into Annales, a lack that despite recent, belated theoretical interest (Hodder 1987a, Bintliff, ed., 1991, Knapp, ed., 1992) was not rectified at this conference, where Gurevich's and Alain Schnapp's papers remained largely undiscussed. Schnapp attempts to tackle the question of why archaeology, particularly in France, has missed this historical line of insight and argues that the discipline has been set since the nineteenth century in a natural science framework. Another reason is the failure of Annales history to produce a body of theoretical literature, part of the general antipathy of professional historians to Hegelian-type philosophy. The postprocessual (in the broadest sense, in order to include Bintliff) interest in Annales history and related social theory will be discussed below, along with the wider issues this raises of the interrelationship between subject and object, structure and agency.

ARCHAEOLOGY AND HISTORY

The responses of Ian Hodder (ed., 1987b) and John Bintliff (1991) to Annales history are interesting for their differences. Hodder is chiefly concerned with the long-term Braudelian paradigm because of its insistence on process – that is historical process – rather than the 'causal functional explanation' (Hodder 1987, p. 2) which characterises 'processual' archaeology. Clearly the possibility of a materialist and truly historical long-term study would appeal to the postprocessual project. But we have already criticised Braudel for the static nature of his long-term *géohistoire*. In fact, to admit process Hodder introduces ideological structures to the *longue durée*, which Braudel would presumably see as part of the medium term. An example is Georges Dumézil's 'trifunctional' ideological structure of Indo-European society. This is a clear prelude to Hodder's ideas about long-term ideological structures in the European Neolithic – the discourses of 'domus' and 'agrios' discussed in *The Domestication of Europe* (Hodder 1990). In accordance with the thrust of this work, Hodder, like Braudel, underplays shorter-term historical change and reproduction. Hodder does recognise Braudel's failure adequately to conceptualise the relationship between events and structures (Hodder, ed., 1987b, p. 6), but *The Domestication* arguably does not follow this through, and Hodder's conference paper, as we shall see, raises the same issues.

Bintliff (1991, p. 4) argues that Annales history may allow us to overcome the problems of the New Archaeology while preserving its central concepts – in other words, a more conservative reading of Annales history than Hodder's: '. . . the Annales methodology can be seen as complementary, rather than contradictory to the central concepts and approaches of the "New" format subjects.' In fact, as Gurevich discussed and I mentioned above, an important strand of Annales thinking has been opposed to the positivism of the 'New' approaches in social science. We must not overlook the influence of figures like Michel Foucault and Paul Ricoeur who, although not part of the Annales scene, have been very influential upon its more recent practitioners (Chartier 1988). As I made clear above, Annales represents a number of different and even opposed modes of thought that do not submit too well to being presented as a unified body of theory, as Bintliff in particular is attempting to do. In suggesting Annales history provides a means for theorising the interaction between structures and events, he overlooks the fact that individual Annales scholars have tended to emphasise one or the other – hence a process more of oscillation than of resolution – largely because, although they were aware of the problem, explicit theorisation of the issues has been lacking.

The most interesting comment with regard to archaeology in Bintliff's volume is that by Anthony Snodgrass (1991, p. 57), who argues that 'to put forward structural history, or indeed any other kind of history, as a model for archaeological approaches to the past is surely to privilege the status of historical archaeology'. Here, indeed, is a way to inject a theoretical perspective into the archaeology of historic periods; for, as Snodgrass and other contributors show, one can fit together the historical and archaeological data more constructively than has been the case up till now by utilising an approach based on Braudelian temporality. Specifically, archaeology can provide evidence of a longer-term nature, allowing investigation of the dialectic between geographical and socio-economic structures on the one hand and historical events on the other. The use of survey data and approaches to the landscape in order to build up a regional picture provides the necessary spatial dimension. But essentially this is a call for advancing the integration of different perspectives rather than for a distinctly new theorisation of past societies.

So what are we to make of Bintliff's implied claim that the approach is relevant also to prehistoric archaeology, the details of which, however, he fails to spell out? Graham Barker (1991, p. 39) in the same volume makes the point that events cannot be discerned in prehistory: '. . . the search for *événements* by cultural prehistorians earlier this century tended to create a narrative prehistory peopled by Beaker Folk, Urnfielders, Marnians and the rest, that is now almost universally recognised to have been pseudo-history rather than prehistory. We make better use of the material at our disposal in evaluating it for trends and processes.'

In Barker's case-study of the Biferno valley in Italy, the dominant figure in the prehistoric sequence is the valley itself, like Braudel's Mediterranean, and its topographical constraints on communication, settlement and agriculture. This is interesting, but far from novel – in this sense archaeologists have been writing 'geohistory' for years. How it relates to people, which is the historical side of the coin, is, however, far from clear – this is where prehistoric archaeology can still learn from historical debates. The reaction to Braudelian history has shown that human agency is a necessary part of *historical* explanation. Archaeology may not be able to produce individuals, but it can produce knowledgeable agents who are more than cultural dupes. However, we find this theorised less well by historians than by some sociologists, to whom I will turn below.

If Bintliff's volume largely fails to demonstrate through case-studies the degree of relevance of Annales approaches for archaeology which he is seeking to show, a second recent book on archaeology and Annales history (Knapp, ed., 1992), deriving from a series of papers presented at an archaeological congress in Baltimore, is more successful and instructive than Bintliff's. The range of case-studies is broader and the willingness to assess Annales approaches critically, rather than merely to borrow, is refreshing, as is the recognition that Annales means more than Braudel.

Most interesting, perhaps, for prehistoric archaeology is the paper by Duke (1992), who has looked at the rhythms of temporal change in the archaeological record of the Northern Plains. Whereas prehistoric cultures have been seen as unchanging, environmentally adapted, 'cold' societies, the historical period's more rapid change characterised it as 'hot'. Archaeology therefore became subordinate to ethnography and history. However, Duke uses Annales ideas of structure and event, taking up the later Annalistes' shift to a greater concern with the event, and their thinking on structural change to enlighten the prehistoric sequence. For instance, he considers the role of a specific event, such as the adoption of the bow and arrow, in producing broader structural changes in society, in this case relating to the valuation of hunting and its associated material culture. Hence Duke uses Annales thinking to approach the problem of the dialectical relationship between events and structures, discussed in more detail below.

In their summary assessments of the volume, Bulliet and Sherratt both emphasise that, while Annales history won't directly advance archaeology, the encounter is intellectually profitable, although the borrowing of ideas is more fruitful at the level of general aims and outlooks, rather than specific approaches like Braudelian models of temporality. Some of these points are drawn out in a perceptive review of both volumes by C. Delano Smith (1992).

NARRATIVIST APPROACHES TO HISTORY

Beyond Annales, historical theory can provide other radically different insights for archaeology, as exemplified by Hodder's paper. He suggests that archaeological periodisations can be understood in a real sense, that narratives structure people's lives in an analogous way to our structuring of the archaeological record. In other words, temporal classifications are not merely imposed on the data but relate to the lived experience of groups and cultures. The more empirical part of the paper suggests a certain strategic unity to the meaning of material culture in different phases of the Scandinavian Neolithic, in other words that ideology has an overall sense to it over long periods. This does raise interesting questions about the social construction of ideologies, but in pursuing these we would need to move beyond what Hodder has presented in *The Domestication of Europe* and utilise a more comprehensive social theory. Hodder's use of the theories of Hayden White and Paul Ricoeur is novel and interesting but not unproblematic. The main themes need some unpacking.

The first is to do with Ricoeur's assertion that real life is structured as a narrative. This raises the fundamental question of the relationship between 'reality' (lived experience) and representations of that reality (texts or memories). The question of what form history should take and whether narrative is an appropriate mode of historical discourse comes to the fore when we acknowledge the limitations of positivist and poststructuralist approaches. The former, which is exemplified by the covering law approach or Collingwoodian hermeneutics, begins with the denial of any essential difference between past and present. The latter, as in the works of Foucault, stresses the absolute difference of the past and denies fixed reference points like human nature or the concept of 'man'. But deconstruction inevitably provides only a partial and unsatisfactory resolution of the problem of capturing the otherness of the past (see J. Thomas 1991a, pp. 2–6). In between lies the narrativist approach to history. Ricoeur's argument, which is outlined in the three volumes of *Time and Narrative*, is complex, and I can present only an unsatisfactory summary here (based on H. White's 1987 discussion). Both Ricoeur and White argue that narrative is an appropriate – indeed, a necessary – discursive mode for history.

For White it is a question of rhetoric. By pointing out why the text of a medieval annals does not satisfy us as history (H. White 1987, pp. 6–16) he helps us to realise that such a non-history lacks plot, continuity, agency and closure: there is no 'structure' to the events other than the temporal scale into which they are inserted; there are large gaps of blank years when (apparently) nothing happened; events are not the results of human action but just occur – hence a battle is equivalent to a natural event like a bad harvest in its lack of historical cause and effect, and seemingly arbitrary position in the sequence; similarly the annals begins and ends without any contextual scene-setting or summing-up.

What makes acceptable history, therefore, is form and coherence, characteristics provided by narrative. Hence any true history is structured as a narrative, that is, it possesses a plot – even Braudel's *longue durée* – although it does not necessarily narrativise, that is, take the form of a story. The key point is that because narrative is not scientific does not deny it truth-value:

> Narrative historiography may very well . . . 'dramatize' historical events and 'novelize' historical processes, but this only indicates that the truths in which narrative deals are of an order different from those of its social science counterparts. In the historical narrative the systems of meaning production peculiar to a culture or society are tested against the capacity of any set of 'real' events to yield to such systems. If these systems have their purest, most fully developed, and formally most coherent representations in the literary or poetic endowment of modern secularized cultures this is no reason to rule them out as merely imaginary constructions. To do so would entail the denial that literature and poetry have anything valid to teach us about reality.
>
> (H. White 1987, p. 44)

For Ricoeur narrative history has the status of a 'true allegory'; it is an allegory of temporality, but true because historical events possess the same structure as a narrative discourse. Our understanding of the world and of history is based on making such an allegory which 'stands for' but is not reality. This process has three aspects or moments: the prior understanding of human action and temporal structures; the historicality achieved when these events are located within a context, which signifies the role of the plot in 'grasping together' disparate factors like events, agents, goals and consequences; and the actualization of the world presented in the text through the act of reading. These are the *mimeses* discussed by Hodder. The use of this term implies a sort of 'real imitation', a symbolic representation of real events that is realistic because the real events are themselves symbolic, appealing ultimately to the level of 'deep temporality' which underlies all history. If all this seems to elide the distinction between history and fiction, it is true that Ricoeur argues they share the same ultimate referent (temporality) but the immediate referent privileges history, that is, real events, the document or 'trace' (Petit 1989) that maintains the difference between past and present.

What this theory does is provide us with a critique of some of the Annales historians' rejection of narrative, because their conceptualisation is based on too narrowly literary a view of the term: the 'trends and processes' discussed by Barker (1991, p. 39: see above) are just as much a narrative as the 'narrative pseudo-history' he decries. There is also here a critique of the Hempelian logico-positivism which underlies the covering law approach in history as well as the New Archaeology. Hempel argued that explanation takes the same form in history as in natural science, but the crux of the narrativist argument is that *explanation* is not the whole story in the case of history – it can be seen as only a means for *understanding*, the grasping together of events within the coherence of narrative, not subsuming a case under a general law but interpolating a law into a story (Ankersmit 1986, p. 21; Petit 1989).

We are left with the problem we began with, of whether real life can itself be conceived of as a narrative. Ricoeur, like Frederic Jameson (H. White 1987, ch. 6), seems to believe life makes sense only in so far as it is worked into a narrative. Kemp (1989), discussing Ricoeur, argues that because we lack experience of our own birth and death the narrative plot of an individual's life is not a given but a task; and for Jameson narrative achieves the status of a mode of consciousness, making sense of what is otherwise the blind play of contingency. There remains therefore a tension between narrative as immanent in the structure of events and narrative as imposed upon them, but even in the case of the latter it is seen as working at a fundamental level of human consciousness. The question of the distinction between historical reality and its textual representation is shown to be irrelevant when we accept that understanding is impossible outside a narrative representation.

We should therefore conclude that narrative is a necessary form of historical explanation, and that any attempt to expunge it leads to inadequacies like those of the New Archaeology. But it needs to be exposed as ideological, however much it is a model of 'reality', so that we can allow an appeal to the 'trace', documents and artefacts, to maintain the distinction between history and fiction.

So, in taking such a line of thought, Hodder has tapped into a rich vein of historical theory which archaeologists concerned with the relationship between subject and object would be well advised to attend to. But we may wonder whether Hodder's version of narrative adequately captures the real structure of events. The main area of criticism has to do with the use of White's ideas of 'metahistory', which was developed as an analysis of nineteenth-century historical writing, and the hidden discourse of historians in applying their own preconceptions of the world to the object of historical analysis. In other words, it is a theory of the production of written texts. By using this theory, Hodder asks us to presume an author of and a motive, albeit a hidden one, to lived experience, since the sequence of 'tropes' he finds in the Scandinavian Neolithic follows the logical sequence set out by White. As we are not presuming an external (that is, divine) agent, we must assume Hodder is arguing for some sort of Durkheimian collective representation and the necessary corollary that society is more than the sum of its constituent human parts. This is the only social theory consistent with the ideas about the unfolding of ideological structures discussed in *The Domestication*, which again suggests a certain sequential necessity in the shift from the 'domus' discourse to that of the 'agrios'. Of course, a similar criticism may be lodged against White's temporal sequence of historians' rhetoric, but Hodder's extension of the theory to the domain of lived experience throws the problem into clearer relief.

What Hodder therefore seeks to give us is a view of society that, like Braudel's or Lévi-Strauss's, reduces agents to epiphenomena of structures. Unlike Braudel and Lévi-Strauss, however, these structures are dynamic and changing, but, for all the fact that they are enacted through the situated practices of agents, they are inevitable and necessary in determining those practices, because they follow a preordained narrative scheme. The effect for archaeological interpretation if this is the case is that material culture may be seen as the direct evidence of ideological structures, and we can effectively ignore the individual agents who produced it. To use a theatrical analogy, their parts have been written in advance, and, however effective their performance, the drama will take place in the sequence scripted. In other words, whatever lip-service Hodder may pay to situated practices, agents' freedom to act otherwise is constrained to an extent that they are no longer agents in the accepted sense.

Although Hodder spoke during the conference discussion of 'dialectical interactive meaning', the interaction he implies is one between archaeologists and long-term ideological structures, not historically situated agents. Hodder seems to make the error of confusing narrative as a means of 'grasping together' disparate factors to make sense of the world with narrative as a causal factor in history at the level of the *longue durée*, going beyond the arguments of White and Ricoeur. Hodder's scheme replaces the Braudelian prison with the necessity of the story that the past reveals, and in a similar way denies agency.

We therefore need to discuss the concept of agency, which many participants felt was not adequately covered at the conference. It is not, however, a magic word that gets us out of the structuralists' problem. Hodder's paper should not be taken, to mix a metaphor, as a straw man to be instantly demolished with a salvo of structuration theory. Attempts to bridge the dichotomy between objectivism and subjectivism are at the heart of contemporary debate in social theory.

STRUCTURE AND AGENCY

Agency, to 'action theorist' philosophers, is characterised by volition and intention, and cannot be reduced to mere events, although unintended consequences, to the extent that they were the product of an intentional action, can be outcomes of agency. For Moya (1990) the core of agency is a commitment to do something in the future. While decision-making is a norm-following process, it is essentially violable. In other words, the ability of agents to act otherwise is the key to their agency. But there are always practical restrictions on the range of feasible options for action, dependent on the individual's social context, itself a specific manifestation of what may be termed 'social structure'. No man (or woman), then, is an island – but the exact nature of the relationship between structure and agency remains a key problem in social theory. The two philosophical extremes which should be rejected can be characterised as pure objectivism and pure subjectivism.

In the first of these, actions are subject to causal determinism by pre-existing structures, be they the 'system behind the Indian' of functionalist systems theory or the 'deep structures' of the structuralist mindset. In these cases external factors constrain unacceptably individual freedom, with potentially disturbing political implications. It is this reef to which Hodder's theory sails uncomfortably close.

But the other extreme is just as erroneous: the pure subjectivism associated particularly with existentialist perspectives. Sartre, for instance, can be seen as a 'libertarian' postulating every action as a kind of antecedent-less confrontation with the world (Bourdieu 1990a, although others see Sartre as more of an action theorist: e.g., Atwell 1980). The critique sees agents' practice as both enabled and constrained by the social and ideological networks of which, as social beings, they are a part. Individualism is another version of the subjectivist fallacy, for it denies the force of interest groups and collectivities as well as the impact of those pre-existing structures into which individuals are socialised.

The conference debate throws some light on these issues as they pertain to archaeology. One comment heard was that: 'You have the individual in history, but the non-literate past is anonymous and collectivist.' This denies the reality of human agency, which is unaffected both by the degree of literacy in a society and by the archaeological knowledge of that society. As John Barrett said, with reference to Hodder's paper: 'What is missing in all this is the idea of situated practice and a proper understanding of agency. Ian [Hodder] has given us once again the structuralist image. But people occurred there as individual agents – something we can grasp in prehistory and in history. The archaeology of agency and situated practice is missing in so much of what has been talked about.'

Barbara Bender attempted to explain the 'confusion between individuals and agency – what we are talking about is the way people effect change'. The key to agency is not individuality but action. In a sense, to be an agent is to be human; it should be taken for granted, but that does not mean it need not be theorised. Nor should we make the mistake of confusing agency with the 'freedom of the individual' that is one of the 'self-evident truths' of the modern worldview. Agency can also be collective, through kin-groups, age-sets and so on. The problem for social theorists becomes one of maintaining a sense of individual autonomy within the wider conception of agency to avoid the concept merely disguising a neo-objectivism.

We should therefore discuss two major perspectives aimed at overcoming the objectivist and subjectivist dualism and constructively integrating structure and agency. The first is that of Pierre Bourdieu, and the notion of 'habitus' (Bourdieu 1990a, 1990b). Bourdieu pursued ethnographic research in Algeria in the 1960s and noticed that the kinship relations stressed in practice were not the full range of logical relations that a structuralist analysis might have discovered. More generally, practical action was merely a subset of theoretically permissible actions. He argued that practice was conditioned by what he termed the habitus, a system of structured, structuring and durable dispositions produced historically. The habitus varies between individuals, but individual habitus are in a relationship of homology. These dispositions constrain and provide for action at the level of practical knowledge, those things which are known and do not need to be consciously articulated: for instance, kinship relations or the performance of certain rituals. Action mediated by the habitus is instinctive and regulated. Bourdieu (1990b, pp. 62–70) uses a sporting analogy: the 'players' have a 'feel for the game', which equips them to pursue conscious strategies:

> I described the double game strategies which consist of playing in conformity with the rules, making sure right is on your side, acting in accord with your interests while all the time seeming to obey the rules. One's feel for the game is not infallible; it is shared out unequally between players, in a society as in a team.

Hence their knowledgeable agency is not compromised. The habitus frequently sacrifices rigour for simplicity, and rites or beliefs that make sense in practice may appear counter-logical or contradictory in a broader view:

> symbolic systems owe their practical coherence – that is, on the one hand, their unity and their regularity, and on the other, their "fuzziness" and their ir-regularities and even incoherences, which are both equally necessary, being inscribed in the logic of their genesis and functioning – to the fact that they are the product of practices that can fulfil their practical functions only in so far as they implement, in the practical state, principles that are not only coherent – that is capable of generating practices that are both intrinsically coherent and compatible with the objective conditions – but also practical, in the sense of convenient, that is, easy to master and use, because they obey a 'poor' and economical logic.
>
> (Bourdieu 1990a, p. 86)

Bourdieu (ibid.) gives the example of occasions when the house is symbolically divided into male and female halves, contradictory to a wider set of beliefs which portrays the whole house as female in contrast to the 'male' land. But such structures are not a neutral symbolic scheme – practice is always a struggle for domination, as Robbins (1991, pp. 148–9) makes clear:

> Bourdieu realised that there were within Algerian society people who possessed the socially delegated authority to retain intellectual mastery over the agrarian calendar which constituted the structure within which social practices oper-ated. . . . Institutionalized rituals excluded the polythetic practices of individuals and functioned as mechanisms of domination.

The habitus may be codified to different extents, that is, the social 'game' may be given explicit rules; and for complex (or 'differentiated') societies Bourdieu intro-duces the notion of the 'field', a historically constituted area of activity with specific institutions (the academic field, the political field, etc.). The habitus can produce different practices dependent on the state of the field, so a dialectic is set up between habitus and field. In other respects, however, the existence of the field limits the operation of the habitus:

> in general, in undifferentiated societies . . . the personal strategies of agents have to be constantly renewed, whereas in differentiated societies objectified fields exist within which and between which power is deployed. To put this in the language of 'field'-studies: the genesis of autonomous and institutionalized 'fields' . . . has the effect of consigning personal strategies . . . to a secondary position.
>
> (Robbins 1991, p. 115)

This is an attractive theory which has been noticed by archaeologists (e.g. Hodder 1986, pp. 70–6) but little applied outside ethnoarchaeological studies (e.g., D. Miller 1985, Moore 1986). One problematic feature concerns the means of transformation of the habitus. Although constituted in practice, the habitus is objectified in material culture and ritual. Perhaps because the model originated as a reaction to structuralist interpretations of traditional societies, explaining social change was less of a concern than showing how social rules were realised in practice. In this sense it may translate less fruitfully to modern society. But Bourdieu (1990b, pp. 118–19) has defended himself on this charge:

> I do not see where my readers could have found the model of circular reproduction which they attribute to me (structure-habitus-structure) . . . it is the structure (the tensions, the oppositions, the relations of power which constitute the structure of a specific field or of the social field as a totality at a given point in time) which constitutes the principle of the strategies aimed at preserving or transforming the structure.

> Although apparently situated between structure and practice, there is little sense of a generative dialectic through the habitus. Bourdieu's realisation that the French education system was largely impervious to re-structuring may have influenced his tendency to abstract structure as something largely unchanging. Bourdieu has difficulty in explaining revolutionary change because he believes that any revolution is dependent on the existence of anticipatory conditions which alone can bring it into actuality. . . . The gradualism which seems inevitable for Bourdieu as a theory of social change also applies in respect of individuals.
>
> (Robbins 1991, p. 173)

However, because archaeology deals largely with change over the relatively long term, we need to clarify the processes of social transformation.

A more self-consciously dialectical approach is Anthony Giddens's theory of structuration (Giddens 1982, 1984, Cohen 1989, Bryant and Jary, eds, 1991). The concept of structuration is similar to that of the habitus but it is not objectified in the same way. Rather, structuration is the set of conditions that intervene between structure and practice to ensure the reproduction or transformation of that structure. Giddens argues that the relationship between structure and agency is one of 'duality' (each is implicated in the production of the other) rather than 'dualism' (categorical opposition). Hence Giddens argues that 'the structural properties of social systems are both medium and outcome of the practices that constitute those systems' (1982, pp. 36–7); or, again, that: 'analysing the structuration of social systems means studying the modes in which such systems, grounded in the knowledgeable activities of situated actors who draw upon rules and resources in the diversity of action contexts, are produced and reproduced in interaction' (1984, p. 25).

Social action, in Giddens's theory, is to the structural properties as an utterance is to the rules of grammar (1982, p. 37). A comprehensible speech-act contributes to the reproduction of the grammatical and syntactical system as a whole. Similarly, agents draw upon the rules and resources to produce and reproduce activities. This is similar to Bourdieu's notion of practical actions abstracted from a notional set of logical relations. For Giddens, continuity in action is achieved by the high degree of routinisation of practice, action that is carried out at the level of practical consciousness, and which does not need to be articulated. Routinised practice is therefore Giddens's equivalent of the durable dispositions of the habitus. But Giddens tries to allow more freedom to agents; in his theory, power is very important – the key to successful action is the ability to mobilise resources, both 'allocative' (material) and 'authoritative' (related to production and organization) in order to achieve outcomes, either at a group or an individual level: 'Power . . . is generated in and through the reproduction of structures of dominance' (Giddens 1984, p. 258). Agents may act to maintain or transform structures, but they are always constrained or enabled by differential access to resources and by their own practical competence.

Change does seem easier to visualise in Giddens's scheme, but it tends to be externalised, occurring at 'time–space edges' between different sets of structures of routinised practices and at the junctions 'between societies of differing structural type' (ibid., p. 244). This means that for 'tribal cultures' where 'the boundaries between different "societies" are usually not clearly marked' (ibid., p. 195) change becomes harder to allow or account for. But it is important to make the point that change and stability are essentially the same, as outcomes of reproductive practice. This is necessary in order to escape the systems theory approach which has to posit a special causality for change as opposed to the natural state of equilibrium. In fact, stability needs explaining just as much as change (Shanks and Tilley 1987b, p. 212).

Nigel Thrift (quoted in Cohen 1989, p. 201) has criticised Giddens's silence on the institutions that establish a linkage between structure and agency. At the level of the latter, an account is needed of how subjects' wants and needs are differentially formed (J. Thompson 1989, p. 74). In stressing that societies are permeable and only loosely articulated, Giddens tends to obscure the mechanism of their transformation or reproduction. Derek Gregory (1989) points out that, although Giddens's time–space model could be made to yield all sorts of transformations, his particular concern with practical consciousness and routinisation overemphasizes the likelihood of social stability.

Giddens (1989, p. 277) does not agree with this criticism. All I can do in the space available is to try to convey the character of an ongoing debate. Giddens's and Bourdieu's theories have not been seriously discussed by archaeologists, or directly compared by anyone. In the context of this brief discussion, we may conclude that Bourdieu's theory better establishes the linkage between structure and agency by positing the intervening habitus; Giddens's is less prone to the reduction of agency that the objectification of the habitus often implies.

The differences probably relate to different psychological conceptions of agency. One problem with structuration theory is its consistent rationality – Giddens seems to assume that human nature has not essentially changed, and does not suggest how or when the 'rational agent' of his theory was generated. His concern with analysing capitalism tends to take the modern worldview as a given. Giddens's 'rational actor' is very much a modern, Freudian concept; Bourdieu in contrast argues against a controlling 'self' and in favour of a persona generated by particular social conditions (Robbins 1991, p. 172). Another factor is the differing empirical origins of the theories: in an ethnographic study on the one hand, with action much regulated by tradition, and in a historical study of modern capitalism and the social fluidity that implies on the other. Archaeologists, especially prehistorians, deal largely with small-scale societies which are regulated by traditions embodied in ritual and material culture, and are socially less fluid: in Giddens's terms, they show low distanciation and high routinisation. Hence the habitus with its 'fuzzy logic' and strategic rather than totalising rationalisations, particularly as objectified in material culture, may be a more helpful concept for archaeologists; but, nevertheless, societies do change and Giddens's ideas of agency, distanciation, and power resources, particularly within a framework deriving from the time-geography of Hägerstrand, may be useful in articulating social trajectories.

Other perspectives in social theory are critical of the structurationist approach. Poststructuralists would argue that the 'knowledgeable actor' is a fiction, under-valuing the constraints operative in modern society. Foucault has suggested that the social sciences are implicated in the legitimation of this society, so this theory cannot be the neutral 'ontology of potentials' (Cohen 1989, p. 11) it claims to be. Boyne (1991, p. 73) suggests that the dissolution of the subject which is part of the poststructuralist project could provide an argument that the agent is merely a 'mytheme generated . . . by the virtual structures of the social unconscious'. But poststructuralism is handicapped, perhaps fatally, by the fact that its attempt to overturn rationalism must be conducted within a rationalist discourse (Callinicos 1991). Ultimately, if, as archaeologists, we accept the existence of a real past (however knowable), we cannot avoid objectifying it to some extent, positing it as other than the present, even while we admit the subjective, hermeneutic nature of interpretation. Indeed, to accept the past as other, to maintain a difference, as Ricoeur does, for instance, allows us to challenge the naturalised, taken-for-granted nature of many aspects of modern society. We cannot therefore afford to ignore the historicity of our discipline, and we must admit this dialectic between structure and agency.

Archaeological interventions into this whole debate have been rather sparse. Much of the postprocessual debate has been concerned with the nature of interpretation of the past and the status of the archaeologist, rather than social theory, which tends to have utilised borrowed structuralist and Marxist approaches. Hence, as Matthew Johnson (1989) points out, important papers like Shanks and Tilley's (1982) or Leone's (1984) lack a historical theory of the agent. John Barrett (1987, p. 9) suggests archaeology can be seen as evidence for practices, and their material situation (a materiality captured better by Bourdieu's habitus than by Giddens): 'Social practices are the object of our study: archaeology is the empirical examination of material evidence to discover how such practices were maintained within particular material conditions.'

Structuration theory can allow us to move beyond the purely descriptive use of time and space that characterises most archaeology, and to show how human lives are structured in time–space. Ultimately archaeology needs to be able to deal with the long-term vista of prehistory and make sense of changes in material culture within a narrative that does not do away with the agent but recognises the play of difference in material culture variability and finds in this variability the contingent circumstances which lead to change and are comprehensible within a narrative structure. Hence we also need to theorise the relationship between material culture and social structure – which is essentially an archaeological problem.

The narrative coherence we will find is one of retrospective necessity – in other words, meaning is clear in hindsight but does not follow any pre-given, structurally determined sequence of change. The contingency of history becomes thinkable, and life becomes livable, only when grasped into this sort of meaningful narrative which endows events with significance on the basis of their retrospective importance.

HISTORY THAT HURTS

Michael Shanks made similar points about narrative, but the key to his contribution lies in the statement that: 'Historical stories told are also . . . of the human pain of history. History is not simply . . . an intellectual act of construction and creation but demands a poetics and the recognition of death and decay, which are the heart of history' (transcript from conference tapes). Shanks asks us to start from the materiality of artefacts, which ties into their history, a history which traces a continuous path through time and space, not separating past from present. But the affective and aesthetic aspects of these artefacts tell a human story, an ideological story which allows us to critique our concepts and assumptions. Hence he argues, for instance, that the assertion of identity, of agency is a contingent, ideological act. The modern notion of the agent, as we saw with Giddens, is just one strategy of assertion. The pots may tell other stories.

Joan Gero in turn saw, following Frederic Jameson, that 'history is what hurts'. In trying to get at the experiential dimension of history we need to look more at the agent and her or his situation in practices that manifest and reproduce absent structures. This is what Shanks has sought to do by the detailed study of a single Korinthian pot.

This is, of course, but one side of the coin: to assess subjectivity in the past demands also a recognition of the subjectivity of the interpreter, in other words a critique of our own discourses and practices. It is this sociology of the discipline that Gero set out to provide a framework for. Her paper demonstrates that there are always stakes in the production of a narrative. Gero points out that they have to do with the following issues:

1 The contingent circumstances of archaeological discoveries. This is similar to Renfrew's (1977) critique of the culture concept, in which he argues that type-sites which serve to define a 'culture' do so only by virtue of the primacy of their discovery. As he puts it (ibid., pp. 94–5):

> If the excavator first digs at P and recovers its assemblage he will subsequently learn that adjacent points have a broadly similar assemblage which he will call 'the P culture'. Gradually its boundaries will be set up by further research, with the criterion that only those assemblages which attain a given threshold level of similarity with the finds from P qualify for inclusion. So a 'culture' is born, centring on P, the type-site, whose boundaries are entirely arbitrary, depending solely on the threshold level of similarity and the initial, fortuitous choice of P as the point of reference.

The situation is no doubt overstated, since in reality all sorts of historical, geographical, practical and personal factors impinge on this sort of pure research. But it makes clear the necessity to be aware of the specific history of any research area.

2 The context of archaeological finds. Here it was the points found in direct contact with extinct animals that allowed the definition of a Palaeoindian culture, and also led to the acceptance of a 'Man the Hunter' paradigm for this research.

3 Cultural preconceptions. Here specifically the corollaries of the idea of 'Man the Hunter', specifically the valuation and gendered reconstruction of the practice of hunting. But we could think of other examples.

For instance, Bernhardt (1986) took the opportunity of a reassessment of the European early Neolithic site of Köln-Lindenthal to study the interpretation of Neolithic houses through the earlier part of this century. Many German archaeologists saw 'dwelling-sites' as indicators of folk customs and ethnic types. The theory was that, while built houses occurred on the culturally advanced tell-sites of south-east Europe, 'barbarian' populations in northern Europe could only recognise earth-holes as dwellings. There was developed an evolutionary typological sequence of: pit dwellings – tents/yurt – roofed houses. Although other scholars saw building types as related more to environment and climate than to ethnicity, when post-built structures began to be encountered in a Neolithic context they were often seen as granaries rather than as dwellings because ethnographers argued that in North America, for instance, granaries were often built more lavishly than houses. Hence the situation of Buttler and Haberey's original (1936) publication of Köln-Lindenthal in which the larger burrow pits were seen as dwellings and the well-built post-houses as granaries. From a modern viewpoint this is a quite bizarre interpretation, but one that is comprehensible as the outcome of a particular historical discourse. As Thomas Kuhn (1970, p. 111) has described for the natural sciences, once a particular paradigm or set of theories is replaced by another, scientists' perception of the world changes so radically that the world itself may as well have altered.

4 Aesthetic judgements. The distinctive style of the Folsom points was important for the development of this discourse as it served to focus attention on this class of artefacts above any other. Similarly the aesthetics of classical archaeology have helped to define the discourse of that subdiscipline (see section below (appendix) on classical archaeology and disciplinary ownership).

5 Research structure and strategies of data collection. In other words, both professional career structures and field methodologies are implicated in the reproduction and persistence of a particular discourse. The same ideas are passed on from one generation of scholars to their students, who become the next generation. Anyone coming in from outside with a new way of looking at the material may not be accepted precisely because they have not had the usual training in the conservative tradition. In fieldwork these traditions may be enshrined in research designs, choice of sites and recording methods. Fieldwork in some areas of the United States may also have its own ideology and set of values, like the Near Eastern archaeology of the later nineteenth century which celebrated 'both the lone male and the machinery of civilisation' and consequently prescribed female gender roles as 'to observe, receive, admire' (Hinsley 1989, p. 94). Hence present archaeological practice may reinforce particular interpretations of the past.

The contingent nature of 'paradigm shifts' in scientific research has been discussed by Thomas Kuhn (1970) in terms of a build-up of problems with an established paradigm. At first they can be accommodated by making small modifications to the existing paradigm, or by ignoring them. This is part of the practice of 'normal science', described by Kuhn (ibid., p. 10) as research based on achievements that some scientific community acknowledges as supplying the foundation for further practice. A particular paradigm operates as a 'criterion for choosing problems that . . . can be assumed to have solutions' (ibid., p. 37), and a project not conforming to the expectations set by the paradigm 'is usually just a research failure, one which reflects not on nature but on the scientist' (ibid., p. 35). Hence a set of theories and research questions and practices becomes self-fulfilling.

But eventually the whole system has to give, and a 'scientific revolution' or 'paradigm shift' occurs. To evoke a crisis, an anomalous result must call into question fundamental principles of the paradigm, or inhibit important practical applications (ibid., p. 82). Many years ago, Max Planck realised that 'a new scientific truth does not triumph by convincing its opponents and making them see the light, but rather because its opponents eventually die, and a new generation grows up that is familiar with it' (quoted in ibid., p. 151).

This is an idea that was echoed by Colin Renfrew in an earlier conference session. But whether paradigm shifts in this sense occur in archaeological theory (such as the transition to the New Archaeology in the USA: Meltzer 1979) is still debated, largely because of Kuhn's own rather vague definition of a paradigm (see Kuhn 1974). In any case, it is arguable that archaeological 'paradigms' are even less easy to upset by anomalous evidence than is the case in hard science, because data require more contextual interpretation and are easier to assimilate into a pre-given framework. The early Neolithic pit-dwellings discussed above are a good example, based on preconceptions rather than on 'objective' assessment of the data. A truly revolutionary change in archaeology was the development of an independent chronology provided by C-14 dates, which upset traditional theories of culture change in Europe (Renfrew 1973). Although that was based on hard science, which archaeologists rarely question, several older scholars with heavy stakes in defending the traditional views, and hence the validity of their work, refused to accept C-14 dating. Its populariser, Colin Renfrew, fitted Kuhn's (1970, p. 90) statement that 'the men who achieve these fundamental inventions of a new paradigm have been either very young or very new to the field whose paradigm they change'.

These are largely historical conditions, and we might now return full circle and conclude by looking again at history. What Joan Gero's paper asks us to consider is why archaeology has not produced a critical history of itself. The main texts for the history of archaeology make little attempt to situate archaeological theory and methodological developments in a social or political context. Glyn Daniel's *The Origin and Growth of Archaeology*, for instance, is very much a 'great man', history-of-ideas approach – the genius of the individual is the key to the development of archaeological theory, and as we meet them first their names are capitalised. Daniel's *The Idea of Prehistory* shows a similar avoidance of social context ('Real prehistory begins with men like these striving to understand man's prehistoric past': Daniel 1962, p. 12) and celebrates the 'great men' with whom the author can sometimes link himself: 'We are, at first, mainly concerned with a very great man [Grafton Elliot Smith] who was a Fellow of my own College in Cambridge' (ibid., p. 88).

Recently, Bruce Trigger's more ambitious *History of Archaeological Thought* has paid more attention to the social context of archaeology, 'the changing relations between archaeological interpretation and its social and cultural milieu', but lacks the detailed exposition of sociological and political dimensions that Gero's case-study eloquently suggests we need. The arguments flowing in archaeological theory about the relations of structure and agency have washed over the history of the discipline, where a social structure is frequently absent. But the example of classical archaeology and the case-study of the Palaeoindian show that the state of the discipline can hardly be understood without these considerations. Stan Green (conference comment) sums this up: 'I learned some; the conference raised some issues; but for the most part it remained paralysed by its politics.'

Critical history is a necessary part of grappling with these problems. It helps us to see how archaeological knowledge is constructed. For instance, C. M. Hinsley (1989, p. 80) sees archaeological narrative as a particular and powerful form of origin myth; Alice Kehoe (1989, p. 106) argues that the Three Age System was a variant of the myth of three offers or tests to which a culture hero must respond. She links it to Jacques Derrida's notion of 'white mythology' and suggests the privileging of technology made archaeology suitable to be an instrument of ideology for the industrial societies of the later nineteenth century.

This sort of historical critique of archaeological methods and concepts ties in with the need for a more critical assessment of how we write and communicate our ideas. A paper deriving from a conference such as this cannot adequately convey what went on just by reproducing the papers, or even by transcribing the discussion. What was not said, who was not asked to attend or speak, who chose not to attend, speak, or submit their papers for publication – these are all issues of the sociopolitics of the discipline, and all play their part in determining the success or otherwise of a particular discourse; all are actions which have some impact on the development of ideas in archaeological theory. Hence theory and history/sociology of this kind cannot be separated – and that realisation is related to the clarity with which there emerges from a big conference like Interpretive Archaeologies a sense of just how much personal, social and political factors influence the discourse on theory represented by the text of the conference proceedings. If we wish to overcome the situation whereby, as Gero puts it, 'those who control the railroads [of epistemology] control the surrounding territory', the answer is not merely to try to build new competing railways, but to understand historically how the existing routes came about.

Chapter 18

The French historical revolution

The Annales school

Aron Gurevich

One of the reasons for the Annales' stunning success was recently suggested by Peter Burke (1990, pp. 105–6). Although all, or almost all, achievements of the school taken separately (a special emphasis on social and economic history, an inter-disciplinary approach to history, interest in *géographie humaine* and *géohistoire*, the demonstration of the multiplicity of time, quantitative, local and micro-history, the history of everyday life and of *mentalités*) have had certain antecedents, their unique constellation is, from Burke's point of view, specific to this direction in historiography. I believe there is something in the very nature of the 'New History' that makes it crucial for understanding the leading tendencies in contemporary historical thought.

The most important contributions of the Annales group to the historical profession are, first, a new assessment of the historian's intellectual and professional status; second, a revaluation of the historian's attitude towards sources; and, third, a pioneering understanding of the specificity of history. The 'silent revolution' in the historian's craft initiated by Bloch and Febvre began from a deep reappraisal of the personal stance of the historian. They proclaimed a complete reversal of the relationship between the historian and the past. Historical reflection and analysis begins not from the past, as the positivist historians imagined, but from the historian who constructs his or her object and studies it from the point of view of his or her own time.

Historians are able to comprehend and explain only because they belong to their own culture and share its values. However, there exists a real danger of anachronism if historians apply their systems of values uncritically to the study of other cultures. Having this danger in mind, Bloch and Febvre initiated the study of *mentalités*, for it is exactly such an approach that affords the best remedy against the modernisation of history. The great attention paid to *mentalités* has had deep methodological significance from the very beginning.

The founders of Annales rejected *l'histoire récit* and substituted for it *l'histoire problème*. The historical problem is dictated by the interests and ideas of the society to which the historian belongs. The interaction between the present and the past which was later qualified as a 'dialogue' constitutes the very essence of the historian's profession.

But does the formulation of the historical problem not resemble the construction of Max Weber's 'ideal type'? Is not the idea of the connection between the present and the past the counterpart of the idealist philosopher Rickert's theory that historical study is related to the values that historians share with their own cultures? I am inclined to find some resemblance between the position of the first 'annalists' and Neo-Kantian theoretical postulates, although I do not insist on any direct influence. Most significant is that this shift seems to be connected with a more general change of attitude of creative people towards their objects which took place during the first half of our century.

It is clear from this point of view that the historians of a new cast are very far from the old illusion of being able to 'resurrect' the past, to 'live themselves into it' and to demonstrate it *'wie es eigentlich gewesen war'*. They clearly understood that historical reconstruction is no more and no less than construction, that the historian's role is incomparably more active and creative than their predecessors believed.

The premise of such a statement is that historical knowledge is not monolithic but consists of different blocks or layers. Historians are able to establish true facts: they possess many material remnants of the past and can decipher texts and understand their contents, not only what lies on the surface but also their hidden sense. However, there exists above all these details a general system of relations which forms the all-embracing historical *context*. It is from the context that all facts and phenomena receive their true meaning. Historians cannot but try to resuscitate this context, and as a result every epoch has (to use Febvre's expression) its own idea of ancient Rome or its particular Renaissance. The historical context is reconstructed not only from the 'bricks' collected from the sources, but also with the help of the 'ideal type' formed by the historian, based on the contemporary view of the past. It is the present that gives the historian an understanding of the general tenor of the epoch under study.

Here I present an example to illustrate the importance of the historical context.

One of the main sources for the study of the Viking Age in Scandinavia is the hoards of silver and gold coins supposedly hidden in the ground to save them from robbery and the other problems widespread in this period. Some scholars see in these hoards a kind of ancient savings bank. But the question arises as to why nobody at this time tried to dig up this wealth and use it to purchase slaves, land or some other valuables. Moreover, a lot of coins were thrown into pits or into the sea without any view to future recovery. There exists a story about the famous Icelandic poet Egill that when he was old and near to death he took his coffers of silver and brought them with the help of two slaves to an uninhabited part of the country, from where he returned without coffers or slaves. It is obvious, says the Egils Saga Skallagrimssonar, that the coins were hidden and Egill then killed the slaves so nobody could know the location of the hoard.

It seems to me that we can understand the problem of the Viking hoards only if we radically change and widen the historical context. Silver and gold were at this time not only material valuables but primarily a materialisation of magical 'luck'. A person who possessed coins, a sword or a precious cloak given by a king or other chief got from the lord a part of his 'luck' or good fortune, and remained its possessor as long as the object was kept. The wish to protect one's 'luck' and use it in the other world as well as in this life was the main reason for creating hoards. Hence to understand the true meaning of Viking hoards they must be set not only in the context of economic life but primarily in the context of religious beliefs, the importance of magic, and the image of the other world.

Returning to the theoretical discussion, the emphasis laid on the historian's procedures seems extremely important, for an inalienable characteristic of our *métier* is a great moral responsibility. This responsibility is double-sided: one aspect is connected to our contemporaries, for they rely on us in their need to establish communication with the people of the past. The historian is the mediator between two worlds, that of the present and that of the past, and the historical consciousness of society depends on the interpretation given by historians. The other aspect of the historian's responsibility consists in his or her relationship with the people of the past. It is the historian who has the ability to transform the world of the speechless dead into the world of living persons.

The choice of historical sources is dependent on the historical model constructed by the scholar. Therefore it is extremely important to distinguish between the record of the past and the historical source proper. The distinction between monument and document is made by Foucault (1969, pp. 13–15). Historical sources *sensu stricto* do not exist independently of the historian, for the remnant of the past by itself is silent and it begins to speak only when the historian communicates with it. It is the historian who makes the choice, transforming a particular record of the past into a source of information. Nobody except the historian can give to some text or artefact the dignity of the historical source. The revaluation of sources is an important part of the revolution undertaken by the 'new historians'. In the first place they learned to read the traditional sources anew, to penetrate deeper into their texture and to decipher new information and additional meanings within them. The historical monument is inexhaustible; but its value as a source depends on the problem raised by the historian.

In the second place, reappraisal of sources led to the reorganisation of their hierarchy. The sources which had been considered second-rate or accessory acquired new meaning in the light of the new problems. The expression 'historical data' seems to be rather delusive, for nothing is 'given' to historians, who extract the necessary information from the sources by applying to them technical skills and sophisticated procedures. The historical source is not a kind of 'window' through which it is possible to glimpse historical reality. The source is not transparent and unblurred, but it takes great effort on the part of the scholar to penetrate its meanings, for it is a 'prism' which refracts the 'rays' coming from the past according to its own complicated structure.

This situation is rather difficult and extremely tense. On the one hand, it is solely by means of historical sources that we can study the phenomena of the past; but, on the other hand, the sources form a kind of obstacle which must be overcome in order to comprehend the past. The study of history appears primarily as a constant struggle between the historian and the sources which oppose his or her will to establish the truth.

The historian's task consists first of all in decoding the language of the sources. 'Language' is used here in a wide semiological sense, for it is not enough to overcome the purely linguistic difficulties, but it is necessary to decipher the meanings hidden in the texts. To 'demystify the document' means not merely to understand the ideological intentions of its author, but, primarily, to locate it within the general cultural context to which the source belongs. It seems appropriate to mention that the methods used by the Annales historians are better suited to the study of static aspects of history than to the study of change, which remains a great and most complex problem.

The Annales historians clearly understood the deep difference between the methods of the natural sciences and those of the humanities. The former discover the laws of nature while the latter try to understand human behaviour through the differences between different cultures. This methodological dissimilarity presupposes that the historian's approach cannot be analogous to that of the scientist. Of course, all scholars must use in their research the set of notions they receive from contemporary thought. Historians apply to the past such general concepts as 'social formation', 'class', 'state', 'society', 'labour' and 'civilisation'. Using this 'set of co-ordinates' given them by their own vision of social life they select and arrange the information taken from the sources.

However, the question arises of whether such notions were used by the people of the past and, if they used some of them, what meaning they acquired in different periods of history. The history of notions and categories (*Begriffsgeschichte*) is a necessary part of historical study. In other words, the problem of the humanities seems to be as follows: What was the 'set of co-ordinates' which was ingrained into the minds of the people of different periods of history?

Thus, unlike the *Naturwissenschaften*, which work 'objectively' from the outside by applying the notions of the researchers, the *Kulturwissenschaften* need two different and complementary systems of notions, one belonging to the historian which reflects the conceptual universe of contemporary culture, and the other which is specific for the culture of the people being studied. The idea of the necessity to study history 'stereoscopically' is one of the greatest achievements of the Annales school. By introducing such a double vision the historical discipline has found its identity for the first time. The principle of the 'dialogue' presupposes both participants: the present and the past, partakers in the dialogue of cultures, at last acquired their own different voices. The inner, psychological impulses of social behaviour became an inalienable aspect of historical research, transforming it from the study of abstract and superhuman social and economic forces into the history of human beings. The co-ordination of both approaches, 'from without' and 'from within', and their integration into the all-embracing system is an interesting question closely connected with the interpretation of historical process. How do the people of a particular culture solve the problem of the relationship between the *imaginaire* and the real conditions of their existence?

Today the leading tendency seems to be the movement from the history of different *mentalités* taken separately towards anthropologically oriented history, or historical anthropology which studies all aspects of human life as a system. The 'annalists' have found the very nerve of our profession. The Annales was not an isolated phenomenon created by the heroic efforts of Bloch and Febvre alone, but seems to be a significant manifestation of contemporary culture and the deep transformations of the human mind occurring during our century.

Chapter 19

The relations between human and natural history in the construction of archaeology

Alain Schnapp

I shall start with a paradox. Why is it that French archaeology has not managed to integrate a movement of history – the Annales school – which accorded such importance to the material basis of society, an interest called by Braudel 'material civilisation' (not to be confused with 'material culture')? The solution to this paradox is to be found in the 'dominated' character of French archaeology, and also in the prevalent representation archaeologists make of their creed as torn between the natural and human sciences.

Let us consider the formation of the earth sciences through such scholars as Thomas Hooke and Buffon. We realise that both see in the sciences of the antiquarians – *sensu* Camden (sixteenth century), Worm (seventeenth), Maffei or Caylus (both eighteenth) – the model for earth sciences. To construct a geology, following Hooke, it is necessary to consider that:

> Shells and other fossils appear as the medals, urns or monuments of nature. They are the greatest and most lasting monuments of antiquity, which in all probability will far antedate all the most ancient monuments of the world, even the very pyramids, obelisks, mummies, hieroglyphics and coins will afford more information in natural history than those others put together will in civil [history].

Buffon goes even further with this antiquarian metaphor:

> As in civil history one consults the deeds, seeks the medals, deciphers ancient inscriptions to determine the epochs of human revolutions . . . so in natural history it is necessary to excavate the archives of the world, draw old monuments from the belly of the earth, collect their detritus, and assemble in a corpus of proof all the indices of physical changes which can make us return to the different epochs of nature.

Buffon does not suggest the opposite: that the history of nature can serve as a basis for human history. On the contrary, he seeks for his (political) tranquillity to demonstrate that the history of nature is as far from human history as is divine history. For, indeed, all of antiquarian archaeology was structured around the opposition made by Varro (first century BC) between *res humanae* and *res divinae*. Varro's successors – notably the founders of prehistory – would strive to demonstrate that there was no solution of continuity between humans and nature, and that the nature/culture couple could profitably replace the divine/human couple. This fundamental reversal is at the basis of the typological revolution introduced by Pitt-Rivers, de Mortillet or Montelius. Indeed, for the last of these, types are living beings to be analysed by archaeology as fossils – thus turning upside down the starting-point of Hooke and Buffon.

The tendency towards a naturalising and evolutionist archaeology would be strongly resisted (e.g., A. M. Tallgren 1937). However, this critical movement conducted archaeology towards culturalism and descriptive typology. In this context, the New Archaeology can be considered as a third critical stage: there is no question here of considering types as living species, but rather of studying societies as functional species (in organic functional terms).

Thesis, antithesis, synthesis – it is difficult to escape this rhetorical model. But I would like to emphasise that any history of humanity must admit the polarity nature/culture as a fertile component of the historical method. Put otherwise, it can be argued that 'archaeology is the continuation of history (or its beginnings) through other means'. If so, it may not be necessary for archaeologists to request of history (even that of the Annales school!) keys to the past – archaeologists already possess such keys, if only they would use them.

Chapter 20

Material culture in time

Ian Hodder

The definition and dating of chronological phases or periods are fundamental to most, if not all, archaeological endeavour. The procedures involved in identifying types, periods and their dates are now sophisticated, but there has been little theoretical discussion about style sequencing and periodisation as cultural processes. The main concern over recent decades has been to use periodisation as a starting-point for studies of settlement, economic or social change. The periodisation itself remains in the background, subservient to evolutionary change, adaptive strategies or ideological manipulations.

In recent decades, too, the sequencing of styles has remained largely untheorised as archaeologists have focused on style as synchronic messaging (e.g., Wiessner 1990) or meaning (e.g., Hodder 1991c). Stylistic change is seen as the active product of social or symbolic strategies, but there has been little account of the ways in which styles are constructed by referencing or responding to earlier styles, as part of diachronic processes.

By way of contrast, earlier generations of archaeologists were absorbed by the patterns in time formed by periods and styles. In particular, they placed periods within a narrative structure which often had a classical narrative plot or story-line with a beginning, middle and end: Early, Middle and Late; Formative, Classic and Post-Classic. Such examples of periodisation as narrative are largely looked upon today with scepticism, since we have no theories which would make sense of the idea that cultural sequences are organised into larger plots. Period narratives would today normally be assumed to have been constructed by the observer rather than to have had any validity to past agents.

In this paper, however, I wish to argue that where chronological sequences of styles can reliably be built by stratigraphic or chronometric means, an attempt can be made to reconstruct the narratives according to which past agents constructed their lives. I am not referring here to individual plots and brief histories, but to the larger-scale narratives which may last millennia and in which we are all enmeshed. For example, I am personally aware of living in a postcolonial Britain. Although others may contest this account of Britain, where I place myself in the long-term narrative of imperial rise and fall affects the way in which I live my life. Most of us are aware of being part of longer-term narratives, such as the Christian era or the British heritage, which we both inherit and transform (rewrite).

It is particularly in the expressive rather than the technological areas of culture that narratives are told. For Neolithic Europe, I have argued (Hodder 1990) that the expressive areas of pottery styles, figurines, burials and house-forms tell two competing stories. The first, the *domus*, is a story about the domination and domestication of nature, used as a metaphor for the domination and domestication of people. The second, the *agrios*, is a story about warring, hunting and drinking, used as an etiquette of power. As archaeologists we have to be wary about reading material culture evidence directly. The material culture might itself have been involved in telling stories or recounting myths. For instance, I argued (ibid., p. 175) that the Corded Ware/Bell Beaker phenomena expressed a story about the foreign, imposed, violent nature of power. The material culture *was made to seem as if* a movement of people had occurred, regardless of how many people had actually moved, and was produced as part of a narrative which explained new forms of power as having been imposed by foreign 'élites' – tales of stranger-rulers.

A narrative can be described as an account which relates events into a sequence with a beginning, a middle and an end. Rhetoric concerns the devices or forms used to persuade an audience of a narrative. In language, such rhetorical devices include irony and figures of speech such as metaphor, metonymy and synecdoche. I wish to demonstrate further that similar devices can be applied to material culture.

Metaphor involves using a word or phrase in a new context in order to express relations of similarity or analogy. New dimensions of the familiar are often opened up in such comparisons. Archaeological examples might include a pot made in the form of a woman, or Neolithic tombs built to represent houses (ibid., pp. 51–2; 149–55).

Metonymy and synecdoche can be seen as forms of metaphor. *Metonymy* as a figure of speech occurs when reference is made to something by substituting an associated idea or object, such as a crown or axe for a powerful leader, and *synecdoche* when a part is used to imply a whole; for instance, a sail standing for a ship. However, because there are difficulties in distinguishing metonymy, where associated elements substitute for the whole but are excluded from that whole, from synecdoche, which includes them as parts, different definitions can be given to these figures of speech. For example, Hayden White (1973) argues that metonymy indicates any case in which a part refers to a whole, while synecdoche occurs when a part stands for a *quality* of the whole, as the heart in the phrase 'she is all heart'. An archaeological example of this definition of synecdoche might include the use of depictions of female breasts to represent nurturing.

Irony is the negation at the figurative level of what is affirmed at a literal level. Ethnographic examples are suggested by the parody of dominant positions in rituals of role-reversal. Archaeological examples might include cases such as Neolithic megalithic burials where inequalities are masked or denied. In terms of historical sequence, irony describes a course of events, the result of which is the direct opposite of what is expected. Thus, the closure and negation of an earlier use of tombs for burial might be described as ironical.

Interpretation of the rhetorical strategies used in material narratives depends on an understanding of context. For example, a figurine of an unclothed, accurately modelled human body could be a metaphor for society as a whole, or for harmony with nature, or it could refer ironically to the frailty of the human condition. Deciding between such interpretations depends on wider understanding of relevant social strategies and cultural meanings.

There is more to rhetoric than metaphor and irony. For instance, there is the dramatic potential of monuments to create feelings of awe or surprise. However, for the moment I wish to focus on situations in which material culture is manipulated in ways comparable to the rhetoric of spoken and written narrative discussed by Hayden White.

White (1973) has argued that narratives, including histories and philosophies of history, are characterised by plot, argument and ideology (Fig. 11). *Emplotment* is the kind of story that is told: for example, romance, which reveals the triumph of good over evil, humans over nature; or satire, which expresses humans as captives of forces beyond their control, caught within unchanging structures. *Argument* concerns the laws of historical explanation that are invoked in order to make a narrative persuasive. For example, a mechanistic narrative is reductive in that it shows that history is the playing out of universal laws (as in Marxist theory). An organicist account, on the other hand, is synthetic, identifying principles which integrate the whole. *Ideology*, in White's account, refers to the ethical element and the narrator's role in social praxis. For example, radicals seek change and the formation of a new society through rational, scientific means, while conservatives are resigned to only gradual change. In my view White's categorisations are less successful in this area, as his ideologies are not concerned with strategies of misrepresentation. An alternative scheme would distinguish ideologies which involved universalisation (legitimating social strategies by claiming them to be universal), naturalisation, and masking or denial (Hodder 1991c).

The importance of White's scheme for archaeologists is that it provides a vocabulary for beginning to identify rhetorical strategies used in material culture. It also allows us to see that material culture might change not simply because of changes in social or economic structures, but also because of changes in form or rhetoric. White also argues that there are elective affinities between plot, argument and ideology (Fig. 11). The narrator's choice of these modes is prefigured by an underlying linguistic coherence which White calls *trope*. These tropes are the deep structures of the historical imagination and have a tendency to change in the sequence shown in Fig. 11.

trope	emplotment	argument	ideology
metaphor	romance	formist	radical
metonymy	tragedy	mechanist	radical
synecdoche	comedy	organic	conservative
irony	satire	contextual	liberal

Figure 11 Hayden White's metahistorical tropes

The metaphorical trope is characteristic of the first phase of a new narrative. It is representational and substitutive, triumphantly bringing in new ideas but with a lot of local variety. In the example of the Scandinavian Neolithic (Fig. 12), the first phase is indeed characterised by the bringing in of ideas from the more southerly TRB areas, but with a considerable variety of local response. The metonymical trope involves reduction, a part for a whole, as in the case of the Early Neolithic tombs, whereby one person buried in a communally constructed tomb was an associated element or part representing a whole. It also involves schism and hierarchy, as suggested by the contrast between those buried in the tombs and those not. White's third, synecdochical trope is also reductive, but involving integration around abstract ideas, as in the use of ritual to integrate all spheres of life in the early Middle Neolithic. Decorated pottery and a range of symbolic relations and oppositions integrate tombs, enclosures and 'cult' houses in a typically organicist way. Material culture undergoes progressive and directed change in a romantic or perhaps comic form. The final ironic trope involves negation and doubt, a self-critical relativising. This is the trope within which White himself writes, and within which my post-imperial (and postprocessual) consciousness takes its form. In the Scandinavian later Middle Neolithic, tombs continue to be used but are no longer built. Such a shift does not necessarily imply new social forces but, rather, a change to a satirical rhetoric whereby humans are expressed as captives of historical forces. As a result a larger number of individuals are placed in the graves. The bones are sorted to deny social asymmetries using a masking ideology and finally the tombs are closed in negational fashion.

trope	Neolithic sequence	narrative
metaphor	**early Neolithic** substitution, adoption, metaphor humanity over nature – agriculture (romance) abrupt break (anarchy)	DOMUS
metonymy	**later early Neolithic** reduction part represents whole in grave schism and hierarchy	
synecdoche	**Fuchsberg to middle Neolithic I** greater integration around abstract ideas expressed in ritual (organicist) progressive change (comedy)	
irony	**middle Neolithic II to V** negational, closing off tombs tombs used not built – lack of change (satire) humans captives of forces	
metaphor	**early Corded Ware/Single Grave** substitution, adoption, metaphor humanity over nature – secondary products heroic warrior elite (romance) abrupt break (anarchy)	AGRIOS

Figure 12 The tropes applied to the south Scandinavian Neolithic

The criticisms of White's account of tropes are numerous. In my view the notion of elective affinities or deep structures which recur in a cycle is doubtful. The case against White's trope cycles is parallel to Collingwood's (1927) critique of Oswald Spengler's theory of cycles in his *Decline of the West*. Collingwood (ibid., p. 316) described the fallacy of attempting 'to characterize a culture by means of a single idea or tendency or feature, to deduce everything from this one central idea', when in fact cultures are made up of opposites in dialectical movement.

But the main criticism of both Spengler and White is that the periodisations and cycles can be seen as arbitrary fictions of the observer. When we divide prehistory or history into periods with beginnings, middles and ends, 'we are talking not about history, but about the labels we choose to stick upon the corpse of history. Better historical thinking ... would show us ... a dynamic interplay of ideas' (Collingwood 1927, p. 324). A 'period' of history is often no more than the observer's fabrication. White has been accused of erasing the distinction between fiction and history, since he has not been interested in exploring the relationships between narrative history (with its tropes) and the real world of action.

The main response to these criticisms should be to focus on the positive idea that material culture is used in rhetorical strategies within narratives. We then need to evaluate the idea that narratives and rhetorics are not only in the domain of the observer. After all, even if we abandon the idea of periods or tropes we are still left with the problem of whether the *domus* narrative, for instance, is in 'my' or 'their' mind. If narrative and rhetoric do play dialectical roles in the way we live our lives, then Collingwood's critique can be bypassed.

An enormous contribution to our understanding of the relationship between narrative, rhetoric and action has been made by Paul Ricoeur (Moore 1990). He argues that historical events, unlike natural events, possess the same structure as narrative, and historians are therefore justified in regarding their narrative representations as explanations. According to Ricoeur, the intentionality of human actions creates lives that seek the coherence of emplotted stories. The stories people live are not only conscious in 'their' minds, but also concern wider consequences and structures. Narratives link agents to the background of forces.

More specifically, Ricoeur sets up a dialectical movement between experience and narrative by showing the relationship between three forms of mimesis. Mimesis1 is our experience of being caught up in stories, of being 'within time'. It is our practical understanding of what it means to raise one's arm in different contexts (ibid., p. 103). Mimesis2 is emplotment and narrative, based on but in tension with Mimesis1. Events are 'grasped together' into a whole plot and given coherence by the identification of an end point. Mimesis3 is the return to practical experience, the relating of the plot to real action. In linking story and experience, people may have their experience 'opened up' in the process.

Over all, then, according to Ricoeur, narrative acts on practical experience to produce a refiguring of our temporal experience. In contrast to White, Ricoeur argues for an eternal interplay between mimesis1 and mimesis2. This discussion is of direct relevance to material culture which is both the result of practical experience and in its symbolic aspects the result of telling stories about and to ourselves. The door is thus opened to consider the narrative and rhetoric of sequences of material culture events; and, although I am not assuming that prehistoric people would have been able to translate terms like irony directly, I would claim that a consideration of archaeological evidence allows an accommodation, a translation between the past and the present. Rhetorical form cannot be interpreted without reference to narrative content. It is only in terms of what a person is trying to 'say' with material culture that rhetoric can be understood, and narrative must therefore be regarded as an emplotted experience of events in time. It is the dual variation of narrative and rhetoric which underlies the dry periodisation of material style sequences.

Chapter 21

Archaeology and the forms of history

Michael Shanks

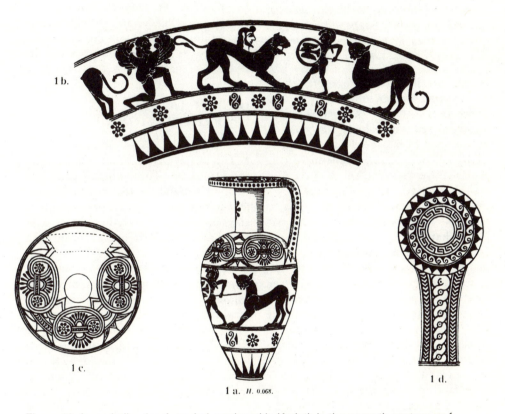

1 b.

1 c.

1 a. *H. 0.068.*

1 d.

Figure 13 An aryballos (perfume jar) produced in Korinth in the seventh century BC.[1]

Archaeology may be of various disciplines, of anthropology, and sometimes of the physical sciences (petrological examination of ceramic thin section at the polarising microscope); archaeology is also of history. I wish to put forward some reminders about archaeological history.[2]

Above: an aryballos (perfume jar) produced in Korinth in the seventh century BC.[2]

How is the design in Fig. 13 (above) to be understood? Some would read the words and literature of the time, searching for clues in myths and legends to the identity of the soldier and his monstrous adversary. Others have scrutinised brush marks and the line of painting for those idiosyncrasies which reveal the

HISTORY *OF*: PASTS AND PRESENTS

History is usually heard as history *of*: history of things, of the Neolithic, of archaeology, of ourselves, of the West. In this history is both the past and its retelling.

> *The tension is a very familiar one between the past (as it may have been) and its continuing existence in the present. Questions arise: can we ever know what really happened, what part do we play in realising the past, in making the past what it is (now)?*

Grammatically, this history *of* is both a subjective and an objective genitive. There is the subject (history, and our historical self), the object (the past or, in subjected form, ourselves). And there is the act of language, generative (the genitive): we write and speak of the past and of ourselves at the same time.

Archaeology, as a history of things, is both those things and their telling. We know that the past is destroyed in its archaeological study; it ought to be told – this is the present's duty, isn't it? But, apart from this *pragmatic* link between past and present, there is a deeper and more substantial one. There is a mystery which arises when the past, conceived as objective and of its own time, is separated from our present which, by whim, chooses to look back then. The mystery is of how to make the link one which can lead to objective knowledge of what happened then, when the link depends as much on subjective and fragile whim, and not some necessity given in the nature of things. The past becomes subject to the bias (political, personal, every) of the present, and so it is no longer pure and untainted, which is the way we should surely wish it? This mystery is resolved in the acceptance of the inextricable unity of the past and its retelling.

Meaning. The meaning of archaeological things does not reside in the past so much as *between* past and present.

individual painter – the line of an ear, paw or knee, drawn in a particular way. These are attempts to realise that which has been lost, and is now longed for – the person in the past with whom the aryballos may be associated.

But the pot is already so much more than the past, now lost. Its design, according to art histories, is one which heralds the transition from Greek Geometric to Orientalising style, a key point in the emergence of classical ceramic excellence, and its representation of bodily form upon fine clay base.

The pot is referred to histories of art style.

DESIGN AND THE INTERPRETATION OF MATERIAL FORM

• The potter acted in accordance with conditions set. The aryballos conforms with a tried and, by its time, traditional technology of clever, deft preparation of clay and slips, manipulation of kiln environment to produce dark on light body.
• The potter worked with an aesthetic vocabulary of animal imagery, of violent soldiery and monsters, composite creatures, grounded with floral pattern. This vocabulary is found far beyond Korinth, has associations in the Near East (as indicated in the designation 'orientalising' style), and even seems to reference themes found on pottery made several hundred years earlier in Greece and Crete.
• The potter used tried and traditional techniques, as of generations ago: pots with strict geometric and austere linear surface, almost entire. Fine and accomplished pieces, products of a workmanship of certainty – all details controlled and regulated according to secure technique. But in space opened between triple lines the potter painted free-hand, no longer with multiple brush and hand steadied against pot upon turntable, no longer according to a strict

A Hegelian term to refer to this relationship is *Aufhebung*, or sublation: to transcend or suspend the opposition between past and present without suppressing either element. Past and present lose their immediacy, but are not destroyed by that loss; loss of immediacy is mediation by the other. This unity without suppression is as in oxymoron, the juxtaposition of opposites to create another sense. It is like metaphor which asserts the identity of two different things or states.[3]

MEMORY AND REMEMBERING

Like memory and remembering, history implies an *act* of historicising, of making history.

> *Memory is sometimes haphazard, is not linear, involves* making *sense; memory evolves, with loss and restitution.*

What does this notion of the *act* of history involve?

THE NARRATIVE ACT

• Something particular is incorporated within something more general, and this is the creation of sense. It may be a narrative. This is a fundamental and human means of making sense of things, even as they happen; we tell to others. Narrative involves emplotment. There may be some idea of system, even in a simple list, even as the antiquarian hoards. There may be meta-narratives: (familiar), often grand or overarching stories which provide a larger sense – stories of the rise and fall of civilisation, of the triumph of power, of corruption and decadence. Narrative also implies a style, a rhetoric, and delivery to an audience.

CONSTRUCTING SCALES

• This is a creative act of *construction*. What constructs history? People do. As and limited range of simple geometric motifs. The potter now risked spoiling the vase with a slipped hand. There was more and indelible risk in the use of incision, scratching through the painted slip, scarring the pot surface with the mark of free hand. Working in miniature upon pots such as this (less than 7cm high) heightens the risk.

The picture upon this pot may be of a myth still known to us (we recognise something of a *chimaira* in the strange composite creature facing the soldier). The myth may be lost, but the picture belongs with a class of imagery (figured and produced in Korinth in relatively small numbers) which focused upon wild animal and bodily form, on floral decoration and violence, soldiers, as here, armoured and animated, and monsters other than the world we know. It is an imagery far removed from the domestic and the everyday, the world of the home and of nurture and nourishment; and it is dominated by the masculine, with hardly any references to the female. It is, I argue, a heterotopia, an other and ideological world of masculine endeavour and wild animal otherness.

And in this the pot references themes familiar still now – an ethos, one of many, of aristocratic masculinity defined in confrontation with wild otherness. Another element of the long term.

And what of the conditions of the potter's act? Is there not an incongruity between the figured imagery and the peasant world of household ceramic workshop? Perhaps production was for aristocratic traffickers or traders; many such pots ended up in the cemeteries of the citizens of the new colonies of the west, at the margins of the Greek world. Pots for the adventure of travel out to worlds at the edge, and to worlds beyond the living.

The hero asserts his identity in facing the otherness of the monster. The risk of the potter's hand (in incised black figure decoration) asserts the part of the potter. Is this coincidence?

in a workshop and under set conditions (which may be altered), within relationships with others. The *nature* of the conditions varies. Sometimes the conditions may be such as to prevent the accumulation of events or circumstances which lead to change. The conditions may be such as to set certain questions which allow only certain answers and modes of action. They may last a long time. In this way scales of change and history are *contingent*, are made; they are not naturally given as short or long, or of the social and of the environment.

CHANGING HISTORY

• There is our contemporary notion of historicity, that people may act (together) to change history, the course of events. This notion has been a significant feature of modernity, that contemporary experience which arrived with industrial labour, urban growth and mechanisation. Revolution, mass and rapid social change, is one of its expressions. More than ever before, people are aware of their historical place.

THE POWER TO ACT

• This awareness is of *agency*, the power to act and change, but also its loss. In modernity the individual is so often felt lost in the flow of change, anonymous, unable to act. History, anonymous change, occurs of its own accord, beyond the ordinary person, on the television; great men, statesmen, power brokers, are the only ones able to assert their will.

POLITICS AND THE PERSONAL

Those things that are intimately personal, possessions, experiences, may be cherished as escaping such a sense of history. The family snapshot of incidental detail references areas beyond history: cycles and rhythms of family

THE INTERPRETIVE ACT

I write of ideologies, systems of images, trade abroad and ultimate deposition in cemeteries (and sanctuaries, for divinities). So much of this is hindsight, unknown to the potter, and the terms and forms of understanding are (inevitably and of course) our own. This intersection is the condition of history, of being able to retell the story of the pots, have them make sense for us now.

The pot is material residue of times past, but it rests in a museum case (in Boston), and is the subject of so many narratives of art history and cultural achievement, but also those stories of potter and aristocratic aspiration. Can it be said to *belong* to the past?

If the pot is treated as a relay or device to get the interpreting present to something else which is desired (the myth represented, the mind of the potter, the artistic person of the potter, or the 'society' which it may be held to express), what explains the *materiality* of the pot? If the meaning of the pot is found in something else (myth, mind of potter, society), and in something else *then* in the seventh century BC, what becomes of the pot *now*? What becomes of its material resistance to the death, loss and decay which have overtaken so much to which it refers?

Are these questions not resolved in the persistence of *acts of interpretation*? The pot is the product of the interpretive act of potter, acting upon clay, interpretation of decoration by potter, trader and whoever placed such pots in graves, but then of the farmer (probably) who found the pot again, the person who bought it and sold it to a museum, and the scholars who have reinterpreted it. This is a *continuity*; there is no separation of original past and secondary present. This is the *life* of the artefact, forever raw material of cultural and historical production.

and life (birthdays, occasions, rites of passage) which are beyond the force of agency and change.

> *The notion of the agent, in control, acting to change, power broking, decisive, goal-orientated, getting what they want, asserting will, is central to an androcentric conception of the person, the political self. Implied here also are conceptions of public and private, within and beyond history.*
>
> *History – nature; public – private; detached – personal; masculine – feminine. Ideas and experiences of historicity are permeated by the dynamics of gender.*

• The personal snapshot refers me to the aesthetic and affective. An act is of practice which, of course, involves thought and feeling as well as action; it also implies an ethics. So history has its affective dimension, is done with an aesthetic. The story told may be eloquent or not, and always involves a style of telling, and a rhetoric. These are inseparable from the historical. Archaeological history is not only of the realm of the cognitive, to do with knowledge that some things happened in the past. The affective dimension demands a poetics or stylistics of change and the human pain of history. (The emotive power of the material past is well known.) And the materiality of the archaeological demands also a recognition of the death, decay and loss which are the heart of its history. These arenas of the affective are so often marginalised in academic archaeology.

I have raised some familiar points about archaeology, but ones which sometimes remain unrelated, yet which would have a considerable effect on the mode of production of archaeological pasts. I am arguing

• for the primacy of interpretation, rather than a past out there and back then;
• for a dynamic unity of past and present in the crafting of culture and history;
• for accepting the loss and decay of the past;
• and therefore the obligation of restitution, our redeeming act of reconstruction.

History sweeps a great pile of debris at our feet. We can hoard fetishistically, be buried by the increasing mass, or use the rich references, evocations and knowledges in our cultural self-production.[4]

NOTES

1 I have written an interpretation of a series of such proto-Korinthian pots at some length in the *Journal of European Archaeology* (1992). For a full presentation, see my forthcoming *Art and the Rise of the Greek City State.*

2 For futher detail and bibliography on time, archaeology and narrative, I refer to Shanks and Tilley 1987a, ch. 1; 1987b, ch. 5; also 1987c, and other articles in the same journal; Shanks 1992. Compare also Hodder 1990 on analogous themes of interpretation, archaeology, the long term, and the present's relationship with the past.

I am less concerned here with being definitive than with suggesting some lines of thought between a particular archaeological artefact and what archaeologists may be doing as historians.

3 I feel I should expand somewhat on the notion of sublation. In a sublated relationship the object from the past is mediated by the subjective self of the present archaeologist. The reality of the past is not simply its factuality, its raw existence as fact, as that which is there remaining after the decay and loss. The full reality of this pot is *realisation* – the process of it becoming something other than itself. This becoming-other-than-itself involves the intercession of subjectivity: that is, the perceiving, feeling, analysing archaeologist. This pot is not defining itself as anything, but depends on its relationship with me now (as I do with it and a factual world

beyond me). The form of the objective world of the past is our subjectivity. To know what something really is, what its concrete reality is, we have to get beyond its immediately given state, which is a tautology (the pot is a pot), and follow the process in which it becomes something else, as in the proposition 'the pot is a work of ideology'. But in this process of becoming the pot still remains a pot, of course. This is sublation – the dynamic of turning into something else and effecting reconciliation.

4 For final words I would like to thank Alain Schnapp and the Maison des Sciences de l'Homme for setting up my stay in Paris where the final version of this piece was completed.

Chapter 22

Railroading epistemology

Palaeoindians and women

Joan Gero

I would like to begin this discussion with Frederic Jameson's solution to a central dilemma of history, addressing the conundrum that historians must ultimately confront only a representation of history because, by definition, the real past has already ceased to exist. The real object of history cannot exist, but Jameson argues its reality lies in its final causal condition, beyond meaning or narration – even beyond knowledge. Jameson concludes that history continues to assert itself – 'history is what hurts' (Jameson 1988b, p. 164).

Here I wish to consider some of the historical aspects of archaeology that 'hurt': that is, I wish to look at the social construction of archaeological knowledge as a means of understanding the sources of epistemological authority and the forces that sustain these over time. I see this exercise as part of a broader interdisciplinary attempt to close down the distance between knowledge and the context in which that knowledge is produced.

As long as we consider that the making of an item of knowledge emerges directly out of natural reality, we stipulate the grounds for admitting science as rational and 'transparent' – anyone can do it, geniuses better than others, and science therefore involves some of the greatest men, great moments and great sites. This combination of individualism, positivism and élitism conspires to confuse the role of scholarly practice in constructions of knowledge. To concentrate on the role of human agency in making knowledge, we undermine the inevitability of what has accrued as knowledge and we clarify the inferential processes that most often lie hidden in data summaries and interpretive conclusions to archaeological work.

My point is to demonstrate that much of our knowledge about the past arises out of particular sets of historically conditioned observations and routine taken-for-granted research practices, and that the most firmly fixed, the 'true-est' ideas and understandings about prehistory are, in the words of Bruno Latour, 'summaries of complicated material situations' (Latour and Woolgar 1979, p. 170). In this view, facts are not simply recorded as they are observed; they are crafted out of a welter of confusing and conflicting observations, modified and reformulated out of knowledge of what other scientists are working on, and accepted more readily if their proponent is well credentialled. Once a 'fact' is arrived at, it is quickly freed from the circumstances of its production and loses all historical reference to the social and contextual conditions of its construction (ibid., p. 106). Thus the processes that account for and produce scientific facts or knowledge are always invisible since practitioners themselves use language and concepts as though the knowledge they produce had no history, no social life, no culture . . . and no *gender*.

A constructivist view of science, then, rejects the individualism of a discovery model and emphasises instead two kinds of contingency: first, historical contingency (or what Haraway (1988, p. 596) calls 'the railroad industry of epistemology, where facts can only be made to run on the tracks laid down from (paradigmatic early work) and those who control the railroads control the surrounding territory'). Second, although I won't deal further with it here, this view emphasises social or relational contingency, where the self-serving, internally related community of knowledge-makers forecloses the very universality and transparency that science is said to embody. In the rest of this discussion I want to turn to the North American Palaeoindians to illustrate how historical contingency has structured archaeological fact, and in the process has erected a singularly well circumscribed, well defended and profoundly androcentric research field.

The establishment of an antiquity for 'man' in the New World that goes back into the Pleistocene has an almost canonical character in the history of American archaeology (Meltzer 1983, Wormington 1957). Following a bitter controversy which lasted several decades of professional dispute, a discovery was made in 1926 just eight miles west of Folsom, New Mexico, of a type of fossil bison believed to have been extinct for thousands of years, together with several pieces of worked flint artefacts. Two of these stone fragments could be fitted together to form the readily distinguishable part of a projectile point characterised most significantly by the removal of a grooved or channelled flake on both faces. After two more seasons of excavation and the total recovery of nineteen of the same distinctive artefact type from the undisturbed Pleistocene matrix, the last hold-outs admitted that 'the men who had flaked the weapon points were contemporaries of the extinct bison' (Wormington 1957, p. 25). Says one modern commentary: 'For once in the long battle over the antiquity of man, the archaeological record had played fair, and the evidence was clear' (Meltzer 1983, p. 38).

A deliberate effort to recover a larger sample of Folsom points was rapidly rewarded and their continued association with extinct bison stood up in every excavated occurrence (Wormington 1957, p. 29). More ambitiously, the subsequent work in the late 1920s included a search for Folsom habitation areas that would yield a larger tool inventory and longer deeper stratigraphic columns in which the relationship of Folsom materials to other tool types could be established. Success on both counts was achieved in the 1934 excavations at Lindenmeier: several thousand stone artefacts were recovered, including newly noted variations within the Folsom forms, a great many knives, scrapers of different forms and spokeshaves. 'All of these objects must have been useful in important activities such as shaping shafts for weapons, butchering animals and preparing hides,' says Wormington (ibid., p. 35), still focusing exclusively on the meat and the hunt of palaeo-existence. But there is no comment on the function of the 'non-distinctive' artefact types. What should we make of the excavators' mention of rubbing-stones with red stains, ground cores of haematite, a bead and a carved bone disc? Was there more to palaeo-life than the slim view illuminated by this particular paradigm?

Because Folsom was the first point type to be recognised as of Pleistocene age, it emerged as a point of reference, with other distinctive Palaeoindian cultural materials described as older or younger than Folsom, and noted geographically in relation to the Folsom area. Bison, together with mammoth, remained the dietary datum, and Palaeo-man was fixed in time, space, occupation . . . and gender.

From these foundational beginnings, Palaeoindian studies have converged with extraordinary singlemindedness on a research construct that has only very recently been questioned. In Gordon Willey's (1966, p. 38) words, 'the big-game pursuit is the most characteristic and diagnostic feature of the culture shared by these particular early Americans. There can be no question that it was an activity of primary importance; it imparted a design, a style to their lives.' The consensus that the distinctive fluted point, invented on the American continent, was responsible for, or at least intimately involved with, the success of Early Man, the Palaeoindian Hunter, made these artefacts centrefold pin-up displays in so many books on prehistory.

The Palaeoindian period ends when the fluted point disappears from the archaeological record. Palaeoindians 'evaporate' (in Marie Wormington's words) with a thoroughness that makes it hard to believe in even the biological, much less the cultural, continuity of humans in America. Without the fluted point there is no Palaeoindian, and the construct falls off with a clarity of boundary that matches the boundedness of the research community.

The historical contingency of the Palaeoindian construction thus becomes clear: before the use of radiocarbon dating, the identification of diagnostic Palaeoindian markers could only be verified as 'early' by direct and uncontestable association with extinct Pleistocene life-forms. In its historic context, early Man could only be a big-game hunter, with all the ideological loading that that entailed and all that it left out: women! Furthermore, the elegant simplicity of a widely distributed and distinctive tool led easily to a conflation of variability into a single Fluted Point tradition, one that was only occasionally and roughly sorted by time and space. For instance, in one of the earliest reports on Palaeoindian materials from eastern North America, W. Ritchie reviewed a substantial amount of data from the Reagan site in Vermont and concluded that all except one of his trait categories 'have parallels in sites attributable to the paleo-Indian in various parts of the United States' (Ritchie 1953, p. 251).

Why this insistence on 'the likenesses outweigh[ing] the differences, both as respects typology and technology' (ibid.)? Shouldn't we expect the differences to be seized upon as temporal and spatial markers, to increase the discriminations in palaeo-dispersals and adaptations? And why dismiss the very intriguing engraved ground-stone pendants from Reagan, which clearly have *no parallels* in the Plains material? The real question then emerges: why has the Palaeoindian construct been used here instead of viewing the at least partially distinct fluted materials as the earliest manifestations of particular occupations in each distinct regional sequence?

Significantly, what was created in this flattening process was a national paradigm, at a time of intense growth in the professional ranks of archaeology. The constructed universality of the Palaeoindian phenomenon, despite the lack of a fine-grained chronology, provided the classic origin story for all American peoples that the almost exclusively male archaeologists could study everywhere in the country. Constructed not locally but nationally, Palaeo-man is an earliest common denominator, a base-line of American technological prowess and ecological efficiency. It is entirely logical within this model that Palaeoindian research concentrates on modes of dispatching Pleistocene fauna as well as on the ecological, climatic and geomorphological reconstructions of the Palaeo-environment. What was available to eat then and how was it taken? But even such narrowly empirical and accessible questions as how this food was prepared are ignored. Continental expansion is never translated into women carrying out productive and reproductive activities, and the social, engendered world of which eating meat must have been only a tiny part is utterly absent.

The question then becomes compelling. How could Palaeoindian studies be otherwise? And, most pressingly, why are women archaeologists and women Palaeoindians so entirely absent from this research? The persistence of Palaeo-man throws us back to constructivist notions of science. How has the railroad industry of epistemology kept Palaeoindian facts running on these same tracks for sixty years? To understand this is to understand the structure of the modern research community, with its divisions of labour and its hierarchies, and its gendered social world. It is also to understand that successful practitioners of research must follow precedent and paradigm in the observation, manipulation and description of material remains: they (we!) must adopt specific technological, social and literary practices defined as central to the research endeavour. The elucidation of these practices, however, takes us into the realm of social contingency – which is another topic.

Part 5

Material culture

Chapter 23

Interpreting material culture
The trouble with text

Victor A. Buchli

A VERY BRIEF HISTORY OF TEXT

Discussions of text have dominated the interpretation of material culture in postprocessual archaeology for over ten years now since the emergent disenchantment with the New Archaeology in the early 1980s. At that time there was a shift from systems-orientated functionalist approaches which minimised the role of symbolic systems and ideology towards postprocessual approaches which placed primary emphasis on systems of meaning and interpretation. This new direction was further propelled by the inheritance of ethnoarchaeology from the New Archaeology and the resultant increased engagement of archaeologists with developments in ethnography, particularly the ethnographic applications of critical theory and literary criticism.

The comparison of material culture with text, however, has been around many years in one veiled form or another as Parker Pearson noted in 1982 (Parker Pearson 1982, p. 100) when he referred to Gordon Childe's insistence that material culture be treated 'always and exclusively as concrete expressions and embodiments of human thoughts and ideas' (Childe 1956; p. 1). The notion that material culture could express or contain ideas as language does lends itself to the application of structuralist and semiotic analysis. However, a purely structuralist approach as evidenced in the work of Leroi-Gourhan (1965, 1982) did not really take off. Ian Hodder writing in 1986 saw this as a tendency for structuralist approaches to be subsumed rather flirtatiously within the New Archaeology for its innate 'systemness' in that both approaches emphasised the role of general systems to explain all aspects of human behaviour. It was then later rejected for its inability to conform to the New Archaeology's positivist requirements of hypothesis testing and falsifiability (Hodder 1986, p. 35). However, as Hodder noted, the attraction survived in one form or another in the works of a variety of authors throughout the seventies and early eighties (1986, p. 34).

It was not really until the early eighties that the comparison with text resurged with increased force. In the preceding years with the publication of Bourdieu's *Outline of a Theory of Practice* (1977) and Anthony Giddens's *New Rules of Sociological Method* (1976) and *Central Problems in Social Theory* (1979) a more satisfactory critique of structuralism arose in the pursuit of understanding systems of meaning, shifting the emphasis from static structures of meaning subordinating all individual actions to the dictates of underlying structures, to actively manipulated generative principles (i.e., rules for making structures) exploited by individuals pursuing various independent social goals – actively manipulating structures of meaning rather than being manipulated by them. This approach inspired those archaeologists dissatisfied with the New Archaeology's treatment of meaning to pursue their interests with renewed vigour and establish a generation of practitioners critical of the New Archaeology more forcefully than ever before. The works of individuals such as Henrietta Moore (1986), Daniel Miller (1982a, b, 1985), Michael Parker Pearson (1982, 1984 a, b), Shanks and Tilley (1987a), Shanks and Tilley (1987b), Mark Leone (1982b), Leone, Potter and Shackel (1987), Ian Hodder (1982a, b, 1986) and others attempted to reassess comparisons with text with the infusion of the poststructuralist critiques of structuralism by Bourdieu and Giddens as well as the critiques of structuralism by Roland Barthes, Jacques Derrida, Michel Foucault, Paul Ricoeur and the Marxist tradition of Critical Theory.

Thomas Patterson (1989, p. 556) sorts out this unruly variety of responses and influences into three reasonably distinct but inevitably forced strains of thought that manage more or less to capture the dominant tone of the works involved. The first, which is essentially 'Hodderian', draws on the work of the historian/theoretician Robin Collingwood and is articulated through the diverse works of Pierre Bourdieu, Clifford Geertz, Anthony Giddens and Paul Ricoeur. Most notable in this tradition are the works, of course, of Ian Hodder himself and Henrietta Moore. They approach the archaeological record as most directly analogous to a text or narrative to be decoded and manipulated by various historical agents and accessible to the archaeologist, 'privileging the cryptographic skill and eloquence of the archaeologist as interpreter' (Patterson 1989, p. 556). The second strain, filtered through the works of Michel Foucault and Marxian critiques, focuses more on relations of power and domination in social practice and the creation of knowledge, particularly emphasising the implications of archaeology to late capitalism and the roles that it plays in reproducing society and how that might be changed. The work of Shanks and Tilley (1987a, b and Shanks 1992a), Shanks and Tilley (1987a, b and Tilley 1989a, b), Daniel Miller (1987), and Miller and Tilley (1984) can be used to characterise this strain. Text here is still understood as a narrative to be decoded but the importance of social conditions under which material culture and other narratives are produced and interpreted to reinforce and reproduce dominant social structures are accorded greater significance. The third strain, very closely related to the second, is more emphatically concerned with the role and implication of communication and ideology in the constitution of archaeological discourse in the present day. The primary influences are the works of Jürgen Habermas, Louis Althusser and the tradition of Critical Theory. From this strain Mark Leone (1982a) Leone, Potter and Shackel (1987), Leone and Potter (1992), and Alison Wylie (1985, 1987) are notable in providing a critique of how archaeological texts themselves and the archaeological record, which constitutes these texts, are produced and disseminated– in short a more overtly political critique of the production of archaeological texts, their uses, and how the raw material, the constituted physical archaeological record, is used to generate these texts and the audiences they serve.

More recently in the past three years there has emerged a certain uncertainty and wavering brought on in part by the expansion and interaction between these arguments. Hodder has reappraised his contextual approach in the light of H. G. Gadamer's hermeneutics (Hodder 1991). This reassessment came at about the same time his critics claimed that his contextual approach was essentialist, presuming a unified narrative text 'out there' to be read as well as the competence of the archaeologist would permit, denying the historically contingent nature of interpretation (Johnsen and Olsen 1992) and the multiplicity of interpretations in the past and the present (Barrett 1987).

Similarly, more Marxist interpretations of the second and third strain have come under increasing scrutiny for their tendencies to create holistic, totalising representations of interpretive and historic processes – another form of alternative 'systemness' akin to the functionalist systems theorising of the New Archaeologists (Barrett 1992, Bauman 1992). Hence a certain uncertainty has developed, particularly amongst more strident Marxists, and a waning of the confidence and vigour of the mid-eighties when postprocessualism and discussions of text broke on the scene. Concurrently there has been an increasing awareness of the unique qualities attributed to material culture distinguishing it from some established definitions of text (Hodder 1989).

Despite these waverings, text is still discussed quite vigorously. The papers presented here point towards, in a rather unexpected way, a certain consensus concerning the viability of the comparison for material culture. Individuals otherwise quite diverse in their approaches stand together to defend the direction. Perhaps the 'death knell' for the undertaking to be is quite premature – 'not all texts after all are literary texts', 'the analogy needs to be stretched' (H. Moore, personal communication). Others somewhat impatient with the highly abstracted discussion on the issue might demand that we finally just implement the comparison 'and put it to use and see how it works' (C. Renfrew, personal communication).

There is a danger of a 'false consensus', however. One of the things that has emerged in the volume is that we still are not quite sure what exactly we mean by a 'text' and on what data we can appropriately apply the comparison. Resolving this issue, however, is fraught with many difficulties. Considering Moore's earlier statement, there is a great deal of disagreement as to the meaning of the terms involved. When we say 'text' do we mean a semiotic system (de Saussure) or structuralist system (Lévi-Strauss), a hermeneutic interpretive system based on structuralism (Gadamer and Ricoeur) or something entirely different? Up to now I have intentionally avoided using the words 'metaphor' or 'analogy' to describe this comparison. However, despite their tendency to be used interchangeably, the two words are not identical and their distinctions are highly problematic. Is material culture analogous to texts structurally and functionally? Or is material culture like a text, a metaphor without structural similarities but imaginatively linked? If it is an analogy, then how do we make the analogy to the things we study, and for what categories of material culture is the analogy appropriate or inappropriate? For the most part, these issues have not been problematised and the distinction is rarely made, with the resulting confusion that the term is often used inconsistently as analogy, metaphor, or just as the thing itself in ways that might contradict the overt intention of the author under consideration.

THE TROUBLE WITH TEXT

Much of the confusion concerning text is related to how one falls along a continuum of belief, from whether one believes a retrievable 'Past' (unified, monolithic and directly retrievable) to many little 'pasts' (multiple, contradictory and oftentimes inferred) or to the opposite belief that there is no past at all that can be meaningfully grasped. This is a question of faith ridden with intense anxiety for the archaeologist concerned with 'The Past' or 'pasts' and for whom an analogic approach to text and material culture can yield useful correspondences with which to 'recover' meaning. Conversely, those archaeologists leaning towards the position that there is no such thing as a retrievable past might find an analogic approach has little value and text is more usefully understood in metaphoric terms in attempting to use the material record to address contemporary concerns and not futilely retrieve past ones.

COMMENTARY

Colin Richards

Such anxieties can be felt in Colin Richards's paper despite his statement that 'there are no past truths, no single meanings any more than there are contemporary truths'. He proposes to view the highly empirical practice of excavation less as the neutral and objective extraction of data, and more as a process of culture contact, drawing on analogies with ethnographic fieldwork. He compares the gradual observation, selection and piecing together of data from an archaeological field site to the process by which an ethnographer comes in contact with an alien culture, by observing, selecting data, and performing an analysis.

This analogy, however, is rather problematic if Richards takes the view that 'there are no past truths'. Ethnographic culture contact is a dialogue whereby two agents, the ethnographer and the informant, are involved in a mutually reconstitutive account of social phenomena. Cultural concepts in a sense are literally being created at the point of contact between the ethnographer and the informant in the form of the ethnographer's description and the 'native' theorising of the informant who attempts to engage the ethnographer's queries thereby re-creating or even articulating cultural concepts, previously left unobjectified. 'Contact' as such in the strict ethnographic sense is clearly not possible in the course of excavation since the numerous individuals responsible for the artefacts excavated, as the artefacts themselves, are not capable of talking back, 'speaking' as it were, engaging themselves with their interlocutors during the course of excavation. 'Contact' never occurs and neither does the mutual reconstitution of cultural practices. Excavation in this sense is profoundly monologic – monologue with a pile of debris, incapable of ever responding on its own to the questions put towards it. Yet Richards claims that 'the past' (as signified by the material record) does indeed speak – 'but only through a dialectical relationship between subject and object, the present and recognised past'. This, however, is not the same sort of dialogue characterising ethnographic cultural contact, but a dialogue with oneself, with a 'recognised past' constituted in the present; a monologue and nothing ever more. 'Contact' as such can be nothing more than contact with oneself mediated through the meaningful constitution of material remains into the material culture and artefacts of the present. This is not to deny the constitution and recognition of patterning in material remains or the constraints such patterning would have to our interpretive endeavours; anything does not go. Our interpretive requirements will always prevail and be meaningful to us but not to 'them', whoever they might be. The 'contact' metaphor is potentially misleading, imputing the sense that a 'past' must exist because one could then retrieve it (take it down from the shelf) and read it, or 'interrogate' it during the course of a mutually constitutive conversation of culture 'contact' with the meaningfully constituted remains of a past people. If one could not engage the archaeological record in this way, it would simply be 'gibberish' and all our endeavours presumably meaningless; without the authority to guide us in our present-day endeavours. If it is 'out there', then it can 'speak', be 'read', or 'coaxed to speak' through dialogue, and amenable to interpretation through its analogy to text.

However, Richards's understanding of 'contact', despite problems with the use of this metaphor, entails a provocative understanding of the interpretation of material culture that suggests better ways of coping with the contingent multiplicities of its interpretation. He questions prevailing excavation techniques that restrictively constitute material culture, forcing it into alien geometries of order; reducing it from three to two dimensions and forcing a loss of complexity of understanding in the excavation process that denies the multiplicity of potential voices used in the production of the monolithic, single-authored, 'objectivising' enterprise we normally call a site report. Rather, Richards calls for alternatives to our excavation practices that might break up the Procrustean hold these techniques have had on our ability to further constitute and elaborate our interpretations of material culture.

Felipe Criado

For Felipe Criado the idea of the archaeological record and material culture as meaningless 'gibberish' is less anxiety provoking and the utility of a textual analogy consequently is limited. Criado proposes an alternative approach to interpreting material culture, replacing the textual metaphor with a visual metaphor of visibility strategies. Criado identifies four visibility strategies: to inhibit, to hide, to exhibit and to monumentalise, and suggests an opposite strategy of a 'will-to-unvisibilising' – to not engage in any visual strategy at all. To do nothing in fact, thereby focusing on the significance of meaninglessness in understanding.

This typology of visibility strategies is proposed as an alternative to existing periodisations which, Criado feels, are implicitly teleological and of questionable use. A periodisation based on visibility strategies therefore has as one of its advantages its obviously stated, consciously assumed strict formal cognitive criteria which serve to recontextualise information into new contexts towards presumably more immediate contemporary 'socio-cultural discourses'. It would not pretend to reveal any pre-existing meanings 'out there' in the 'Past'. Similarly the designation of a particular visual strategy or 'will-to-visibility' does not imply a specific meaning; rather, it intuits the existence of a meaning or intentions towards the articulation of something inherently indeterminable.

However, as Criado points out, the temptation to characterise socio-economic formations in terms of specific strategies towards visuality can become problematic. In his scheme one senses the presence of lingering deterministic ideas of evolutionary stages of society. One could imagine passing through stages of complexity from unvisibility, inhibition (prehistory), hiding (Palaeolithic), exhibition (Neolithic) and monumentalisation (Late Neolithic and early states); reproducing established periodisations of history. Rather than describing an aspect of material culture in a particular society with the very likely possibility that several of these strategies might be pursued simultaneously, these stages are presented as discrete representations of a dominant and determining social quality (hierarchical, within nature, without nature, nature and culture opposed) at the expense of other competing strategies. In keeping with this it follows that any combination of strategies represents some social instability involving the competition between two or more tendencies for domination in the next stage of social development, rather than the coexistence and interdependence of multiple strategies.

Criado, in his system of visibility strategies, recognises no 'pre-existing meaning' to be revealed in the course of analysis, but, rather, the 'reading' of his system 'would involve the recombinations of relations into new contexts involving codes from other social-cultural discourses'. In short the material remains of past behaviour become the raw material of which new contexts – that is, present concerns and discourses – are constituted. The exploitation and engendering of meaning of otherwise meaningless material remains is not some empty intellectual exercise, but integral to the constitution of our being.

Julian Thomas

'The "Past" has "to be" for us to structure existence' (J. Thomas, conference comments). Humans can only think in narratives or totalities; 'totalities don't exist but we need to create them' (ibid.) otherwise how would we cope as individuals, as societies and as a species with the meaningless chaos surrounding us? In producing these necessary fictions Thomas sees significant problems relating to the use of the textual analogy leading to a dichotomy between symbolism and materiality. Central to this dilemma is the role of time in interpreting material culture, particularly as time and time-depth are considered one of the unique insights archaeology provides within anthropology. Thomas notes that discussions of time are frequently separated from the often structuralist and synchronic discussions of material culture, creating a changeless and fossilised representation of material culture that belies its constantly changing significance.

By reintroducing the element of time and time-depth to the interpretation of material culture, Thomas proposes to overcome this false dichotomy between symbolism and materiality and break free from the ossifying effects inherited from structuralism. Rather than seeing material culture as embodying anything in particular, Thomas suggests that material culture be viewed as the raw material for the creation of narratives, recontextualised and redeployed as agents continuously change their use of material culture in the creation of narrative expressions of identity. More significantly, he proposes to shift from the artefact of material culture itself to the agent herself and her manipulation of material objects in the world as a way of locating herself in that world. The object itself loses primacy and is viewed merely as the vehicle of multiple, mutating interpretations, uses and fetishisations. These manipulations, though constantly changing and shifting, are organised by certain pre-understandings or hermeneutic perspectives that are the standpoints from which the world is perceived, interpreted and acted upon. As Thomas writes, we hear soundwaves as motorcycles or as birds and debate understanding material culture as texts. These are all pre-understandings which establish a specific vanishing-point about which the field of our discursive perspective is delineated and structured. Consequently, Thomas's suggestion places the agent and her actions as the fulcrum about which material culture is to be understood as Parker Pearson and others have sought to do. Material culture does not function 'as text' in Thomas's scheme but, rather, it is the stuff of which texts or narratives are made to help us cope with the contingencies of our existence.

Michael Parker Pearson

Parker Pearson, like others, found the textual analogy strictly problematic (Parker Pearson, conference presentation). He suggested an understanding of text more as the object of semiotic analysis and less the hermeneutic interpretive process. Material culture should not conform stictly to semiotic analyses of text; material culture's uses are often far more utilitarian than communicative. Rather, texts should be seen as just another category of material culture. The analogy to Parker Pearson seemed overstretched and even downright misleading since it denied the opportunity to adequately incorporate notions of agency and structure in understanding material culture because of the rather fixed communicative nature of literary texts.

Parker Pearson's use of the word 'text' implied that it was static, sealed off, and unidirectional in that it had the specific function of communicating written information. It was not as polysemous as an item of material culture such as the crown that he mentioned, which could be interpreted and used in a variety of ways such as headgear, a symbol of rank, or as a gloss for the state. Such a definition of text assumed there was in fact something explicit and essential to be grasped, uncovered, deconstructed towards, which with discipline, good hard work and critical vigilance would yield through the investigator's labours that which was true, intended, and explicitly communicated. However, much poststructuralist understanding of literary texts, notably the work of Jacques Derrida, would not accept such a fixed definition of literary texts and would see it as similarly fluid if not more so than material culture.

In referring to how much texts and material culture were not alike, Parker Pearson observed several significant contrasting characteristics. Material culture was more use-bound, less abstract and more practical; it was more directed towards the physical exploitation of the environment rather than being explicitly communicative. It therefore did not primarily function to represent directly, though it could and often did as in the crown metonym mentioned above. It was more likely to be taken for granted, since once constituted it no longer required constant reiteration. One simply picks up a hammer and uses it, once its function and the rules for its use have been established without second thoughts or reinterpretations. Literary texts require reiteration and reinterpretation, in short reinvention, in order to function. In this respect the banality of much of material culture's use is much like the rules of grammar, not conscious, taken for granted until a rule has been misapplied and one uses a wrench to chop down a tree. The last and probably most salient distinction Parker Pearson observed was the durability of non-textual items of material culture. Their ability to exist mutely, survive physical degradation and remain visible makes them qualitatively distinct in most respects from ordinary literary texts. There were dangers, however, in attributing specific qualities to this durability. The primacy of material culture in contemporary consumerist postindustrial societies was not to be assumed in past societies. There was the risk of fetishising such material goods and inappropriately attributing meaning. The sheer physicality of material cultural data, pregnant with expectant meaning, could exert a very seductive and transfixing force within the dearth of contextual data, obscuring pressing questions of agency and context.

Parker Pearson, however, pointed towards something far more provocative to our interpretive practices as archaeologists. We transform one type of material culture, the material record, into another: a literary text, site report or academic publication. What were the advantages of this transformation of something so rich into something so two-dimensional as a site report contained within a three-dimensional object we call a 'text'? The once rich environment of three-dimensional objects situated meaningfully within the context of three-dimensional space was lost for ever through the course of our controlled destruction of a site. This environment is resurrected again as a literary text, illustrated and supported only by objects that have now become artefacts pulled out of their contexts, forever dependent on that text and the structure of the process of destruction which brought those objects into the world. What are the advantages of such transformations to our endeavours when they might involve considerable gain or loss to our experience? Parker Pearson suggests that maybe we could consider other ways of transforming the archaeological record. If we as archaeologist are to be considered the legitimate specialists charged with transforming and interpreting the archaeological record, maybe our consumption and experience of the archaeological record and the experience of other publics consuming and experiencing the fruits of our labours might be meaningfully expanded by not just creating one form of material culture such as archaeological texts but others as well.

Underlying several of the papers in this volume is the old issue of theory and practice: how to relate our theories of material culture to the actual interpretation of material culture in our work. Parker Pearson's paper in this volume attempts to alleviate this problem with an actual case-study. This paper challenges the accepted wisdom that the Sutton Hoo burial is associated with the Kingdom of East Anglia. Armed with better chronologies, a revaluation of previous 'culture historical' approaches and a broader sensitivity to the symbolic and idiosyncratic associations of certain items of material culture at the burial, Parker Pearson suggests an alternative association that is East Saxon, and very persuasively argues for a specific identification of the burial as that of the East Saxon king, Saebert. The argument is presented as an example of the utility of the use of multiple interpretive or theoretical approaches in gaining a better understanding of material culture. Parker Pearson here proposes an understanding of multiple interpretations, less as the simultaneity and management of multiple views in the pursuit of various immediate goals (political, academic, or social) as some others have suggested. Rather, the dynamics of multiple interpretations are seen more as the competition of various viewpoints to interpret the data most persuasively where the best interpretive fit prevails until a better one challenges the existing order.

Maurice Bloch

Maurice Bloch offers an example of how the analogy to text, especially when understood in semiotic or structuralist terms as something to be 'read' or decoded, can be entirely inappropriate. To illustrate the difficulties of analogy, he discusses the problems entailed in dealing with carvings on Malagasy house-posts. The carvings on these posts, Bloch suggests, do not in fact mean anything, even though they might be evocative or representative of specific things such as the rain or the moon. The figures do not in fact mean those things; they simply have some superficial resemblances to these things so they can be more easily named and referred to. In short, they do not signify. That is, they do not function as signifiers revealing something signified – the way a literary text would signify constituted by arbitrary signifiers. Signifying nothing, the best Bloch can do in light of our disciplinary requirements to ascribe meaning and significance to these figures is to say they 'magnify' something. They are expletives, exclamation points, crescendo marks of several generations in the 'magnificat' of a lineage's founders who erected these posts.

The lesson of Bloch's cautionary tale is that we should use our analytical tools where appropriate and not make everything have to behave as text and signify, however compelling the objects at hand may be. This naturally creates a problem as to when to use this analogy and when not to. The preoccupation of ethnographers and archaeologists alike with ascribing significance to all manner of observed phenomena can result, as Bloch's cautionary tale so clearly points out, in demanding answers to entirely irrelevant questions, as witnessed by the frustration experienced by Bloch and other researchers. To insist on the equation that elaborately incised patterns of circles must represent some thing, be a signifier with a corresponding signified, is one of the fundamental operations associated with the textual analogy. It insists, rather tautologously, that the observable universe is constituted by signifiers, much like Foucault's medieval episteme: everything means, signifies something and is waiting for someone to read it (Foucault 1970). The possibility of non-significance or, more specifically, some thing that does not follow the equation of signifier/signified becomes lost.

Bloch's Malagasy carvings, however, illustrate in many ways what Thomas was theorising: that objects participate in a greater associated context of shifting meanings, rather than having any specific designative sense. In the case of the carvings, they participate in a larger cultural sensibility that is more connotative than denotative, where a larger narrative of family history and growth are played out against commonly shared Malagasy sensibilities and aesthetics. Ironically, 'fossilisation' actually does occur here but in a somewhat playful and metaphoric sense of 'hardening': that is, making more 'physical' and 'enduring' the meditation of a lineage on its origins and its maintenance or, rather, the 'magnification' of this expression within in a common cultural practice. In short, a metaphoric exploitation of the physical properties of a material, to fix and magnify a certain idea, in this case the longevity of a founding couple. This is not unlike the 'fossilisation' of archaeological data or any other 'hard' data – that is, the process of making it 'bony', structuring it (not to mention actually hardening it and preserving it from physical decay), fixing it in time and space, as in a field report or collection and having it 'vouloir dire' and constituted to designate a very specific something. The irony here is that the archaeologist when queried might not respond like the Malagasy carver that he is just making some thing or other, making it beautiful or honouring it. The archaeologist might actually believe that he is designating something like the 'moon', 'social contradiction' or 'incipient state formation' rather than performing a 'magnificat' elaborating the very serious myths of his own origins.

Material culture and physicality

In discussing the appropriateness or inappropriateness of 'text' towards the understanding of material culture, a common distinctive feature of material culture has been continuously invoked either distinguishing it at times from literary 'texts', subsuming literary 'texts' to it, or alternately functioning alongside with literary 'texts' in the creation of narratives – namely the fact that material culture is a thing, hard, durable and physical. This might seem banal and horribly obvious at first, but the constituted physicality of material culture is what distinguishes it most specifically from other data. It is the cornerstone of Criado's 'will-to-visibility' scheme, essential to the poetry of Malagasy carving in Bloch's discussion, the point of 'culture contact' in Richards's presentation, and the fulcrum about which narratives are spun out in Thomas's paper. It is the one thing that distinguishes most saliently the data of the archaeologist from any other anthropologist (see the extensive discussions of materiality by Shanks 1992a, 1992b, 1993a).

The attribution of physicality – the constitution of otherwise inchoate matter with physical attributes, beyond being a statement that that which is under consideration assumes three dimensions, implies an intention towards imbuing a particular expression with durability to sustain physicality over time for some specified or indefinite period. The constitution of physicality and durability is almost without question one of the central preoccupations of archaeologists (the generation and elaboration of artefacts) and others who attempt meaningfully to constitute and appropriate physical properties in the material world. In short the constitution of physicality implies a desire for some form of sustained expression or utility, be it a literary text to be circulated indefinitely, a house to be built for a generation or several, or a cup to be used once or for an entire lifetime. The produced durability of an object often has everything to do with how long one wants the expressive quality of the object of material culture to be sustained – built for eternity in stone, or out of paper to last just the day. Or conversely, as in the case with rubbish, something to be forgotten becomes an artefact through incidental preservation and subsequent reconstitution as artefact. The critical quality of durability associated with material culture by Richards often falls out of the conscious discursive realm precisely because it is so familiar and taken for granted. Similarly, overlooking the relation of physicality to expressive significance is one of the central dichotomies Thomas refers to affecting archaeology. And lastly the production of durability predicates all of Criado's visibility strategies.

Of course, the production of physical attributes in the generation of material culture is what we constitute and document so obsessively – the size, material composition, position, weight and number of discrete objects. Empiricism as such is nothing more than this obsession with the production and documentation of physical attributes of the material world. This predilection of our highly empirical discipline has been pointed out as having its pitfalls. Overenthusiastic documentation without explanation is decried as 'facticism' (Moore), 'fetishism' (Parker Pearson) or 'obsessive systematisation' (Richards). The prevailing belief has been the more we constitute and document physical attributes of the material world, the more we can become 'objective' and get a better 'picture' of what actually 'is there' and understand its essence. The poststructuralist disenchantment with the enterprise of establishing 'totalities' and 'essences' can only call into question the tools of objectivising enterprises that try to document something – to know what it really and truly 'is'. To continue incessantly to constitute and document the physicality of the material world and know that 'there is no there there' to document (apologies to Gertrude Stein) is only to come up with an increasingly 'harder', 'two-dimensional image' (Moore) of the material world that resists interpretation of its obsessive, speedy and somewhat ecstatic documentation. Such a process can potentially disempower disfranchised groups and individuals trying to establish control over interpretations and representations that oppress them by consistently denying any form of 'authentic' interpretation. Abject obsession with the physicality of data can be seen as just as potentially harmful to the disfranchised as any claims to objectivity that silence others.

But the physicality we have produced is all we really are left with after we have purged ourselves, as most poststructuralists would have us do, of most of our essentialist yearnings. Physicality as such is probably the last bastion of such essentialism – a banal vice, however, I would argue, and for purely pragmatic reasons very necessary for the production and sustainment of our narratives. We know the objects we have created cannot 'really' denote 'incipient state formation' or 'clouds', but we can safely collect any references made about the object, photograph it, X-ray it, thin-slice it, irradiate it, conserve it, digitise it and put it in a database on disc or CD and relay it within split seconds on computer networks to all our colleagues around the world. Such obsessiveness with the production of objectivity in the pursuit of the objectification of the myriad refractions of the physical world is generally met with the accusation of 'fetishisation'. Clearly if such exercises are not fixed, denotative, explanatory, 'anchored in an adequate social theory', they are simply highly indulgent, irresponsible practices whose only aim is simply to continue endlessly in this self-reproducing and self-referencing process – producing objectifications without a subject, signifiers without a signified, hollow, empty and two-dimensional – fetishes of bourgeois scholarship.

The derogatory associations related to fetishisation seem to stem from a lingering Marxian contempt of excrescences beyond use-value (Marx 1983) – the persistence of the idea that a commodity or object has inherent use-value true to the amount of physical labour exerted to produce it, its physical nature and its utility. This is contrasted with exchange-value which attaches increasing value to the commodity and its culturally (not naturally inherent) determined value as ever-increasing superfluous non-utilitarian embellishments or 'fetishisations' of the commodity. This characterisation of exchange-value betrays a contempt for contingent, culturally determined superfluity of associative meaning in deference to a utilitarian, directed and fundamentally essentialist use-value. In this scheme some 'thing' must be doing something other than just being itself for its own sake, fetishised, with no 'thing' to designate, refer to or have use-value for. To claim innocence while signifying without signification at best is highly superficial and fetishistic, even silly, while highly suspect and pernicious at worst.

However, it is material culture's apparent ability to subvert and resist the metaphysics of use-value through various commodifications and fetishisations that makes it so dynamic, particularly in comparison with its kindred objects, literary texts, which are often attributed (arguably so) with rather stable fixed values and referents. The ambiguous and polysemic attributes of material culture so frequently referred to in the course of this conference attest to material culture's stubborn resistance to meaning in terms of functionalist use-value. Rather, it is precisely these associated qualities of ambiguity that are critical to understanding material culture and the role it plays in human affairs (J. Thomas). In short, it is all the various permutations, fetishisations and recontextualisations which make material culture important. Its constituted physicality, ironically, is precisely what enables it to pass so freely from one context to another. You can pick it up and move it from a grave-site to a museum vitrine or buy it and use it as a flower-vase rather than a funeral urn. Precisely because it is rendered durable it can accommodate a great degree of ambiguity regarding its associative meanings in various recontextualisations, repeatedly moved or seen many different times and ways in many different contexts (Thomas).

Obviously, since any attempt to fix a single referent to any material object in light of its continuously shifting recontextualisations and reconstitutions with the concomitant loss of any single meaning leaves us with just material culture itself, the object, in all its produced, dazzling and compelling physicality infinitely pregnant with potential meanings. Since it is considered by most of us now distasteful if not immoral to fix a single meaning, how are we to negotiate the plurality of associative meanings let forth? Once we have relinquished our authority we cannot say that only certain kinds of associative meaning sanctioned by our professional institutions are legitimate and others (say, the claims of New Agers, historical theme parks, Druids, or my next-door neighbour) are not. How, then, is this cacophony to be managed and, more important, how can it be maintained and preserved against attempts to silence it?

The raw material used to generate this cacophony is material culture itself in all its constituted and evocative physicality. Managing physicality involves the establishment of parameters for access to the objects themselves (the establishment of Criado's visibility strategies) and for the constitution and expression of that physicality (that is, the representation of the object in varying contexts, its physical reconstitution as coded data, exhibit, video, public database, or theme park) in tune with deliberately chosen visibility strategies. As professionals, one of the things we most certainly do best is create the data, constituting it and giving it form. John Fritz has asked why it is that the data of older, less theoretically sophisticated archaeologists are so much richer than the data produced by problem-orientated 'one-shot' investigations of more recent, theoretically sophisticated archaeologists (John Fritz, conference comments). Christopher Tilley's multiple interpretations of rock carvings at Nämforsen (Tilley 1991) attest to the richness of the data set provided by his highly empirical and non-theoretical predecessor G. Hallström, who compiled the data used by Tilley. Hallström's otherwise fetishistic constitution and recording of the objects at hand in all their various aspects elaborated a physicality of the carvings in such a way as to create an even greater trove of material in more readily accessible and visible form for the further elaboration of new and different associative meanings. The interpretations otherwise reached by Hallström might have little but purely historical value at the present time in light of pre-existing disciplinary concerns, but the data so richly constituted are invaluable.

Hallström in his desire for creating the conditions by which his conclusions could be reproducible and his authority confirmed, ironically created the conditions whereby his authority could be challenged – not in terms of whether he did the job properly or not, but in terms of the constitution and maximisation of visibility and physicality and creating the conditions of multiple authority as evidenced in the text by Tilley. Parker Pearson criticised highly theoreticised postprocessual texts as inaccessible and consequently stifling of meaning and called for 'developing new media of experience' (Parker Pearson, conference presentation) to break the hold of these rather constrictive texts on interpretation. Similarly, Richards, in his paper, challenges the authority of the site report or final text as the culmination of the interpretive process. He proposes to break it up, expose the various localised authorities and interpretations in the course of excavation, refracting and document-ing the interpretive process at as many points as possible of interpretive 'encounters' in archaeological procedure, thereby breaking up the authority of the fictive single author of the site report into an elaboration of archaeological procedure producing many authorities and interpretations.

Elaborating on and constituting the material culture of archaeological work in so many media, expanding upon all the intricacies of the interpretive process cannot but be susceptible to the accusation of 'fetishisation' and 'commodification' of questionably commodifiable objects. Such materialist concerns, however, are un-avoidable and integral to the sort of society we find ourselves in. As Thomas points out, the objects and things we produce are the touchstone from which we weave narratives about ourselves, others and the past, probably something we as a species have been doing for quite some time, emphasising certain things, intentionally forgetting some and simply disregarding others. What becomes critical and problem-atic is managing this process. It is probably unquestionable that we want to constitute and consolidate material culture in the production of our pasts and presents. This production is vital for the creation and maintenance of our narratives in the present. This might be a violation of the attributed intentions of past authors associated with the artefacts we have produced and preserved who may have intended their productions to decay and be forgotten. But, then, archaeology has always been particularly aggressive and violent against notions of origins and intent through its destructive excavation practices and interpretive contortions whether in the name of 'Science' or creating the necessary physical conditions for creating our and other pasts. To mourn this violence is to believe in loss – a loss of something 'true' and 'original', a rather false sentimentality in light of much that is discussed in this volume. Our material concerns and 'fetishisations' are very much non-issues in this respect. It is difficult to see how the inclusion of day-to-day reports of excavation observations and multiple conclusions in site reports is very different in degree of fetishisation from the techno-empirico-fantasies of some hardline New

Archaeologists. They both, however, elaborate and constitute data, making it more accessible for other authors to use and weave further narratives.

This all brings us back to the problem of how to manage all these voices, all these 'authorities' and archaeologies regarding material culture. A general feeling is that no one should be prohibited access to the material cultural data produced and denied legitimacy in interpreting it outside the profession. But John Fritz did bring up the question of whether other groups ought to be actually allowed to constitute the data and dig up sites as pot-hunters in North America often do (John Fritz, conference comments). A possible criterion for deciding these issues and the exertion of professional authority might be to ask what acts inhibit the constitution of potential data least. Pot-hunters often lose much detail regarding the deposition of artefacts in their work, constituting the data poorly in its detail and inhibiting the circulation of these artefacts by maintaining them in virtually inaccessible collections. The physicality and visibility of these objects are obviously hindered, severely inhibiting the richer constitution and use of these artefacts of material culture by others. One of the goals of the profession ought to be to ensure maximal access while maximising the constitution of the artefacts of material culture. Such a goal is largely curatorial and preservational and dominated by the questions of what gets preserved, why, by whom, for whom, and how to allocate resources towards these goals.

Peter Fowler noticed an interesting shift from theory to money in the discussions above (Peter Fowler, conference comments). Mark Leone spoke of his concerns of how to tie all our 'high falutin' theory to the actual management of resources in producing the archaeological record (Mark Leone, conference comments; see Leone and Potter 1992 for an in-depth discussion). How do we decide to spend the money we have and what are the bases of these decisions? Fowler himself called for archaeologists to be more bold about demanding money for archaeological work. What started out as esoteric discussions of 'text' ended up on how to get more money and how to use it. So how did we get from text to money? Was it disillusion with theoretical meanderings, even a rejection of the enterprise in light of the overwhelming pragmatics of getting things done in an environment where such meanderings leave the discipline distracted and unable to deal with the realities of competing interest groups? The reburial of Native American human remains, the archaeologies competing for recognition of under-represented groups (racial, ethnic and sexual), government intervention, funding, commercialisation, and threats by rapid development to the archaeological record all force themselves upon us in the course of our interpretive labours. Much of the discipline's previous efforts to establish 'origins', 'scientific objectivity', or 'anchoring in an adequate social theory' have more or less failed to provide us with the tools to contend with this increasingly cacophonous environment. After all the theoretical fervour of the past ten years we are finally left with the constituted objects themselves and the seemingly banal but vital question of their management. This preoccupation with physicality in our discussions of 'text', focuses our attention on the issues surrounding our notions of durability, interpretation, and contextualisation that favours increasingly new constitutions of material culture. Consequently, this current in our theoretical debates on 'text' demands a new concern with management, pragmatics, access and presentation to ensure the fundamental and equitable conditions of interpretation.

Chapter 24

The visibility of the archaeological record and the interpretation of social reality

Felipe Criado

The questions which are posed in this article are based on a series of specific characteristics of the archaeological record which, although essential and well known, are nevertheless important and useful for the analysis of this record and the social practices which created it. These self-evident facts can be listed as follows.

- For the greater part of prehistory human action did not significantly alter the surrounding environment.
- The construction of artificial 'monuments' only took place in relatively recent times.
- Despite many specific exceptions, in general it is true that the use of precious, imperishable materials in the creation of material culture is an equally recent phenomenon.

The late occurrence of these features shows that the construction of a social landscape using artificial elements of material culture is a rare event, and not the universal which it is erroneously taken to be within modern ideology. Moreover, this event (the construction of a social landscape) is paralleled by the simultaneous appearance of other phenomena which are inextricably bound up with the intensification of social complexity. Under our interpretation the emergence of these social facts implies that the societies involved were fundamentally transformed.

Now, if we examine these transformations, we can clearly see that they are based upon a previous modification of cultural orientation towards nature and a new understanding of the relationship between society and the latter. Some points which support this interpretation are as follows.

- The absence of 'technology' in primitive societies and its subsequent emergence as a specialised and autonomous domain of social activity underlines the dislocation of society and nature in order to further the social control of nature by technological means.
- There is an accompanying growth of 'production' and economic rationalities which tend towards the maximisation of production.
- There is the fact that the first long-lasting monumental constructions of human societies were intimately bound up with the exercise of power and its ideological control.
- The first social images of time (understood as tradition or social memory) are correlated with the development of the first monuments, an increase in social inequality, and the appearance of social groups 'wielding' power.

In the light of these observations we believe that the social transformations imply a change in the management of spatial rationality within the societies involved. The change would, by the same token, also imply new ways of conceptualising time and space as basic correlates of new social strategies involving the *construction* of the landscape.

Given this interpretation and the theoretical perspective which underlies this text, it must be acknowledged that the modification of concepts of space and time is not merely 'bound up' with social transformations: it constitutes the fundamental horizon of their possibility.

This argument can be made more specific if, in the light of anthropological evidence, we consider different conceptions of space as these are documented within different socio-cultural complexes. The idea may be developed that some forms of landscape construction are related to a cultural rationality typical of primitive societies and the 'savage mind', so we have tried to relate this dynamic of the social construction of the landscape in prehistory with a (pre)historicisation of Lévi-Strauss's model (1966 and after) of the 'savage mind' and the 'domesticated mind'.

This does give rise to several problems. The first is that the 'savage mind' does not lend itself to being historicised in this way. To cope with this problem we propose a reading which isolates and excludes the generic and abstract component of Lévi-Strauss's 'savage mind' and concentrates on the concrete and historical aspects which can be applied to specific social configurations. Put in another way, our reading distinguishes between a 'savage' syntax and a 'savage' semantics. While it maintains the first to denote what Lévi-Strauss terms 'mind' or 'thought', it adopts the second (semantics) to further our understanding of specific social formations.

We also assert that, since the 'savage mind' has not always existed, but came into being at a determinate point in time, it must have been preceded and followed by qualitatively distinct modes of 'thought'. While any comments on the possible predecessors of the 'savage mind' remain hypothetical, its successors are accessible through historical and anthropological analysis.

In this way we can formulate a general model of which the salient features are outlined below. However, it is difficult to explore this field of possibilities in prehistory, through archaeology. In order to exhaust this field of possibilities we shall try to formulate a theoretico-methodological limit which permits us to read and characterise the archaeological record in accordance with the interpretive scheme just outlined. This model derives from our conviction that the *conditions of visibility* of the archaeological record and material culture are one of the most important resources which can be deployed to understand the relationship of the latter with the social reality from which they derive. In this way we can come to understand the cultural rationalities, attitudes towards space, and modes of conceptualisation of the nature/culture relationship which characterise specific archaeological contexts. To this end we have adopted a strict materialist perspective, of which, as it underlines all aspects of our analysis, we shall give a brief account.

Our perspective is based on four fundamental and complementary principles which are causally linked.

- Reality is produced through human labour, social practices. This principle is linked to the thought of the young Marx in which 'infrastructure' was originally understood as human labour, and 'superstructure' as the results of that labour.
- The real is criss-crossed by a fundamental material unity which implies that all segments of reality are linked and mutually determined.
- Reality is not simply constituted by the material, but also by the ideal and the imaginary. So the 'real' character of a phenomenon does not derive from its physical attributes, but from its ability to produce real effects (this is defined by Foucault as the materialism of the incorporeal).

- The ideal is frequently the basic infrastructural condition of the material world, since objects and labour itself must be thought before they can be practised.

POSITIONS

We adopt the definition of material culture (elaborated by Shanks and Tilley) as the objectification of social being. This is a useful definition as it implies that the transformation of a brute material thing into a cultural object involves the gathering together of a series of determinate traces of the socio-cultural context within which the object is produced.[1]

Now, in order to remain consistent with a materialist perspective we must acknowledge that these traces are not confined to the domain of material culture: they permeate all forms of social action and are the results of these actions. To the extent that the material reality of the archaeological record is, in fact, *constituted* by these effects, we must pay careful attention to the comments above.

So the archaeological record should be thought of as not simply being the traces which have survived the effects of cultural postdepositional factors which remain accessible to the archaeologist through an analytical process realised within a determinate contemporary social and economic context. It must also be stressed that these formal elements are patterned by specific attitudes towards surrounding 'reality'. Thus we can speak of three distinct moments in the formation of the archaeological record: the pre-existing social reality, the physical processes of decay and preservation, and the contemporary act of reading.

We suggest in this article that within the first set of social factors or 'attitudes' underlying social action we can isolate a specific 'will' to render the result of social action visible or invisible.[2] This 'will' is evident where the efficacy of a social process depends upon its manifest visibility (rituals, displays of power, military manoeuvres, etc.). The formal aspects of the results of social action can clearly be influenced by this 'will' to visibility, and can, in fact, be divided into two distinct groups, in each of which action 'corresponds' to pre-existing social reality in a different way. In the first the formal elements of the action and its results are intrinsic, in the second, extrinsic.

The first group consists of 'products'; that is, the results of a process of 'production', whether intentional or not, which gather together their social conditions and preconditions within a formal unity. The second are simply 'effects'; that is to say, the traces or indirect consequences of social actions. This dual classification will act as a fundamental schema with which we shall classify the effects of social action on the environment.

If we take into account the necessary correspondence between social being and social action, then we must recognise that the 'will to visibility' can be explicit and conscious, or implicit and unconscious, quite independently of whether the related social actions are intentional or non-intentional. By this we mean that the actors involved are not necessarily capable of representing such a 'will to visibility' to themselves. Instead, to the extent that ideological functions which presuppose the visibility of a social grouping or subset of social actions are in operation, we can legitimately infer and describe such a 'will to visibility' from the manifest cultural effects of such a will. Similarly we must remember that it is the rationality of a specific socio-economic formation which determines which cultural traces will be visible and which will not. For example, we should not expect to find traces of the fundamental transformation of nature in hunting societies, nor should we expect traces of permanent settlements from mobile communities.

We must stress that the term 'will' does not refer to individual psychology or intentionality, or imply that the 'will to visibility' expresses a conscious intention. Instead it represents an intrinsic, rational, non-empirical ground of social processes. In some cases it is consciously used by these processes, in others it is identical with them, while in others its existence must be inferred as part of our own contemporary reading.[3] The first case would be exemplified by the construction of a commemorative monument which perpetuates an ideological discourse of domination. An example of the second class would be the iconic message purveyed by medieval sculptures which presuppose visibility but are not explicitly preoccupied with it. An example of the third group is the way in which we must interpret the *absence* of oppressed groups such as the result of a dominant ideology which secures their visibility.

So in some cases the 'will to visibility' is an intrinsic part of social action which is explicit in the archaeological record (the minority of cases); in other social contexts (the great majority) it is *we* who must posit such a will in order to understand this record. In both cases, however, we believe that this model can legitimately be used in archaeology, as it manifests a logic which is homologous to that which constructed the record being analysed.[4] Therefore we can expect that the various components of material culture and the results of social action will demonstrate different degrees of visibility in accordance with the underlying social rationality. We will refer to those formal characteristics of social actions which relate to their degree of visibility as *conditions of visibility*. These conditions indicate a variety of modes of emphasising the process of objectivication which gives rise to material culture, and the orientation of society towards the world. We shall label these as *strategies of visibility*.

DEVELOPMENTS

Having arrived at this point, we want to go beyond a set of empty theoretical imperatives and convert them into concrete methodological proposals. We shall attempt to do so by tackling the following questions:

- How can we recognise and characterise *strategies of visibility* within the archaeological record?
- Once we have recognised those strategies, how do we reconstruct the 'will to visibility' which they represent and analyse how this is related to a specific cultural rationality?
- Finally, how do we relate this will to visibility with determinate historical social formations?

THE RECOGNITION AND DEFINITION OF STRATEGIES OF VISIBILITY

In order to resolve the first of these questions we must define how these strategies operate, what mechanisms they function through and, most important, the system of existence of such strategies of visibility.

The latter is constituted through a combination of specific elements, dimensions and resources of diverse kinds. Different strategies of visibility, the achievement of specific forms of visibility or invisibility, depend on such unique combinations.

So, from a logical point of view, the existence of a determinate strategy of visibility presupposes that a choice has been made whether to render social action visible or invisible. As noted above, this choice can be conscious (intentional). In the latter case the 'choice' corresponds to the intrinsic logic of the socio-cultural formation concerned. This very duality, which is inherent in all social/human action, is necessarily found in the subsequent choices made in the construction of visibility; from here on the repertory of possibilities is doubled.[5]

The 'will to visibility' is objectified through a variety of elements. We may call these the *raw material* from which visibility is constructed. Essentially, they fall into three categories: material culture products, the effects of social action, and social practices themselves. Considered dynamically we must ascribe a genetic priority to the last of these 'raw materials'; that is, social practices. Visibility is manifested first in this domain, then through its effects (whether conscious or unconscious), and lastly through material culture itself. So the presence of any of these classes of elements might imply the visibility of the 'genetically prior' elements.

Once an element of raw material has been mobilised for the production of visibility we must consider the dimensions along which this process is projected. From our point of view these are, essentially, those of *space* and *time*. The first refers to an essentially episodic, temporally discontinuous visibility manifest *only in space*. The second refers to visibility which persists through time, which has a definite duration. Logically we might isolate different forms of this temporal visibility according to the extent of the duration implied.

Lastly, the construction of visibility presupposes specific material resources which help determine the unique character and configuration of a form of visibility. They assist in determining, for example, whether cultural acts are projected along a spatial or temporal dimension. As these resources are dependent on highly specific social, cultural and historical factors, it is impossible to list the repertory of choices. However, they do seem to fall into two basic categories: the reutilisation of natural elements, and the construction of artificial elements.[6]

If we consider the totality of logical possibilities formed by combining these four levels (relying only on the principal choices within each class), we obtain a total of 384 different combinations, each denoting a distinct strategy of visibility. Obviously, many of these 'possibilities' have only a theoretical significance, logically conceivable but not practically significant options.

However, despite the great number of such possible strategies, we can take four principal types to represent most of the variability present.

- First we have the cases where there is absolutely no interest in highlighting (or hiding) the presence of social action, and its results. This context implies the absence of any strategy designed to render social products visible *as* products. For this reason we might call such strategies *inhibitory*. We can assert the presence of this 'inhibition' as it produces neither intentional results or products nor non-intentional results. It can, however, give rise to non-intentional products which survive in the archaeological record and reveal the presence of human groups marked by this 'absence'. These groups have probably constituted the majority of human societies on the earth.
- We can also pick out a second group of strategies concerned with *hidings*. These are characterised by a conscious strategy to hide or mark the presence of social action and its results. This strategy leads to the disappearance of social products as products. It is distinct from the previous strategy, which simply involved the *lack* of recognition of such products, not an active attempt to hide their existence.
- A third group of strategies are those which aim to exhibit the processes or results of social action *within* the social present. They are concerned solely with

spatial exhibition through which they emphasise the natural character of social products as products. So we can label them strategies of *exhibition*. These strategies produce intentional results in space, but some of them may also have an involuntary temporal dimension. Moreover, in this way they can generate products and effects which have both a spatial and temporal character.

- Lastly we have strategies similar to the previous group but through which social processes and results are projected temporally. These strategies attempt to highlight the visibility of social creations both within the social present and through time, controlling and overcoming the temporal dimension of change. These strategies can be described as *monumental*. Monumentality produces intentional results (both products and effects) projected both in space and time. But it can also produce non-intentional results which project in both dimensions.

The most representative product of such strategies is the *monument*. From our point of view, a monument can be defined as a cluster of intentional results, made concrete in the form of an artificial product which is visible through space and which maintains this visibility through time.

Now, if we were to interpret this definition in simple univocal terms, it would obscure subtle distinctions between monuments which do not fit within such categories easily. However, although there are cultural creations which do not present the correlated and complementary elements which we consider to characterise monumentality (material product – artificial element – spatial visibility – temporal duration), we may legitimately label everything which has some form of spatio-temporal projection as a specific type of monument.

The first consists of natural elements, rocky outcrops, topographical peculiarities (caves, hills) which are endowed with a specific social significance. By nature these features are visible through space and time, and this facilitates their use by social groups as symbols of the continuity and perpetuation of the group, a means of naturalising social discourse. Therefore it would seem reasonable to describe them as genuine monuments. Here we have a configuration of the following four elements: imaginary product – natural element – spatial visibility – temporal projection. The principal difference from the category of monumentality outlined above is that once the event which ascribes meaning to the natural element is over, and the social group involved has disappeared, there is no easy way to recognise such natural elements *as* monuments. Sometimes, however, cultural continuity has preserved traces of the significance of these elements: a fact often attested amongst peasant societies which may incorporate natural features into their own cultural traditions which were once significant in proto- and pre-historic societies. We shall call this type of monument (for reasons to be explained later) a *savage monument*.

Another type of monument is that which displays the classic configuration of elements, but in which spatial visibility is *not* clearly manifested. An example would be human constructions which are endowed with monumentality through the proximity of an older natural feature which contributes to their spatial visibility and temporal duration but which may be difficult to detect without prior knowledge of the social rationality at work in each specific context. We could label such a feature an *ambiguous monument*. An example would be those megaliths which occur near rocky summits or outcrops. Their presence is both emphasised and partially hidden by such natural features. Similarly, petroglyphs carved on conspicuous outcrops may be invisible from a distance owing to the slight alteration of the rockface.

THE INTERPRETATION OF THE WILL TO VISIBILITY

Our proposals so far simply provide a means of ordering and systemising the archaeological record. However, we think that its usefulness can be taken for granted as we can employ it to reconstruct the presence of a specific 'will to visibility' and then go on to interpret the cultural values which it presupposes. We must begin by examining the conditions of visibility of the results of social action as revealed in the formal and contextual characteristics of that part of the archaeological record being studied. This does not mean that we *assume* a specific meaning behind a strategy of visibility; instead we carry out a formal analysis deriving from our own operational logic outlined above.

Once we have achieved a formal self-contained description, we must proceed to the next level of analysis. This presupposes that the will to visibility implements specific concepts of space and time, which are themselves related to the way in which the society concerned conceptualises its own relation to nature and the environment. A regularity is established between all these domains which determines that each will to visibility reflects a specific cultural rationality and is related to social representations and ideological discourses, as it constitutes a fundamental mechanism whereby such discourses operate.

If we examine the visibility of human action, society and people as they emerge from these strategies, we can refine our understanding of the concepts of space and time underlying these four general types of strategy of visibility (defined above) by using analogies derived from anthropology.

So, although our interpretations offer a way of ascribing meaning to the archaeological record, they are themselves derived from the anthropological models we discussed earlier (we shall return to this point in the last section).

THE CONTEXTUALISATION OF WILL TO VISIBILITY AND STRATEGIES OF VISIBILITY

The regularities which we can establish between a will to visibility and a specific pattern of social and cultural rationality can be interpreted in two different ways.

First, as a diachronic succession: that is, a series of cultural constructions which follow each other and represent different social formations. However, this does *not* imply an evolutionary progression from one state to the next.

Second, they can be interpreted in a synchronic and social manner. Here they are seen as a means of constructing distinct cultural identities within specific historical contexts in terms of the conflicts present in the relevant social formations and the specific nature of the social formation as a totality. So each society can be characterised by a unique will to visibility or this will may be interpreted in terms of conflicts between social formations or tensions within a social grouping. The latter case may seem more relevant to complex societies, in which an increase in social distinctions leads to a greater variety of social expectations and aspirations. However, we must remember that the construction of gender is virtually a universal social process and a basis for the development of inequality within the 'simplest' societies. So we may posit the existence of conflicting strategies of visibility within such societies which played an important role in expressing and elaborating the conflicts arising from the social construction of gender.

'Monumental' material culture characterises a 'divided society' (in the sense developed by Clastres). On the archaeological level it represents late-Neolithic peasant communities and their proto-historic successors; ceremonial monumentality is the most important expression of such a divided society.

Strategies which simply 'exhibit' material culture characterise those societies based on the maximal exploitation of nature where we can detect the opening of a rupture between society and nature; post-glacial art exemplifies this form of cultural rationality.

Strategies of 'hiding' characterise those societies which remain immersed in the natural order, and do not risk the opening of a gap between nature and culture; this would be exemplified by Palaeolithic art.

Strategies of 'inhibition' would have dominated the greater part of human prehistory. Here people did not consider themselves the masters of creation and world. The fragility and scarcity of archaeological evidence for such societies in itself constitutes a significant marker of such 'inhibition'.

PROBLEMS

The previous points suggest that we adopt a visual metaphor to understand the archaeological record.

The validity of this metaphor is based on the fact that the will to visibility is a condition of the constitution of the archaeological record as such. So the morphology of this record, with all its inherent absences and failings, can itself be turned into a core of meaning, through which a specific will to visibility is revealed. 'Absent' archaeological events are pregnant with meaning, as their lack of existence can in fact be understood as their most intrinsic and intimate mode of being.

This model offers a profoundly different set of perspectives on the archaeological record from those which dominate at the present time: the physical metaphor of the New Archaeology and the textual metaphor of postprocessual archaeology.

Given that the former has been superseded by the latter, we must refine our analysis, which, we believe, enables us to go beyond the textual metaphor. Although this textual metaphor has encouraged the development of archaeology through the last decade,[7] we feel that it has been incapable of solving the basic problem of *reading* material culture. This problem lies in presupposing a meaning lying within the text which demands and solicits a reading.

As is well known, this is not a problem as such for hermeneutics which asserts that the act of reading is an interpretive act which, rather than providing a transparent interpretation of an external text, increases our self-understanding *through* the text. This solution is acceptable on the condition the text and its reader share a single cultural and linguistic horizon. For it is only within a single horizon of understanding that comprehension of the text is necessarily converted into the self-understanding of the world obtained by the reader. What proponents of a hermeneutic approach tend to forget is that Archaeology, Anthropology and History are, for the most part, concerned with radically *different* cultural horizons. In this case interpretation as self-understanding is simply not feasible, for self-understanding through a (pre-) text is simply an excuse for the tyrannical domination of that text by the reading subject.

This follows from the structuralist and poststructuralist position that the meaning of a sign is found in a system of differences between signs. However, as most signs are absent within the text their 'original' meaning can never be discovered. To do so would imply an external perspective on the text or phenomenon being interpreted. Now, this external rationality would be an imposition on the text-phenomenon by an alien subjectivity – rationality. So, when Derrida (for example) states that there is nothing outside the text, he is not so much saying that there is no *meaning* within the text, but that this meaning is not *present*, it does not *exist now*, and if it ever did 'exist' its meaning would in fact be a redoubling of the context through which the reader faces the text. This meaning would in fact be a form of subjective reification.

It is for this reason that, as poststructuralism has pointed out, the presupposition of an implicit meaning necessarily reinforces the philosophy of consciousness and the modern conception of subjectivity. This simply maintains the traditional values of the subject, time, History, universality. . . .

This debate has preoccupied archaeologists for the last few years. Although there seems to have been a provisional victory for the hermeneutic camp which reconstructs archaeology as an interpretive practice (developed by Shanks and Tilley, 1987a and 1987b) (which merely concedes that the interpretive process must recognise certain 'natural' limits of the text which contain any subjective excesses), this simply conceals the fact that from a poststructural perspective archaeology as such *is not possible*.

If we acknowledge the absence of many of the signs which constitute meaning from the archaeological record, we must also admit that 'our discipline' simply cannot gain access to any original meaning owing to the fragmentary nature of the totality of signs as this is presented to us. The only way of 'solving' this problem is through an excess of subjectivity which functions by supplying the 'missing signs' which are absent from the record.

Now, placing ourselves in this abyss of madness, engaged in a debate over the possibility of limits, we must acknowledge that the very same problems can arise through our own use of a visual metaphor. For if we assume that a specific will to visibility represents a distinct rationality, are we not ourselves imposing a universal rationality on the specific configurations of material independently from their unique social and historical context? Are we not simply reconstructing an evolutionary, taxonomic scheme typical of modernist discourse, one which should be firmly excluded by a postmodern epistemology?

The limitations of the visual metaphor are revealed by the fact that it be seen as reinforcing the ideology of exhibition and social visibility which seems so typical of the will to power-knowledge of the 1980s.

It would be ingenuous to argue that these problems are foreign to our text because they are not amongst its explicit aims and its basic proposals and their development render such an outcome impossible. We have known for a long time that the text goes beyond the intentions of its author and in order to solve these problems we must subject the text to a quite different discipline.

So I have tried to construct a methodology and practice which is not based on a super-interpretation but on the development of an intuition (namely, that the production of the archaeological record is criss-crossed by a will to visibility) which then leads on to a systematic description of material culture based on merely *formal* relations. This system consciously adopts *our own* perspective to study the archaeology. Our interpretation widens out from this point: *not* based on the reading of a given meaning but on the reordering of formal relations, their significant juxtaposition with relations preserved in other codes and deriving from other social contexts. In particular, we rely on insights provided by anthropological theory. Nevertheless, these procedures, however rigorously applied, are not in themselves sufficient to subvert the risk of meaning.

From a theoretical and interpretive perspective this risk can only be dissolved through an operation which has been the ground of success of structural anthropology. This operation consists in basing interpretations on patterns of rationality and subjectivity which are radically different from our own.

Archaeology, faced with the dilemma of excessive subjectivity or its disappearance as a discipline, can only mitigate these difficulties and reduce the subjective risk of positing absent meanings by grounding its interpretations in patterns of rationality which are not exclusively our own. Or, in other words, if there is nothing outside the text we must insinuate new texts within the traditional text.[8] We believe that most of postprocessual archaeology has failed in this task; but has, instead, simply extended the domain of the archaeologist's subjectivity – a modern Western subjectivity – however much this process is disguised using the conceptual apparatus of hermeneutics and the ethical justification of political radicalism.

So what begins as *our* analysis ends up as something quite different (by using concepts derived from the work of rationality which are attested anthropologically). At the very least these facts and models permit us to use this starting point heuristically and convince us that our hypothesis is a legitimate framework for archaeological analysis. Our method would have the advantage of corresponding to the very patterns of rationality which constitute the archaeological record; patterns which subvert our own traditional values and rationality.

It is precisely for this reason that we believe our visual metaphor is not simply an extension of the ideology of the 1980s; instead we believe that the application of this model can lead to conclusions which radically subvert and invert our starting point.

We assert these proposals in the knowledge that, if they are true, they are so at global level and not necessarily true at some specific levels. However, have we really escaped the risk of meaning, of conjuring up meaning with subjective strategies? Have we really put forward an alternative which owes more to poststructuralism than to hermeneutics? Perhaps in the end we haven't. For if we perform a phenomenological reading of Lévi-Strauss, we realise that a hermeneutic approach does underlie his work. If we observe that structural anthropology postulates a radical homology between the cultural and natural orders, that the very possibility of structural analysis is grounded on this homology and that the scientific pretensions of structural analysis presuppose the identity of structures of the human spirit with nature, then must we not admit that, to the extent that it goes beyond the subject/object division, it does so by recuperating the phenomenological *Lebenswelt*. Does this not acquire an ontological priority upon which the configuration and explanation of reality must be based?

If we recognise that the work of Lévi-Strauss is based on a form of radical objectivism which destroys the subject/object distinction on which the project of modern consciousness is built and that as a result it dissolves humanity in nature, can we not accept that what differentiates it from both positivist objectivism and phenomenological subjectivism is the absolute refusal to base this new (postmodern) project on a founding subjectivity and to recuperate this subjectivity through the results of the analysis? When Lévi-Strauss defines his work as neo-Kantianism without a transcendental subject he is referring precisely to this duality, one pole of which is absent. For while it tries to construct a theoretical model of transcendental objectivity which takes account of the relationship between nature and culture, it attempts to do this *without* elevating the notion of man as a transcendental subject.

The death of man, as postulated by anthropological structuralism, is nothing more than a piece of *a priori* and *a posteriori* caution, designed to avoid the recuperation of the classical philosophy (metaphysics) of consciousness. Anti-subjectivism becomes an ethical option which enables us, at the last moment, to prevent the speaking subject from recuperating discourse. In the absence of any emerging new pattern of subjectivity we must resort to nihilism. At the end nothing guarantees that our text will not have reproduced the pattern of subjectivity from which it originated and will not have been converted into a useful tool for reproduction of the system.[9] For us, the only option in this situation is the ethical position asserted above. We must consciously or deconstructively choose to remain outside discourse casting a philosophical smile (to quote Foucault) on discourse once it has been accomplished. At the same time we must exhaust the risks of basing archaeological practice on other patterns of subjectivity, because it is only in this way that archaeology can contribute to the urgent project (urgent in the present crisis situation) of constructing new patterns of subjectivity through which to contrast the adaptation of society to nature with the very bases of social reality.

NOTES

1 Obviously, as asserted through post-processualism, these traces are not the direct reflections of the social circumstances in which they were produced.

2 Although we shall be dealing with the first of these moments within this article, we must admit that this partially influences the other two. Depending on whether the will to visibility is present in the first moment, the effects of the second and third on the archaeological record are altered. If, for example, an ornamental item is made out of perishable material, it is unlikely to survive in the archaeological record, whereas an object made from precious metal is much more likely to survive the effects of natural destructive agents and also acquire greater significance within the traditional processes of archaeological interpretation.

3 This use of the term 'will' derives from the concept of a will to power-knowledge in Nietzsche and Foucault.

4 Although the facts already cited tend to justify this assertion, we realise that this is in fact the primary root of the practical, methodological, theoretical and empirical problems which attend our proposals. These are considered at length throughout this article, particularly in the last section.

5 To support this statement we must firmly reject the theory of consciousness prevalent in the Anglo-Saxon world according to which human activity is always conscious or intentional. This position, exemplified in behavioural psychology, follows from the dominant strategy of the construction of the individual in modern societies as a conscious intentional agent; one who is always responsible for his or her acts. This process of individuation is particularly prominent, in Saxon, Nordic and Germanic societies; less so in Latin ones. It has constructed the type of subject on which Western bourgeois democracies are based. Despite the fact that Freud and psychoanalysis have radically deconstructed the bases of this position, it remains strong.

6 All these questions presuppose that we are dealing with non-literary societies. Given that writing (first epic, then as history) itself constitutes a specific form of visibility, and functions as a strategy of exhibition we must consider its effects on the other strategies of visibility listed. We must also take into account that in non-literary societies the function of writing is largely taken over by orality and oral tradition. The difference is that, whereas orality creates an episodic form of visibility and, therefore, ought to be treated as a specific form of strategy of exhibition, writing creates authentic 'monuments' and must therefore be classed as a strategy of monumentality.

7 In the sense that, as a form of discourse, it has changed the way we *see* things through and despite the dominating force of the words we use.

8 Thus, although History is faced with the same set of problems, it sets about solving them in a different way. Through written texts and historical documents it can gain access to the discursive systems of the society being studied. Using structural analysis or historical semantics it can uncover the pattern of rationality being expressed.

9 Some critics suggest (not without reason) that this is the very outcome of Lévi-Strauss's 'Structural anthropology' to the extent that it reproduces the context and subject/object of post-industrial culture.

Chapter 25

Tombs and territories

Material culture and multiple interpretation

Michael Parker Pearson

Different theoretical perspectives on material culture can lead to radically different interpretations of archaeological evidence. The competition of multiple interpretations can cause considerable controversy if one interpretation of the evidence has previously been accepted as 'fact' rather than hypothesis. This raises questions about the extent to which belief in the conventional wisdom may constrain the search for new interpretations. The overdetermination of facts by interpretive frameworks has been recognised for some time in archaeology, but few empirical examples have been produced to illustrate the issue.

In 1939 archaeologists discovered the remains of a ship, laden with treasure, buried under a mound on the east bank of the River Deben in south Suffolk. This ship burial from Sutton Hoo has been studied in more detail than any individual burial in Europe. Recent innovative excavation of other mounds and burials in the Sutton Hoo cemetery by Martin Carver has also produced new evidence. Using the wealth of evidence and observations published by Rupert Bruce-Mitford (and by many other researchers working on this and related topics), it is possible to interpret the same material evidence to reach different conclusions on the attribution and significance of this ship burial.

The association of the burial with the East Anglian kingdom is generally treated as a 'fact' beyond dispute. Indeed, many specialists consider that this was the grave (or cenotaph, since no body was found in the bone-dissolving sand) of Raedwald, king of the East Angles, who died around AD 625.

There are stylistic links between Sutton Hoo and similar but smaller boat burials in eastern Sweden. These similarities include the practice of burial in a boat under a mound, and a distinctive style of animal ornament in the jewellery. Partly as a result of these material links, the early kings of East Anglia, the Wuffing dynasty, are considered to have had Swedish ancestry. But are stylistic similarities in metalwork style and funerary rite incontrovertible grounds for establishing that the man honoured by this burial had Swedish ancestry? We reach such conclusions by using assumptions about culture and style within a 'culture history' paradigm. The similarities of mound burial, use of boats in graves and techniques of ornament in precious metals are considered to represent ethnic groupings in a direct and reflective manner. But does this assumption give sufficient consideration to the social and archaeological context, both locally in eastern England and across northern Europe?

Metalwork of the Sutton Hoo/eastern Swedish style has been taken to indicate strong cultural links specifically between Sutton Hoo and eastern Sweden. But there is the distinct possibility that the Sutton Hoo style metalwork was circulating more widely throughout north-west Europe in the early seventh century. Since élites in southern England and Scandinavia had largely abandoned the practice of burying these kinds of grave goods by that time, it is possible that these high-status artefacts

remained in circulation among the living and are therefore rarely visible archaeologically, since they did not form ritual deposits. There may have been a broad
network of élite use and exchange of this metalwork across much of Scandinavia as
well as southern England. Finds from the Baltic islands of Bornholm and Oeland
suggest that such styles were being manufactured there, among other places.

The similarities between Sutton Hoo and eastern Sweden are evident in the use of
similar prestige grave goods and the funerary symbolism of ships and boats. The
existence of small boat burials in East Anglia has been used to stress the association
between East Anglia and eastern Sweden, but boat-associated burials are found
throughout south-east England. Similar prestige grave goods are found with burials
in Essex, Buckinghamshire and Oxfordshire. A few stray finds of this animal
ornament style of metalwork are known from East Anglia (amongst other places),
but their uncertain contexts and unknown processes of deposition constrain the
archaeologist's ability to identify them firmly as East Anglian products.

The Sutton Hoo burial also contains items of Frankish origin and Frankish style.
A purse contained a hoard of gold coins, each struck in a separate Frankish mint.
The sword came from the Rhineland. There are close similarities in the dress items,
such as the massive gold belt-buckle, with those from Frankish élite burials.
However, some of the intricacies of the gold-working and garnet setting were unique
to England. The quantity of Frankish material indicates a link to Francia, and the
many items from the Mediterranean and further east can be argued to have passed
through Francia. This link does not demand an ascription of simple ethnic or
political identity. Similarly, links between Sutton Hoo and eastern Sweden may have
been far more complex than direct political or ethnic identities.

This is not a Swedish or a Frankish burial, although it contains material of
Swedish and Frankish origin. Aspects of dress style are unique to southern England.
This was the ceremonial uniform of a ruler who lived in England, but where was his
kingdom? Was it East Anglia, or was it a smaller 'emergent' polity within south
Suffolk?

We have presumed that Sutton Hoo was a 'central place' at or near the centre of
a political territory, in contrast to the comparable eastern Swedish boat burials which
were placed at the forest and upland margins of their communities. Were élite burials
and cemeteries necessarily constructed at the centres of their kingdoms, rather than
on their peripheries? We should consider the possibility that the Sutton Hoo cemetery
might be the burial ground of rulers from the kingdom to the west, the East Saxons
(broadly coextensive with the county of Essex, of which the present boundary lies
10 miles to the west). Sutton Hoo lies within a region where the funerary costumes
of fifth- and sixth-century women may be considered as ethnic markers of the Angles.
Some of these dress fittings are of styles common in Norway and Sweden – further
confirmation for some archaeologists that by the seventh century Sutton Hoo was in
East Anglia. A few examples in England are found outside Anglia (a region stretching
from Lincolnshire to Northamptonshire to East Anglia), in Essex and Kent. However,
there is no doubt that women buried in south Suffolk were symbolising Anglian and
not Saxon identities. But such styles were not confined by the boundaries of political
territories; ethnic identity is not necessarily contiguous with political territory. This
is not to deny the importance of ethnicity at that time; such stress on regionality in
personal dress and weaponry styles indicates that it was an important issue.

But within the 'culture history' paradigm there has often been uncritical acceptance that the ethnic groupings mirrored territorial power polities. There may well
have been an approximate match of Anglian ethnicity with political territories, but
the boundaries between ethnicities were fluid and variable.

Were there grave goods in the ship burial which could indicate that here also were the ethnic identifiers of an East Angle? Most of the grave goods were imported to England – a cape from Syria, garnets from India, bowls from Egypt, a sword from the Rhine, drinking-horns from Sweden and coins from France. The hanging-bowls, cauldrons, buckets and other items were probably of English manufacture but cannot be localised. The shoe-buckles are of a style found in Essex, Kent and Francia. The unassuming, poorly made pottery flask was also probably made in Kent or the South-East. There was just enough surviving of the three bone combs to identify them as Saxon styles (which were very rare in East Anglia). Three of the nine spears were of a style found in graves within the Saxon and Kentish kingdoms. None of the items from the ship can be labelled as East Anglian. Perhaps everything in the burial was imported and nothing will reveal the occupant's local origins. Given the modesty of some of the items and the size of the assemblage, this seems unlikely.

Those items in the burial which are regionally specific have East Saxon or Kentish affinities, but not East Anglian associations. But, if this was not an 'East Anglian' burial, what was it doing in an area which was probably East Anglian by the eighth century and which already had a sizeable population of women wearing Anglian costume? Sutton Hoo lies on an economic boundary between communities using gold coinage as a medium of exchange and those to the north using it for personal ornament. There are also other types of trade goods which rarely find their way north of the Chilterns and Suffolk clay watershed. Intriguingly, Sutton Hoo also lies on a former political boundary zone between the Late Iron Age and early Roman territories of the Iceni and the Trinovantes, whose territory extended into what is now south Suffolk. These tribal and subsequently cantonal territories have been identified largely for coin distributions. Are political boundaries from the Roman period relevant for the post-Roman era? We cannot know whether the boundaries altered in the Roman period, but it is certainly possible that the East Saxon kings had inherited the administrative structure and political territory of the Late Roman Trinovantes.

The new hypothesis we can consider now is that Sutton Hoo is the burial of an East Saxon ruler. The grave is unusual in containing items which have been interpreted as regalia: a whetstone sceptre and an iron 'standard'. The bejewelled uniform, based on late Roman parade armour, is also interpreted as a royal attribute. As a prehistorian, I have always been wary of identifying historically recorded people and events in the archaeological record. But in this case I am curious. There are documented king-lists, and a detailed study of the East Saxon Seaxneting dynasty has recently been published. The early seventh century is essentially a prehistoric period since most 'historical' records relating to that time were not written down until later. Nevertheless, the dates of accession and death of various kings are not known from the writings of Bede.

Although there are undoubted problems in textual criticism with Bede's motives and interpretations, his historical accuracy is broadly accepted. Indeed, the identification of the Sutton Hoo burial as that of Raedwald is drawn largely from Bede's history.

One individual who seems a good candidate is the East Saxon king, Saebert, son of Sledd and sister's son of Aethelbert, king of Kent. Aethelbert was married to Bertha, a Frank. As a favoured sister's son, whose maternal uncle was married to a Frankish princess, Saebert was just the man to have had access to élite alliance systems in Europe and the gifts which cemented them. His baptism was sponsored by his maternal uncle, Aethelbert, around AD 604. He died in AD 617/618 and was succeeded by his three pagan sons who, unusually, shared the kingship together.

Within the burial are artefacts which have aroused considerable interest for their symbolic associations. On the right side of where the corpse's head would have rested were two silver spoons (inscribed 'Saulon' and 'Paulos' in Greek) and ten silver bowls decorated with cruciform motifs. Similar crosses adorned the scabbard and the belt buckle incorporated a hollow cavity, comparable to Frankish belt-reliquaries. Some archaeologists have been dubious as to whether English élites of that period would have been aware of the Christian symbolism of these items. However, a closer analysis of the context of material culture use suggests that the baptismal spoons had not lost their Christian meaning. Their careful placing, together with cruciform-decorated bowls, to the right-hand side of the spot where the head would have lain suggests that they were considered by the mourners as highly significant to the deceased. Some archaeologists accept the association of Christian meaning but consider that it constitutes further evidence that this grave was that of Raedwald who, Bede tells, converted to Christianity yet retained his pagan idols.

This compromise has been used to explain the pagan nature of the ship burial with all its grave goods, combined with the Christian possessions of the individuals commemorated. Of course, the dead do not bury themselves, and I suggest that this burial is more plausibly interpreted as the memorial of a Christian (Saebert had been baptised) by pagans according to invented or elaborated custom.

Saebert seemed a good candidate owing to his relationships with his Christian maternal uncle and his pagan successors. My interpretation of the material culture, in particular the curious mix of Christian grave goods and pagan rites, indicated Saebert as a possibility. The coin dates, however, were firmly fixed in the mid-620s. This was far too late for the Sutton Hoo to have been Saebert's monument. But the dating of the Sutton Hoo hoard has just been completely reassessed in an as yet unpublished paper.

This paper concludes that the coins could have been brought together between 600 and 630 but were probably collected by around 613. This was an extraordinary coincidence and made me think that, on this evidence, we really might put a new name to the Sutton Hoo burial.

Finally, I came across an association which convinced me that this was Saebert's monument. This was an association which goes further in the interpretation of material culture as manipulated ethnic identifiers. There are aspects of the selection of grave goods and their placing within the grave which direct our attention to the way that meaning is manipulated through the selection and placing of material culture. Looking through the grave assemblage, I noticed that particular grave goods appear in threes. There are three buckets, three hanging-bowls, three cauldrons and nine spears in three different styles. Might these have been the funerary gifts of the three sons? No other individual grave of this period in the whole of Europe contains similar multiples of these types, although groups of three shields occur in graves in eastern Sweden and Buckinghamshire. Even more interestingly, all of them (with the exception of one spear) were placed outside the personal space where the body (or its representation) was laid. The placing of these sets-of-three items, above the head end and below the feet end, suggests that these were treated as a different category of objects from those items in the 'personal space' of the body area – perhaps funerary gifts of the sort mentioned in *Beowulf*, as opposed to personal possessions of the deceased.

The details of this interpretation, with full references to the Sutton Hoo literature, are available in a paper (by myself, Alex Woolf, and Robert van der Noort) entitled 'Three men and a boat: Sutton Hoo and the Saxon kingdom', which has been submitted to *Anglo-Saxon England*. That paper, and an earlier version, produced a wide range of responses when circulated in draft. Some archaeologists could not see, when they were moving towards postprocessual approaches, why I was apparently running back the other way into 'culture history' and what they saw as outmoded historical and particularist interpretation. Others failed to see why it mattered who was buried in that mound, presumably oblivious of – amongst other things – the implications for the continuity of Roman to Saxon political territories, the confrontation of Christianity and paganism, and the cultural and political relationships between the East Saxons and eastern Sweden, as well as Francia. Perhaps a hallowed 'fact' was threatened by a new theory. Most specialists in the subject do not believe my interpretation (as one said, 'Doesn't that suggest to you that you're wrong?'). Some do not know whether to believe it.

My reading of material culture – at a number of different levels – leads me to interpret the evidence thus. There is an association with eastern Sweden; there is an association with Francia; there are no associations in the grave with East Anglia. Anglian material is found in south Suffolk, but there is evidence that this was a boundary zone, both politically and economically. It is therefore constructive to consider the possible East Saxon rulers as occupants of Sutton Hoo, and Saebert fits by his dates and by his Frankish, Christian and pagan connections. This opens up the question of links between eastern Sweden and the East Saxons, rather than the East Angles as the relationship is currently read. The reinterpretation also has considerable implications for our understanding of the continuity of power relationships at the end of the Roman period and of the confrontation of Christianity and paganism and its political context.

We will never know which interpretation is closer to the 'truth'. There are and will be other competing interpretations. Some will say that such questions about individual identification should not be asked by archaeologists any more. Are there ways that competing interpretations can be tested against fresh evidence? It is probably unlikely that unequivocal and unambiguous discoveries will be made that resolve the dilemma. We can detail some of the archaeological linkages that we would like to recover, but they will offer congruence with one or other theory, rather than proof.

For example, we need to locate sixth- and seventh-century deposits in London and look for evidence of contact with eastern Sweden or the manufacture of animal ornament metalwork. Conversely, future research may demonstrate that contact between eastern Sweden and England occurred only in the East Anglian kingdom. But, whatever new information we uncover, at the roots of our beliefs are theoretical assumptions about the relationship between material culture, ethnicity, territory and power and also the ways in which material culture is used. Whatever evidence is recovered in future, we still disagree over *how* it is interpreted.

Chapter 26

Reconciling symbolic significance with being-in-the-world

Julian Thomas

I would like to argue that the debate on material culture within archaeology is presently characterised by a number of dichotomies which need to be overcome. Prime amongst these is the separation between the symbolic significance of objects and their materiality. This is predicated upon the different theoretical approaches which concern themselves with these two aspects of the material world. However, another related problem lies in the way that we have kept our discussions of time and of material culture separate: in different chapters of books, or in different sessions of a conference like the present one. We have rich descriptions of the way in which material culture is ordered and employed in the negotiation of social position, yet when we turn to a consideration of time, 'history' is invariably seen as something which happens to human beings and social relations, not to things. When we start to think about change through time, material culture tends to be relegated to the status of the type fossil: the record of past social processes.

Thus, although we have what could be described as a poststructuralist archaeology, it is the structuralist heritage of the tradition which has been foregrounded in its consideration of material culture, which is seen as a system of objects described largely with spatial metaphors. Obviously, this is only compounded by a grounding in ethnoarchaeological studies which can rarely encompass great time-depths. We need to consider the temporal characteristics of material culture. This requires a consideration of time which is involved less with periodisation or with the periodicities of particular kinds of event and process and more with how human existence is stretched across time.

In a recent article, Ian Hodder has suggested that archaeology should undertake a turn towards the hermeneutic tradition. However, his discussion is largely concerned with the way in which we should interpret the past, rather than with the strand of hermeneutic phenomenology which considers how beings operate in the world, encountering and interpreting other beings. One aspect of this set of concerns is an interest in the way in which material things intervene in the process of social life and the way in which human beings engage with the ready-to-hand. We can argue that investigating the temporality of material things requires an understanding of the temporal structure of human beings. In Western thought, the understanding of time has revolved around the opposition between a physical, external continuum, a cosmological time, and time as a purely subjective and internal aspect of human consciousness, centred on a moment which we think of as 'now'. An alternative is to see temporality not as a facet of consciousness, but of Being, quite distinct from any centred intentionality, yet finite and given by the structure of Being-in-the-world. In such a conception, the present cannot be given any priority over past or future. Just as poststructuralism de-centres the subject in language, such an approach denies that the subject can be whole and self-present within each of a succession of 'nows'. Past, present and future constitute a unity which cannot be dissolved. I only have a sense of selfhood because I have a past to draw on and a future into which to project myself. What is essential, though, is to avoid the conclusion that some kind of totalised authenticity, some 'being a whole' can be achieved by an individual or a collectivity through some resolute grasping and drawing together of past, present and future in a moment of vision. It is in this relict essentialism that the real political dangers of these ideas lie. Rather, we could suggest that the only way in which human beings can conceptualise self-identity is in narrative. The self is dispersed through time and is drawn together in a kind of story. Material things fit into this structure of narrative by being engaged in, or encountered in the course of human projects. Objects change their status from the merely present-at-hand thing which is simply there, in the environment, to the ready-to-hand, caught up in the operation of a human purpose. This slipping back and forth in our concern, and the associated way in which tools eventually become forgotten in the process of their use, conditions the way in which we build up an awareness of the world and recursively create our own identity. Things, locations, settings are fixed points between which the narrative of human existence is spun out. Thus while material things form nodes within a signifying system structured by metaphor and metonymy, they are also conceptually ordered according to narrative temporal structures, appertaining to an individual or to groups. This sequential ordering may be at variance with any structural coherence and may be one source of the restructuration of the symbolic system. Thus, while accepting the textual metaphor for material culture, it is possible to start to accommodate an awareness of objects as co-present things within the world. This requires an investigation of the way in which things are incorporated into the symbolic order and either retained or forgotten, as memory, trace or tradition. These different forms of retention obviously need to be investigated in concrete instances, but it is my suspicion that they set up the conditions under which items come to be encountered and interpreted. The things of the world are always experienced-as, through a structure of pre-understanding. Thus we never hear a pure soundwave, we hear a motorcycle or a bird singing. What we have to consider in archaeology is the way in which human beings, in their concernful dealings in the world, come to restructure their symbolic orders through a process of encounter and forgetting played across time. Central to this, as I have suggested, is the way in which material things are incorporated into personal biographies and group myths in the production of a sense of identity. It is thus through considering the linked but independent temporal structures of human beings and things that we can start to reconcile the materiality and the symbolic significance of material culture.

Chapter 27

Questions not to ask of Malagasy carvings

Maurice Bloch

This paper is a cautionary tale or a short history of the attempts at interpretation of the carvings of a group of people in Madagascar: the Zafimaniry.

The Zafimaniry are swidden cultivators living in the eastern forest of Madagascar and they number about 20,000. However, they are famous because they are one of the few groups which originally produced the kind of things museums and tourists can take away and display, and subsequently they have developed a tourist-goods industry of some significance. Here I am concerned with their traditional carvings. These are low reliefs or engravings of relatively elaborate geometrical patterns which cover the wooden parts of their houses – especially the shutters and, most beautifully, the three main posts (Fig. 14). Since the 1920s, at least, professional and amateur anthropologists and archaeologists have bothered the Zafimaniry by asking them what these carvings 'meant'. Included among these, in the recent past, has been myself.

I say what these carvings 'meant', but this is a tricky word indeed. What I am talking about is in part the trickiness of the word. There is of course a massive, almost infinite literature in philosophy and linguistics on the topic, but here I simply want to consider the problems of the word when applied to this type of material culture and then in a rather matter-of-fact way, since this is one of the kind of cases which anthropologists and archaeologists deal with.

The people who interrogated various Zafimaniry and then went on to write articles or books in order to report the answers they were given did not use the word 'meant', because they were writing in French. This is not quite such a trivial point as it might seem, because already in French there is no equivalent to the English verb 'to mean'. One can ask the 'sense' (which perhaps corresponds to the English meaning) or one can use the phrase (and that is the phrase used by the writers) *vouloir dire*, 'try to say'. These authors tell us, then, what these carvings are 'trying to say'. If there is a problem between French and English, it is not surprising that there is also one between French and Malagasy. All the writers concerned purport to report Zafimaniry answers to their question – but to what question? First of all, the authors fall into two categories. Two of them can speak Malagasy, in both cases probably better than I can (one of them is a native speaker); the others must have used an interpreter who was presumably landed with the critical task of rendering into Malagasy the French phrase *vouloir dire*. How did they do it? I can only guess from my attempts to ask the same thing in Malagasy. One can ask something which is a bit like the English 'what is the point of', a phrase which is the rare positive of a commonly used catchphrase which means 'there is no point to it' (*antony*); or one can use a rather ontological phrase which asks, 'what is the root cause of this?' (*fotory*); or one can ask for the engravings, 'what are those pictures of?'; or you can ask people as they are doing the carvings, 'what are you doing?'

Figure 14 Malagasy carvings

None of these questions really conveys what either the French or English terms convey. In any case, when I asked these questions of the Zafimaniry during my first fieldwork there I obtained rather disappointing answers. To the question 'what are those pictures of?' I was answered with great certainty that they were pictures of nothing. When I asked for a cause or the point of the carvings I triggered the ready-made phrase that there was no point, and when I asked what people were doing I was told 'carving'. There was actually one answer I was given very often, but I felt it was so bland and therefore frustrating that I payed no attention to it and did not even put it down in my field notes. It was that 'it made the wood beautiful'.

I want to return to this in a moment; but first, a word about what the other writers say they were told. Apparently they did not have the same frustrating experience as I did – or, at least, give no hints of this. My first reaction to their apparent success, when I knew perfectly well that all these people had merely been passing through, when I had spent a considerable time with the Zafimaniry and spoke their language, was that these authors were mainly making it up. Now I am a little more charitable – at least, in the case of two of them, one of whom is the native speaker I referred to above. I don't think these two were lying – simply that they were misleading. These authors report that various parts of the carvings are representational; that, for example, the ubiquitous circular designs represent the moon and that some of the designs which appear like shading are rain.

I think I now know what they are talking about. As a result of subsequent fieldwork I was told by certain expert carvers somewhat similar things about various designs commonly used by the Zafimaniry. However, in following these up it was made very clear that what was meant was that these were 'the names' of these designs. It is not that they represent the phenomena but that the names indicate a trivial similarity which can be used as an indicator of the design when, for example, you ask a carver to do a particular design for your house. It is rather like herringbone tweed. Clearly the tweed is not a picture of the osature of the fish.

All this, however, does not mean that I have nothing to say about these carvings, and I shall try to explain how I feel able to move on. This is partly as a result of the fact that someone once elaborated the remark that the carvings make the wood beautiful by adding 'they honour the wood'. Immediately I realised that the bland statement was not so bland after all since its focus was not beautification in general but beautification of the wood. But really this was only a hint. In fact the only useful answer the Zafimaniry could have given me and the other researchers to our questions was the famous one: 'If I were you, mate, I would not be starting from here.'

Where one needs to start is with an understanding of the significance of houses and the wood the carvings decorate, and I briefly shall try to indicate this.

For the Zafimaniry, houses are the basis of ordered society and the mark of a successful life; this is because they are the outward side of a successful marriage. For the Zafimaniry, going through life successfully is a gradual process of settling down, of which marriage is an essential element, and growth through the production of children, grandchildren, etc., who are the continuation of the couple. When children are young they are undetermined in place, substance or morality. Their bodies are malleable so that they are permanently affected by their environment. They don't have a home of their own. They don't take part in agriculture, but they hunt and gather all over the place, they play in a chaotic way, their language is not well rounded. The attachments they form – and these include sexual attachments very early on – are chaotic and impermanent. But then, gradually, they settle spatially, physically and psychologically as they move towards marriage – and marriage takes material form in the house they begin to build and furnish. The young man will put the central house-posts and a flimsy outer wall of reeds and mats, the young woman will bring the furniture of the hearth. This building is the flimsy beginning of marriage; but if the relation settles down (which may or may not happen) – above all, if the couple start to produce children – the house will harden. That is, the flimsy materials will, little by little over many years, begin to be replaced by massive vertical pieces of wood. It is as if the body of the pair as individuals begins to fade in significance and instead it is replaced by the building of their mutuality. This is expressed in a number of ways but, above all, by the oft-stressed observation that the house is acquiring bones: that is, the pieces of wood. And the wood that is used is not any wood; it is wood from the hardest, longest-lasting trees, and it is not any part of the tree, but the hardest impacted heartwood of these woods which the Zafimaniry call by a word which literally means 'to last'. The aesthetic and moral value of the hardness of such wood, especially the fact that it is a hardness produced from an original softness (the young plant), totally dominates Zafimaniry discourse in a way which would almost be impossible to overemphasise. This house and this wood can be seen as material culture, but to an extent this is misleading in that such a phrase suggests something different from non-material culture. It would be quite misleading to see Zafimaniry houses as expressing Zafimaniry marriage and society or containing married pairs. The house is the marriage. With time, the original couple (in human form) will die and the children, grandchildren, great-grandchildren will disperse, but ideally neither of these processes will occur completely. This is because these descendants will gather on occasion in the house to settle disputes or ask blessings from the original couple – or, rather, from the house or parts of that house such as the cooking pot and posts. The original couple therefore survives and continues to grow as their progeny multiply – and so will the house. The descendants soon take over the business of the house, at first during the life of the original couple and then without interruption after their death. The house will continue to harden and become more and more bony. This is a process which is never complete, partly because some wood will need replacing but also because the hardening is in fact endless. Even if the wood of the house is very hard and sound there is a continuation to the process of hardening and transformation, and that continuation is carving. Carving which 'honours' the hardness of the heartwood and makes it even more evident and beautiful.

The carvings are therefore the continuation of the process of human maturation and settling down, of marriage and house creation, of hardening, of growth, of acquiring bones. The carvings are not separate from this process, they are not representing, they are part of the finishing of a task which should never finish as it should grow for ever. The carvings are a celebration of the material and the building and of a successful life which continues to expand and reproduce (and, by the way, this is why the carvings must remain shallow engravings because otherwise they would be negating their very purpose by weakening the wood).

The carvings are not pointing outwards – mutely trying to say something, *voulant dire* as the questions expected – they are an essential element of the material and the social principle on which they occur; they are not referring or signifying. The beautifying is merely the extension of the making and being of the wood and the house and growth of the original marriage. The carvings are the continuation and magnification (as in *magnificat*) of the growth and success of the couple transcending the impermanence of life.

Chapter 28

Knowing about the past

Colin Richards

In this brief statement I wish to address the problems surrounding the interpretation of material culture in one area of archaeological practice which, to all intents and purposes, has remained virtually untouched by recent re-orientations in archaeological theory. Despite discussion of the nature of an 'archaeological record', the practice of excavation, perhaps the closest form of past culture contact that archaeologists experience, maintains some form of immunity. Fieldwork methodology has, in fact, remained the last bastion of the 'New Archaeology'. This, as far as I can see, constitutes a major failing of a postprocessual archaeology.

Doing archaeology, as I assume, should imply at least some interest if not excitement about the past, as opposed to fulfilling an indulgent introspection, otherwise the opportunity provided by the physical and intellectual confrontation between ourselves and a totally different and alien culture is wasted. This point of contact is all-important since if any reading or experience of the material remains of another culture is to occur it will be effected in its purest form at precisely this time. Despite pleas to the contrary it is not possible to re-create this situation at a later date and expect the same encounter. Excavation is, therefore, a unique aspect of an ongoing project of evaluation and interpretation which forms the basis of knowledge of the past. Again the question must be asked, where is the agenda for a re-examination of archaeological practice in the face of a rejection of the division between practical and theoretical archaeology?

Material culture as experienced by the archaeologist is a distortion of its past realities; there were no past truths, no single meanings, any more than there are contemporary truths. Yet we maintain the fallacy of the possibility of compiling an objective account of the past through data collection. Here an immediate concern is the rejection of positivism without turning to the excesses of complete relativism.

As Chris Tilley (Tilley 1989) has recently observed, a major problem in British archaeology is the mistaken status of excavation as a scientific exercise of data collection, constituting an end or goal in itself. This view promotes the role of the excavator as an independent detached observer compiling an objective record of the observable and detectable. This procedure is deemed essential since the excavator is apparently conducting the unrepeatable experiment. Hence excavation, in its claim to be scientific, has built up a battery of techniques, and methodology itself has virtually become an object of study. This is excavation as technique conducted by technicians, which reaches absurdity in the commonplace application of technologies for no other reason than their availability. The question why seems inappropriate in the obsession to conduct systematic excavation of things in an objective manner. The apparent objectivity manifest in the context-recording sheet is a prime example of this illusion while even the area of excavation, regardless of the aims, is shaped to conform to geometric principles of order. In this practice we see an obvious conflict between the urge to accrue valid scientific knowledge and the awareness that this knowledge be based on logical and empirical truths or certainties, which through human mediation are inaccessible. This situation is compounded by an implicit belief that the more data we obtain the more we will know about the past. On the whole this image of data collection is not at all restricted to archaeological rescue situations but also embraces the majority of 'research' excavations. Ironically, 'rescue' excavations, owing to the time and financial constraints, are often less encumbered by the trappings of objectivity.

The interpetation of the past through material culture is not necessarily dependent on the nature of the archaeological evidence as observable facts. The archaeological record is neither fact nor fabrication, and because it represents an engagement with the material remains and conditions of other people's lives our understanding of it is sometimes little more than impressions or feelings. Hence, interpretive practice involves far more diversity of thought than the subscription to a single mode of practice or theoretical stance allows. Similarly, our understanding of the material residues which we wish to interpret is just as tainted and context-dependent as the interpretations we place upon it. Hence, in some ways, there is no inconsistency between different conceptions of an archaeological record. The inconsistency lies in the manner of interpretation as opposed to our everyday experience of the lived world.

The evidence cannot speak for itself; it requires some form of reading through experience. However, regardless of the distortions or deficiencies which are manifest in its constitution, none compares to the impediments we impose during the transformations of excavation. This is not merely a question of methodology but one of perception. Here it is interesting that the success of claims to knowledge of the past are engaged and assessed on the accepted status of links between past actions and behaviour and the representation of that past, as opposed to the status of a wide range of evidence which shapes our interpretive abilities. Accepting that the people being studied are no longer present, we still feel constrained by the notion that this somehow removes temporality from the equation. Consequently, the interpretation of material culture, we know, although being a production of everyday routines of people engaged in various social practices, an existence embodying space and time, is perpetually curtailed through our limited expectations. This limitation is manifest in methods of depiction and ordering of the data. For instance, everyone is aware that it is the spatial component of archaeological evidence which is given primacy, from the recording system of excavated finds to the production of wider geographic distributions of artefacts and monuments. These spatial constructs are then reinterpreted as if containing a reality of past practices. Frequently this spatial analysis comes to represent the material conditions of past living society, reducing it to a two-dimensional representation. We do not experience our social world in this manner, so why create and then be imprisoned by such an artificial image of the past?

Again I wish to liken excavation to culture contact and ask how this encounter should be treated. In practice the technique of excavation has hardly altered over the last fifty years. The recovery of data remains the goal, and its collection is chronologically ordered through the removal of layer and contexts within a strict rationale of moving systematically backwards in time. The definition of the observer/excavator as a technician acts on the one hand effectively to divorce the observer from the historical specificity of the context; hence removing the burden of possessing or attempting to accrue a detailed knowledge of the past. On the other hand this monopolises the privilege of direct contact with another past society. The counter-productivity of this situation is clearly revealed when the act of excavation is seen as interpretive practice, as opposed to neutral observation – the latter being continually endorsed through appeals to simple common sense and possession of technical skills and practical knowledge. Under the conditions of excavation, as culture contact, where a constant series of decisions are taken, observation and understanding come together. However, this is not a one-way operation – the past does speak – but only through a dialectical relationship between subject and object, the present and recognised past.

Excavation, as we are continually informed, is destructive by definition. Despite claims to the contrary, the experience involves transformations which can never be replicated. Archaeological contexts, unlike the anthropological, can never be revisited and re-examined after a period of reconsideration. Archaeologists totally destroy the contexts they visit.

If excavation is conceived in these terms and viewed as a physical and personal engagement with another culture, then it involves a slowly developing sense of recognition embodying incremental leaps in understanding. Therefore, the responsibility of the excavator far exceeds the safe detachment of the technician. Interpretation of contexts of human action, admittedly self-defined, must occur at the point and moment of contact. This, as Tilley (1989b, p. 279) states, is 'thought in action'. Interrogation of the material remains must form part of this action since 'immediate' analysis is actualised in any reading of material culture.

A reconsideration of procedure to allow such a relationship to develop does not merely rely on methodology or the asking of new questions, but on a revaluation of practical archaeology. The 'correct' and accepted sequence of field archaeology, that of excavation – post-excavation – report, tends to be synonymous with observation/ data collection – analysis – interpretation. Interestingly, this procedure is mirrored in the structure of written excavation reports. At a practical level this separation of observation and interpretation maintains a temporal and spatial structure. Although weakly justified in terms of logistics and tradition, the reinforcement of this structure has far more to do with the control and monopoly of knowledge. Hidden within the spatial and temporal structure of excavation to publication is a steadily decreasing access to the data until finally it lies in the hands of a single individual to interpret the past. Here it is suggested that all the stages of excavation should represent merely an ongoing project of learning as opposed to a vehicle for authoritative statements about the past.

Thus, the separation of observation and interpretation in time and space becomes an invalid and redundant exercise. It is now seen as creating an unnecessary cleavage in interpretive practice. This necessitates the collapse of the sequence of excavation, post-excavation and report-writing; they are now part of a unitary project and cannot be seen as isolated components. Analysis and revaluation now occur during the physical process of excavation, questions are asked and resolved at this point of contact with the data. A record of this process constitutes the 'excavation report' which will be made available through different appropriate media. Moreover, through the nature of these changes excavation is no longer the domain of a single person and again this requires a far greater responsibility on the part of the excavator.

This proposal has the intimate effect of unifying people within an excavation and in different areas of archaeological specialisation who have become increasingly alienated over the last decade, not least those concerned with a theoretical archaeology. It is, after all, part of a much larger project of attempting to know about the past.

ACKNOWLEDGEMENTS

I greatly appreciate the comments made by John Barrett, David Breeze, Steve Driscoll, Alan Leslie and Niall Sharples on an earlier draft of this paper. I would also like to thank Ian Hodder and Mike Shanks for inviting me to speak at the Interpretive Archaeologies conference.

Appendix

Further comment on interpretive archaeologies

In an attempt to do justice to the variety of issues and points raised and discussed at the conference (upon which this book is partly based), appended here are some comments provided by participants.

Classical archaeology: a case-study in disciplinary ownership

Jonathan Last, Cambridge: At the start of the floor discussion on Part 4, Mark Leone posed the question of whether archaeology can be owned. Shortly afterwards the discussion revealed a fine example of disciplinary closure and ownership: the case of classical archaeology. This exchange is transcribed here. We should not, however, assume that other areas of archaeology, be they concerned with a particular region or period (for example, Palaeoindian research) or a particular theoretical approach (for example, Cambridge postprocessualism), are any less 'owned' or exclusionary to those who do not join in with the conventional methodology or discourse. Nevertheless, classical archaeology is a useful case through which to expound these issues.

*   *   *

Louise Hitchcock: I asked Michael Shanks if he considered his work on Proto-korinthian pottery part of the tradition of classical archaeology, or a rupture or discontinuity – this has to do with the question of ownership. He said classical archaeologists would probably ignore his work. Given the power of the institution of classical archaeology, how will it ever really change if there is no dialogue with it?

Michael Shanks: I wasn't aware I was going to be picked up on this! . . . Can classical archaeology be changed? When I said that the discipline might well ignore my work, I was basically thinking that I didn't want very much to do with its practitioners. Not because I don't value the dialogue, but I'd rather read what they have to write and use it as I wish than have to go through all the structures and procedures which represent the *discourse* of classical archaeology.

To begin anecdotally – I moved towards classical archaeology about four years ago because of the nature of the material and its disciplinary location – classical archaeology, particularly of the eighth to sixth centuries BC, is a very *marginal* discipline, since various disciplinary fields have an interest in that time: classical studies, literary studies and traditional classics, an anthropological angle, ancient history, art history and the grander philosophy of history, including the metahistory of the West. My immediate experience was of an enormous problem with the discourse that classical archaeology represents, and that means very basic things such as types of question considered reasonable, styles of publication, career paths considered creditable – all that comes under that very useful notion of discourse and its structures. Consider citation. I know it's supposed to be very scholarly and undoubtedly it is in some ways, but the hyper-citation is incredible: every sentence needs at least five footnotes which return the reader to numerous minor and often third-rate precedents. Yet – what I find to be fundamental – usually conceptual, philosophical or theoretical matters may remain unreferenced. I do not find this at all 'scholarly'. I think this is part of the character of the discipline. A nineteenth-century discipline still, classical archaeology hasn't had the sort of ruptures which have been experienced in archaeology. In terms of the theoretical literature there are various watersheds in archaeology and you need not make reference to works before certain dates as they will not be dealing with what you're talking about. In classical archaeology, however, an empirical and theoretical continuity goes way back – citation can take you back well into the nineteenth century. Generally the mode of presentation in these papers is a very difficult one to get into. You feel, 'It's intimidating, it's scary'; you feel edgy and reluctant to say anything. This is one reason why I'm reluctant to engage with classical archaeologists in the contexts of their disciplinary discourse – not that I don't want dialogue, but the context just scares me, and, though it may be sacrilege to say so, it requires a lot of *useless* work to produce a paper acceptable to classical archaeology. On the other hand, I like the material and want to get on with it – I think it's very rich and very valuable, and there has been some helpful stuff written in classical archaeology.

As for ownership, I certainly feel that classical archaeology is owned. One of my reasons for moving into the field was the personal one that I'd had a traditional Classics education. It happened to me in my teens. I didn't want this part of me to be not me – I experience a split through a disciplinary discourse which doesn't have much to do with me, even though its subject was part of my upbringing. I wanted to make some of Classics my own; but at the same time it isn't, so there's that strange sense of contradiction. A lot of people may feel that sense of loss of ownership on a personal level much more generally – local pasts, for example, may not be perceived as belonging to ordinary local people, but as being in the control of others.
Joan Gero: . . . One of the main things all research paradigms contend with is keeping the discord out. You must keep out the conflicting noise and so you must, like the recent Palaeoindian [research], concentrate on redundancy. Its firmest implications are very hard to take, very overdetermined and very exclusionary, but that in a sense is its success in evolutionary terms: it has retained stability for all these decades, and an integrity. Whether the tone of the story can say that – I think it can only get me in trouble!
Michael Shanks: That's what I was trying to get across about structures.
James Whitley: Your problem is not structures, it's your inability to acquaint yourself with the material. It's very simple – it's much, much less complicated than you make it out to be. . . . I believe that the basic problem with theoretical archaeology and the attempts to create dialogues between kinds of archaeology is that archaeologists don't read books. If you want to have a career in theoretical archaeology, what you do is read the introductions, you read the conclusion, you flick through the middle, and turn it into a slogan which you can then use to construct a kind of new theoretical book on archaeology. Close reading does not exist in archaeology. It's a kind of minimal condition for what might be called interesting – close reading neither of the material nor of other archaeologists' texts. What you do is turn them into straw men which you then use to construct. It's chiefly true of theoretical archaeology and if you have to produce a book every four years that's the way to do it, so scholarship goes out the window, close reading and

awareness of what people are actually saying goes out the window, and a close reading of material culture goes out the window; and this is the way theoretical archaeology advances, and why it's so comic – or should I say farcical? – in the way it's developed.

* * *

Is Shanks excluding himself by apparently denigrating traditions of research in classical archaeology because they do not fit with the kind of approach he wishes to take?

Is Whitley cutting himself off from insights developed in other areas because of a belief in the superiority of classical archaeology's detailed textual and empirical research?

We should not allow their rhetoric to obscure the fact that there have been many connections between classical archaeology and other areas of the discipline, both in the past, because many archaeologists had a classical training, and in the present, when many classical archaeologists are aware of broader theoretical developments (e.g., Hall 1991).

We might suggest that traditional classical archaeology maintains its separateness and its practices because:

- it developed early on its own body of literature and research practices, which are still cited. Hence there is an appeal to ancient precedent; but little critical work on the history of classical archaeology (Dyson 1989, p. 129).
- for historical reasons, classical and prehistoric archaeology have been intellectually and spatially separate. Consider the case of Cambridge, where the Classics (and classical archaeology) department is physically distant from the archaeology department; or the importing of European professors of classical archaeology to America ensuring, by linking in to a different intellectual tradition, a separation from other branches of archaeology and anthropology (Dyson 1989, p. 130).
- it deals with literate societies where texts are highly privileged in social interpretation. Hence classical archaeology looks to Classics as much as to archaeology. As Dyson (1989, p. 131) puts it, sacred objects are closely associated with sacred texts.
- this privileging of classical literature, largely because it is seen as shedding light on the origins of our own civilisation, leads to a concern with aspects of high culture (philosophy, political history, art) that classical archaeology defers to. The texts in question were written by and for a literate élite; classical archaeology's belief in the humble task of the archaeologist to recover these cultural high points is very different from the credo of the New Archaeologists that 'archaeology is anthropology or it is nothing' (Dyson 1989, pp. 128–9)
- hence art-historical approaches are central to classical archaeology, and contextual or social archaeology approaches are far less important (cf. Whitley 1987).
- therefore there is often more concern with the recovery of objects for their own sake than detailed contextual recording in excavation. This is also partly related to the frequently large scale of classical sites, but it serves to rule out the possibility of certain interpretive approaches.
- in addition, the long time-span and rigid hierarchy of many Greek and Roman excavations tends to instil this conservatism into each generation of field workers. Of course, this is not exclusive to classical archaeology and the same phenomenon may be observed in other areas (for example, Flannery's (1976) characterisation of the Real Mesoamerican Archaeologist).

This reaction to Mike Shanks's paper, attempting to gain new insights from the study of a single artefact type, which is a typical approach in classical archaeology, exemplifies the problem. All the above points mean that there are vested interests in classical archaeology maintaining a sense of apartness, achieved largely by prescribing a set of research practices based on supposed detailed knowledge and a close reading of texts and artefacts which largely excludes disciplinary 'outsiders' from making any authoritative contribution to classical archaeology. Hence if Shanks merely refuses to play by the rules requiring a demonstration of one's knowledge of textual and art-historical evidence his work will be considered suspect and thereby marginalised.

If Interpretive Archaeologies is going to be useful as a conference or as a publication, it should be concerned with hastening the recognition of the plurality of voices, discourses and approaches by promoting both critiques of practice and dialogue across disciplinary boundaries.

All areas of the discipline have their accepted norms in both methods and theoretical approaches. The challenge is one of stimulating fruitful cross-fertilisation rather than withdrawing into exclusive worlds with labels like 'Classical Archaeology' or 'British Prehistory'.

Further comment from and about the discipline and classical archaeology

James Whitley, Cardiff: This has been a disappointing conference. Many now well-worn ideas have been recycled, and we have had, on prominent display, the theoretical archaeologists' unwillingness to engage either with a particular set of data or with intellectual traditions outside of Anglo-American 'anthropological' archaeology. Consequently there is much of a feel of 'déjà écouté' about many of the papers, and a sense of frustration in much of the audience.

Louise Hitchcock, American School of Classical Studies, Athens: It was clear from Shanks's description of the Korinthian perfume-jar and firing technique that he 'knows the material'. However, it was equally clear from Whitley's discussion of theoretical archaeology that he knows little to nothing about theory and the years required to do the reading and rereading of difficult texts, or about the difficulties involved in applying it to material culture also known as 'data'.

Whitley's misconceptions serve to reify the split between theory and practice, rendering difficult the realisation of a *meta*-discipline of Material Culture Studies.

This misconception and split will not go away without confronting the issues of authority, anti-theoreticism and anti-intellectualism, ownership and particularly institutionally created rules of exclusion – not on an intellectual level, but on a practical level. Classical archaeology as a discipline is a too real metaphor for these issues.

The problem of authorising archaeological accounts

Anonymous: Many, if not most, of the participants agreed in discussion that a crucial issue is that of the authority of different interpretations of the past, and the place of values in archaeological work and writing. It is clear that the debates in the literature of archaeology and the social sciences have not resolved the problem of how to justify particular accounts of the past when science's authority of objectivity has been challenged and undermined, as it has since the 1970s. Whereas the necessity of a pluralism of archaeological pasts seems accepted, perhaps for political rather than philosophical reasons, judging and authorising particular accounts remains the key issue, an issue of the *political responsibility* of archaeologists.

On meaning

Frands Herschend, Uppsala: There is an overflow of meaning, and that goes for the hand-axe as well as for the smile that the baby sees in its mother's face. There is a real potential in such material patterns which makes it reasonable to call them 'works', and therefore they should be put alongside more complex works like the Roman villa or a piece of writing.

Lack of meaning is in itself hardly a problem, and potential meaning not a specific human quality.

The essential problem is that of analysing meaning into understanding. This, in its turn, is a matter of partly or totally ruling out the overflow of meaning. It is an interactive process among any number of persons to create significant symbols that are, at best, social and factual truths. Together with understanding, one also creates the meaningful misunderstanding of others with whom there is only a modest base for interaction.

If we succeed in making a work nothing but a significant symbol, then it turns into an indisputable fact. If, for example, the breaking down of Carbon-14 in an analytical interaction can be seen as only a significant symbol of the lapse of time, then it has the status of a fact. Obviously, even lapse of time may lose its symbolic significance; human works tend never to become stable significant symbols. This means that they are only partially and temporarily factual or true in an analytical sense. The interesting thing with understanding is, in other words, the balance or tension between understanding and misunderstanding. This goes for cultural history as well as conferences.

On the origins of meaning

Meg Conkey, Berkeley: I would take the position that many, if not all, of the core concepts we employ to inquire into the so-called origins of meaning (and by such concepts I am referring to things that we banter about regularly – symbolism, consciousness, meaning, self-awareness, all often taken to be interchangeable) are cultural constructions that have changed with time. We have long-held academic conceptualisations of these phenomena and we should keep in mind that our consideration of these concepts is deeply rooted in the anthropology of knowledge. I merely want to remind ourselves what is obvious but, however, hasn't always been, as Clive Gamble's example of Boucher de Perthes would tell us: namely, that since consciousness, self-awareness, cognition, and cognitive meaning are categories that have particular historical cultural meanings and histories, to take these categories out into the wider world in search of a phenomenon such as the emergence of symbolism or meaning is itself a cultural enterprise. I would like to remind us in particular that the specific history of how anthropology has approached these questions of consciousness, thought, symbolism and meaning-making in other societies is relevant to any of our concerns. For myself in particular I just look at the dramatic way in which the very concept of art or the concept of aesthetics has changed through and since the eighteenth and nineteenth centuries.

What it means to be conscious, to be aware, to be a meaning-maker, to be symbolic has varied in Euro-American culture ever since the seventeenth century. It was once thought that consciousness referred to public knowledge. Today it is more used to refer to private, individual knowledge, and the term implies self-awareness, which is somewhat different from awareness of the self in interaction or awareness of relationship. And so I think out of today's usage of such concepts as consciousness it is not surprising to see that many of the related package of terms that we are interested in have become reified as a property of mind, rather than as an emergent property in and of social action.

I am taking maybe a more than somewhat constructionist view here, but it does not necessarily preclude the possibility that there are universal aspects or features. However, I think that these things must be problematised, not given. For example, I would be willing to accept the idea that the category of person appears so widespread as to be universal, but the specific definition of person is surely culturally constructed and highly variable.

This is a general point, too – we have to think harder, deeper and historically about some of the terms we regularly employ. In her book *The Man of Reason* (1984) Genevieve Lloyd, for example, showed that the only constant in Western philosophers' thinking about rationality on the one hand, and masculinity on the other hand, is their association. What each is said to be changes historically, but their association seems to go on.

In writing the narrative of the development of human engagement with meaning-making worlds, there will never be a *Figure 1*, there will never be the first illustration, but I am willing to sacrifice this origins kind of notion for more contextualised, nuanced, reflexive accounts that entertain both evidential and conceptual critiques.

Biological anthropology, ethology and archaeology: a problem of interdisciplinary communication

Anonymous: The issues of this session are interdisciplinary. The metaphor of language has come to dominate discussions of meaning in (material) culture studies; but, then, what are the implications when some animals seem to interpret and attribute or have meanings for things, but no language? And how does post-processual or an interpretive archaeology deal with animal language and meanings and their *continuity* with our own human meanings? However, people did not seem to get through to each other in this session. The contention was assumed by many that Palaeolithic archaeology of the earlier hominids is different and distinct from archaeologies of later periods, and that study of earlier periods involves or indeed requires biological, ethological or other approaches which have been criticised in archaeology, rightly or wrongly, as deterministic and so unacceptable. Many found the disciplinary boundaries between biological anthropology, ethology and archaeology too strong to overcome, even though questions asked in common make it desirable that they are.

It was accepted that there are both continuities and discontinuities between humans and the higher apes, but the complexities and subtleties of interpretive behaviour are only recently being appreciated. The implications of this real continuity between nature and culture have yet to be fully realised.

A note on untangling meaning

Matthew Johnson, Durham: Several times in discussion at the conference speakers made a key assumption about 'meaning': that, however defined, past meaning could be more easily untangled for recent, complex, literate societies than for distant, prehistoric societies. This assumption is particularly manifested in the notion that written texts afford a more direct access to meaning than the archaeological record. I want to explore, and hopefully undermine, this assumption in this note.

It is one of the more useful insights of poststructuralism, of course, that texts do not denote meaning in any straightforward or direct way. Therefore, we can't 'read off' the meaning from a text and apply it uncritically to a set of archaeological material, though this is precisely what some traditional and processual archaeologists have attempted to do in the past. It is also apparently what some prehistoric archaeologists assume their text-aided counterparts think is possible.

It is useful to remember at this point how cultural anthropologists go about constructing meaning. As Maurice Bloch's contribution to the conference showed so elegantly, meaning resides most fundamentally in the implicit, the taken-for-granted, the unspoken of a culture. The process of unravelling meaning is almost akin to excavation – of unpeeling the layers of overt discourse to get down to the fundamental categories and metaphors that constitute a culture.

Written texts were, of course, produced by societies that if they were still around would be subjected to the same technique (as that of cultural anthropology). Thus, when we take any particular text, the process of moving from its overt face to its underlying meaning is a complex one. Direct and commonsensical readings must be questioned. Divisions taken from Western thought must be laid aside.

Let us take a classic text that recurs constantly in English archaeological research and whose meaning is, apparently, overt: Domesday Book. Domesday is a tax record. Its aim is to record the wealth of England, community by community, systematically, for the purposes of the State. There are, of course, innumerable scholarly difficulties in the minutiae of its interpretation, but its broader meaning is, it would seem, transparent.

Of course, it is nothing of the sort. To take one aspect among many: Domesday records the forms and amounts of 'rent' paid by householders. We all understand rent, or at least we all experience it on a day-to-day basis. But medieval rent is not the same thing as modern rent. The Soviet scholar Kosminsky showed many years ago that the medieval concept of rent is one that is socially and culturally embedded. It is not determined by market forces: it has social, legal and moral parameters. Its genealogy, its transformation into the rent of Adam Smith, Ricardo and modern economics, is a long and complex one; but that is another story.

So, in fact, the seduction of the text lies not in its apparent ease of reading, but in the perceived cultural proximity, the lack of difference of the past that produced it to our own present. Neolithic chambered tombs or Palaeolithic cave art are clearly alien and take some work at decoding; the meaning of medieval tax records is apparently obvious, because many of its institutions and beliefs are apparently close to our own. This is complete nonsense. The past is a foreign country, and there is no *a priori* reason to believe they did things more differently in the Palaeolithic than in the Middle Ages, unless a naïve evolutionary or progressive model of social change is assumed. Few scholars even in the processual camp would subscribe to such a model – at least, overtly.

In this sense the struggle to explore the meanings of texts is a struggle to denote difference where sameness has been assumed, to denote foreignness where common sense has been taken for granted. It is, of course, a political struggle, since the notions of sameness and common sense serve to present capitalist values as timeless and unchanging. Perhaps this is the real reason why the ease of reading the text is such a difficult concept to undermine.

Interpretive archaeologies: a reaction from a British Prehistorian

J. D. Hill, Cambridge: My main theoretical criticism concerns the lack of the social. I accused (in another written comment) the conference of being Thatcherite in its avoidance of the social – both society in the past and society in the present. It is issues of a social archaeology, albeit radically recast by symbolic and structural archaeology and structuration theory, that are of pre-eminent concern for myself and those I claim to speak for. It is the issues of agency and structure, power, the practical and the symbolic, etc., which are those theoretical issues that concern us most. These issues were raised, especially in Part 5 on the character of material culture, but never discussed – but outstanding issues they are. They also lay behind a range of issues actually discussed, such as the textual analogy in archaeology and the 'objective' reality of something past out there. This new form of social archaeology would say there is something out there and perhaps the archaeological record is less a text for free reading in the present than a set of material evidences for specific social practices in the past intimately intertwined in the duality of agency and structure – blood, sweat and power.

Yet surely it is the lack of an explicit understanding of the nature of the social that is also lacking in the archaeological present. At times it appeared that we were in the relativist debates of the early 1980s, and surely a major weakness of 'interpretive archaeologies' as discussed is their ineffectual, Angst-ridden, liberal-relativist nature. Without a real understanding of the social in the present, particularly power, this will always be the case. It will also be the case that, however intellectually and morally correct such positions are, there will be others who will happily use their power in archaeology.

What is all this saying? Perhaps to recognise that postprocessual archaeology is not, or never was, a single coherent entity. It became clear that there are at least two major dialogues within postprocessual archaeology. At the conference we heard the Cambridge-North-American discourse; the British Prehistory discourse (increasingly a project exploring the issues of structuration and the active role of material culture) was largely silent – or misinterpreted when it wasn't. While in the past the distinctions have been blurred in our confrontations with processual archaeologists, it is time to recognise the distinctive nature of these different discourses. This isn't harmful, but a recognition of the maturity of postprocessual archaeology. As such I, like at least one other Cambridge research student, came out of the conference with a new sense of identity. We were not 'Interpretive Archaeologists' but committed to a new, postprocessual, structurationist, social archaeology that has become British Prehistory.

Processualism, postprocessualism and the politics of academia

Felipe Criado, Santiago: Could you, Anglo-American archaeologists, realise that, from an *abroad* and *broader* perspective, the debate between processualism and postprocessualism is not any more an intellectual one and is mostly a matter of academical fighting, power within academia. This is the reason why Latin (Mediterranean as well as American) archaeologies become suspicious about postprocessualism and recent debates in English-language archaeological literature. From the very moment that the debate is put into a different context the positions involved are no longer useful for other archaeologies. In order to use postprocessualism or cognitive-processual archaeology as reference points in archaeologies which are not Anglo-American, it is necessary to reproduce, through this dialectical model of confrontation, the inherent academical strategies of power, and this does not seem a good solution at all.

A comment upon agency, experience, and a Japanese perspective

Koji Mizoguchi, Cambridge: In Japan there are literally thousands of professional archaeologists, mainly employed by local government, digging thousands of sites every day. Excavation reports are now said to number about 1,500 a year. The intellectual framework shared by many Japanese archaeologists is still dominated by a rather mechanistic view of the relationship between the object-world as constraining and subjects as constrained, mainly in Marxist terms. Another dominant norm of archaeological practice – at least, until the 1970s – was that archaeologists could have some effect upon society by telling a kind of political narrative to the general public, alongside following a specific party-political line. In this framework archaeologists' day-to-day practice only had its effect at a level where their own day-to-day *experience* had no meaning.

Although the dominance of this framework has declined since the late seventies, because of worldwide disappointment with socialism, the myth that archaeologists can do nothing effective in changing society through their day-to-day practice remains as the dominant structure sanctioning archaeologists' 'creative' activity. Now, archaeologists in Japan seem to me to be trying to obtain their ontological security by routinising their practice with obsessively detailed descriptions of artefacts.

Having said all this, I can also say that the encounter with the book *Symbolic and Structural Archaeology* (edited by Ian Hodder and published in 1982) was certainly a joyous relief to some, at least, Japanese archaeologists, because, through emphasising the role of active agents in the reproduction of social systems, the book told that our day-to-day practice can have a significant effect upon social change through unintended consequences of action and our reflexive monitoring of those consequences. A group of my colleagues came to believe that we could de-routinise the practice and free an archaeological imagination in our day-to-day experience.

But to come across, in some papers and particularly Ian Hodder's, a re-emergence of the notion of unconscious motivation as constraint was shocking and disappointing. On the one hand it must be accepted that we have emphasised the importance of the active social subject by misunderstanding the definition of agency as only *intentional* transformation of things. Nevertheless, it seems, and still is in Japan, vital to realise the importance of unintended consequences of action in day-to-day practice and their effects upon structure through human knowledgeability.

On the politics of field archaeology

Louise Hitchcock, American School of Classical Studies: The privileged access to archaeological sites is institutionally situated and reified, not only by institutions that provide funding, but also by those that grant permits – not just governments, but also foreign archaeological schools. Then there are the field-directors who decide who will be permitted to gain excavation experience and how the site will be written up. The theoretical orientation of field archaeology will not change until the controlling/sanctioning institutions are changed.

Some comments on the discipline of archaeology

Anonymous: The use and value of a conference such as Interpretive Archaeologies lies in what appears to be an integration of opinion and thinking in what is emerging as an international discipline of archaeology – at least, in its philosophical role if not in its practical mode. The strong aspect of nationalism, which has appeared at the level of individuality, has been subsumed in an overall agreement about the way that archaeological thought should progress as a coherent whole. If this can continue, then the input of concepts from people operating from within slightly different paradigms from those of Cambridge can only assist in an understanding of humans in all contexts, which is what archaeology is about.

On the politics of an archaeological conference

Stan Green, South Carolina: Although the conference was meant to be a conversation, it soon became clear that the sociopolitical power relationships were controlling the discussion of issues. Several good issues were raised, but their discussion soon deteriorated toward personal, programmatic and even ideological levels. In most cases people would or could not take the step that was necessary to push the issue, it would seem (according to my instant analysis), because it would be 'dangerous' or threatening to their position. I am not sure much learning occurred and that is my main disappointment. Different views, some ideas were expressed, but not much learning occurred. People came with positions and remained there, not least on the outside. . . . So I learned some; the conference raised some issues, but for the most part it remained paralysed by its politics.

On facts and interpretation

Anonymous: Why are primary sources considered so important in writing archaeological papers, compared to secondary sources? Are secondary sources considered unreliable? Surely a fact is a fact?

On disciplinary boundaries

David Lowenthal, London: A greater effort should have been made to transcend merely *archaeological* foci. For all of us, the understanding, use and creation of the past is an enterprise for which disciplinary boundaries are meaningless and obfuscating.

On text and understanding material culture

Marek Zvelebil, Sheffield: The papers on the interpretation of material culture are poor, revolving around the question whether the analysis of text is an appropriate analogy for interpreting material culture. Most papers think not. For some of us this seems a banal conclusion which we have never doubted. Could we now move on to address *much more* interpretive issues concerned with the *understanding* of material culture?

On the gender of a presentation

John Fritz, Vijayanagara Project: Why did Michael Shanks, as it seems to me, give a masculine presentation, in terms of his body language and way of speaking?

Body language: a spring coiled, uncoiling wire. Wound or contained but giving out in pulses of energy. Expanding outward from a protected or defended centre of power, hence authority. Occupying space exclusively, as a boxer, and not like a dancer whose space can flow together with a partner.

Mode of speaking: explosive and non-linear. Like fireworks where we must figure, configure or figure out the patterns. (Not the usual male presentation, it must be said, of a flow of inherent, logical and authoritative statement.) This could be engaging because we must participate in creating the message, but possibly off-putting.

Was it related to the subject-matter – gendered imagery of men, violence, fighting with and against nature; animals and their masters?

Writing archaeology for professional and general readers

Catherine Hills, Cambridge: The conventional view of publication puts a great gulf between specialist, technical papers on one hand and popular books, articles, radio and television on the other. Both specialists and journalists guard their own territory and maintain that each cannot write for the other's audience. This can cause considerable problems of communication, not least because it allows both sides to disguise their different shortcomings.

Academics use technical terms, and assume their readers both already have much knowledge of the subject and, more insidiously, share the author's perceptions of the significant issues. There is a need for technical publications and for the presentation of data which no non-specialist will ever refer to. But that is no excuse, especially when writing synthetic or analytical papers, for writing in an obscure and confusing manner. The best academic writing is clear and logical, often deceptively simple in expression even when dealing with complex issues. Such works can convey new ideas while not being beyond the grasp of intelligent non-specialists.

Academics also patronise popular writing, and its readership. In many countries, including Britain, popular works count less than specialist papers, or even negatively, in assessing academic achievement. For younger academics this can be a powerful disincentive. There is a feeling that such stuff can be left to journalists because it doesn't really matter. This attitude is unfair both to journalists and to the general public, and ultimately dangerous to the academic world. If we are perceived as an inturned secret society, public funds will dry up: this process may already have begun. We have a responsibility to communicate our knowledge to everyone, not just to our colleagues. This does mean that complex issues have to be boiled down to their essentials, and subtle arguments summarised, which inevitably risks ending up with the wrong overall message. That is why it is actually more difficult to write for a general than for a specialist audience: they don't already know the language, nor do they already accept the basic value of the research topic. It is a very good discipline to have to return to first principles and explain what you are doing, and why the results should be of interest to anyone except yourself. Not all academics can be expected to write in a popular style, but they should be able to sort out their ideas clearly enough to communicate them accurately to someone else, perhaps a journalist co-author.

If we don't help them, we cannot expect non-specialist authors to stop writing books in a superficial scissors-and-paste manner. Approaching a subject from the outside, piecing together snippets from different textbooks without appreciating how those snippets were themselves created, cannot produce a balanced up-to-date account of anything.

Each year fresh glossy books are created by recycling outdated information from old books, and old pictures, to perpetuate ideas discredited fifty years ago. This is not the fault of the writers so much as of the current publishing scene, with its demand for rapid turnover and quick shelf-clearance. This is a fundamental problem for academic writing of all kinds. It both demands the constant, instant book: 'we have to get a million words out every week'; and threatens even specialist books. Reports worked on for years, embodying the information recovered from long and expensive excavations, are now distributed by commercial publishers who pulp them after a few years. What price 'preservation by record', then?

There is not an easy answer to these problems. We have to alter our own attitudes, as specialists. Our knowledge is not our private preserve; it should be widely communicated while not compromising either our research time or the complexity of some of our findings. If it is worth finding out, it is worth telling people about. On the other hand, we must resist the commercial world's instantly disposable and recyclable approach to information of all kinds. At the very least we must protect what should be permanent findings in excavation reports from the market-place. This is not so far as it might seem from my starting-point: I would never advocate complete abandonment of specialist publications, although I believe even they could often be far clearer and more accessible. But we should also take very seriously our responsibility to communicate with a wider public.

Theory and practice

Anonymous: The central problem in archaeology has ceased to be a lack of theoretical tools, but is now a lack of people who are skilled in using the tools to create interesting and valuable accounts of the past.

Glossary

To provide orientations within the extensive fields covered in this discussion of interpretation and archaeology a glossary of some key concepts is here provided. Many concepts which would come under the closely related topics of social and critical archaeology are omitted. Comment and definitions of the latter – and, indeed, many of the concepts which follow here – can be found, for an Anglo-American context, in Shanks and Tilley 1987a and 1987b, Shanks 1992a, Tilley (ed.) 1990, Hodder 1991c; wider reference can be found in the excellent *Dictionary of Human Geography*, edited by Johnston, Gregory and Smith (1994).

No attempt has been made to be definitive. Concepts such as these that follow are constantly subject to shifts of meaning and redefinition through the manoeuvres of cultural politics. Cross-references are in italics.

the aesthetic and the affective A great deal of recent *social archaeology* has concentrated on a rather narrow (and, some would argue, gendered) spectrum of social *experience*. In addition to rational action, decision-making processes, structures of *power*, hierarchy, and the control of resources within ecological systems, archaeologists (especially, but not solely, *postprocessual*) are coming to theorise and work upon the aesthetic dimension, considering the affective component of art and style and social *practice* generally. This can be interpreted as part of wider project of *embodiment*.

The aesthetic and affective dimensions of the past are often prominent in the constructions of *heritage* and those cultural works which deal with the presence of the past, being vital sources of energy in nationalist and regional identities.

agency Agency is a variety of social power relating to intentional and meaningful action. The concept refers to the capabilities of people and is a major dimension of social *practice*. In contrast with the determinism of functionalist (q.v. under *structure*) or *structuralist* approaches which subject people to determining *structures*, humanistic approaches, such as many variants of *postprocessual archaeology*, stress the creative role of human agents who intend, have motivations, rationalise and reflexively monitor action. Any account of past societies must therefore take account of these micropolitical aspects of everyday social *practice* and *experience*. The relation between agency and social *structure* is explicitly considered in the *structuration theory* of Giddens which attempts to transcend a rigid dualism of agency and *structure*, corresponding to a dualism of determinism and voluntarism.

For some the concept of agency is part of a project of empowerment: generally a stress on agency is an important recognition of the creative and productive power of people.

Problems with agency concern its relation to the idea, sometimes criticised as ethnocentric, of the individual and autonomous human subject; *poststructuralism*, for example, has effectively criticised the centrality of this figure of traditional humanism. Human agency, an important idea in any theory of historicity (the capacity to act as a historical agent), might also be regarded as historical itself, changing in its character and experiences (q.v. *genealogy*).

alterity, the other, heterogeneity Classification always has to simplify, asserting the importance of some attributes of an artefact, for example, over others. Taxa or classes are characterised by relative homogeneity. The heterogeneous is that which escapes or embarrasses the procedures of classification. Alterity and otherness are closely related terms which refer to what is in opposition to a particular phenomenon and so, by being different, give shape to it and mark its boundaries. In sexist discourse, for example, masculinity may be defined by the expulsion of what it is not, the feminine; the feminine becomes the other. For Bataille heterogeneity refers to a whole range of unassimilable experiences and phenomena such as sexuality, excretion, destruction, bestiality, ecstasy, trance, which are often the focus of sacred energies and taboo.

Heterogeneity and alterity are important interpretive terms because they refer to the relative independence of what it is we are trying to understand (it always somehow escapes us), remind us that there is always more to learn, that any classification or typology is provisional. The concepts also point to the perpetual presence of horror in social *experience* – that which cannot be rationally assimilated.

authority The authority of the archaeologist may still be conceived to lie in his or her expertise and relationship with the *objectivity* of the past or of explanation. But awareness of the constructed and located character of knowledges has undermined this source of authority – the subject and object of archaeological knowledge have been brought together in a focus on archaeology as acts of cultural production (appropriating the past and producing knowledges of it). The empirical past is not in itself enough to justify archaeological knowledge, it has been argued. Other sources of authority for archaeological *interpretation* may be political, ethical, aesthetic or pragmatic; it depends on local circumstances. It may be argued, for example, that an archaeologist's authority should be rooted in his or her skill in interpreting the past. A variety of contexts of archaeological work would, following this line of argument, entail *pluralism* – different knowledges suited to different local contexts, interests and needs. The issue of authority is one of *cultural politics* and the relationship between *power* and the legitimation of knowledges. An associated problem or criticism is that of *relativism*.

behaviour See under *practice*.

body See under *self, body and subject*.

commodification When artefacts, which can be argued to represent bundles of social relationships, are turned into objects which appear separate and simple, they are commodified. A commodified artefact is one which is abstracted from the contexts and relationships which make it what it is. Full understanding is thereby prevented. To treat artefacts only as commodities is a basic feature of capitalist ideology. Some archaeological approaches and some cultural appropriations of archaeological artefacts (for example, museum exhibitions) have been criticised for commodifying the past.

constructivist philosophy and sociology of science The social character of knowledge is the focus of much philosophy and history of science since the 1970s. The basic contention found in various forms is that knowledge is a social construction or achievement, hence such work often comes under the label of 'constructivism'. It is important to note that this does not necessarily challenge the efficacy, technical success or 'reality' of knowledge, although the issues of *relativism* are involved. *Postprocessual archaeologies* often emphasise the constructed character of archaeological knowledges of the past (q.v. *paradigm*).

context The physical context of archaeological finds has long been recognised as essential to archaeological *explanation* and *interpretation*. *Processual social archaeology* has emphasised the systemic context of *behaviour* – the necessity of locating behaviour within functioning social wholes. More recently *postprocessual* material culture theory has considered it vital to refer the production, style, exchange and consumption of artefacts to wider contexts of social *practice*, social *structures*, symbolic codes and formal organising grammars. Such a position has taken influence from *structuralism* and *poststructuralism*. Hodder's contextual archaeology is to be mentioned here. The concept of context can profitably be connected with an interest in *agency* such as that found in *structuration theory*: the temporal and spatial settings of human practice are considered essential to its constitution, with *place* and *temporality* actively constructed through practice. Human *agency* is always and unavoidably situated. More generally, in the work of Shanks, Tilley and McGuire, the concept has been widened with a philosophy of relationality which examines the forms of connectedness found in human *lifeworlds*. The background to such philosophy is varied – from Hegelian Marxism and *critical theory* through to *poststructuralism*.

critique Critique may simply refer to the critical element of liberal and academic debate: criticism (usually conceived as 'open') of the opinion and work of others.

But, more important, critique is a tradition within Western philosophy. After Kant critique is reflection on the conditions of possible knowledge, a rational reconstruction of the conditions which make language, cognition and action possible. After Hegel and Marx critique is negative thinking. This involves an opposition to neat systems of thought on the grounds that they are always inadequate to reality (q.v. *heterogeneity*). Critique aims to subject everything to rational scrutiny, unveiling and debunking, reflecting on the constraints to which people succumb in the historical process of their self-formation (q.v. *ideology*). Critique asks questions of people's *identity*, their subjectivity, questions of *power* as *agency* and involving subjection to powers beyond. Negative thinking includes *ideology* critique as the scrutiny of sedimented meanings within cultural works which serve particular social interests; often it is associated with a political project of liberation from distortions, constraints and tradition via critical insights into the working of *power*. Anglo-American Critical Archaeology (a term applied to the work of Mark Leone and others usually belonging within a *postprocessual* outlook) has adopted such a project.

Critique is not a methodology but more an attitude which focuses on the social construction of knowledge. The tradition is thus very relevant to a self-reflective discipline.

cultural politics Many things have contributed to archaeology becoming explicitly considered a field of cultural politics. The cultural changes associated with *postmodernity* (for example, resurgent nationalisms feeding searches for local *identity)* and in particular the frequent referencing and appropriation of the archaeological past in *heritage* concerns are important factors. Archaeology has been brought forcibly to confront its place in the present by interests normally considered external to the academy. The philosophical and methodological challenges to *value freedom* in critical theory (q.v. *Western Marxism*) and *ideology critique*, and sociologies of knowledge which treat knowledges as cultural productions or achievements (q.v. *constructivist philosophy of science*) have made it impossible, in the view of many, to maintain a belief in archaeological knowledge as essentially neutral and finding its *origin* in a *real past* detached from the present. The concept of discourse is here central to a position which would have archaeology a mode of cultural production with accompanying inseparable political issues regarding the form, purpose and content of archaeological work.

discipline While common usage treats discipline as simply a branch of knowledge or field of study, critical approaches in the sociology of knowledge stress the dimensions of *power* in the concept of discipline. Disciplines, as a part of *discourse*, are regimens, rules, procedures which are part of the conditions for the production of knowledges – they enable or power the production of knowledge. With such a definition attention is directed as much to the structure as to the content of knowledge, to bodies of knowledge which are located in history and in social practices as much as in the object of knowledge. For Foucault in his later work, discipline is a technology of power located in attitudes towards the body and related to the constitution of subjectivity – what it is to be a subject in society.

discourse Discourse refers to all the conditions required for the production of knowledge. Archaeology constructs its object past through the workings of discourse. This is a key concept in directing attention not so much to the content, but to the conceptual, social and historical conditions within which *disciplines* produce their statements, texts, knowledges and values. Discourse can be treated as the structured conditions within which statements may be made, texts constituted, interpretations made, knowledges developed, even people constituted as subjectivities. Discourse may consist of people, buildings, institutions, rules, values, desires, concepts, machines and instruments These are arranged according to systems and criteria of inclusion and exclusion, whereby some people are admitted, others excluded, some statements qualified as legitimate candidates for assessment, others judged as not worthy of comment. *Disciplines* mark areas of legitimate interest and supply procedural rules, patterns of acceptable practice. There are patterns of authority (committees and hierarchies, for example) and systems of sanctioning, accreditation and legitimation (degrees, procedures of reference and refereeing, personal experiences, career paths). Discourses include media of dissemination: talk and speeches, books, papers, computer and information systems, galleries, or television and radio programmes. Archives (physical or memory-based) are built up providing reference and precedents. Metanarratives, grand systems of narrative, theory or explanation, often approaching myth, lie in the background and provide general orientation, framework and legitimation.

embodiment A humanistic project of widening interpretation to include all dimensions of social *practice* or, better, *experience* – the cognitive and intellectual, physical, *aesthetic and the affective*. Embodiment is a project of rooting social *experience* in all the senses of the body (q.v. *self, body and subject*; *sense and sensibility*).

empiricism The theory that all knowledge derives from the senses; empiricism is therefore an *epistemology*. One form of empiricism asserts that all knowledge comes from sense impressions (of the object of knowledge) and the mind plays no role whatsoever in forming that knowledge – this is the traditional empiricism of British philosophers such as Hume and Locke, where the mind is depicted as a blank slate, and is closely associated with the rise of modern science. Since Kant changed the frame of philosophy, which had been one of empiricism versus rationalism (i.e., knowledge derived from the senses versus knowledge derived from the mind), by mediating these two theories, a modified empiricism has been adopted, whereby some role is given to the mind in forming knowledge, though the problem has always been how to relate the two adequately. For *positivism* this has centred on the problem of induction, i.e., how to infer general knowledge from particular sensory data. Empiricism of various forms is the dominant epistemology in archaeology; empirical data, achieved particularly through controlled observation, are the base or origin of knowledge and are to be kept separate from the distortions of subjectivity (q.v. *values and value-freedom*). The problem with empiricism in general is that it is self-refuting or at least dependent upon a separate metaphysics, since the claim that all knowledge is dependent on empirical data cannot itself be accommodated in this thesis and has to be justified externally.

emplotment The process by which a historian 'grasps together' elements of historical data into a sensible and coherent narrative whole, characterised according to narrativist philosophy by various rhetorical modes or devices (q.v. *narrative and narrativity*).

epistemology and knowledge Epistemology is that branch of philosophy which deals with the character of knowledge. It is the study of what constitutes knowledge, considering its construction, its limits and its validation. An epistemology is a theory of knowledge. Since Descartes in the seventeenth century much philosophy has in various ways centred on the problem of knowledge. It was not until the end of the nineteenth century with Nietzsche, and then in the twentieth century with Heidegger, that epistemology was dropped from its prime position in philosophy, though it still remains there in *positivism*. The turn in Anglo-American archaeology in the 1960s to the question of what constitutes knowledge of the material past was (and still is) an interest in *positivism* (q.v. *constructivist philosophy* and *sociology of science*).

A recent interest of British *postprocessual social archaeology* is in the importance to social reproduction of knowledge, practical and propositional or discursive (available to expression in *discourse*). An interest in technical knowledge and practice has a long standing in French archaeology. This concern with knowhow, skills and technology seems very appropriate to a field of study centred upon material culture. The reference in social theory is to people as knowledgeable *agents*, skilled in social *practice* and who monitor the consequences of *practice* (q.v. *intentionality and agency*).

essentialism The idea that particular things have essences which serve to identify them as the particular things that they are. Such a belief and premiss is often found in archaeology: society itself or types of society, for example, may be held to have an 'essence' (though it may not be termed such) which is expressed in what archaeologists observe. Essentialism is most often associated with abstraction: the essential features of a society are identified abstractly (perhaps in theory) and empirical expressions of the set of abstracted essential features sought. Typology and artefact classification may also tend to essentialism if the categories used to identify artefacts are treated abstractly and if the origins and meanings of the categories or taxa are not fully considered (q.v. *heterogeneity*).

Essentialism is usually a term of criticism in archaeology because of the metaphysical problem it introduces of the origin of the essences: if society is essentially a functioning system of patterned behaviours (a position held by some *processual archaeologists*), what is the origin of this necessary logic? Why is society necessarily like this? The abstract categories of essentialism also belittle human *agency*. Can society exist as a set of essential features prior to its human subjects? Opponents of essentialism would usually stress human *agency*: the origin of those categories treated abstractly as essences is to be found in social *practice*. So society is a human construction, as is 'the past', as are the categories we use to understand societies in the past; there is no abstracted or logical and neutral necessity to any of them.

experience Social *practice* has become a key concept of *postprocessual social archaeology*. Experience is a related but wider and less abstract term, a means of *embodying* the concept of *practice*. Lacking from experience can be notions of intentionality (an experience may just happen to you). Experience can be passive and contemplative, personal as well as social, emotional as well as intellectual or physical. Someone who is experienced has knowledge acquired through practice (they may be considered 'expert') or through having undergone things. Etymological roots are the Greek *peirao*, try, and *perao*, pass through. A peril (a related word) is a trial undergone, and all aspects of perception are invoked – from intellectual awareness to physical suffering. Experience is knowledge acquired through trial. An experiment is a tentative procedure which makes trial of things. Here experience may contain a notion of knowing reality not through simply having been told, but by having undergone trial, or by making trial of things; reality comes to be that which has resisted trials made of it. An experience is an event by which one is affected, an action or condition viewed from the person or *self*, subjectively. Concomitantly to experience is the condition of being consciously the *subject* (in all senses) of a *practice*, state or condition.

explanation and understanding The essential openness of *interpretation*, which aims at understanding, may be contrasted with the aim of closure (logical, causal, teleological or genetic) between explanans and explanandum, which is usually considered the aim of explanation – defining, analysing and modelling entities and processes held to be the reason for what is observed of the object of interest. The contrast between explanation and understanding has been taken as a dichotomy or dualism referring to the appropriate aims of the social and natural sciences respectively (q.v. *hermeneutics*).

genealogy Included here for its technical sense, found in the work of Foucault, of a historical project which aims to reveal, via careful and particularistic interpretation, the discontinuities, difference and *heterogeneity* in what was considered regular, stable and continuous (for example, human sexuality or rationality).

heritage A heterogeneous field of collage. In the constructions of heritage objects, images, ideas, sentiments, practices, not necessarily pertaining to the past, may be assembled and associated with global, national or local *identity* and/or promoted as educational or diverting entertainment.

hermeneutics and the hermeneutic circle In particular hermeneutics is a method for interpreting texts, but more generally the word refers to the art, skill, theory and philosophy of interpretation and understanding. Contemporary hermeneutics is partly derived from nineteenth-century German historians such as Dilthey, where a central issue was the distinction between natural and social phenomena, and hence the natural and social sciences, with their different modes of acquiring knowledge, i.e. understanding (verstehen) versus explanation (erklaren) (q.v. *explanation and understanding*). It was given a new basis through *phenomenology* by Heidegger, who saw understanding as constitutive of human existence, and thus a phenomenology of human existence is a phenomenology of understanding. Of importance here is Heidegger's concept of pre-understanding, which Gadamer took up in connection with the notions of prejudice, tradition and authority which are of central importance to contemporary hermeneutics, and constitute the basis of the hermeneutic circle.

The hermeneutic circle encapsulates the act of understanding or interpretation. Understanding, according to hermeneutics, is always historically located, within a tradition credited with authority, from the viewpoint of whoever wishes to understand. So we never understand something as given, but always as something, having a pre-understanding or anticipation of what it is we engage with or are looking upon, just as when we read a particular part of a text, we always already have some grasp of that text as a totality or a whole. This prejudice (pre-judgement) is considered essential to understanding; it is not a barrier but the medium of understanding. If modified in an interpretive encounter with something we desire to understand, it forms a new basis of the next engagement, and so on: this is the hermeneutic circle.

Implicated in the hermeneutic circle is the problem of the universality of hermeneutics – that is, if all understanding is also a pre-understanding, then there is no point from which to make external judgements, independent of tradition, and this has serious consequences for a critical hermeneutics which wishes to provide a *critique* of the power structures implicated in a tradition (q.v. *explanation and understanding, interpretation*).

heterogeneity See under *alterity*.

identity The implications of the material past in personal, local and national cultural identity have been foregrounded by the constructions of the *heritage* industry. A frequent focus in the relationship between past and present, identity is thus a vital issue in any archaeological *cultural politics*.

The identity of an artefact is also a concern of (archaeological) classification. Whether stable identities should or can be sought has been challenged particularly by *poststructuralism* (q.v. *heterogeneity*).

ideology A complex term of social and political theory, ideology may refer (and not exclusively) to a set of ideas held by a group of people, to ideas about social reality which are false (false consciousness), or to ideas, knowledges or practices which result in the reproduction of social relationships characterised by inequality or contradiction. It is thus a key term in sociologies of knowledge. Ideology has been found a useful concept in *social archaeology* and in critical archaeology (q.v. under *critique*) aiming at a critically self-reflexive discipline of archaeology aware of the location of archaeological knowledges in contemporary society (q.v. *discourse*).

intentionality Some approaches in the human sciences hold that people should be considered not as passive tabulae rasae, through whose *behaviour* society may be traced, but as active subjects. This is a feature of *postprocessual* archaeologies. The contrast is between an interest in *behaviour* and an interest in active social *practice*. To understand and explain *practice*, account must be taken of faculties and capabilities of intending, choosing and ordering – people's self-reflexive monitoring of their lifeworlds. Human *agency* is an important associated concept. The implications for *social archaeology* are profound – accounts of past societies and their material culture *lifeworlds* very different from those of traditional and *processual* archaeologies are hereby implied. This has been a major development of *postprocessual social archaeology*. There are also implications for understanding the practice of archaeology – the past is less 'discovered' (traces to be recorded by the observing archaeologist) than it is worked with and upon according to creative acts of intention and choice made under particular social interests.

interpretation With a particular archaeological aim of understanding the past and a wider interest of providing edifying learning experiences, interpretation is a never-ending process of making sense (q.v. *meaning and sense*). Interpretation is essentially open and never final: more can always be said or learned, and interpretation is anyway historically located (q.v. *hermeneutics*, *explanation and understanding*).

landscape Landscape is the result of a social construction of space, containing a bundle of practices, meanings, attitudes, values. It is thereby a term appropriate to a humanistic understanding of the environment and to be contrasted with a naturalistic approach (q.v. under *processual archaeology*).

Landscape archaeology is now a major subdiscipline uniting historical geography, human geography, history and archaeology (q.v. *space, place and locale*).

lifeworld see under *phenomenology*.

meaning and sense Meaning has become a key word in archaeology (especially *postprocessual*). The meaning (past and present) of the things found by archaeologists is an important question. However, in accordance with ideas concerning the openness of *interpretation* and the multiplicity of the interpreted world (q.v. under *pluralism* and *poststructuralism*), it may be better to think not of the meaning of things, but of the process of making sense of them.

mentalité A term found in the historiography of the Annales school which covers the non-material aspects of culture – *ideologies*, beliefs and worldviews, particularly of the type which are not easily rendered verbally. These are revealed through the contextual interpretation of texts or material culture.

narrative and narrativity Versions of historical narrative remain for many the ultimate aim of archaeological work – combining the particulars of the archaeological past into meaningful wholes with features such as events and plot. With a renewed interest in *writing* and *text*, the forms and character of narrative in archaeology (actual and potential) have come under scrutiny by some. The subject is a wide one. Narrative is a basic human means of making sense of the world, and narratives form a basic component of self-*identity*. Narratives accordingly feature prominently in nationalist and *heritage* appropriations of the archaeological past. The concept emphasises the active character of making sense (q.v. *meaning and sense*) – constructing meaningful plots out of what was uncertainty, and plots which have or will have meaning and significance for an audience or *public* (q.v. *emplotment*).

Narrativity is a concept associated with an explicit philosophical concern with the writing of historical texts; the theory that meaningful history can only be presented in a narrative form characterised, according to Hayden White, by plot, continuity, agency and closure. Opposed to this is, for example, a covering-law approach which, influenced by positivist philosophy of science, concentrates on historical explanation through explicit causal relationships rather than the historical understanding exemplified by the narrativist approach (q.v. *explanation and understanding*).

negotiation Negotiation is an important aspect of the interpretive character of social reality and the *lifeworld*. The world is not just given to people and their senses, according to such an argument, but argued over, reinterpreted, negotiated (q.v. *interpretation*).

object, artefact and materiality While most archaeologists can generally be held to be dealing with aspects of the object world, distinctions can be made (at least) between objects of knowledge, raw materials worked upon in (cultural) production, artefacts, and the realm of materiality. All are part of the field of material culture studies, which potentially includes archaeology. Questions of the social life of things, people's self-creation through material production, of technology, practical knowledge and reason, philosophical issues of the character of materiality are addressed in this interdisciplinary field.

objectivity The notion that things or statements about things exist or are true independently (and therefore absolutely) of human existence or belief. It is often opposed to subjectivism, which states that knowledge and truth are not thus independent. The debate between *processual* and *postprocessual* archaeology has been characterised as a polarisation between objectivist and subjectivist approaches. This is held by some archaeologists (traditional, processual and postprocessual) to be a very damaging and unnecessary polarisation. The point should not be to polarise but instead to relate the knower and the known.

ontology Much Anglo-American archaeological thought of the last thirty years has focused on *epistemology* and methodology. Recently some archaeologists (*postprocessual*) have come to consider what may be termed archaeological or social ontology – asking questions of the character of the object of archaeological inquiry (ontology is the branch of philosophy concerned with what exists). Such archaeological ontology asks what is the character of material culture, what is social *practice*, just what is it that archaeologists are attempting to interpret or explain, and more generally what is the character of materiality as it is experienced archaeologically?

origins Some of the conventional big questions of archaeology concern origins: the origins of humanity, of agriculture, of civilisation, of social complexity, of the West, for example. That there can be coherent answers to these complex questions has been doubted by some on the grounds that the search for origins is a project which aims to reduce the multiplicity and equivocality of social reality to coherent systems, and consoling metanarratives (q.v. under *discourse*) imposing present interests and categories on the past. A search for origins is also opposed by a *genealogical archaeology*.

More philosophically, that the origin of archaeological knowledge is to be found in the past as it was (*the 'real' past*) has also been doubted, particularly by certain strains of *poststructuralism* (q.v. also postmodern attitude under *postmodernity and postmodernism*).

paradigm Paradigm is a term used and popularised by Thomas Kuhn to refer to the theories and methods shared by a scientific community practising 'normal science', when basic assumptions and orientations are left uncriticised. The term has been criticised for its vagueness, although Kuhn subsequently attempted to distinguish paradigms in the wider sense of the shared commitments of a scientific group (the 'disciplinary matrix') from the narrower sense of the concrete problem solutions or exemplars they hold in common. Nevertheless, paradigm is an important concept for understanding *discourse* and the social construction of knowledge. Different paradigms in archaeology have been identified and proposed.

phenomenology In the modern sense this is a philosophy initiated by Husserl in the early part of this century and which aimed to return to a Cartesian attitude of doubt by constructing a presuppositionless analysis of human experience as it is lived. It involved the method of bracketing-off assumptions or presuppositions about the world and so to reach the essence of the phenomena under investigation. The major criticism of Husserl came from his pupil Heidegger, who disagreed with Husserl's starting-point, the Ego, holding that this starting-point itself presupposed something about the world. Heidegger's phenomenology worked not from the Ego but from an existence which is always already situated in the world – Being-there (Dasein).

More generally a phenomenological interest is one in people's lived *experience*, a unity of subject and object worlds with the subjective being the form that the objective world takes. A key term here is that of *lifeworld* – the environment ('natural', artefactual and human) as it is lived by people.

pluralism Pluralism is a corollary of certain aspects of interpretation: the irreducibility of the world to categories of understanding means that things can always be interpreted differently. The world is polysemous and characterised by multiplicity. A plurality of *interpretation* corresponds with this multiplicity. Multivocality refers to the political requirement that different interpretations are given equal opportunities and resources to voice themselves and be judged.

poetics An archaeological poetics is an explicit concern with the technicalities of the production of archaeological works in the widest sense: for example, archaeological *writing* and illustration. It is thus part of a self-reflexivity concerned with *discourse* and *discipline*.

positivism Although there are varieties of philosophical positivism, in archaeology positivism is a general position which gives primacy to *epistemology*, and one which is essentially *empiricist*. The natural sciences are usually taken as the paradigm of an *empiricist epistemology*, and hence positivist archaeologists will invoke not necessarily laws but a generalising explanatory framework wherein a particular event, for example, is explained by reference to or subsumption beneath a general relationship. There is an emphasis on empirical data as the primary means of testing such explanations because of their *objectivity*. By asserting the identity of natural and social phenomena, the application of the methods – and assumptions – of natural science is imported into social science, with quite serious consequences for how social phenomena are subsequently perceived. Quantitative and mathematical techniques are liberally applied in *processual archaeology*, sometimes, it is criticised, without adequate reflection. Positivist archaeology differs quite radically from a hermeneutic tradition which distinguishes explanation from understanding achieved through interpretation (cf. *hermeneutics*).

postmodernity and postmodernism It is suggested here that it is convenient to distinguish postmodernity as an extension of modernity – the cultural condition of late capitalism – from postmodernism – a recent movement in the arts, philosophy, the social sciences, style and popular culture – and from a postmodern attitude. So Harvey has characterised postmodernity as a cultural component of a new phase of capitalism, post-Fordist and concerned with strategies of flexible capital accumulation. The postmodern condition is characterised as fragmented, dislocated, interested in style, eclectically pillaging the past and other cultures without regard for traditional forms of authenticity, building on the demise of the certainties of old class cultures and institutional forms of the nation state. Within postmodernism, architecture has left the international style of modernism with an attention to the decorative, to variation of façades with pastiche, diversity of colour, design elements and iconography. Within the humanities postmodern method (notably deconstruction – q.v. under *poststructuralism*) is a mode of *interpretation* which aims to elaborate the multiple relations between culture, class and gender positioning and their effects upon cultural production and consumption, destabilising easy and univocal readings of cultural products. A major criticism is that the resulting interpretive multiplicity (q.v. *pluralism*) is politically disabling because it challenges single authoritative readings which may provide legitimation for particular cultural or political strategies (q.v. *authority*). This is allied with the more general criticism that a postmodernist celebration of *pluralism* may be *relativist*. A postmodern attitude is characterised by a radical scepticism towards the claims of grand theory, towards totalising theoretical schemes produced from single and privileged vantage points (for example, the claims of *positivist* social science or orthodox Marxism). Instead an openness to difference and *alterity* is celebrated, with multivocality (q.v. under *pluralism*), experimentation and the empowerment of marginal political and cultural constituencies.

postpositivism This is not so much a coherent theory as a general reaction and move away from *positivism*; in philosophy it was associated first with the work of Kuhn and Feyerabend who, to different degrees, criticise the empiricist basis of positivism. More generally, the term is applied to alternative approaches such as *hermeneutics*.

 Postprocessual archaeology can certainly, though only partly, be associated with postpositivist philosophy because of its constitution as a reaction against the *positivist* bias of much *processual archaeology*. The postpositivist strain in *postprocessual archaeology* is a reinstatement of the social foundations and responsibilities of archaeological inquiry, a refusal to separate archaeological 'science' from *discourse*, and a suspicion of the value of unrestrained application of quantitative techniques.

postprocessual archaeology Postprocessual archaeology is not so much a coherent body of thought as a reaction against the positivist base in *processual archaeology* (q.v. *positivism*), and many of the implications of that base, such as 'naturalism' (q.v. *processual archaeology*) and 'scientism' – natural science taken as the model for archaeology. Postprocessual archaeology incorporates many different approaches derived from *Western Marxism, hermeneutics, poststructuralism* and *constructivist philosophy of science*. One topic of interest is social *ontology* – the character of social reality which may be taken as the object of archaeological study. Attempts have been made to provide archaeology with more sophisticated and differentiated conceptions of past society and to explore these conceptions through archaeological materials. Dimensions which have been theorised and explored are social power, structure, contradiction and social change, and gender. Here a key concept is *agency* (an aspect of social power). People are knowledge-able agents – attention should be paid to intention, meaning and signification in order to understand past social phenomena. This has involved many post-processual studies of systems of signification, and studies which recognise the social importance of symbolism and *ideology*. Another topic of interest is the past in the present – archaeology as a mode (one among many) of cultural production, archaeology as *discourse*.

poststructuralism Poststructuralism refers to the ideas and works, developed since the 1960s, of a number of mainly French intellectuals; Derrida, Lacan, Foucault, the later Barthes, and Kristeva are some of the most prominent names. Roots reach back into Hegel, Nietzsche, Husserl, Heidegger, Freud and Marx. The main currents of *structuralist* thought are extended and, arguably, radicalised in this disparate body of thought: first, in relation to language, *identity* and *meaning*, and, second, in relation to the human subject. Derrida, notably, argues against the totalising and fixed character of a structuralist analysis of language and texts, holding that the relations between signified and signifier (within the sign) are indeterminate and that meaning is slippery and irreducible to structures of difference (the classic structuralist premiss). The notion of a unified and rational subject *self* has been replaced with a subjectivity in process and the product of *discourses*; much poststructuralism opposes the notion of any essential *self* – or, indeed, any sense of the real outside of cultural systems of discourse. Foucault's investigations of the history of *discourses* extended into social power, conceptions of the human body and *self*, sexuality, architecture, and the spatial organisation of society.

A general trend of poststructuralist method, often termed deconstruction, is against *essentialism* and towards an unsettling of any firm, detached and neutral conclusions; truth claims are internal to any particular discourse, it is claimed, and any fixed transcendental *origins* of knowledge are denied. Deconstruction is best seen perhaps as a destabilising method throwing into doubt the authority claims of established interests and traditions, opening up alternative spaces, readings and meanings. With regard to the challenge to neutrality, fixed origins and identities there is a similarity to some trends of *postpositivist* philosophy which insist on situating knowledges as social and cultural achievements.

The implications of poststructuralism for any field of social inquiry are immense. Influences are readily apparent in *postprocessual archaeology* regarding *epistemology*, method and social *ontology*.

power Much *postprocessual social archaeology* has focused on power as a key dimension of *practice*. Relations of power (particularly concerning economy and resources) are also often central to *processual* accounts of past societies. With respect to archaeological practice, power is also implicated in the concepts of *discourse* and *discipline*. Power is a manifold concept encompassing *agency* as well as power over others and over things, authority and might, institutional and informal operations. It is as much productive as constraining. All this should, it may be argued by theorists, be considered in accounts of past societies.

practice and behaviour Practice refers to the meaningful actions of knowledgeable *agents*, but is often used in terms of routinised actions – those actions which are mundane, conventional and repeated, produced through practical knowledge or knowhow rather than propositional knowledge open to discursive elaboration (q.v. *discourse*). An interest in practice rather than behaviour is a feature of *postprocessual archaeology*.

Behaviour, in contrast, refers to the activities of social actors without reference to *agency* and *meaning*. Motivation, knowledge and rationalisation may be considered in behavioural explanation, but usually in terms of rational processes of decision-making (cross-cultural), or decisions made according to social norms. Whatever, the term does not carry the interest in creativity and reflexive monitoring that practice does.

processual archaeology Deriving from New Archaeology of the 1960s and early 1970s, processual archaeology generally takes an anthropological and *positivist* position. The latter has had strong implications for the manner in which archaeologists interpret the archaeological record. Through its *paradigm* of natural science, the past is imbued with a 'naturalism' in that social phenomena are regarded like natural phenomena: society is treated as a second nature. Drawing particularly on biology, systems theory became a dominant model in which to view the past, where societies are seen as systems with various parts, each interlinked most notably by feedback relationships. Ecological models are commonly invoked to explain various phenomena, and 'natural' factors, such as subsistence and the environment, play a strong role in explanation. Problems which are recognised include previous assumptions about what constitutes 'efficiency' in such systems, and therefore a wider interest in symbolic and cognitive spheres is developing.

public Particularly since the late 1970s the *cultural politics* of archaeology has become, for many, a vital issue. As archaeology's cultural space in the present has come under scrutiny, it is no longer enough to justify the *discipline* by reference to the assumed intrinsic value of the pursuit of knowledge (of the material past) for its own sake. The issue of for whom archaeologists work and write is on the agenda: be they employers, audiences, clients, publics, other archaeologists. That there are many constituencies and audiences for whom archaeologists write implies *pluralism* – many publics. An ethic of professionalism would seem to require attention to modes of report and address: for example, forms of *narrative*, *writing* and illustration (q.v. *poetics*).

the 'real' past Many archaeologists might aim to discover what happened in the past, but the feasibility and reasonableness of this simple aim has been seriously questioned. To hold that social life is always open to (re)interpretation, that the social world is polysemous and multiple, rather than single and deterministic (positions now widely found in the humanities; q.v. also *pluralism*), means that there never was a single 'real past' to discover archaeologically. The pre-understanding which we take to the past as archaeologists is the condition for understanding according to *hermeneutics*, and *constructivist philosophy of science* indicates that knowledge is always socially situated.

These all indicate that the past cannot be held as the real and objective *origin* of what archaeologists do. And, anyway, it no longer exists as it was lived, is much lost and decayed. But this is not necessarily to deny that the past did indeed happen as it did. The best we can do perhaps is learn in an encounter with the past. Mediation is a key term here – the archaeologist conceived as mediating the past and the present; the archaeologist working a space between past and present. A more reasonable aim thus might be to work upon the traces of the past recovered archaeologically to produce knowledges which are considered relevant, edifying and justifiable by contemporary interests.

realism A philosophy (usually of science) which has been found attractive to many wishing to overcome the problems of *positivism*, but who also see *structuralism* and *poststructuralism* as flawed (q.v. also *postpositivism*). The basic contention is that real mechanisms or causes can be identified (abstractly, by and with the abstractions of science) behind specific and contingent occurrences or events.

relativism In general relativism is the claim that there is no knowledge independent of the knower, that all knowledge is created within a cultural system. One implication may be that there can be no absolute or independent means of judging between different knowledge claims, including science. Such a relativism is self-refuting since what it states about knowledge (that there are no independent means of assessment) must apply equally to that claim itself (it cannot be upheld). It also contradicts a substantive experience of the intercommunicability of human cultures. However, a relativism which stops with the argument that knowledges are constructed, are temporally and spatially located, does not necessarily have these problems. Relativism is a charge often directed against *postprocessual archaeologies*. It is a primary concern of *constructivist philosophy of science*.

scientific method Many archaeologists would wish to adhere to scientific method to ensure *objectivity*. The term refers not so much to the everyday practice of how scientists work (which has been studied by *constructivist philosophers of science* with very different results), as to an idealised and prescriptive notion of how science in general works, and therefore how knowledge is generated (q.v. *epistemology*). Such scientific method is characterised by a critical process of general hypotheses tested against particular observations, which either corroborate or refute the original hypothesis – as such it may often be labelled critical rationalism (q.v. also *explanation* and *positivism*). Earlier difficulties were associated with trying to solve the problem of induction, which, for example, Popper's falsification principle attempted to do; however, the problem of the interdependency of the test observations with the theoretical assumptions of the hypothesis make the whole idea of the scientific method as an objective route to knowledge extremely implausible.

self, body and subject A project of *social archaeology* attempts to explain and interpret past societies through their material remains. Social *practice* is a concept held by many now to be central to this project. Society is hereby considered to be more than patterns of regularised behaviours, but involves the *agency* and intentionality of human subjects. Accordingly there is need to consider the construction of the self, of the acting subject. And *practice* is more than the mental and verbal. *Practice* is embodied, rooted in the body (as flesh) and its senses. Account needs to be taken of *the affective*, of all aspects of sensibility and the senses. The *lifeworld* is multidimensional. Metals shine and glitter as well as cut, architectures resonate as well as shelter from the weather. A humanistic project of embodiment aims to accommodate within *interpretation* the full manifold character of (social) *experience*.

sense, sentiment, sentience and sensibility A family of concepts belonging with any interpretive and embodied (q.v. *embodiment*) project aiming to make sense (q.v. *meaning and sense*) of the social *experience* of knowledgeable and sentient *agents*. Encompassing *the aesthetic and affective* dimensions of *experience* in *interpretation* perhaps requires an education of the sentiments – attending to the many varied textures of the *lifeworld*.

social archaeology This refers to archaeology operated under the contention, now widely held in Anglo-American archaeology, that understanding the archaeological past must involve reconstruction of past societies and social practices – artefacts and other archaeological finds must be placed in social *context*. This requires an anthropological and sociological bias to the *discipline* of archaeology. Classification and descriptive *narrative* are not sufficient ends in themselves.

space, place and locale Place is a portion of neutral or mathematical space occupied, taken up by a person or thing. Locale is a setting in which social *practices* occur. Mention should also be made here of a sense of place as a part of a local 'structure of feeling'. The terms 'place' and 'locale' are thus central to humanistic and phenomenological geography, and to any interpretive social science which aims to understand the *lifeworld* and the constitution of social *practices*.

A sense of place is also arguably vital (in its absence as well as its presence) to the postmodern condition (q.v. *postmodernity and postmodernism*).

structuralism Structuralism is a very influential approach and body of cultural theory derived ultimately from work in linguistics, particularly associated with Saussure. A major distinction is between language as it is spoken (parole) and language as the underlying system of signs (langue). Structuralism focuses on the latter, and makes a further distinction within the sign, between the signifier (for example, a word) and the signified (that which the sign refers to). The emphasis is on the system of signs, and their differences, rather than on the individual signs. In anthropology, the approach has been most famously adopted by Lévi-Strauss, who analysed, among other things, native myths in the same manner, and particularly made use of binary oppositions such as culture:nature, hot:cold, or raw:cooked. It is through this kind of analysis that it is perhaps most widely known in archaeology, while a more pervasive influence has been through the linguistic or textual analogy, that cultural phenomena are structured as in a language.

The major problem with structuralism is its privileging of structure (langue) over *agency*. There is the crucial, but often unanswered, question of the genesis and maintenance of *structure*, a question which *structuration theory* and human-istic approaches which stress creative *agency* attempt to address.

structuration theory The structuration theory developed by Giddens since the 1970s has had a significant influence on *postprocessual social archaeologies*. It is concerned to overcome the dualism, found in most of the social sciences, of individual *agency*, meaning and understanding versus social structure. Its major thesis is the replacement of the dualism with a duality wherein social *structure* is both the medium and the outcome of the social *practice* of knowledgeable social *agents*. The later work of Giddens has emphasised how time and space are basic constituents embedded within social life: the limitations of individual presence are transcended by the stretching of social relations across time and space through processes of time–space distanciation (q.v. *temporality*).

Structuration is best seen less as a theory to be applied than as a set of tools to be used with a new sensitisation to the character of social *practice*. This is how it has been received in *postprocessual social archaeology*.

structure Generally structure refers to the basic framework or form of society, though social theory has attempted various refinements of the term. Elements of a physical structure such as an artefact are often associated with function, hence functionalist and structural functionalist theory which treats society as analogous to an organism, with each institutional part (religion, the economy, etc.) function-ing to maintain the whole. Such theory is related to systems theory, and both have generally received much application in *processual social archaeology*. More particularly structure refers to the longue durée in Braudel's temporal scheme (q.v. *temporality*), the fundamental baseline of a historical period, seen by the earlier Annales historians as essentially geographical or environmental in character. Analysis of society in terms of structure has often been at the methodological expense of the social individual or subject, with a dualism between structure and *agency*. In *structuration theory*, which attempts to overcome this, structure means those ideas, resources and rules shared by a society and drawn upon in practice by knowledgeable *agents*.

In spite of such refinement of the concept, it is perhaps overworked in the social sciences, 'structured' being used often to mean little more than organised, patterned or appearing non-random.

subject See under *self, body and subject*.

temporality See under *time and temporality*.

text and intertextuality As with *writing*, the concept of text refers to more than the written word. Text refers to extended sequences of written discourse. The text as a work (of *discourse*) is more than the sum of its sentences; it is produced in accordance with rules and procedures, its genre; and a text has a style. Far from being dependent upon an author, the text has its own separate career, is partially autonomous, and as a material form is separate from its conditions of production. The text, constructed from a mosaic of quotations of all kinds, is necessarily interdependent with a mass of texts and statements which precede, accompany and succeed it – this is the concept of intertextuality (after Kristeva) which again demotes the importance of the author and their intentions. The concept thus implies a denial of univocity and searches for the essential meaning of a text or author – a critical understanding of text is that of an open work susceptible to multiple readings which are intimately linked to cultural and political positioning (q.v. *pluralism*). The *authority* of the author is challenged.

The concept of text is an important tool in the understanding of archaeology as a *discipline* and *discourse*; textualisation has already attracted great attention in anthropology and history. It has also been influential in the interpretation of material culture through a textual analogy – the proposition that material culture is structured and operates like text. The work of Ricoeur and Barthes particularly is relevant to both perspectives.

time and temporality In spite of archaeology being a discipline prominently concerned with time there has been little reflection upon time in the discipline. Time is most often identified with chronology and secondarily with social change. But a concern with time as experienced in history (temporality) rather than as objectified (and perhaps *commodified*) chronology is to be found, for example, in Braudel's different temporal scales or Ricoeur's suggestion that historical narratives are 'allegories of temporality', a discursive mode used to convey something of the experience of time. An attention to the experience of time is part of a *phenomenological* project. *Structuration theory* also treats time (and space) not as a neutral dimension but as constituted within social practices. A manifold concept of temporality is arguably a vital part of any *social archaeology*.

values and value-freedom Scientific and objective method (taken as a model by many archaeologists) might well aspire to value-freedom – exclusion of value-words and value-judgements. This does not mean that selection of material for investigation does not involve value-judgement about how interesting or relevant it may be, or that judgements about the validity of inference may not be made. Facts are to be kept separate from values, and what is to be excluded is the making of value-judgements about the *people* in the field of study (q.v. *empiricism*, *objectivity*, *positivism*, *scientific method*). That this is possible or desirable has been widely challenged. An alternative to value-freedom argues that archaeologists should take full responsibility for their work and not detach themselves from issues of *cultural politics*, now so frequent in archaeology; archaeologists should not retreat into conceptions of a discipline claimed to be concerned with neutral knowledge separable from its conditions of production in the present.

Western Marxism With the failure in the early decades of this century of socialist revolution in Western Europe exponents of Marxist thought turned from political economy to investigate and theorise cultural phenomena and focused on drawing out the implications of Marx's ideas about *ideology*. Western Marxism is a term used to denote those in the tradition thus initiated. It includes philosophers and sociologists such as Horkheimer, Marcuse and Adorno, political theorists such as Gramsci, Althusser and Habermas, and many others. Those on the fringe include Sartre and Benjamin. The Frankfurt School of Social Research was an early institutional focus. Critical Theory is a term often associated with the School and with Western Marxism. In Britain and America the publishing efforts of the New Left have greatly contributed to its dissemination.

Some effort was concentrated on demonstrating how *ideology* affects our understanding of the world, and works to maintain and create social *structure* and particularly the *power* differences in society; a central concern is the relation between *agency* and the *structure* of society. Debate over political and social theory has been deep and continuous. The importance of the tradition to archaeology is in the sophisticated treatment of cultural phenomena, in its persistent questioning of the relations between the theory and practice of *cultural politics*, and in its sustaining the tradition of cultural *critique*. A problem has been a retreat into theory from a practical engagement with political practice.

writing Archaeologists translate material remains (of the past) into reports, papers and books. The question of how to publish and write has long been recognised as important. More recent foregrounding of the relationship between archaeologists and their present has sharpened the question. For whom, how and why? – audiences, constituencies and *publics* are crucial factors, as are those of political purpose and cultural relevance. Philosophical issues here are to do with the representation of historical and social reality – of what do the latter consist and what is to be made of them? For a critical and self-conscious perspective (after, among others, Roland Barthes) concerned with the production of archaeological knowledge, writing is less to do with a work or set of marks upon a page and is less about the communication and representation of ideas and things established elsewhere (as many archaeologists might hold) but is a much wider and heterogeneous space within which meaning is produced. In *poststructuralism* writing is not about conveying the presence of things in marks upon a page but may be conceived to be a system of differences, networks of signifiers which classify and constitute meanings through differentiation (rather than by transporting the presence or essence of something). Attention is called to all manner of contexts (material, conceptual, political, social and cultural) of the production of archaeological meanings (see also *text* and *discourse*).

Bibliography

'Access without conflict: a general desire' (1991) *Country Life*, 12 September.

Adorno, T. (1973) *Negative Dialectics*, London: Routledge.

Aiello, Leslie and Dean, Christofer (1990) *An Introduction to Human Evolutionary Anatomy*, London: Academic Press.

Althusser, Louis (1971) 'Ideology and ideological state apparatuses', in *Lenin and Philosophy*, New York: Monthly Review Press.

Anderson, J. R. (1984) 'Monkeys with mirrors: some questions for primate psychology', *International Journal of Primatology*, 5:81–98.

Andresen, J. T. (1992) 'The behaviorist turn in recent theories of language', *Behaviour and Philosophy*, 20: 1–19.

Ankersmit, F. (1986) 'The dilemma of contemporary Anglo-Saxon philosophy of history', *History and Theory*, Beiheft 25: 1–27.

Appadurai, A. (ed.) (1986) *The Social Life of Things: Commodities in Cultural Perspective*, Cambridge: Cambridge University Press.

Appleton, J. (1986) *The Experience of Landscape* (paperback reprint), Hull: Hull University Press.

Archaeological Review from Cambridge, 9:1 (1990), *Technology in the Humanities*.

Archaeological Review from Cambridge, 9:2 (1990), *Affective Archaeology*.

Arlott, J. (1988) *The Coloured Counties: Poems of Place in England and Wales*, London: J. M. Dent.

Ashbee P. (1972), 'Field archaeology: its origins and development', in P. J. Fowler (ed.) *Archaeology and the Landscape*, London: John Baker.

Ashworth, G. J. and Tunbridge, J. E. (1990) *The Tourist-Historic City*, London/New York: Bellhaven Press.

Aston, M. (1985) *Interpreting the Landscape*, London: Batsford.

Aston, M. and Rowley, T. (1974) *Landscape Archaeology: An Introduction to Fieldwork Techniques on Post-Roman Landscapes*, Newton Abbot: David & Charles.

Atwell, J. (1980) 'Sartre and action theory', in H. Silverman and F. Elliston (eds) *J.P. Sartre: Contemporary Approaches to His Philosophy*, Pittsburgh, Pa: Duquesne University Press, 63–81.

Bagguley, P., Mark-Lawson, J., Shapiro, D., Urry, J., Walby, S., and Warde, A. (1990) *Restructuring: Place, Class and Gender*, London: Sage Publications.

Baker, D. (1983) *Living with the Past: The Historic Environment*, Bletsoe, Bedford: David Baker.

Baker, F. and Thomas, J. (eds) (1990) *Writing the Past in the Present*, Lampeter: Saint David's University College.

Bapty, I. (1990) 'The agony and the ecstasy: the emotions of writing the past', *Archaeological Review from Cambridge*, 9:2: 233–42.

Bapty, I. and Yates, T. (eds) (1990) *Archaeology after Structuralism*, London: Routledge.

Bard, K. A. (1990) '"Social tool use" by free-ranging orangutans: a piagetian and developmental perspective on the manipulation of an animate object', in S. T. Parker and K. R. Gibson (eds) *'Language' and Intelligence in Monkeys and Apes*, Cambridge: Cambridge University Press.

Barker, G. (1991) 'Two Italys, one valley: an Annaliste perspective', in J. Bintliff (ed.) *Annales History and Archaeology*, Leicester: Leicester University Press, 34–56.

Barrett, J. (1987) 'Contextual archaeology', *Antiquity*, 61:468–73.

Barrett, J. (1988) 'Fields of discourse: reconstituting a social archaeology', *Critique of Anthropology*, 7:5–16.

Barrett, J. (1992), Comment, *Archaeological Review from Cambridge*, 11:1:157–62.

Barrett, J. *et al.* (1991) *Landscape, Monument and Society: The Prehistory of Cranborne Chase*, Cambridge: Cambridge University Press.

Barth, F. (1987) *Cosmologies in the Making*, Cambridge: Cambridge University Press.

Bauman, Z. (1992) *Intimations of Postmodernity*, London: Routledge.

Bazerman, Charles (1981) 'What written knowledge does: three examples of academic discourse', *Philosophy of the Social Sciences*, 11: 361–87.

Beaudry, Mary (1990), review of Leone and Potter (1988) *The Recovery of Meaning in the Eastern United States*, *Historical Archaeology*, 24:3:115–18.

Beaudry, Mary, Cook, Lauren and Mrozowski, Stephen (1991) 'Artifacts and active voices: material culture as social discourse, in Randall McGuire and Robert Paynter (eds) *The Archaeology of Inequality*, Cambridge, Mass.: Basil Blackwell, 150–91.

Bender, Barbara (1985) 'Prehistoric developments in the American Midcontinent and in Brittany, northwest France', in T. D. Price and J. A. Brown (eds) *Prehistoric Hunters and Gatherers*, London: Academic Press.

Bender, Barbara (1991) 'Twenty years of history, evolution and social change in gatherer-hunter studies', in T. Ingold, D. Riches and J. Woodburn (eds) *Hunters and Gatherers*, Vol. 1, *History, Evolution and Social Change*, Oxford: Berg.

Bernhardt, G. (1986) 'Die linearbandkeramische Siedlung von Köln-Lindenthal: eine Neubearbeitung', *Kölner Jahrbuch für Vor- und Frühgeschichte*, 18/19; 9–165.

Bettinger, R. (1991) *Hunters and Gatherers: Archaeological and Evolutionary Theory*, New York: Plenum.

Bhaskar, R. (1979) *The Possibility of Naturalism*, Hassocks: Harvester Press.

Biben, M. and Symmes, D. (1991) 'Playback studies of affiliative vocalizing in captive squirrel monkeys: familiarity as a cue to response', *Behaviour*, 117:1–19.

Binford, L. (1972) *An Archaeological Perspective*, London: Academic Press.

Binford, L. (1977) general introduction, in *For Theory Building in Archaeology*, London: Academic Press.

Bintliff, J. (1991) 'The contribution of an Annaliste/structural history approach to archaeology', in J. Bintliff (ed.) *Annales History and Archaeology*, Leicester: Leicester University Press, 1–33.

Bintliff, J. (1992) comment on Thomas and Tilley, *Antiquity*, 66:111–14.

Bintliff, J. (ed.) (1991) *The Annales School and Archaeology*, Leicester: Leicester University Press.

Birks H. H. *et al.* (eds) (1988) *The Cultural Landscape – Past, Present and Future*, Cambridge: Cambridge University Press.

Black, Robert, (1982) 'Ancients and moderns in the Renaissance: rhetoric and history in Accolti's *Dialogue on the Preeminence of Men of His Own Time*', *Journal of the History of Ideas*, 43:3–32.

Black, Robert (1985) *Benedetto Accolti and the Florentine Renaissance*, Cambridge: Cambridge University Press.

Bleicher, J. (1980) *Contemporary Hermeneutics: Hermeneutics as Method, Philosophy and Critique*, London: Routledge & Kegan Paul.

Bleicher, J. (1982) *The Hermeneutic Imagination: Outline of a Positive Critique of Scientism and Sociology*, London: Routledge & Kegan Paul.

Blunden, J. and Curry, N. (eds) (1985) *The Changing Countryside*, The Open University in association with the Countryside Commission, London: Croom Helm.

Blunden, J. and Turner, G. (1985) *Critical Countryside*, London: BBC.

Blythe, R. (1972) *Akenfield: Portrait of an English Village*, Harmondsworth: Penguin.

Blythe, R. (1982) *From the Headlands*, London: Chatto & Windus. Republished as *Characters and Their Landscapes* (1984), San Diego/New York/London: Harvest/Harcourt-Brace Jovanovich.

Boesch, C. (1991) 'Teaching among wild chimpanzees', *Animal Behaviour*, 41:530–6.

Boesch, C. and Boesch, H. (1983) 'Optimization of nut-cracking with natural hammers by wild chimpanzees', *Behaviour*, 83:265–86.

Boesch, C. and Boesch, H. (1984) 'Possible causes of sex differences in the use of natural hammers by wild chimpanzees', *Journal of Human Evolution*, 13:415–40.

Boesch, C. and Boesch, H. (1990) 'Tool use and tool making in wild chimpanzees', *Folia primatologica*, 54:86–99.

Bord, J. and C. (1978) *The Secret Country*, London: Paladin.

Boucher de Perthes, J. (1847) *Antiquités celtiques et antédiluviennes. Mémoire sur l'industrie primitive et les arts à leurs origines*, Vol. 1, Paris: Treuttel & Wurtz.

Bourdieu, P. (1977) *Outline of a Theory of Practice*, Cambridge: Cambridge University Press.

Bourdieu, P. (1988) *Homo Academicus*, Cambridge: Polity Press.

Bourdieu, P. (1990a) *The Logic of Practice*, Cambridge: Polity Press.

Bourdieu, P. (1990b) *In Other Words*, Cambridge: Polity Press.

Boyne, R. (1991) 'Power-knowledge and social theory: the systematic representation of contemporary French social theory in the work of Anthony Giddens', in C. Bryant and D. Jary (eds) *Giddens' Theory of Structuration: A Critical Appreciation*, London: Routledge.

Bradley, R. (1983) 'Archaeology, evolution and the public good: the intellectual development of General Pitt-Rivers', *The Archaeological Journal* 140: 1–9.

Braudel, F. (1972) *The Mediterranean and the Mediterranean World at the Time of Philip II*, 2 vols, London: Collins.

Brodeur, Paul (1985) *Restitution: The Land Claims of the Mashpee, Passamaquoddy, and Penobscot Indians of New England*, Boston, Mass.: Northeastern University Press.

Brown, C. H. and Hauser, M. D. (1990) 'Primate vocal gestures' [abstract], *American Journal of Primatology*, 20:177–8.

Brown, D. E. (1991) *Human Universals*, Philadelphia, Pa.: Temple University Press.

Brown, Marley (1992). 'The archaeology of Virginia's Golden Age: new insights and future directions', paper presented at Council of Virginia Archaeologists Symposium VI, Charlottesville, Va, 22–3 May 1992.

Bryant, C. and Jary, D. (eds) (1991) *Giddens' Theory of Structuration: A Critical Appreciation*, London: Routledge.

Burke, P. (1990) *The French Historical Revolution: The Annales School, 1929–1989*, Cambridge: Polity Press.

Burling, R. (1986) 'The selective advantage of complex language', *Ethology and Sociobiology*, 7:1–16.

Buttler, W. and Haberey, W. (1936) *Die bandkeramische Ansiedlung bei Köln-Lindenthal*, Berlin: de Gruyter.

Byrne, D. (1991) 'Western hegemony in archaeological heritage management', *History and Anthropology*, 5:269–76.

Byrne, R. W. and Whiten, A. (1992) 'Cognitive evolution in primates: evidence from tactical deception', *Man* (n.s.) 27:609–27.

Byrne, R. W. and Whiten, A. (eds) (1988) *Machiavellian Intelligence: Social Expertise and the Evolution of Intellect in Monkeys, Apes, and Humans*, Oxford: Clarendon Press.

Callinicos, A. (1991) 'Against post-modernism: a Marxist critique?' paper given at TAG Conference, Leicester.

Callon, M. (1986) 'The sociology of an actor-network: the case of the electric vehicle', in M. Callon, J. Law and A. Rip (eds) *Mapping the Dynamics of Science and Technology*, London: Macmillan.

Callon, M. (1991) 'Techno-economic networks and irreversibility', in J. Law (ed.) *A Sociology of Monsters: Essays on Power, Technology and Domination*, London: Routledge.

Candland, D. K. and Kyes, R. C. (1986) 'Introduction: the human primates' theory of the primate mind', in J. G. Else and P. C. Lee (eds) *Primate Ontogeny, Cognition and Social Behaviour*, Cambridge: Cambridge University Press.

Cannadine, D. (1983), 'The context, performance and meaning of ritual: the British monarchy and the invention of tradition', in E. Hobsbawm, and T. Ranger (eds) *The Invention of Tradition*, Cambridge: Cambridge University Press.

Carlyle, T. (1832) 'Boswell's Life of Johnson', in *Thomas Carlyle's Works*, Ashburton Edition, London: Chapman & Hall, 1885–8, Vol. 16.

Carman, J. (1990) 'Commodities, rubbish and treasure: valuing archaeological objects', *Archaeological Review from Cambridge*, 9:2.

Carman, J. (1991) 'Beating the bounds: archaeological heritage management as archaeology, archaeology as social science', *Archaeological Review from Cambridge* 10:2:175–84.

Cartmill, M. (1990) 'Human uniqueness and theoretical content in palaeoanthropology', *International Journal of Primatology*, 11:173–92.

Cathcart, Brian (1992) 'A world that sings imperfect harmony', *Independent on Sunday*, 8 March.

Cavalli-Sforza, L. L. *et al.* (1988) 'Reconstruction of human evolution: bringing together genetic, archaeological and linguistic data', *Proceedings of the National Academy of Sciences*, 85:6002–6.

Cavendish, R. (ed.) (1989) *Encyclopedia of the Unexplained*, London: Arkana (Penguin).

The Cereologist (formerly *The Cerealogist*), *The Journal for Crop Circle Studies* (1990–2), London: Specialist Knowledge Services, Frome.

Chapman, W. (1989) 'The organisational context in the history of archaeology: Pitt-Rivers and other British archaeologists in the 1860s', *The Antiquaries Journal* 69:1:23–42.

Chartier, R. (1988) *Cultural History: Between Practices and Representations*, Cambridge: Polity Press.

Cheney, D. L. and Seyfarth, R. M. (1986) 'The recognition of social alliances among vervet monkeys', *Animal Behaviour*, 34:1722–31.

Cheney, D. L. and Seyfarth, R. M. (1990) *How Monkeys See the World*, Chicago, Ill.: University of Chicago Press.

Cheney, D. L., Seyfarth, R. M. and Smuts, B. B. (1986) 'Social relationships and social cognition in nonhuman primates', *Science*, 234:1361–6.

Chiappe, J.F. (1989) preface, in Henry Servieu, *Petite histoire de France*,. Montreuil: Éditions de Chire.

Childe, G. (1956) *Piecing Together the Past*, London: Routledge & Kegan Paul.

Chippindale, C. *et al.* (1990) *Who Owns Stonehenge?* London: Batsford.

Christian, R. (1977) *Vanishing Britain*, Newton Abbot: David & Charles.

Cicero (1979) *De oratore*, ed. E. W. Sutton and H. Rackham, Loeb Classics, Cambridge, Mass.: Harvard University Press.

Citron, S. (1991) *Le Mythe nationale: l'histoire de France en question*, 2nd edn, Paris: Éditions Ouvrières.

Clare, D. (1973) 'Archaeology: the loss of innocence'. *Antiquity*, 47:6–18.

Clark, G. (1986) *Symbols of Excellence*, Cambridge: Cambridge University Press.

Clark, G. A. (1988) 'Alternative models of Pleistocene biocultural evolution: a response to Foley', *Antiquity*, 63:153–62.

Clarke, D. (1968) *Analytical Archaeology*, London: Methuen.

Cleere, H. F. (ed.) (1989) *Archaeological Heritage Management in the Modern World*, London: Unwin Hyman.

Clifford, J. (1986) 'Introduction: partial truths', in J. Clifford, and G. E. Marcus (eds) *Writing Culture: The Poetics and Politics of Ethnography*, Berkeley, Calif.: University of California Press.

Clifford, J. (1988) *The Predicament of Culture: Twentieth-Century Ethnography, Literature and Art*, Cambridge, Mass.: Harvard University Press.

Cobbett, W. (1967) *Rural Rides*, Harmondsworth: Penguin.

Cohan, S. and Shires, L. S. (1988) *Telling Stories: Theoretical Analysis of Narrative Fiction*, London: Routledge.

Cohen, I. (1989) *Structuration Theory: Anthony Giddens and the Constitution of Social Life*, London: Macmillan.

Coles, B. and J. (1986) *Sweet Track to Glastonbury: The Somerset Levels in Prehistory*, London: Thames & Hudson.

Collingwood, R. (1927) 'Oswald Spengler and the theory of historical cycles', *Antiquity*, 1:311–25.

Collis, J. S. (1975) *The Worm Forgives the Plough*, Harmondsworth: Penguin.

Colls, P. and Dodd, P. (eds) (1986), *Englishness: Politics and Culture, 1880–1920*. London: Croom Helm.

Committee for the Preservation of Rural England (1987) *England's Glory: A Photographic Journey through England's Threatened Landscapes*, London: Weidenfeld & Nicolson.

Conkey, M. (1990) 'Experimenting with style in archaeology: some historical and theoretical issues', in M. Conkey and C. Hastorf (eds) *The Uses of Style in Archaeology*, Cambridge: Cambridge University Press.

Conkey, M. and Hastorf, C. (eds) (1990) *The Uses of Style in Archaeology*, Cambridge: Cambridge University Press.

Conkey, M. with Williams, S. H. (1991) 'Original narratives: the political economy of gender in archaeology', in M. di Leonardo (ed.) *Gender at the Crossroads of Knowledge: Feminist Anthropology in the Postmodern Era*, Berkeley, Calif.: University of California Press.

Connerton, P. (ed.) (1976) *Critical Sociology*, Harmondsworth: Penguin.

Cooke, P. (1989), 'Locality, economic restructuring and world development', in P. Cooke, (ed.) *Localities*, London: Unwin Hyman.

Coones, P. (1985) 'One landscape or many? A geographical perspective', *Landscape History*, 7:5–12.

Cosgrove, D. and Daniels, S. (eds) (1988) *The Iconography of Landscape: Essays on the Symbolic Representation, Design and Use of Past Environments*, Cambridge: Cambridge University Press.

Costen, M. (1992), *The Origins of Somerset*, Manchester: Manchester University Press.

Crawford, O. G. S. (1953), *Archaeology in the Field*, London: Phoenix.

Creighton, M. (1898) *The English National Character*, Romanes Lecture, London: Henry Frowde.

Cresta (1992) *Holidays to Paris and Euro Disney Resort*, Altrincham: Cresta.

Cundy, B. (1991) 'The analysis of the Ingaladdi assemblage', PhD dissertation, Australian National University.

Daniel, G. (1962) *The Idea of Prehistory*, Harmondsworth: Penguin.

Daniel, G. (1967) *The Origins and Growth of Archaeology*, Harmondsworth: Penguin.

Darvill, T. (1987a) *Prehistoric Britain*, London: Batsford.

Darvill, T. (1987b), *Ancient Monuments in the Countryside: An Archaeological Management Review*, English Heritage Archaeological Report no. 5, London: Historic Buildings and Monuments Commission.

Dasser, V. (1988a) 'A social concept in Java monkeys', *Animal Behaviour*, 36:225–30.

Dasser, V. (1988b) 'Mapping social concepts in monkeys', in R. Byrne, and A. Whiten (eds) *Machiavellian Intelligence: Social Expertise and the Evolution of Intellect in Monkeys, Apes, and Humans*, Oxford: Clarendon Press.

Davis, B. (ed.) (1992) *Ciphers in the Crops: The Fractal and Geometric Circles of 1991*, Bath: Gateway Books.

Dawkins, R. and Krebs, J. R. (1978) 'Animal signals: information or manipulation', in J. R. Krebs, and N. B. Davies (eds) *Behavioural Ecology: An Evolutionary Approach*, Oxford: Blackwell Scientific.

de Waal, F. (1977) 'The organization of agonistic relationships within two captive groups of Java monkey', *Zeitschrift fur Tierpsychologie*, 44:225–82.

de Waal, F. (1982) *Chimpanzee Politics*, London: Jonathan Cape.

de Waal, F. (1989), 'Dominance "style" and primate social organization', in V. Standen, and R. A. Foley (eds) *Comparative Socioecology*, Oxford: Blackwell.

Deacon, T. W. (1988) 'Human brain evolution: I. Evolution of language circuits', in H. Jerison and I. Jerison (eds) *Intelligence and Evolutionary Biology*, Berlin: Springer.

Debenham, Tewson & Chinnocks (1991) *Stonehenge: Conservation and Management Project*, London: Debenham, Tewson & Chinnocks.

Deetz, J. (1977) *In Small Things Forgotten*, New York: Anchor, 1992.

Deleuze, G. (1969) 'Platon et le simulacre', in *Logique du sens*, Paris.

Deleuze, G. and Guattari, F. (1988) *A Thousand Plateaus: Capitalism and Schizophrenia*, trans B. Massumi, London: Athlone Press.

Dennett, D. C. (1987) *The Intentional Stance*, Cambridge, Mass.: MIT/Bradford Books.

Dennett, D. C. (1988) 'The intentional stance in theory and practice', in R. Byrne and A. Whiten (eds) *Machiavellian Intelligence: Social Expertise and the Evolution of Intellect in Monkeys, Apes, and Humans*, Oxford: Clarendon Press.

Derrida, J. (1972) 'La double séance', in *La Dissémination*, Paris: Seuil.

Derrida, J. (1976) *Of Grammatology*, Baltimore, Md: Johns Hopkins University Press.

Detienne, M. and Vernant, J.-P. (1978) *Cunning Intelligence in Greek Culture and Society*, Hassocks: Harvester.

Devereux, P. (1991) *Earth Memory*, Yeovil: Quantum.

Devereux, P. (1992) *Symbolic Landscapes: The Dreamtime Earth and Avebury's Open Secrets*, Glastonbury: Gothic Image Publications.

Dogan, M. and Pahre, R. (1990) *Creative Marginality*, Boulder, Colo.: Westview.

Dower, M. (1992) 'Protecting our total heritage', *Countryside* (newspaper of the Countryside Commission), 56: 3.

Duby, G. (1980) *The Three Orders*, Chicago, Ill.: Chicago University Press.

Duke, P. (1992) 'Braudel and North American archaeology: an example from the Northern Plains', in A. B. Knapp (ed.) *Archaeology, Annales and Ethnohistory*, Cambridge: Cambridge University Press.

Dunbar, R. I. M. (1988) *Primate Social Systems*, London: Croom Helm.

Dunbar, R. I. M. (1991) 'Functional significance of social grooming in primates', *Folia primatologica*, 57:121–31.

Durkheim, E. (1915) *The Elementary Forms of the Religious Life: A Study in Religious Sociology*, London: George Allen & Unwin.

Dyson, S. L. (1989) 'The role of ideology and institutions in shaping classical archaeology in the 19th and 20th centuries', in A. L. Christenson (ed.) *Tracing Archaeology's Past: The Historiography of Archaeology*, Carbondale, Ill.: Southern Illinois University Press.

Eagleton, T. (1983) *Literary Theory*, Oxford: Blackwell.

Eagleton, T. (1986), *Against the Grain*, London: Verso.

Eccles, J. C. (1989) *Evolution of the Brain: Creation of the Self*, London: Routledge.

Eco, U. (1987) *Travels in Hyperreality*, London: Picador.

Enzensberger, H. M., (1990) *Europe, Europe: Forays into a Continent*, London: Picador.

Essock-Vitale, S. and Seyfarth, R. M. (1987) 'Intelligence and social cognition', in B. B. Smuts, D. L. Cheney, R. M. Seyfarth, R. W. Wrangham, and T. T. Struhsaker (eds) *Primate Societies*, Chicago, Ill.: University of Chicago Press.

Evans, E. Estyn (1973) *The Personality of Ireland*, Cambridge: Cambridge University Press.

Evans, G. Ewart (1965) *Ask the Fellows Who Cut the Hay*, 2nd edn, London: Faber & Faber.

Evans, G. Ewart (1969) *The Farm and the Village*, London: Faber & Faber.

Fenton, A. (1985) *The Shape of the Past I: Essays in Scottish Ethnology*, Edinburgh: John Donald.

Fiske, A. P. (1992) 'The four elementary forms of sociality: framework for a unified theory of social relations', *Psychological Review*, 99:689–723.

Flannery, K. V. (1976) *The Early Mesoamerican Village*, New York: Academic Press.

Fleming, A. (1988) *The Dartmoor Reaves: Investigating Prehistoric Land Divisions*, London: Batsford.

Foley, R. (1987a) *Another Unique Species*, London: Longman.

Foley, R. (1987b) 'Hominid species and stone tool assemblages: how are they related?', *Antiquity*, 61:380–92.

Foley, R. (1990a) 'How useful is the culture concept in early hominid studies?', in R. Foley (ed.) *The Origins of Human Behaviour*, London: Unwin Hyman.

Foley, R. (ed.) (1990b) *The Origins of Human Behaviour*, London: Unwin Hyman.

Foley, R. and Lee, P. C. (1991) 'Ecology and energetics of encephalization in hominid evolution', *Philosophical Transactions of the Royal Society of London*, B 334:223–32.

Foucault, M. (1969) *L'Archéologie du savoir*, Paris, Gallimard.

Foucault, M. (1970) *The Order of Things*, London, Tavistock.

Foucault, M. (1972) *The Archaeology of Knowledge*, London: Tavistock.

Foucault, M. (1973) *Ceci n'est pas une pipe*, Montpellier.

Foucault, M. (1977) *Discipline and Punish: The Birth of the Prison*, Harmondsworth: Penguin.

Foucault, M. (1979) *The History of Sexuality, Vol. 1, An Introduction*, trans. R. Hurley, Harmondsworth: Penguin.

Foucault, M. (1981) 'The order of discourse', in *Untying the Text*, ed. R. Young, London: Routledge & Kegan Paul.

Foucault, M. (1984a) *Histoire de la sexualité*, Vol. 2, *L'Usage des plaisirs*, Paris: Gallimard.

Foucault, M. (1984b) *Histoire de la sexualité*, Vol. 3, *Le Souci de soi*, Paris: Gallimard.

Fowler, P. J. (1992) *The Past in Contemporary Society: Then, Now*, London: Routledge.

Fowler, P. J. (ed.) (1972) *Archaeology and the Landscape*, London: John Baker.

Fowler, P. J. and Sharp, M. (1990) *Images of Prehistory*, Cambridge: Cambridge University Press.

Frye, Northrop (1983) *The Great Code: The Bible and Literature*, London: Routledge & Kegan Paul/Ark.

Gadamer, H.-G. (1975), *Truth and Method*, New York: Seabury.

Gadamer, H.-G. (1977) 'The universality of the hermeneutic problem', in *Philosophical Hermeneutics*, Berkeley, Calif.: University of California Press.

Gamble, C. S. (1991a) comment on P. C. Lee, 'Biology and culture', *Cambridge Archaeological Journal*, 1:2.

Gamble, C. S. (1991b) 'Brilliant – rock art and art rock in Australia', *Nature*, 351:608.

Gamble, C. S. (1992) 'Reflections from a darkened room', *Antiquity*.

Gathercole, P. and Lowenthal, D. (eds) (1989) *The Politics of the Past*, London: Unwin Hyman.

Gero, J. (1991), 'Palaeoindians and the social construction of knowledge', lecture delivered to the Department of Archaeology, University of Cambridge.

Gero, J. and Conkey, M. W. (eds) (1991) *Engendering Archaeology: Women and Prehistory*, Oxford: Blackwell.

Gero, J., Lacy, D. M. and Blakey, M. (eds) (1983) *The Sociopolitics of Archaeology*, Research Report 23, Department of Anthropology, University of Massachusetts, Amherst.

Gibson, K. R. (1986) 'Cognition, brain size and the extraction of embedded food resources', in J. G. Else and P. C. Lee (eds) *Primate Ontogeny, Cognition and Social Behaviour*, Cambridge: Cambridge University Press.

Giddens, A. (1976) *New Rules of Sociological Method: A Positive Critique of Interpretive Sociologies*, London: Hutchinson.

Giddens, A. (1979) *Central Problems in Social Theory*, London: Macmillan.

Giddens, A. (1982) *Profiles and Critiques in Social Theory*, London: Macmillan.

Giddens, A. (1984) *The Constitution of Society: Outline of the Theory of Structuration*, Cambridge: Polity Press.

Giddens, A. (1989) 'A reply to my critics', in D. Held and J. Thompson (eds) *Social Theory of Modern Societies*, Cambridge: Cambridge University Press.

Glassie, H. (1975) *Folk Housing of Middle Virginia*, Knoxville, Tenn.: University of Tennessee Press.

Godwin F. (1990) *Our Forbidden Land*, London: Jonathan Cape.

Goodall, J. (1970) 'Tool-using in primates and other vertebrates', *Advances in the Study of Behaviour*, 3:195–249.

Gould, P. and White, R. (1974) *Mental Maps*, Harmondsworth, Penguin.

Gould, S. J. (1987) *Time's Arrow, Time's Cycle: Myth and Metaphor in the Discovery of Geological Time*, Harmondsworth: Penguin.

Gould, S. J. and Vrba, E. S. (1982) 'Exaptation – a missing term in the science of form', *Paleobiology*, 8:1:4–15.

Greenaway, P. (1991), *The Physical Self*, Rotterdam: Boymans-van Beuningen Museum.
Greenaway, P. (1993) *Some Organising Principles/Rhai egwyddorion trefn*, Swansea: Glyn Vivian Art Gallery.
Greenblatt, S. (1991) *Marvellous Possessions: The Wonder of the New World*, Oxford: Clarendon Press.
Greenfield, P. M. and Savage-Rumbaugh, E. S. (1990) 'Grammatical combination in Pan paniscus: processes of learning and invest in the evolution and development of language', in S. T. Parker and K. R. Gibson, (eds) *'Language' and Intelligence in Monkeys and Apes*, Cambridge: Cambridge University Press.
Greeves, T. (1987a) *Parish Maps: Celebrating and Looking After Your Place*, London: Common Ground.
Greeves, T. (1987b) *The Parish Boundary*, London: Common Ground.
Greeves, T. (1989) 'Archaeology and the Green movement: a case for perestroika', *Antiquity*, 63: 659–65.
Gregory, D. (1989) 'Presences and absences: time–space relations and structuration theory', in D. Held and J. Thompson (eds) *Social Theory of Modern Societies*, Cambridge: Cambridge University Press.
Gregory, S. W., Jr (1986) 'Social psychological implications of voice frequency correlations: analyzing conversation partner adaptation by computer', *Social Psychology Quarterly* 49:237–46.
Gregory, S. W., Jr, *et al.* (1993) 'Voice pitch and amplitude convergence as a metric of quality in dyadic interviews', *Language and Communication*, 13:195–217.
Griffin, D. R. (1984) *Animal Thinking*, Cambridge, Mass.: Harvard University Press.
Grigson G. (1984) *The English Year*, Oxford: Oxford University Press.
Gruet (1976) 'Les civilisations du Paléolithique moyen dans les Pays de la Loire', in H. de Lumley (ed.) *La Préhistoire Française*, Vol. 2, Paris: CNRS.
Habermas, J. (1976) *Legitimation Crisis*, trans. T. McCarthy, London: Heinemann.
Habermas, J. (1980) 'The hermeneutic claim to universality', in J. Bleicher (ed.) *Contemporary Hermeneutics*, London: Routledge.
Habermas, J. (1984) *The Theory of Communicative Action*, Vol. 1, *Reason and the Rationalization of Society*, Boston, Mass.: Beacon Press.
Habermas, J. (1989) *The Theory of Communicative Action*, Vol. 2, *System and Lifeworld*, Boston, Mass.: Beacon Press.
Haines, G. H. (1973) *Whose Countryside?* London: J. M. Dent.
Hall, J. (1991) 'Practising post-processualism? Classics and archaeological theory', *Archaeological Review from Cambridge*, 10:2:155–63.
Halsall M. (1992) 'Unearthing new applications for our oldest asset', *Guardian*, 18 May, 13.
Hannah, A. and McGrew, W. (1987) 'Chimpanzees using stones to crack open oil palm nuts in Liberia', *Primates*, 28:31–46.
Haraway, D. (1988) 'Situated knowledges: the science question in feminism and the privilege of partial perspective', *Feminist Studies*, 14: 575–99.
Haraway, D. (1989) *Primate Visions: Gender, Race, and Nature in the World of Modern Science*, London: Routledge.
Harcourt, A. H. and de Waal, F. B. M. (eds) (1992) *Coalitions and Alliances in Humans and Other Animals*, Oxford: Oxford University Press.
Harvey, D. (1989) *The Condition of Post-Modernity*, Oxford: Basil Blackwell.
Hawkes, C. (1954) 'Archaeological theory and method: some suggestions from the Old World', *American Anthropologist*, 56:155–68.
Hawkes, J. (1978) *A Land*, rev. edn, Newton Abbot: David & Charles.
Hebdige, D. (1979) *Subculture: The Meaning of Style*, London: Methuen.
Heffner, H. E. and Heffner, R. S. (1989) 'Cortical deafness cannot account for the inability of Japanese macaques to discriminate species-specific vocalizations', *Brain and Language*, 36:275–85.
Heiberg, Marianne (1989) *The Making of the Basque Nation*, Cambridge: Cambridge University Press.
Heidegger, M. (1962) *Being and Time*, Oxford: Blackwell.
Heidegger, M. (1972) *On Time and Being*, New York: Harper & Row.
Held, D. (1980) *Introduction to Critical Theory: Horkheimer to Habermas*, London: Hutchinson.
Heritage, J. (1984) *Garfinkel and Ethnomethodology*, Oxford: Polity Press.
Hewison, R. (1987) *The Heritage Industry. Britain in a Climate of Decline*, London: Methuen.
Hexter, J. H. (1968) 'The rhetoric of history', *International Encyclopedia of the Social Sciences*, 6:368–94.
Hinde, R. A. (1976) 'Interactions, relationships and social structure', *Man*, 11:1–17.

Hinde, R. A. (1987) *Individuals, Relationships and Culture*, Cambridge: Cambridge University Press.

Hinde, R. A. (1992) 'A biologist looks at anthropology', *Man*, 26:583–608.

Hinsley, C. M. (1989) 'Revising and revisioning the history of archaeology: reflections on region and context', in A. L. Christenson (ed.) *Tracing Archaeology's Past: The Historiography of Archaeology*, Carbondale, Ill.: Southern Illinois University Press.

Hobsbawm, E. and Ranger, T. (eds) (1983) *The Invention of Tradition*, Cambridge: Cambridge University Press.

Hodder, I. (1982a) 'Theoretical archaeology: a reactionary view', in I. Hodder (ed.), *Symbolic and Structural Archaeology*, Cambridge: Cambridge University Press.

Hodder, I. (1982b) *Symbols in Action*, Cambridge: Cambridge University Press.

Hodder, I. (1984) 'Archaeology in 1984', *Antiquity*, 58:25–32.

Hodder, I. (1985) 'Postprocessual archaeology', in M. Schiffer (ed.) *Advances in Archaeological Method and Theory*, London: Academic Press.

Hodder, I. (1986) *Reading the Past; Current Approaches to Interpretation in Archaeology*, Cambridge: Cambridge University Press.

Hodder, I. (1987) 'The contribution of the long-term', in I. Hodder (ed.) *Archaeology as Long-Term History*, Cambridge: Cambridge University Press.

Hodder, I. (1989) 'This is not an article about material culture as text', *Journal of Anthropological Archaeology*, 8:250–69.

Hodder, I. (1990) *The Domestication of Europe*, Oxford: Blackwell.

Hodder, I. (1991a) 'Postprocessual archaeology and the current debate', in R. W. Preucel (ed.) *Processual and Postprocessual Archaeologies. Multiple Ways of Knowing the Past*, Southwestern Illinois University Occasional Paper 10.

Hodder, I. (1991b) 'Interpretive archaeology and its role', *American Antiquity*, 56:7–18.

Hodder, I. (1991c) *Reading the Past*, 2nd edn, Cambridge: Cambridge University Press.

Hodder, I. (ed.) (1982) *Symbolic and Structural Archaeology*, Cambridge: Cambridge University Press.

Hodder, I. (ed.) (1987a) *Archaeology as Long-Term History*, Cambridge: Cambridge University Press.

Hodder, I. (ed.) (1987b) *The Archaeology of Contextual Meanings*, Cambridge: Cambridge University Press.

Hodder, I. (ed.) (1989) *The Meanings of Things*, London: Unwin Hyman.

Hodder I. (ed.) (1992) *Archaeological Theory in Europe: The Last Three Decades*, London: Routledge.

Hodges, R. (1991) *Wall-to-Wall History: The Story of Roystone Grange*, London: Duckworth.

Hofer, M. A. (1984) 'Relationships as regulators: a psychobiologic perspective on bereavement', *Psychosomatic Medicine*, 46:183–97.

Hollis, M. and Lukes, S. (eds) (1982) *Rationality and Relativism*, Oxford: Blackwell.

Hooper-Greenhill, E. (1992) *Museums and the Shaping of Knowledge*, London: Routledge.

Hoskins, W. G. (1955), *The Making of the English Landscape*, London: Hodder & Stoughton.

Hudson, K. (1987) *Museums of Influence*, Cambridge: Cambridge University Press.

Hudson, W. H. (1923) *Nature in Downland*, London: J. M. Dent.

Hunter, M. (1975) *John Aubrey and the Realm of Learning*, New York: Science History Publications.

Jameson, F. (1988a) 'Cognitive mapping', in C. Nelson and L. Grossberg (eds) *Marxism and the Interpretation of Culture*, London: Macmillan.

Jameson, F. (1988b) 'Marxism and historicism', in *The Ideologies of Theories: Essays, 1971–1986*, Vol. 2, *The Syntax of History*, London: Routledge.

Jameson, F. (1991) *Postmodernism, or the Cultural Logic of Late Capitalism*, London: Verso.

Jellicoe, G. and S. (1975) *The Landscape of Man: Shaping the Environment from Prehistory to the Present Day*, London: Thames & Hudson.

Jenkins, J. Geraint (1976) *Life and Tradition in Rural Wales*, London: J. M. Dent.

Jennings, P. (1968) *The Living Village*, London: Hodder & Stoughton.

Jerison, H. J. (1973) *Evolution of the Brain and Intelligence*, New York: Academic Press.

Johnsen, H. and Olsen, B. (1992) 'Hermeneutics and archaeology: on the philosophy of contextual archaeology', *American Antiquity*, 57:3:419–36.

Johnson, M. (1989) 'Conceptions of agency in archaeological interpretation', *Journal of Anthropological Archaeology*, 8:189–211.

Johnston, R. J., Gregory, D. and Smith, D. M. (eds) (1994) *A Dictionary of Human Geography*, Oxford: Blackwell.

Jones, M. (1986) *England before Domesday*, London: Batsford.

Jones, R. and White, N. (1988) 'Point blank: stone tool manufacture at the Ngilipitji Quarry, Arnhem Land 1981', in B. Meehan and R. Jones (eds) *Archaeology with Ethnography: An Australian Perspective*, Canberra: Department of prehistory RSPacS, Australian National University.

Kains-Jackson, C. P. (1880), *Our Ancient Monuments and the Land around Them*, London: Elliot Stock.

Kaiser, H. J. (n.d.) 'Oral history interviews with former residents of Franklin Street and Gott's Court, Annapolis, Maryland', unpublished manuscript on file at the Banneker-Douglass Museum, Annapolis, Md.

Kaplan, J. R. (1978) 'Fight interference and altruism in rhesus monkeys', *American Journal of Physical Anthropology*, 47:241–9.

Kehoe, A. B. (1989) 'Contextualising archaeology', in A. L. Christenson (ed.) *Tracing Archaeology's Past: The Historiography of Archaeology*, Carbondale, Ill.: Southern Illinois University Press.

Keith, W. J. (1974), *The Rural Tradition: A Study of the Non-Fiction Prose Writers of the English Countryside*, Toronto: University of Toronto Press.

Kellner, D. (1989) *Critical Theory, Marxism and Modernity*, Cambridge: Polity Press.

Kemp, T. P. (1989) 'Toward a narrative ethics: a bridge between ethics and the narrative reflection of Ricoeur', in Kemp and Rasmussen (eds) *The Narrative Path: The Later Works of Paul Ricoeur*, Cambridge, Mass.: MIT Press.

King, B. J. (1991) 'Social information transfer in monkeys, apes and hominids', *Yearbook of Physical Anthropology*, 34:97–115.

Knapp, A. B. (ed.) (1992) *Archaeology, Annales, and Ethnohistory*, Cambridge: Cambridge University Press.

Knight, C. (1983) 'Lévi-Strauss and the dragon: *Mythologiques* reconsidered in the light of an Australian Aboriginal myth', *Man*, 18:21–50.

Knight, C. (1991) *Blood Relations*, New Haven, Conn.: Yale University Press.

Knorr-Cetina, K. D. and Mulkay, M. (eds) (1983) *Science Observed: Perspectives on the Social Study of Science*, London: Sage Publications.

Kopytoff, I. (1986) 'The cultural biography of things: commoditisation as a process', in A. Appadurai (ed.) *The Social Life of Things: Commodities in Cultural Perspective* Cambridge: Cambridge University Press.

Krebs, J. R. and Dawkins, R. (1984) 'Animal signals: mindreading and manipulation', in J. R. Krebs and N. B. Davies (eds) *Behavioural Ecology: An Evolutionary Approach*, 2nd edn, Oxford: Blackwell Scientific.

Kuhn, S. L. (1991) '"Unpacking" reduction: lithic raw material economy in the Mousterian of west-central Italy', *Journal of Anthropological Archaeology*, 10:76–106.

Kuhn, T. (1970) *The Structure of Scientific Revolutions*, Chicago, Ill.: University of Chicago Press.

Kuhn, T. (1974) 'Second thoughts on paradigms', in F. Suppe (ed.) *The Structure of Scientific Theories*, Urbana, Ill.: University of Illinois Press.

Kurland, J. A. (1977) *Kin Selection in the Japanese Monkey*, Basel: S. Karger.

Lane, P. and C. (1992) *Key Stage Three. History (Age 11–14 National Curriculum)*, London: BPP (Letts Educational).

Larsen, M. T. (1989) 'Orientalism and Near Eastern archaeology', in D. Miller, M. Rowlands and C. Tilley (eds) *Domination and Resistance*, London: Unwin Hyman.

Latour, B. (1987) *Science in Action: How to Follow Scientists and Engineers through Society*, Milton Keynes: Open University Press.

Latour, B. (1988) *The Pasteurization of France*, trans. A. Sheridan and J. Law, Cambridge, Mass.: Harvard University Press.

Latour, B. (1990) 'Drawing things together', in M. Lynch and S. Woolgar (eds) *Representation in Scientific Practice*, Cambridge, Mass.: MIT Press.

Latour, B. and Woolgar, S. (1979) *Laboratory Life: The Social Construction of Scientific Facts*, London: Sage Publications.

Law, J. (1987) 'Technology and heterogeneous engineering: the case of Portuguese expansion', in W. E. Bijker, T. P. Hughes and T. Pinch (eds), *The Social Construction of Technological Systems*, Cambridge, Mass.: MIT Press.

Law, J. and Callon, M. (1992) 'The life and death of an aircraft: a network analysis of technical change', in W. E. Bijker and J. Law (eds) *Shaping Technology/Building Society*, Cambridge, Mass.: MIT Press.

Law, J. and Williams, R. J. (1982) 'Putting facts together: a study of scientific persuasion', *Social Studies of Science*, 12:535–58.

Lawson, H. and Appignanesi, L. (eds) (1989) *Dismantling Truth: Reality in the Postmodern World*, New York: St Martin's Press.

Layton, R. (ed.) (1989a) *Conflict in the Archaeology of Living Traditions*, London: Unwin Hyman.

Layton, R. (ed.) (1989b) *Who Needs the Past: Indigenous Values and Archaeology*, London: Unwin Hyman.

Le Roy Ladurie, E. (1975) *Montaillou: Cathars and Catholics in a French Village, 1294–1324*, London: Scolar.

Lee, P. C. (1981) 'Ecological and social influences on the development of vervet monkeys', PhD thesis, University of Cambridge.

Lee, P. C. (1991) 'Biology and behaviour in human evolution', *Cambridge Archaeological Journal*, 1:207–26.

Leggatt, H. (1978) quoted in Roy Reed, 'Once again, British art lovers raise cry against heritage drain', *International Herald Tribune*, 11 July.

Le Goff, J. (1985) *The Medieval Imagination*, Chicago, Ill.: Chicago University Press.

Leinonen, L. *et al.* (1991) 'Vocal communication between species: man and macaque', *Language and Communication*, 11:241–62.

Leone, M. (1982a) 'Some opinions about recovering mind', *American Antiquity*, 47:742–60.

Leone, M. (1982b) 'Childe's offspring', in I. Hodder (ed.) *Symbolic and Structural Archaeology*, Cambridge: Cambridge University Press.

Leone, M. (1984) 'Interpreting ideology in historical archaeology: the William Paca garden in Annapolis, Maryland', in D. Miller and C. Tilley (eds) *Ideology, Power and Prehistory*, Cambridge: Cambridge University Press.

Leone, M. and Potter, P. B., Jr (1992) 'Legitimation and the classification of archaeological sites', *American Antiquity*, 57:1:137–45.

Leone, M., Potter, P. and Shackel, P. (1987) 'Toward a critical archaeology', *Current Anthropology*, 28:283–302.

Leone, M. (1986) 'Symbolic, structural and critical archaeology', in D. Meltzer, D. Fowler, and J. Sabloff (eds) *American Archaeology Past and Future: A Celebration of the Society for American Archaeology, 1935–1985*, Washington, DC: Smithsonian Institution.

Leone, M. and Preucel, R. W. (1992) 'Archaeology in a democratic society: a critical theory perspective', in L. Wandsnider (ed.) *Quandaries and Quests: Visions of Archaeology's Future*, Carbondale, Ill.: University of Southern Illinois.

Leroi-Gourhan, A. (1965) *Préhistoire de l'art occidental*, Paris: Mazenod.

Leroi-Gourhan, A. (1982) *The Dawn of European Art*, Cambridge: Cambridge University Press.

Lev-Tov, J. (1987) 'Information privy to a doctor: report on faunal analysis from the privy at Main St. (18AP44)', report on file Archaeology Laboratory, Department of Anthropology, University of Maryland, College Park.

Lévi-Strauss, C. (1966) *The Savage Mind*, London: Weidenfeld & Nicolson.

Levin, B. (1989) 'Shakespeare – the history man', *The Times*, 18 September.

Levine, J. M. (1987) *History and Humanism: Origins of Modern English Historiography*, Ithaca, NY: Cornell University Press.

Lewin, R. (1989) *Bones of Contention: Controversies in the Search for Human Origins*, Harmondsworth: Penguin Books.

Lewis-Williams, D. (1991) 'Wrestling with analogy: a methodological dilemma in Upper Palaeolithic art research, *Proceedings of the Prehistoric Society*, 57:149–62.

Lieberman, P. (1991) *Uniquely Human: The Evolution of Speech, Thought, and Selfless Behavior*, Cambridge, Mass.: Harvard University Press.

Lipe, W. (1984) 'Value and meaning in cultural resources', in H. F. Cleere (ed.) *Approaches to the Archaeological Heritage: A Comparative Study of World Cultural Resource Management Systems*, Cambridge: Cambridge University Press.

Livingston, Eric (1987) *Making Sense of Ethnomethodology*, London: Routledge.

Lloyd, G. (1984) *The Man of Reason: 'Male' and 'Female' in Western Philosophy*, Minneapolis, Minn.: University of Minnesota Press.

Logan, G. (1990) Project Director Evaluation for Maryland Humanities Council Grant #032-L, 'Historical archaeology and African American heritage in Annapolis: a program of public interpretation for the community'.

Logan, G. (1991) Project Director Evaluation for Maryland Humanities Council Grant #729-M, 'The Maryland Black experience as understood through archaeology'.

Lowenthal, D. (1985) *The Past Is a Foreign Country*, Cambridge: Cambridge University Press.

Lowenthal, D. and Binney, M. (eds) (1981) *Our Past Before Us: Why Do We Save It?* London: Temple Smith.

Lubbock, J. (1900) [1865] *Pre-historic Times, as Illustrated by Ancient Remains and the Manners and Customs of Modern Savages*, London: Williams & Norgate.

Lumley, R. (ed.) (1988) *The Museum Time Machine*, London: Comedia/Routledge.

Lunn J. (ed.) (1988) *Proceedings of the First World Congress on Heritage Presentation and Interpretation, Heritage Interpretation International and Alberta Culture and Multiculturalism*, Edmonton, Alberta.

Lutz, C. (1990) 'Culture and consciousness', in P. Cole, D. Johnson and K. Kessel (eds) *Self and Consciousness*.

Lynch, K. (1960) *The Image of the City*, Cambridge, Mass.: MIT Press.

Lynch, M. (1982) 'Technical work and critical inquiry: investigations in a scientific laboratory', *Social Studies of Science*, 12:449–534.

Lynch, M. and Woolgar, S. (eds) (1990) *Representation in Scientific Practice*, Cambridge, Mass.: MIT Press.

M'Bow, Amadou-Mahtar (1979) 'A plea for the return of an irreplaceable cultural heritage to those who created it', *Museum*, 31:1:58.

McCurdy, G. G. (1931) 'The use of rock crystal by Palaeolithic man', *Proceedings of the National Academy of Sciences*, 17:633–7.

McDonald, J. D., Zimmerman, L. J., McDonald, A. L., William Tall Bull and Ted Rising Sun (1991) 'The Northern Cheyenne outbreak of 1879: using oral history and archaeology as tools of resistance', in R. H. McGuir and R. Paynter (eds) *The Archaeology of Inequality*, Oxford: Blackwell.

Macdonell, D. (1986) *Theories of Discourse: An Introduction*, Oxford: Blackwell.

McGrew, W. C. (1979) 'Evolutionary implications of sex differences in chimpanzee predation and tool use', in D. A. Hamburg, E. R. McCown (eds) *The Great Apes*, Menlo Park: Benjamin/Cummings.

McGrew, W. C. (1989) 'Why is ape tool use so confusing?', in V. Standen and R. A. Foley, (eds) *Comparative Socioecology*, Oxford: Blackwell Scientific.

McGrew, W. C. (1990) 'Chimpanzee material culture: what are its limits and why?', in R. A. Foley (ed.) *The Origins of Human Behaviour*, London: Unwin Hyman.

McGrew, W. C. and Tutin, C. E. G. (1978) 'Evidence for a social custom in wild chimpanzees', *Man*, 13:234–51.

McGuire, R. (1992) *A Marxist Archaeology*, London: Academic Press.

Macinnes, L. and Wickham-Jones, C. R. (1992) *All Natural Things: Archaeology and the Green Debate*, Oxford: Oxbow Books.

McKendrick, Scott (1992) 'La vraye histoire de Troye', in Mark Jones (ed.) (forthcoming) *Fake?* London: British Museum Publications.

McKenzie K. (1983) *The Spear in the Stone*, a film in 18mm, Canberra: Australian Institute of Aboriginal Studies.

McWilliams, J. (1991) 'Historical title search and documentation: 163 Duke of Gloucester Street report', unpublished report prepared for Port of Annapolis, Inc., February 1991.

Marten, C. H. K. (1905), quoted in Raphael Samuel (1989) 'Continuous national history', in his *Patriotism: The Making and Unmaking of British National Identity*, Vol. 1 *History and Politics*, London: Routledge.

Martin, R. D. (1983) 'Human brain evolution in an ecological context', 52nd James Arthur Lecture on the Evolution of the Brain, American Museum of Natural History.

Martlew, R. (1988) 'Optical disk storage: another can of worms?', in C. N. Ruggle and S. P. Rahtz (eds) *Computer and Quantitative Methods in Archaeology*, BAR International Series 393, Oxford.

Martlew, R. (1990) 'Videodisks and the politics of knowledge', in D. Miall (ed.) *Humanities and the Computer*, Oxford, Clarendon Press.

Martlew, R. (forthcoming) 'Multi-media in museums: potential applications of interactive technology', *Society of Museum Archaeologists Journal*, proceedings of the 1990 conference in Hull, England.

Marx, K. (1983) *Capital*, Vol. 1, London: Lawrence & Wishart.

Mason, W. A. (1986) 'Can primate political traits be identified?', in J. G. Else and P. C. Lee (eds) *Primate Ontogeny, Cognition and Social Behaviour*, Cambridge: Cambridge University Press.

Massey, A. (1977) 'Agonistic aids and kinship in a group of pigtail macaques', *Behavioural Ecology and Sociobiology*, 2:31–40.

Matsuzawa, T. (1985) 'Use of numbers by a chimpanzee', *Nature*, 315:57–9.

Maurus, M. *et al.* (1988) 'Acoustic patterns common to human communication and communication between monkeys', *Language and Communication*, 8:87–94.

Mazel, A. D. (1989) 'People making history: the last ten thousand years of hunter-gatherer communities in the Thukela Basin', *Natal Museum Journal of Humanities*, 1:1–168.

Mazur, A. C. (1985) 'A biosocial model of status in face-to-face primate groups', *Social Forces*, 64:377–402.

Mazur, A. C. and Cataldo, M. (1989) 'Dominance and deference in conversation', *Journal of Social and Biological Structures*, 12:87–99.

Mbunwe-Samba, P. (1989) 'Oral traditions and the African past', in R. Layton (ed.) *Conflict in the Archaeology of Living Traditions*, London, Unwin Hyman.

Mellars, P. (ed.) (1991) *The Human Revolution: The Archaeological Evidence*, Edinburgh: Edinburgh University Press.

Mellars, P. and Stringer, C. (eds) (1989) *The Human Revolution*, Edinburgh: Edinburgh University Press.

Meltzer, D. (1979) 'Paradigms and the nature of change in archaeology', *American Antiquity*, 44:644–57.

Meltzer, D. (1983) 'The antiquity of man and the development of American archaeology', *Advances in Archaeological Method and Theory*, 6:1–51.

Menzel, E. W. (1971) 'Communication about the environment in a group of young chimpanzees', *Folia primatologica*, 15:220–32.

Menzel, E. W. (1973) 'Chimpanzee spatial memory organization', *Science*, 182:943–5.

Merleau-Ponty, M. (1962) *Phenomenology of Perception*, London: Routledge.

Merriman, N. (1991) *Beyond the Glass Case: The Past, the Heritage and the Public in Britain*, Leicester Museum Studies Series, Leicester: Leicester University Press.

Michell J. (1982) *Megalithomania: Artists, Antiquarians and Archaeologists at the Old Stone Monuments*, Ithaca, NY: Cornell University Press.

Midgley, M. (1979) *Beast and Man: The Roots of Human Nature*, Brighton: Harvester.

Miller, D. (1982a) 'Artifacts as products of human categorisation processes', in I. Hodder (ed.) *Symbolic and Structural Archaeology*, Cambridge: Cambridge University Press.

Miller, D. (1982b) 'Structures and strategies: an aspect of the relationship between social hierarchy and cultural change', in I. Hodder (ed.) *Symbolic and Structural Archaeology*, Cambridge: Cambridge University Press.

Miller, D. (1985) *Artefacts as Categories: A Study of Ceramic Variability in Central India*, Cambridge: Cambridge University Press.

Miller, D. (1987) *Material Culture and Mass Consumption*, Oxford: Basil Blackwell.

Miller, D., Rowlands, M. and Tilley, C. (eds) (1989) *Domination and Resistance*, London: Unwin Hyman.

Miller, D. and Tilley, C. (1984) 'Ideology, power and prehistory: an introduction', in D. Miller and C. Tilley (eds) *Ideology, Power and Prehistory*, Cambridge: Cambridge University Press.

Miller, J. H. (1992) *Illustration*, London: Reaktion.

Milton, K. (1988) 'Foraging behaviour and the evolution of primate intelligence', in R. Byrne and A. Whiten (eds) *Machiavellian Intelligence: Social Expertise and the Evolution of Intellect in Monkeys, Apes, and Humans*, Oxford: Clarendon.

Milton, K. (1990) *Our Countryside Our Concern: The Policy and Practice of Conservation in Northern Ireland*, Northern Ireland Environmental Link.

Mingay G. E. (ed.) (1981) *The Victorian Countryside*, London: Routledge & Kegan Paul.

Moore, H. (1986) *Space, Text and Gender*, Cambridge: Cambridge University Press.

Moore, H. (1990) 'Paul Ricoeur: action, meaning and text', in C. Tilley (ed.) *Reading Material Culture*, Oxford: Blackwell.

Morphy, H. (1989) 'From dull to brilliant: the aesthetics of spiritual power among the Yolngu', *Man*, 24:21–40.

Morris, R. (1989) *Churches in the Landscape*, London: J. M. Dent.

Morse, R. (1991) *Truth and Convention in the Middle Ages: Rhetoric, Representation, and Reality*, Cambridge: Cambridge University Press.

Moya, C. (1990) *The Philosophy of Action: An Introduction*, Cambridge, Polity Press.

Muir, R. (1985) *Shell Guide to Reading the Celtic Landscapes*, London: Michael Joseph.

Muir, R. (1989a) *Portraits of the Past*, London: Michael Joseph.

Muir, R. and N. (1989b) *Fields*, London: Macmillan.

Mullins, P. and Warner, M. (n.d.) 'Archaeological excavations at the Maynard-Burgess site, 18AP64', report in preparation.

Murray, T. (1987) 'Remembrance of things present: appeals to authority in the history and philosophy of archaeology', PhD dissertation, University of Sydney.

Murray, T. (forthcoming) *Encyclopaedia of the History of Archaeology*.

National Trust (1992) *Countryside Matters: The National Trust at Work in England, Wales and Northern Ireland*, London: The National Trust.

Newby, H. (1988) *The Countryside in Question*, London: Hutchinson.

Nicholson-Lord, D. (1991) 'Fossil-hunters are hammering our heritage', *The Independent*, 2 June.

Nietzsche, F. (1967) *The Genealogy of Morals*, trans. W. Kaufmann, New York: Random House.

Nietzsche, F. (1968) *Twilight of the Idols or How to Philosophize with a Hammer*, Harmondsworth: Penguin.

Nishida, T. (1987) 'Local traditions and cultural transmission', in B. B. Smuts *et al.* (eds) *Primate Societies*, Chicago, Ill.: University of Chicago Press.

Noble, W. and Davidson, I. (1991) 'The evolutionary emergence of modern human behaviour', *Man*, 26:223–54.

Norwegian Archaeological Review (1989) 22. Discussion issue: Shanks and Tilley.

Ollman, B. (1971) *Alienation: Marx's Conception of Man in Capitalist Society*, Cambridge: Cambridge University Press.

Olsen, B. (1986) 'Norwegian archaeology and the people without (pre)history: or, how to create a myth of a uniform past', *Archaeological Review from Cambridge*, 5:25–42.

Olsen, B. (1991) 'Metropolises and satellites in archaeology: on power and asymmetry in global archaeological discourse', in R. W. Preucel (ed.), *Processual and Postprocessual Archaeologies: Multiple Ways of Knowing the Past*, Carbondale Ill. University of Southern Illinois.

Parker, S. T. and Baars, B. (1990) 'How scientific usages reflect implicit theories: adaptation, development, instinct, learning, cognition, and intelligence', in S. T. Parker and K. R. Gibson (eds) *'Language' and Intelligence in Monkeys and Apes*, Cambridge: Cambridge University Press.

Parker, S. T. and Gibson, K. R. (eds) (1990) *'Language' and Intelligence in Monkeys and Apes*, Cambridge: Cambridge University Press.

Parker Pearson, M. (1982) 'Mortuary practices, society and ideology: an ethnoarchaeological study', in I. Hodder (ed.) *Symbolic and Structural Archaeology*, Cambridge: Cambridge University Press.

Parker Pearson, M. (1984a) 'Economic and ideological change: cyclical growth in the pre-state societies of Jutland', in D. Miller and C. Tilley (eds) *Ideology, Power and Prehistory*, Cambridge: Cambridge University Press.

Parker Pearson, M. (1984b) 'Social change, ideology and the archaeological record', in M. Spriggs (ed.) *Marxist Perspectives in Archaeology*, Cambridge: Cambridge University Press.

Passingham, R. (1982) *The Human Primate*, San Francisco, Calif.: Freeman.

Patrik, L. (1985) 'Is there an archaeological record?', in M. B. Schiffer (ed.) *Advances in Archaeological Method and Theory*, London: Academic Press.

Patterson, T. (1986) 'The last 60 years – towards a social history of American archaeology', *American Anthropologist*, 88.

Patterson, T. (1989) 'History and the post-processual archaeologies', *Man*, 24:555–66.

Pearce, S. (1992) *Museum Objects and Collections*, Leicester: Leicester University Press.

Pearce, S. (ed.) (1989) *Museum Studies in Material Culture*, Leicester: Leicester University Press.

Pearson, M. (1994) 'Theatre/archaeology', *The Drama Review*, Summer.

Petit, M. (1989) 'Thinking history: methodology and epistemology in Paul Ricoeur's reflections on history from "History and Truth" to "Time and Narrative"', in Kemp and Rasmussen (eds) *The Narrative Path: The Later Works of Paul Ricoeur*, Cambridge, Mass.: MIT Press.

Piattelli-Palmarini, Massimo (ed.) (1980) *Language and Learning. The Debate between Jean Piaget and Noam Chomsky*, London: Routledge & Kegan Paul.

Pickering, A. (ed.) (1992) *Science as Practice and Culture*, Chicago, Ill.: University of Chicago Press.

Ponting C. (1991) *A Green History of the World*, London: Sinclair-Stevenson.

Potter, P. B. (1990) 'The "what" and "why" of public relations for archaeology: a postscript to DeCicco's Public Relations Primer', *American Antiquity*, 55:608–13.

Potter, P. and Leone, M. (1987) 'Archaeology in public in Annapolis: four seasons, six sites, seven tours and 32,000 visitors', *American Archaeology*, 6:1:51–61.

Premack, D. (1988) '"Does the chimpanzee have a theory of mind?" revisited', in R. Byrne and A. Whiten (eds), *Machiavellian Intelligence. Social Expertise and the Evolution of Intellect in Monkeys, Apes, and Humans*, Oxford: Clarendon Press.

Preucel, R. W. (ed.) (1991) *Processual and Postprocessual Archaeologies: Multiple Ways of Knowing the Past*, Carbondale, Ill.: University of Southern Illinois.

Pryor, F. (1990), 'The reluctant Greening of archaeology', *Antiquity*, 64:147–50.

Purser, M. (1992) 'Oral history and historical archaeology', in Barbara J. Little (ed.) *Text-Aided Archaeology*, Boca Raton, Fla.: CRC Press.

Rackham O. (1986) *The History of the Countryside*, London: J. M. Dent.

Rackham, O. (1990) *Trees and Woodland in the British Landscape*, London: J. M. Dent.

Rahtz, P. A. (ed.) (1974) *Rescue Archaeology*, Harmondsworth: Penguin.

Ralston, I. and Thomas J. (ed.) (forthcoming) *Archaeology and Environmental Assessment*.

Redman, C. (1991) 'In defence of the seventies – the adolescence of New Archaeology', *American Anthropologist*, 93:295–307.

Reeves, M. (1980) *Sheep Bell and Ploughshare: The Story of Two Village Families*, London: Paladin/Granada.

Reitz, E. J. (1987) 'Preliminary analysis of vertebrate remains from features 5 and 121, at the Calvert House, Annapolis, Maryland', Report on file Historic Annapolis Foundation.

Renfrew, C. (1972) *The Emergence of Civilisation: The Cyclades and the Aegean in the Third Millennium BC*, London: Methuen.

Renfrew, C. (1973) *Before Civilisation*, Harmondsworth: Penguin.
Renfrew, C. (1977) 'Space, time and polity', in J. Friedman and M. Rowlands (eds) *The Evolution of Social Systems*, London: Duckworth.
Renfrew, C. (1982) 'Explanation revisited', in C. Renfrew, M. Rowlands and B. Segraves (eds) *Theory and Explanation in Archaeology*, London: Academic Press.
Renfrew, C. (1983) 'Divided we stand: aspects of archaeology and information', *American Antiquity*, 48:3–16.
Renfrew, C. (1989) Comments on 'Archaeology into the 1990s', *Norwegian Archaeological Review*, 22:33–41.
Renfrew, C. and Bahn, P. (1991) *Archaeology: Theories, Methods, and Practice*, London: Thames & Hudson.
Richman, B. (1987) 'Rhythm and melody in gelade vocal exchanges', *Primates*, 28:199–223.
Ricoeur, P. (1981a) 'Phenomenology and hermeneutics', in J. B. Thompson (ed.) *Hermeneutics and the Human Sciences*, Cambridge: Cambridge University Press.
Ricoeur, P. (1981b) 'Hermeneutics and the critique of ideology', in J. B. Thompson (ed.) *Hermeneutics and the Human Sciences*, Cambridge: Cambridge University Press.
Ricoeur, P. (1981c) 'The model of the text: meaningful action considered as a text', in J. B. Thompson (ed.) *Hermeneutics and the Human Sciences*, Cambridge: Cambridge University Press.
Ricoeur, P. (1981d) *Hermeneutics and the Human Sciences*, trans. J. B. Thompson, Cambridge: Cambridge University Press.
Ricoeur, P. (1989) *Time and Narrative*, Vol. 3, trans. K. McLaughlin and D. Pellauer, Chicago, Ill.: Chicago University Press.
Rimmon-Kenan, S. (1983) *Narrative Fiction: Contemporary Poetics*, London: Methuen.
Ritchie, W. (1953) 'A probable paleo-Indian site in Vermont', *American Antiquity*, 18:249–57.
Rivière, G. H. (1985) 'The ecomuseum – an evolutive definition', *Museum*, 148:182–3.
Robbins, D. (1991) *The Work of Pierre Bourdieu: Recognizing Society*, Milton Keynes: Open University Press.
Rogers, A., Blunden, J. and Curry, N. (1985) *The Countryside Handbook*, London: Croom Helm.
Rorty, R. (1980) *Philosophy and the Mirror of Nature*, Oxford: Blackwell.
Ruggles, C. and Newman, I. (1991) 'The MRRL's meta-information retrieval and access system', in D. Medyckyj-Scott *et al.* (eds) *Metadata in the Human Sciences*, Loughborough: Group D Publications.
Rumbaugh, D. M. (1986) 'Animal thinking – by stimulation or simulation?', in J. G. Else and P. C. Lee (eds) *Primate Ontogeny, Cognition and Social Behaviour*, Cambridge: Cambridge University Press.
Sahlins, M. (1985) *Islands of History*, Chicago, Ill.: Chicago University Press.
Said, E. (1978) *Orientalism*, London: Routledge & Kegan Paul.
Sambrook, J. (1973) *William Cobbett*, London: Routledge & Kegan Paul.
Sands, S. F. and Wright, A. A. (1980) 'Primate memory: retention of serial list items by a rhesus monkey', *Science*, 209:938–40.
Sartre, J.-P. (1956) *Being and Nothingness*, New York: Washington Square Press.
Savage-Rumbaugh, E. S. (1986) *Ape Language: From Conditioned Response to Symbol*, Oxford: Oxford University Press.
Savage-Rumbaugh, E. S., Rumbaugh, D. M. and Boysen, S. (1978) 'Linguistically mediated tool use and exchange by chimpanzees (Pan troglodytes)', *Behavioural and Brain Sciences*, 1:539–54.
Savage-Rumbaugh, E. S. *et al.* (1993) 'Language comprehension in ape and child', *Monogr. Soc. Res. Child Devel.*, 58:[3–4].
Sayer, D. (1987) *The Violence of Abstraction: The Analytical Foundations of Historical Materialism*, Oxford: Basil Blackwell.
Schiffer, M. B. (1976) *Behavioural Archaeology*, New York: Academic Press.
Schiffer, M. B. (ed.) (1985) *Advances in Archaeological Method and Theory*, London: Academic Press.
Schneider, A. (1993) 'The art diviners', *Anthropology Today*, 9:3–9.
Schulz, P., Rivers, B., Hales, M., Litzinger, C. and McKeen, E. (1980) *The Bottles of Old Sacramento: A Study of Nineteenth-Century Glass and Ceramic Retail Containers*, Part I, California Archaeological Reports No. 20, Department of Parks and Recreation, State of California.
Schutz, A. (1967) *The Phenomenology of the Social World*, Evanston: Northwestern University Press.
Seamon, D. (ed.) (1993) *Dwelling, Seeing and Designing*, Albany, NY: State University of New York Press.
Seamon, D. and Mugerauer, R. (eds) (1989) *Dwelling, Place and Environment*, New York: Columbia University Press.

Serres, M. (1968–80) *Hermès*, Vols 1–5, Paris: Minuit.

Serres, M. (1982) *Hermès: Literature, Science, Philosophy*, trans. J. V. Harari and D. F. Bell, Baltimore, Md: Johns Hopkins University Press.

Seymour, J. and Girardet, H. (1988) *Far from Paradise: The Story of Human Impact on the Environment*, Basingstoke: Green Print.

Shackel, P. (1986) 'Archaeological testing at the 193 Main Street site, 18AP44, Annapolis, Maryland', report on file at the Archaeology Laboratory, Department of Anthropology, University of Maryland, College Park.

Shanks, M. (1992a) *Experiencing the Past: On the Character of Archaeology*, London: Routledge.

Shanks, M. (1992b) 'Artifact design and pottery from archaic Korinth: an archaeological interpretation', PhD thesis, University of Cambridge.

Shanks, M. (1992c) 'Style and the design of a perfume jar from an archaic Greek city state', *Journal of European Archaeology*, 1:77–106.

Shanks, M. (1992d) 'The life of an artifact', paper presented to the Department of Archaeology, University of Wales, Lampeter.

Shanks, M. (1993a) 'Archaeological experiences and a critical romanticism', in A. Siriaiinen *et al.* (eds) *The Archaeologists and Their Reality: Proceedings of the 4th Nordic TAG Conference 1992*, Helsinki.

Shanks, M. (1993b) *Art and the Rise of the Greek City State*, London: Routledge.

Shanks, M. (1994) 'The archaeological imagination: creativity, rhetoric and archaeological futures', in M. Kuna and N. Venclová (eds) *Whither Archaeology? Archaeology in the End of the Millennium*, Prague.

Shanks, M. and McGuire, R. (1991) 'The craft of archaeology', paper delivered at the Society for American Archaeology Meetings, New Orleans.

Shanks, M. and Tilley, C. (1982) 'Ideology, symbolic power and ritual communication: a reinterpretation of Neolithic mortuary practices', in I. Hodder (ed.) *Symbolic and Structural Archaeology*, Cambridge: Cambridge University Press.

Shanks, M. and Tilley, C. (1987a) *Re-Constructing Archaeology*, Cambridge: Cambridge University Press.

Shanks, M. and Tilley, C. (1987b) *Social Theory and Archaeology*, Oxford: Polity Press.

Shanks, M. and Tilley, C. (1987c) 'Abstract and substantial time', *Archaeological Review from Cambridge*, 6.

Shanks, M. and Tilley, C. (1989) 'Archaeology into the 1990s', *Norwegian Archaeological Review*, 22:1–12.

Shoard, M. (1980), *The Theft of the Countryside*, London: Temple Smith.

Shoard, M. (1987), *This Land Is Our Land*, London: Paladin/Grafton.

Sigg, H. (1986) 'Ranging patterns in hamadryas baboons: evidence for a mental map', in J. G. Else and P. C. Lee (eds) *Primate Ontogeny, Cognition and Social Behaviour*, Cambridge: Cambridge University Press.

Sigg, H. and Stolba, A. (1981) 'Home range and daily march in a hamadryas baboon troop', *Folia primatologica*, 36:40–75.

Smith, C. D. (1992) 'The Annales for archaeology?', *Antiquity*, 66:539–42.

Smith, F. (1926) *Prehistoric Man and the Cambridgeshire Gravels*, Cambridge: Heffers.

Snodgrass, A. (1991) 'Structural history and classical archaeology', in J. Bintliff (ed.) *Annales History and Archaeology*, Leicester: Leicester University Press.

Snowdon, C. T. (1990) 'Language capacities of non-human animals', *Yearbook of Physical Anthropology*, 33:215–43.

Spector, J. (1991) 'What this awl means', in J. M. Gero, and M. W. Conkey (eds) *Engendering Archaeology*, London: Blackwell.

Sperling, S. (1991) 'Baboons with briefcases vs. langurs in lipstick: feminism and functionalism in primate studies', in M. di Leonardo (ed.) *Gender at the Crossroads of Knowledge: Feminist Anthropology in the Postmodern Era*, Berkeley, Calif.: University of California Press.

Spiegel, G. M. (1983) 'Genealogy: form and function in medieval historical narrative', *History and Theory*, 22:43–53.

Spiegel, G. M. (1986) 'Pseudo-Turpin, the crisis of the aristocracy and the beginnings of vernacular historiography in France', *Journal of Medieval History*, 12:207–23.

Spiegel, G. M. (1990) 'History, historicism, and the social logic of the text in the Middle Ages', *Speculum*, 65:59–86.

Stetie, S. (1981) 'The Intergovernmental Committee: mechanisms for a new dialogue', *Museums*, 31:2:116–17.

Stetie, S. (1982) 'Les objets d'art ont-ils une patrie?', *Historia*, 433:4–61.

Stewart, S. (1984) *On Longing: Narratives of the Miniature, the Gigantic, the Souvenir, the Collection*, Baltimore, Md: Johns Hopkins University Press.

Stocking, G. W. (1987) *Victorian Anthropology*, New York: Free Press.

Stoianovich, T. (1976) *French Historical Method: The Annales Paradigm*, London: Cornell University Press.

Street, A. G. (1932) *Farmer's Glory*, London: Faber & Faber.

Stringer, C. B. (1984) 'Human evolution and biological adaptation in the Pleistocene', in R. A. Foley (ed.) *Hominid Evolution and Community Ecology*, London: Academic Press.

Stross, B. (1974) 'Speaking of speaking: Tenejapa Tzeltal metalinguistics', in R. Bauman and J. Sherzer (eds) *Explorations in the Ethnography of Speaking*, Cambridge: Cambridge University Press.

Sturt, G. (1922) *A Farmer's Life*, London: Cape.

Taçon, P. (1991) 'The power of stone: symbolic aspects of stone use and tool development in western Arnhem Land, *Australia Antiquity*, 65:192–207.

Tallgren, A. M. (1937) 'The method of prehistoric archaeology', *Antiquity*, 11:152–61.

Tannen, D. (1987) 'Repetition in conversation: toward a poetics of talk', *Language*, 63:574–605.

Tayeb, M. (1979) 'Algeria', in 'Viewpoint: the return and restitution of cultural property', *Museum* 31:1:10–11.

Taylor, C. (1975) *Fields in the English Landscape*, London: J. M. Dent.

Taylor, C. (1983) *Village and Farmstead: A History of Rural Settlement in England*, London: George Philip.

Taylor, C. (1985) *Philosophy and the Human Sciences: Philosophical Papers 2*, Cambridge: Cambridge University Press.

Taylor, C. (1988) Introduction to and commentary on a special edition of Hoskins 1955, London: Guild.

Taylor, C. and Muir, R. (1983), *Visions of the Past*, London: J. M. Dent.

Tegner, H. (1970), *The Charm of the Cheviots*, Newcastle upon Tyne: Frank Graham.

Terrace, H. S. (1984) 'Apes who "talk": language or projection of language by their teaching?', in J. De Luce and H. T. Wilder (eds) *Language in Primates*, New York: Springer-Verlag.

Thomas, C. (1985) *Exploration of a Drowned Landscape: Archaeology and History of the Isles of Scilly*, London: Batsford.

Thomas, J. (1991a) *Rethinking the Neolithic*, Cambridge: Cambridge University Press.

Thomas, J. (1991b) 'Science or anti-science?', *Archaeological Review from Cambridge*, 10:27–36.

Thomas, J. (1993a) 'The hermeneutics of megalithic space', in C. Tilley (ed.) *Interpretative Archaeology*, London: Berg.

Thomas, J. (1993b) 'The politics of vision and the archaeologies of landscape', in B. Bender (ed.) *Landscape, Politics and Perspectives*, London: Berg.

Thompson, D. (ed.) (1980) *Change and Tradition in Rural England: An Anthology of Writing on Country Life*, Cambridge: Cambridge University Press.

Thompson, F. (1973) *Lark Rise to Candleford*, Harmondsworth: Penguin.

Thompson, J. (1989) 'The theory of structuration', in D. Held and J. Thompson (eds) *Social Theory of Modern Societies*, Cambridge: Cambridge University Press.

Thompson, M. (1982) 'A three-dimensional model', in M. Douglas (ed.) *Essays in the Sociology of Perception*, London: Routledge & Kegan Paul.

Thorpe, Benjamin (1851) *Northern Mythology*, London: Edward Lumley.

Tilley, C. (1984) 'Ideology, power and prehistory: an introduction', in D. Miller and C. Tilley (eds) *Ideology, Power and Prehistory*, Cambridge: Cambridge University Press.

Tilley, C. (1989a) 'Excavation as theatre', *Antiquity*, 63:275–80.

Tilley, C. (1989b) 'Discourse and power: the genre of the Cambridge inaugural lecture', In D. Miller, M. Rowlands and C. Tilley (eds) *Domination and Resistance*, London: Unwin Hyman.

Tilley, C. (1990a) 'Michel Foucault: towards an archaeology of archaeology', in C. Tilley (ed.) *Reading Material Culture*, Oxford: Blackwell.

Tilley, C. (1990b) 'On modernity and archaeological discourse', in I. Bapty and T. Yates (eds) *Archaeology after Structuralism*, London: Routledge.

Tilley, C. (1991) *Material Culture and Text*, London: Routledge.

Tilley, C. (1993) 'Interpretative archaeology and an archaeological poetics', in C. Tilley (ed.) *Interpretative Archaeology*, London: Berg.

Tilley, C. (forthcoming) *A Phenomenology of Landscape: Places, Paths and Monuments*.

Tilley, C. (forthcoming) *Art, Architecture, Landscape (Neolithic Sweden)*.

Tilley, C. (ed.) (1990) *Reading Material Culture: Structuralism, Hermeneutics and Post-structuralism*, Oxford: Basil Blackwell.

Tilley, C. (ed.) (1993) *Interpretative Archaeology*, London: Berg.

Tindall, G. (1980) *The Fields Beneath: The History of One London Village*, London: Paladin/Granada.

Tomasello, M. (1990) 'Cultural transmission in the tool use and communicatory signaling of chimpanzees?' in S. T. Parker and K. R. Gibson (eds) *'Language' and Intelligence in Monkeys and Apes*, Cambridge: Cambridge University Press.

Trigger, B. (1989a) *A History of Archaeological Thought*, Cambridge: Cambridge University Press.

Trigger, B. (1989b) 'Hyperrelativism, responsibility and the social sciences', *Canadian Review of Sociology and Anthropology*, 26:776–97.

Turner, J. H. (1987) 'Toward a sociological theory of motivation', *American Sociological Review*, 52:15–27.

Turner, J. H. (1992) 'Overcoming humanities babble: searching for universal types of human social relations [review of Fiske 1991]', *Contemporary Sociology*, 21:126–8.

Turner, V. (1980) 'Social dramas and stories about them', *Critical Inquiry*, 7:141–68.

Ucko, P. *et al.* (1991) *Avebury Reconsidered. From the 1660s to the 1990s*, London: Unwin Hyman.

Uzzell, D. L. (ed.) (1989) *Heritage Interpretation*, Vol. 1, *The Natural and Built Environment*, London: Belhaven Press.

Vergo, P. (ed.) (1990) *The New Museology*, London: Reaktion.

Veyne, P. (1971) Comment on *Écrit l'histoire*, Paris.

Vilar, P. (1985) 'Constructing Marxist history', in J. Le Goff and P. Nora (eds) *Constructing the Past: Essays in Historical Methodology*, Cambridge: Cambridge University Press.

Visalberghi, E. (1987) 'Acquisition of nut-cracking behaviour by two capuchin monkeys (*Cebus apella*)', *Folia primatologica*, 49:168–81.

Visalberghi, E. (1988) 'Responsiveness to objects in two social groups of tufted capuchin monkeys (*Cebus apella*)', *Folia primatologica*, 18:349–60.

Walsh, K. (1992) *The Representation of the Past: Museums and Heritage in the Post-Modern World*, London: Routledge.

Warner, M. (1991) 'African American Annapolitans: social dominance and material negoti-ation', paper presented at the Conference on Historical and Underwater Archaeology, 9–13 January, Richmond, Va.

Warner, M. (1992a) 'African Americans in nineteenth-century Annapolis: material con-sumption and the negotiation of identities', paper presented at the 57th Annual Meeting of the Society for American Archaeology, 8–12 April, Pittsburgh, Pa.

Warner, M. (1992b) 'Test excavations at Gott's Court Annapolis, Maryland 18AP52', report on file at the Archaeology Laboratory, Department of Anthropology, University of Maryland, College Park.

Warner, R. M. (1992) 'Cyclicity of vocal activity increases during conversation: support for a nonlinear systems model of dyadic social interaction', *Behavioral Science*, 37:128–38.

Warnke, G. (1987) *Gadamer: Hermeneutics, Tradition and Reason*, Cambridge: Polity Press.

Washburn, W. (1987) 'A critical view of critical archaeology', *Current Anthropology*, 28:4:544–5.

Watson, P. (1990) 'The razor's edge: symbolic–structuralist archaeology and the expansion of archaeological inference', *American Anthropologist*, 92:613–21.

Watson, P., LeBlanc, S. and Redman, C. (1984) *Archaeological Explanation: The Scientific Method in Archaeology*, New York: Columbia University Press.

Watson, R. A. (1990) 'Ozymandias, King of Kings: postprocessual radical archaeology as critique', *American Antiquity*, 55:673–89.

White, G. (1977) *A Natural History of Selborne*, Harmondsworth: Penguin.

White, H. (1973) *Metahistory*, Baltimore, Md: Johns Hopkins University Press.

White, H. (1987) *The Content of the Form: Narrative Discourse and Historical Repre-sentation*, Baltimore, Md: Johns Hopkins University Press.

White, L. (1943) 'Energy and the evolution of culture', *American Anthropologist*, 45:335–56.

Whitley, J. (1987) 'Art history, archaeology and idealism: the German tradition', in I. Hodder (ed.) *Archaeology as Long-Term History*, Cambridge: Cambridge University Press.

Wiessner, P. (1990) 'Is there a unity to style?', in M. Conkey and C. Hastorf (eds) *The Uses of Style in Archaeology*, Cambridge: Cambridge University Press.

Willey, G. R. (1966) *An Introduction to American Archaeology*, Vol. 1, *North and Middle America*, Englewood Cliffs, NJ: Prentice-Hall.

Willey, G. R. and Sabloff, J. A. (1980) *A History of American Archaeology*, San Francisco, Calif.: Freeman.

Williams, R. (1973) *The Country and the City*, London: Chatto & Windus.

Wilson, William A. (1975) *Folklore and Nationalism in Modern Finland*, Bloomington, Ind.: Indiana University Press.

Wobst, H. M. (1977) 'Stylistic behaviour and information exchange', in C. E. Cleland (ed.) *Papers for the Director: Research Essays in Honour of James B. Griffin*, Anthropological Papers, Museum of Anthropology, University of Michigan, No. 61.

Wolfe, A. (1990) 'Social theory and the second biological revolution', *Social Research*, 57:615–48.

Wormington, H. (1957) *Ancient Man in North America*, 4th edn, Denver, Museum of Natural History, Popular Series No. 4.

Wright, P. (1985) *On Living in an Old Country: The National Past in Contemporary Britain*, London: Verso.

Wright, P. (1991) *A Journey through the Ruins: The Last Days of London*, London: Radius.

Wylie, A. (1985) 'Putting Shakertown back together: critical theory in archaeology', *Journal of Anthropological Archaeology*, 4:133–47.

Wylie, A. (1987) Comment, *Current Anthropology*, 28:297–8.

Wynn, T. (1989) *The Evolution of Spatial Competence*, Chicago: University of Illinois Press.

Wynn, T. (1990) 'Archaeological evidence for modern intelligence', in R. Foley (ed.), *The Origins of Human Behaviour*, London: Unwin Hyman.

Yarnell, T. (1992), 'Forest archaeological sites', *Forest Life*, March, 5, Edinburgh: Forest Enterprise.

Yearley, S. (1981) 'Textual persuasion: the role of social accounting in the construction of scientific arguments', *Philosophy of the Social Sciences*, 11:409–35.

Yentsch, A. (1991) 'Access and space, symbolic and material, in historical archaeology', in Dale Walde and Noreen D. Willows (eds) *The Archaeology of Gender: Proceedings of the Twenty-Second Annual Conference of the Archaeological Association of the University of Calgary*, The University of Calgary Archaeological Association.

Yoffee, N. and Sherratt, A. (eds) (1993) *Archaeological Theory: Who Sets the Agenda?*, Cambridge: Cambridge University Press.

Young, I. M. (1990). 'The ideal of community and the politics of difference', in L. J. Nicholson (ed.) *Feminism, Postmodernism*, New York: Routledge.

Index